Britain and Japan

MANCHESTER
UNIVERSITY PRESS

Britain and Japan
A comparative economic and social history since 1900

Kenneth D. Brown

Manchester University Press
Manchester and New York

Distributed exclusively in the USA by St. Martin's Press

Copyright © Kenneth D. Brown 1998

Published by Manchester University Press
Oxford Road, Manchester M13 9NR, UK
and Room 400, 175 Fifth Avenue, New York, NY 10010, USA

Distributed exclusively in the USA by
St. Martin's Press, Inc., 175 FifthAvenue, New York,
NY 10010, USA

Distributed exclusively in Canada by
UBC Press, University of British Columbia, 6344 Memorial Road,
Vancouver, BC, Canada V6T 1Z2

British Library Cataloguing-in-Publication Data
A catalogue record for this book is available from the British Library

Library of Congress Cataloging-in-Publication Data applied for

ISBN 0 7190 5290 4 *hardback*
    0 7190 5291 2 *paperback*

First published 1998

02 01 00 99 98   10 9 8 7 6 5 4 3 2 1

Typeset in Great Britain
by Servis Filmsetting Ltd, Manchester

Printed in Great Britain
by Biddles Ltd, Guildford and Kings Lynn

Contents

Tables

Acknowledgements

Works of synthesis inevitably depend very heavily on the studies of others. The references and the text make clear the extent of my abundant debts in this respect and I wish to thank all those whose writings have been so freely plundered. Statistical tables from N. F. R. Crafts and N. Woodward (eds), *The British Economy Since 1945* (1991), A. H. Halsey, *Change in British Society* (1978), W. Lockwood, *The Economic Development of Japan* (1968), A. Maddison, *Dynamic Forces in Capitalist Development* (1991), and P. Waller, *Town, City and Nation* (1983), are used by permission of Oxford University Press. Acknowledgement is due to Cambridge University Press for the use of material from P. Deane and W. Cole, *British Economic Growth Since 1688* (1962), A. Maizels, *Industrial Growth and World Trade* (1963), and B. R. Mitchell and P. Deane, *Abstract of British Historical Statistics* (1971). Table 5.3 is reproduced by permission from K. Yamamura and Y. Yasuba (eds), *The Political Economy of Japan* copyright 1987 by the Board of Trustees of the Leland Stanford Junior University. Tables from T. Nakamura, *Lectures on Modern Japanese History, 1926–1994* (Tokyo, 1994) appear by permission of the LTCB International Library Foundation. Macmillan Ltd. gave permission for the reproduction of statistical material from G. C. Allen, *A Short Economic History of Modern Japan* (1981), copyright G. C. Allen; A. H. Halsey, *Trends in British Society Since 1900* (1972), copyright A. H. Halsey; A. H. Halsey, *British Social Trends Since 1900* (1988), copyright A. H. Halsey; R. Minami, *The Economic Development of Japan: A Quantitative Study* (1986), copyright R. Minami. In American editions material from copyright R. Minami from *The Economic Development of Japan: A Quantitative Study* (1986) by R. Minami is reprinted with permission of St Martin's Press, Incorporated. Other figures are used by permission from G. C. Allen, *The Japanese Economy* (1981), Weidenfeld and Nicolson; G. C. Allen, *British Industries and Their Organization* (1951), Addison, Wesley Longman Ltd; P. Francks, *Japanese Economic Development* (1992), Routledge; J. Hendry, *Understanding*

Japanese Society (1987), Routledge; H. Patrick (ed.), *Japanese Industrialization and its Social Consequences* (1976) copyright the Regents of the University of California; S. Pollard, *The Development of the British Economy* (1992), Arnold. Extracts from tables in P. Johnson (ed.), *Twentieth Century Britain: Economic, Social and Cultural Change* (1994), and B. W. Alford, *Britain in the World Economy Since 1880* (1996) have been reprinted by permission of Addison Wesley Longman Ltd. Extracts from statistical tables in T. Nakamura, *Economic Growth in Prewar Japan* (1971) appear by permission of Yale University Press.

I wish also to thank the Japan Society for the Promotion of Science for the award of a Research Fellowship which allowed me to visit Tokyo in 1994, and the City University of Osaka where I spent a month as a Foreign Research Fellow in 1996. My visits on these occasions were organised respectively by Professors Onishi Haruki of Meiji Gakuin University and Tamai Kingo of City University, Osaka. Both arranged my activities with exemplary efficiency and enormous kindness: wittingly and otherwise, both taught me a great deal about Japan. Neither is responsible for anything in this present book, but I trust that they will accept it as an appropriate token of my esteem and friendship.

Kenneth D. Brown

Note: Throughout the book I have observed the usual Japanese practice in which surnames precede given names.

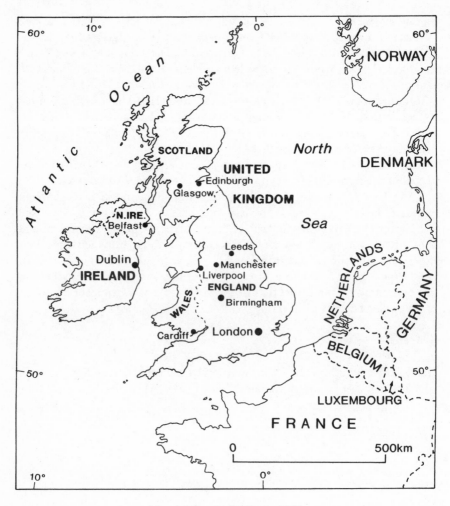

Map 1 (above): Britain in 1900

Map 2 (opposite): Japan in 1900

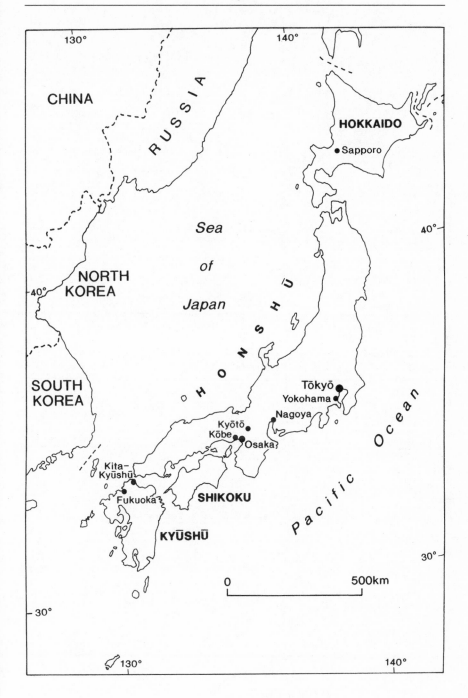

Introduction

When Britain signed its first formal alliance with Japan in 1902, *The Times* remarked in rather patronising fashion that for the Japanese it would provide a new sense of confidence and stability following a period of astonishingly rapid economic development (*The Times*, 25 February 1902). The paper erred, however, in adding that prior to the overthrow of the Tokugawa Shogunate and the Meiji Restoration of 1868 Japan was economically backward, locked into social and economic frameworks reminiscent of medieval feudalism. Nevertheless, a similar interpretation of Japanese development was later adopted by Marxist scholars committed to the view that such outmoded institutional arrangements were a major hindrance to earlier economic change. Subsequent research has done much to modify this analysis, emphasising that many of the economic and social developments initially associated with the Meiji period had antecedents well back in the preceding Tokugawa era, and indicating that the term feudal has often been used rather loosely in the Japanese context (Cullen, 1993; Smith, 1988: 15–49; Macpherson, 1987: 24–31). Conversely, it has also been suggested that change after 1868 was less rapid and comprehensive than has sometimes been assumed, being much modified by longer term and local influences (Wigen, 1995). What does remain broadly true, however, is that until the Meiji Restoration the Japanese were cut off from significant contact with the West, partly as a matter of deliberate policy, partly as a result of near-neighbour China's own insular outlook before it was opened up to increasing European influence in the nineteenth century.

Thereafter, it was only a matter of time before Japan, too, became a part of the international community; indeed, the express objective behind the restoration of imperial power in 1868 was that it allowed the country 'to rank equally with the other nations of the world' (Storry, 1990: 105). By the turn of the century the Japanese had modernised their government, economy and armed forces sufficiently to defeat first China and then Russia. The Anglo-Japanese agreement might be seen, therefore, as the first formal recognition

1

both of Japan's progress and of its aspirations to great power status, although Britain's primary motivation was to safeguard her own strategic interests in the Far East. The treaty acknowledged Japan's claims for a free hand in Korea and also guaranteed Britain's stance in the event of a Japanese clash with Russia. Following the Russo-Japanese conflict of 1904–5, Britain further recognised Japan's achievements by elevating its legation to an embassy, diplomatic convention being that ambassadors were assigned only to great powers.

The 1902 alliance also represented the coming together of two nations with much in common. Both had well-established traditions of central government. Both were islands lying off the coasts of major continents and on the edge of great oceans. Their agreement was a diplomatic concordat between the land of the rising sun and the world's most extensive empire on which the sun was popularly said never to set. That empire was linked together and protected by the world's most powerful navy. Its warships guarded the sea lanes for the world's largest merchant marine which carried coal, cotton, iron and other products so widely over the globe that almost a third of international trade in manufactured goods was British. In addition, some £4,000 million of British investment in 1900 provided much of the capital on which overseas economic development largely depended. London emerged as the centre of the world money market in the years following the Franco-Prussian War of 1870–71, the integrity of sterling providing the essential stability for the gold standard which governed international exchange operations. In terms of industrial output, railway mileage and energy consumption Britain stood second only the United States in 1900. In the same league table, Japan was about eleventh, although the quality of available contemporary statistics precludes precision.

Shortly before the conclusion of the 1902 treaty, *The Times* sounded a cautionary note when the Japanese announced that foreign exhibitors would be allowed to attend the Osaka industrial exhibition. This, the paper declared, would pit the British manufacturer 'against a new rival . . . whose extraordinary progress in the world of industry may well have caused him some uneasiness as to the result of her future rivalry' (*The Times*, 22 November 1901). It was a perceptive observation, for since the beginning of the twentieth century and more markedly since the 1950s the economic destinies of the two nations have followed different trajectories. By the 1990s it was the Japanese who had built the world's second or third most powerful industrial economy, whose merchant fleet was the most numerous, and who owned nine of the world's ten largest banks, reflecting the emergence of the yen as the strongest international currency. By 1994 Japan accounted for about 16 per cent of world manufactured exports and had a balance of trade surplus of some $146 billion. At 2.1 per cent a year between 1990 and 1994 real growth rates were markedly lower than in the heady days of the 1950s and 1960s, but they were still higher than those of most contemporary advanced industrial countries (JISEA, 1996: 17).

Britain by contrast was largely bereft of empire by this time, maintained a navy smaller than that of Japan, and possessed a mercantile marine so diminished that it did not even appear as a separate entity in a 1995 list of the world's principal fleets. Manufacturing industry had contracted significantly and her share of world exports was down to 5 per cent by 1992 (JISEA, 1995: 44). Growing import penetration was reflected in a balance of trade deficit of some $16 billion by 1994 (JISEA, 1996: 66). Even in the 1960s there was a growing concern with Britain's perceived economic decline. Any lingering doubts were quashed by the experience of the 1970s when inflation, falling growth rates, and industrial unrest culminated in the 1979 Winter of Discontent. 'Everything they have read in their newspapers is true', wrote one despairing journalist of foreign visitors, 'and we, as a nation, have had it' (*Toys International*, March 1979: 3).

The intellectual climate was thus particularly favourable when Professor Wiener's controversial book, *English Culture and the Decline of the Industrial Spirit, 1850–1980*, appeared in 1981. Wiener asserted that current British problems originated in the late nineteenth century as old fashioned values associated with the landed gentry began to suffocate industrial dynamism. Soon afterwards Correlli Barnett's *The Audit of War* (1986) attributed Britain's decline to the inappropriate policies pursued after the Second World War. Both books struck receptive chords among journalists, businessmen and politicians alike, all very willing to blame past generations for what seemed to be the national plunge into a sort of post-imperial miasma, compounded by a failing currency and a declining manufacturing base. A cartoon in the Chinese communist paper, the *People's Daily*, effectively caught the prevailing mood. It depicted the British lion, emaciated, near sighted, with spectacles, greying mane and a walking stick, peering at a portrait of himself at an earlier age, ferocious, aggressive and sharp toothed. The accompanying caption read: 'to remember is unbearable' (*Independent*, 5 February 1994). For some, memories of past glories were made all the more poignant by the further evidence of decline which they perceived in the surrender of national sovereignty implied by Britain's growing involvement in the European Economic Community (Supple, 1994: 318–46; Alford, 1996: 331–8).

In fact, of course, Britain remained an immensely wealthy country and as a member of the EEC was part of one of the world's three most powerful economic blocs (the others being Japan and the United States). Aggregate growth rates were quite healthy in historical terms, certainly until the early 1970s, and late twentieth-century Britons enjoyed unprecedentedly high standards of living. Much of this was obscured, however, by the native British penchant for a particularly masochistic form of navel contemplation in which most aspects of economic and social life were, not surprisingly, found wanting when compared, as they generally were, with best practice overseas. Most statistics of improvement appeared less impressive when set against those of other countries. As the economist Nicholas Kaldor observed in 1966, 'Britain appears almost invariably near the bottom of the league tables' (Kaldor, 1966: 1). His particular focus was on economic growth and it was in this context that Britain compared particularly badly with Japan, a rapid mover up these international league tables. From the late 1950s onwards the Japanese growth rate, described by Kaldor as 'outstanding', was significantly and consistently higher than that of Britain (Kaldor, 1966: 2). In 1950 British per capita GDP was almost four times that of the Japanese. By 1994 Japan's was more than twice as large as Britain's (JISEA, 1996: 17). By this time, too, average Japanese living standards, whether measured in terms of income or health, exceeded those of the British. A Japanese child of either sex born in 1993 could anticipate living between three and four years longer than an equivalent British infant (JISEA, 1996: 13).

Economic progress and decline, of course, are relative concepts and, resting as they usually do on statistical measures, have little to say about non-quantifiable indicators of human welfare. Growth statistics might be of little import in societies placing a lower premium on material advance than on, say, individual freedom or equality. Japan's high growth rates certainly masked, for a time at least, high environmental and qualitative costs, while others have questioned the very notion of Japanese economic success and power (Tasker, 1987; Morishima, 1982; Woronoff, 1996a, 1996b). Neither these arguments nor the often overstated versions of British decline, however, can gainsay the reality of the economic role reversal which occurred between Japan and Britain over the course of the twentieth century. The change was symbolised in the contrasting levels of each nation's involvement in the other's economic and social life. In 1900 Britain provided a quarter of Japan's imports, and British vessels were prominent among the foreign ships still carrying a sizeable proportion of Japan's overseas trade in 1913 (Davenport-Hines and Jones, 1989: 218–22). British nationals made up almost a half of the 3,000 or so foreigners recruited by Meiji governments between 1868 and 1912 to assist with modernisation, and British models inspired Japan's new railways, telegraph systems, and imperial navy. By the end of the twentieth century, however, British influence on and in Japan was much reduced. The (mainly) American occupation which followed the Japanese surrender in 1945 ensured that the country was pulled into the cultural orbit of the United States. One small measure of this perhaps was the long popularity of professional baseball compared with soccer, which the British had exported to virtually the entire world. More importantly, by 1993 Britain supplied only 2.1 per cent of Japanese imports by value, making her only Japan's fourteenth most important overseas provider. Japan sold to Britain two and half times as much as she purchased in return. There was also a significant upsurge of Japanese activity in Britain. A number of firms set up manufacturing plants, often as a means of getting inside the tariff barriers of the EEC, while the volume of inward investment rose. Although this represented only a small proportion of the total foreign investment in Britain, both its existence and growth were clear indicators of a major historical shift in economic power occurring over a relatively short space of time. So, too, was the fact that while Meiji Japan had borrowed heavily from Britain in terms of personnel and expertise, by the 1980s British firms were beginning to draw on Japanese manufacturing and management practices (Oliver and Wilkinson, 1988).

Businessmen were not alone in seeking to learn from the Japanese. Other decision-makers and opinion formers also extolled Japan as the exemplar on which economic success could be modelled. Sometimes such comparisons reflected the hidden agendas of British observers, whether a desire to heap the blame for the country's contemporary difficulties on poor management, irrelevant educational provision, misdirected government intervention, or militant trade unionists, for example, but the conclusions were the same. 'The lessons of Japan's business success are no secret', wrote the Conservative minister, Michael Heseltine, in 1990. 'They are there to be learned and the UK has more to learn than most' (*Independent*, 25 February 1990).

All too often, however, such appeals and comparisons lacked much sense of historical perspective, even though they were nothing new. Japan had been used as a reference point by supporters of the National Efficiency movement in Britain even before the First World War (Stead, 1906; Searle, 1977). Caution has to be exercised in providing this historical dimension, however, since comparative national history raises several methodological issues (Black, 1966; Skocpol and Somers, 1994: 72–98). Generally, Japan has been interpreted in terms of Western values and prejudices, too often presented as a society of internal paradoxes (imitative innovators, hard-working hedonists, cruel but cultivated aesthetes) and invariably utterly different from the West (Littlewood, 1996). Thus comparative analysis of Japan's economic and social institutions entails a danger of confusing what has been distinctive with what has been causally significant (Marsh and Mannari, 1976: 336–7). More specifically, the evidence on growth rates for early periods is ambiguous. The quality of the national income accounts on which growth calculations usually rest is very different as between Britain and Japan, while the statistics themselves are error prone. Even if the causes of Japan's economic success can be identified as something more than the unique product of a particular conjunction of historical circumstances and events, it does not follow that they could have been replicated in the very different British context. For this reason one recent book warns against viewing Japan's unique forms of industrial organisation as a universal panacea for less successful economies (Fruin, 1992). Finally, there is no reason to assume that Japan's success is permanent. By definition, international league tables of economic performance imply rankings which change over time. As the twentieth century draws to a close the main surge of Japanese growth has slowed and other South East Asian economies have forged ahead. As one British writer shrewdly observed in 1960,

> from a vantage point two centuries hence Far Eastern history may be seen broadly as a tale of Chinese supremacy, interrupted for a mere hundred years or so; and in this perspective the rise of Japan will be no more than a relatively minor, though interesting episode. (Storry, 1990: 267)

Nevertheless, comparative studies of past economic and social development are still valuable, not least because they undermine the notion that any one national experience is the norm. Thus Britain's industrial revolution, the first in the world, was very different in character from that of Japan, the first non-Western nation to follow suit. British industrialisation occurred spontaneously and took a long time: in Japan it was rapid and consciously sought after by the state. Equally, however, many of the changes thought to have been instrumental in Japanese industrialisation had also occurred in China yet without producing an industrial revolution (Moulder, 1977). Again, a comparative perspective has largely demolished Wiener's assertions concerning the detrimental economic implications of social values in late nineteenth-century Britain (James, 1990: 91–128; Pollard, 1990: 153–74; Berghoff and Muller, 1994: 262–87). Comparative approaches in other words can open up new avenues of exploration or provide correctives to received wisdom, as is apparent from the numerous historical studies which have appeared comparing particular aspects of the British and Japanese economies, especially for the period since 1945.

A general comparison of social and economic development in the two countries covering the whole of the twentieth century does avoid one important methodological problem, namely that of incompatible chronologies. There are very real pitfalls, for example, in applying to modern third world economies models of industrialisation derived from the pioneering experience of eighteenth-century England (Supple, 1963; Kemp, 1989). Both Britain and Japan, however, operated in the same international economy, responding to and affected by the same set of exogenous influences and shocks – two world wars, the emergence of American economic might, the crash of 1929, the depression of the 1930s, the long postwar boom, the oil crisis and subsequent economic instability. These provide some common benchmarks. Different national reactions to these events shaped the economic fortunes of both countries and yet their responses were also conditioned by the peculiarities of their own histories and social institutions. A related point is that while there have been disagreements over the precise timing of Britain's downturn and Japan's take off, it is generally agreed that the key decades in each case lay in the thirty or forty years before 1914. The beginning of Japan's modern economic growth has been located respectively between 1878 and 1900 by Professor Rostow, 1874 and 1879 by Professor

Kuznets, and even more exactly in 1886 by Professor Rosovsky (Rostow, 1971: 38; Kuznets, 1971: 24; Rosovsky, 1966: 92). In the same way, although scholars have differed in their explanations of Britain's comparative decline, variously blaming the early start, entrepreneurs, or institutional rigidities, there is a broad consensus about its location in the half century before the First World War when, in the words of Professor Floud, 'Britain lost the unchallenged position which it had gained as the first industrial nation' (Floud and McCloskey, 1981: 1; Kirby, 1994: 21–37). It is the subsequent outworking of these two different processes, relative decline and growth, with which this book is concerned.

To compare Britain and Japan over the course of the twentieth century is, initially at any rate, to juxtapose two societies at very different stages of development. It is all the more essential, therefore, to devise an appropriate analytical framework to avoid both a merely impressionistic portrait and the slide into parallel history which so often masquerades as comparison. Sociologists have generally agreed that the fundamental concept underpinning their discipline is that of social structure, but they have found it difficult to define society precisely and authoritatively. In the absence of any such agreed definition, therefore, and because the historian must be concerned with aspects of social psychology such as change, experience, and perception, the structural model adopted in this book is a modified version of that utilised by A. H. Halsey in his 1972 statistical survey of twentieth-century Britain. He organised his material around the institutional systems characteristic of any society: production or the economy; reproduction or social structure; power and authority or the system by which government is appointed, laws made, and order maintained; and ritual and communication which asserts and maintains values, thus providing the basis of communal cohesion and identity (Halsey, 1972: 4–19).

Halsey's model naturally reflects Western sociological categorisations and, particularly those aspects of it dealing with social class, might be thought inappropriate to Japan, where status has been more important and the concept of class traditionally carries behavioural and even ethical connotations. But so long as the model is thought of as an organisational device rather than a normative statement, it can be applied to Japan. It might also be reasonably objected that there are inevitable overlaps between Halsey's different institutional systems because historical reality was inevitably much more complex and dynamic than a deconstruction of its component parts can ever convey. Religious organisations can be presented as part of both the ritual and the power systems, propagating commonly held values but simultaneously acting as informal or even formal controls to ensure compliance with them. The beliefs and customs bound up in the system of ritual are often linked to the system of power in that a ruling group may sometimes impose its own dominant culture on society at large. Again, the possession of overseas territory can be treated as an integral part of a mother country's economy, supplying raw materials, labour, and markets, while also providing outlets for capital and people. Equally, however, in so far as empire has been used to reinforce notions of racial and national superiority, it provided part of the social cement within the imperial power, and might be considered as part of the system of ritual. Education also fits into several systems, depending on whether it is being considered as a provider of skilled manpower (production), a vehicle for social mobility (reproduction), or as an agency of socialisation (power and ritual). Such ambiguities and overlaps notwithstanding, however, the comprehensiveness of Halsey's model does make it an appropriate conceptual and organisational framework for the long term comparison of two societies evolving in the same international environment. Furthermore, the inclusion of the systems of power and ritual brings a healthy corrective to those interpretations of the past which have relied too exclusively on the influence of economic forces (Elliott, 1991).

1

Endings and beginnings? Britain and Japan before the First World War, c.1900–1914

The system of production

Agriculture

By 1900 Britain's industrial revolution was complete. Japan's, it is generally agreed, was just beginning, although the late Tokugawa economy was considerably more advanced than older writers sometimes allow. Britain had long since ceased to be self sufficient in food although about 70 per cent of England and Wales was still under cultivation when Edward VII succeeded to the throne in 1901 (Ashworth, 1960: 58). Agricultural employment actually rose slightly during the Edwardian period as did productivity, the latter a result – in part at least – of the trend towards larger farms although there were still 340,000 holdings of less than 50 acres (Ojala, 1952: 152–5). However, by this time less than a tenth of the labour force worked on the land, producing only between 6 and 7 per cent of the national income. Both figures represented a significant decline since 1850, reflecting the relative expansion of the manufacturing and service sectors as well as the great advances made in overseas agriculture and Britain's steadfast adherence to free trade. Huge increases of cheap food imports effectively dethroned King Corn, encouraging a degree of diversification away from arable towards dairy produce and market gardening. By 1914 British farmers were supplying about a quarter of the country's wheat consumption, less than half its butter, cheese, and pig meat, and only about 60 per cent of its requirements for beef, mutton, and lamb.

Farming in Japan had been shaped by a very different physical environment. Although there was some modest increase in acreage before the First World War, the mountainous terrain and generally damp climate restricted cultivation to about 14 per cent of the land mass, and even that was liable to disruption by typhoon, earthquake, flooding or landslide. Animal husbandry remained relatively rare, protein in the predominantly vegetable diet being provided mainly by soya beans and fish. With more than half of all farm land devoted to it, rice was even more dominant in Japanese farming than wheat had once been in Britain's, although most farmers grew other crops as well. All in all, agriculture remained far more central to the Japanese than to the British economy. Its contribution to the GDP was falling, but it still accounted for 34.7 per cent in 1900 and 30 per cent in 1913 (Ohkawa and Shinohara, 1979: 278–9). Similarly, while the proportion of the workforce engaged in farming began to decline after 1905, more than 60 per cent of occupied Japanese were still working on the land by 1911. About a third of farmers were land owners and just over a quarter were tenants, although by 1914 tenants occupied almost half of the cultivated land. As in Britain, the majority of farms were small, although their actual size was much smaller, about 70 per cent having one hectare or less in 1908 (Francks, 1992: 133). Nevertheless, until 1905 real output per worker in agriculture remained higher than in industry and with both output and productivity rising indigenous farmers were able to provide an improved diet to a population which increased by roughly a quarter between 1894 and 1914 (Francks, 1984). Rice productivity was higher than in many Asian countries in the 1960s (Nakamura, 1971: 49). As a consequence, only about 10 per cent of Japan's imports comprised foodstuffs in 1900.

Industry and trade

Along with foodstuffs, raw materials made up about three quarters of total British imports in the prewar years, both indicators of the dominance in the economy of industry. By 1913 manufacturing and mining together accounted for a fifth of capital and a third of national output, while employing almost two fifths of the labour force. Newer industries such as electrical engineering and motor cars were developing, but the major activities remained those on which the industrial revolution had been based – coal, textiles, iron and steel, and engineering. Most were labour intensive. Only 6 per cent of coal was mechanically cut in 1913, for example, the rest being won by skilled hewers using nothing more sophisticated than picks and shovels. Mining was also characteristic of the British economy in another respect, in that on the eve of the war a quarter of all collieries still employed fewer than seventy five workers. The growing scale of business enterprise apparent from the 1880s was confined to a few sectors of the economy and in 1900 almost a half of the manufacturing labour force was still to be found in small workshops and factories (Kropotkin, 1900: 270). With 70 per cent of firms remaining as family concerns, traditions of pride, independence, and tight control all acted as constraints on the effectiveness of the larger concerns into which competitive pressures sometimes forced them from the latter part of the nineteenth century.

All the major industries relied to a significant extent on foreign markets. Almost a third of coal production and three quarters of cotton output were sold abroad in 1913. Cotton exports alone earned £123 million in that year and accounted for almost a quarter of the nation's total overseas sales. About a quarter of the ships constructed between 1900 and 1914 were for overseas buyers. All told, Britain was responsible for about a third of world manufactured exports (table 1.1).

Table 1.1 *Share of world manufactured exports (%)*

	1899	1913
UK	33.2	30.2
Japan	1.5	2.3

(Maizels, 1963: 189)

Although the underlying trend of both imports and exports was upwards, growing international competitiveness left Britain with annual commodity trade deficits (table 1.2). There were those, notably Joseph Chamberlain, who called for tariff protection but their economic logic was flawed. British commercial networks were more complex and widespread than those of any other nation and this trade depended upon the ability of customers to pay for British goods by the reciprocal export of food and raw material. An import tariff would have reduced that capability, thereby affecting Britain's own export sales. In any case, the deficit was easily offset by earnings from invisibles such as shipping and insurance services, interest, and dividends. In 1913, therefore, the surplus on the current account stood at about £206 million.

Table 1.2 *UK imports and exports, 1870–1913 (£mn: current prices)*

	Imports	Exports
1870	303.3	199.6
1880	411.2	223.1
1890	420.7	263.5
1900	523.1	291.2
1910	678.3	430.4
1913	768.7	525.2

(Mitchell and Deane, 1971: 283–4)

Japan by contrast was not nearly so heavily involved in the international economy but had a substantial and accumulating deficit on the current account by 1913. Tokugawa policy had actively discouraged contact with foreigners, although some limited trade links had been allowed to develop. Meiji governments adopted a much more open policy but apart from a little coal and copper Japan had very few desirable raw materials while her own manufactures included little of appeal to Westerners save textiles. Initially, therefore, exports consisted mainly of primary products although progressive industrialisation gradually changed the ratio of manufactured to primary exports. On the eve of the Great War manufactures accounted for nearly 90 per cent of total exports which altogether accounted for a fifth of the GNP, three times their share in the 1880s (Ohkawa and Shinohara, 1979: 315–16). However, they were heavily outweighed by the substantial imports necessary to sustain the drive to modernisation in a country lacking a significant industrial base and raw materials.

By the turn of the century cotton textiles had become a factory-based activity. Output rose more than seven fold between 1903 and 1913 and half the total was exported, but by the standards of the contemporary British industry Japanese factories and production were insignificant. In 1913 the UK had 55.7 million spindles against Japan's 2.4 million, while Japan's exports of cotton piece goods represented only 2 per cent of the British total (Robertson, 1990: 89). The provision of construction bounties enabled Japan's shipbuilders to produce a hundred vessels a year by 1914. Their combined tonnage was minuscule when compared to British output but still represented a considerable achievement in a short space of time. Early attempts to foster iron and steel by importing modern plant failed. Experience in the war against China (1894–95), however, underlined the need for a heavy industrial capacity and in 1901 the furnaces at the state-sponsored Yawata works, built by Germans, were fired for the first time. The tempo of heavy industrial development accelerated further after the war with Russia in 1904–05, as the state gave its official sanction to a number of joint ventures with foreign entrepreneurs. Nevertheless, general economic expansion was such that by 1914 Japan still had to import half of its pig iron and two thirds of its steel.

Along with encouragement for industry went direct state investment into modern telecommunications and a railway network of 7,000 miles by 1914. This was a third of the length of British track, but Japanese railways were not encumbered with the under-used and duplicate lines which so detracted from the efficiency of the contemporary British system (Gourvish, 1980: 41–9). Operating subsidies in the form of postal contracts and navigation bounties gradually helped Japan to assume greater control of her own shipping and by 1914 two thirds of the carrying trade was in her own hands as against the 10 per cent which was all she had been able to support in the 1890s. These subsidies were channelled through new financial institutions, part of a banking modernisation programme promoted from the 1870s. An Industrial Bank was established in 1902 partly for the purpose of providing long term loans to modern industry. The Hypothec Bank was created primarily to lend money for land improvement and non-residential construction, although in practice it also provided loans for light industrial development. The remit of the Yokahama Specie Bank was to provide a more efficient market for

foreign exchange transactions and to end foreign domination of such activities. Underpinning the reforms was the Bank of Japan, set up in 1882 to
function rather like the Bank of England as an internal regulator and lender
of last resort. From 1899 it was the only bank authorised to issue paper
money. With the aid of a massive indemnity from the defeated Chinese, this
financial modernisation enabled Japan to join the gold standard in 1897.
The value of the yen remained remarkably stable right through until 1920 at
about Y10.1 : £1.00.

It is important, however, to keep this prewar economic progress in perspective. As tables 1.1, 1.3 and 1.4 indicate, Japan's manufacturing output
and exports were still dwarfed by Britain's. Factory workers were few in
number and industry was still predominantly small scale. The majority
worked in plants of fewer than five people and even of those in bigger factories in 1914 about 40 per cent were in units employing between five and forty
nine (Minami, 1986; 318). Although the balance between light and heavy
industry shifted in the latter's favour after the war with Russia, the most significant contribution to Japan's high if occasionally uneven rate of economic
growth still came from what has been described as the cottage sector (table
1.5). Not until 1914 did factory output move significantly ahead.

Table 1.3 *Shares of world manufacturing output (%)*

	1880	1900	1913
UK	22.9	18.5	13.6
Japan	2.4	2.4	2.7

(Bairoch, 1982: 296, 304)

Table 1.4 *Comparative total output index (UK = 100)*

	1890	1913
UK	100	100
Japan	27.5	32.5

(Maddison, 1991: 198)

Table 1.5 *Shares of Japanese manufacturing output (Ymn)*

	Factory	Cottage
1884	6.5	212.4
1892	16.7	426.9
1909	881.0	919.0
1914	1518.0	1090.2

(Nakamura, 1983: 80)

Economic growth

Overall, Japanese manufacturing output grew at more than 4.7 per cent a year from the middle 1870s until 1900. Thereafter it accelerated even more under the impetus of the government's drive to encourage heavy industry. By 1914 factory production accounted for 10.8 per cent of the national income. With trade also expanding at 7.5 per cent a year between 1880 and 1913, the GNP rose fairly steadily from the 1880s, although calculations of the actual rate vary according to the assumptions made about the Tokugawa period. One estimate gives an annual figure of 3.6 per cent between 1870 and 1913, although others have revised this downward to 2.4 per cent (Tachi, 1991: 23). Measured in terms of GDP per man year the economy grew at 1.8 per cent a year between 1899 and 1913 (Matthews, Feinstein and Odling-Smee, 1982: 31).

This was considerably higher than the equivalent figure for Britain over the same period – 0.5 per cent. At about 30 per cent, Britain's share of world manufactured exports in 1913 was impressive for a small island nation but still significantly smaller than the 41.4 per cent held in 1880 (Pollard, 1989: 271). An 18.5 per cent share of total world industrial output in 1900 was similarly remarkable but again represented a substantial drop from the 36 per cent produced in 1860. When set against the background of growing German military and economic power and taken in conjunction with the loss of world leadership in certain major industries and the apparent failure of new industries to develop apace, such statistics gave rise to considerable concern among contemporaries. They were interpreted by some, most famously perhaps E. E. Williams in his publication, *Made in Germany* (1896), as symptomatic of Britain's declining position in the world.

It was perhaps to be expected that as a newly industrialising country Japan should have enjoyed a higher rate of growth than the more mature Britain, but analyses of the mechanics behind their respective economic performances have thrown up a number of interesting comparisons: comparisons which, moreover, in the opinion of many observers, were of long term significance in explaining the contrasting economic fortunes of the two countries over the whole of the twentieth century. Generally speaking, the argument is that in Britain the actions of banks and governments, the quality of entrepreneurship, and the structure of business enterprise discouraged industrial dynamism, whereas the reverse was true in Japan. Thus retardation in late nineteenth-century Britain has often been attributed to the banks' indifference to industry's needs and their penchant for directing funds overseas (Kennedy, 1987). This contrasted with Japan where, as indicated above, some banks had very specific industrial functions. Yet Japan's banks were by no means uniformly successful in fulfilling their industrial roles: indeed, British institutions remained as important suppliers of capital to Japan right up to 1914. The Industrial Bank's industrial initiatives incurred such heavy losses that it had to be propped up by loans from the government and the Yokahama Bank. As for Britain's financial institutions, there is little evidence that they were ever regarded as significant sources of investment capital, which businesses more usually generated internally (Capie and Collins, 1992). Finally, it is worth pointing out that between 1907 and 1913 about 44 or 45 per cent of British overseas investment was not in the form of port-folios at all, but rather represented overseas acquisitions made by manufac-turing interests (Corley, 1994: 71–88). None of this appears to support notions of a parasitic banking sector, of British industry hampered by a lack of finance, or indeed of entrepreneurial lethargy.

Another school of thought attributes Japan's progress primarily to the directive role of the government, the implication sometimes being that the lack of such central guidance explains Britain's relatively slow growth (Patrick and Rosovsky, 1976). The contrast between the interventionist Japanese and the laisser faire British epitomised in the latter's staunch adher-ence to free trade, should not be overdrawn, however. British governments were generally more interventionist than might at first appear although the effects of their actions upon the economy were not always positive. While in most cases coming too late to explain a slowing of growth rates which began in the 1890s, a number of measures subsequently acted as brakes on the economy. These included fixing railway freight charges at rates that were not economically viable; handing control of electricity supply to local author-ities, most of whom had vested interests in gas, reducing the working hours of miners after 1908, and imposing charges upon employers as part of the welfare legislation introduced by the Asquith government. All of these mea-sures placed extra costs on British industry. The difference between Britain and Japan would thus appear to be not the fact of state intervention but its nature.

But it is not certain that government intervention was the main cause of Japan's progress anyway. Growth was sustained primarily by small scale, labour intensive enterprises in the town and countryside, rather than by government initiative and big factories (table 1.5). It cannot be assumed either that those responsible for formulating Japan's economic policy in the Restoration period had a clearly thought out, consistent programme which was successfully implemented. Government motives were often mixed and occasionally mutually contradictory. Many of the early national business ini-tiatives failed and the state factories, mines and shipyards were sold off after 1882. Similarly, despite government intentions, banking developed primarily along lines desired by private investors. Indirect intervention in the form of subsidies was equally uneven in its effects with the favoured institutions not noticeably outperforming their competitors.

Meiji governments certainly set out to modernise the country, although it is debatable as to whether the creation of an appropriate infrastructure can be regarded as the equivalent of conscious economic planning. They dismantled many of the formal structures of the previous regime, introducing socio-economic and legal frameworks conducive to modernisation. This was particularly so in the case of primary education where, despite its relatively late start, Japan virtually kept pace with Britain. The Meiji Educational Ordinance announced universal education for Japanese children in 1872, only two years after a national primary system was established in Britain. Compulsion came in 1879, a year before Mundella's bill made British elementary education mandatory. With the establishment of institutions such as the College for Advanced Technical Education, the Japanese appeared to be equally precocious in providing the technical education appropriate to industrialisation. By comparison, it has sometimes been suggested that Britain's faltering economic performance was caused by the government's failure to create an adequate system of technical educational. Yet although the output of science and technology graduates remained comparatively low, the late nineteenth century did see a significant increase in the provision – though on local initiative – of higher technical education (Guagini, 1991: 69–72). Equally, it can be suggested that well established apprenticeship schemes ensured that adequate levels of working skills were sustained. Here, too, therefore, the most significant difference between Japan and Britain was a matter of form rather than degree. On balance, Britain's relatively low output of technically qualified graduates reflected a lack of demand rather than a failure of provision. In modernising Japan such personnel were rapidly absorbed by business (Uchida, 1991: 112–35). This seems to confirm that whatever the aspirations of government and however well conceived they might have been, economic success depended in the last analysis on the response of private firms and individuals who proved receptive to modernisation and organised themselves accordingly.

This perhaps points to a third and potentially more fruitful area of Anglo-Japanese comparison, that of entrepreneurship. It has been claimed that the drive to Japanese industrialisation was facilitated by entrepreneurs drawn mainly from the *samurai* whose training, with its emphasis on dedication, loyalty, and the acceptance of hardship, provided ideal business virtues, while their innate patriotism and sense of community caused them to share in the state's desire to create an economically strong nation (Smith, 1988: 133–47). This is a mirror image of the situation prevailing in Britain, where according to Weiner a process of cultural atrophy was under way, with businessmen being seduced by the essentially anti-industrial values of the country's ruling elites. In the process of marrying into the land, sending their sons to public schools, and aspiring to some idealised version of aristocratic country life, they lost their combative business edge, and manufacturing failed to develop the close links with government characteristic of Japan (Wiener, 1981).

There is a pleasing symmetry in these hypotheses and their underlying assumptions about the relationship between economic growth and social values, but neither is wholly convincing. Detailed case studies of Japanese businessmen have indicated that the connections between the *samurai* and entrepreneurship were rather tenuous, the division between the *samurai* and everyone else being blurred even before the Restoration (Yamamura, 1967: 141–60). Some of those who claimed *samurai* status were very recent entrants, while not every economic development depended on a *samurai* input. Commoners were twice as important as *samurai* in providing share capital for the banks which developed after the passage of the 1876 Banking Act (Yamamura, 1967b: 198–220). Nor is there much solid evidence to support the view that those who established the successful large scale *zaibatsu* enterprises such as Mitsubishi and Yasuda owed anything specifically to their alleged *samurai* origins as opposed to sheer acquisitiveness. 'An entrepreneurial motivation deduced by over-emphasising cultural uniqueness', it has been argued, 'is clearly in conflict with the evidence' (Yamamura, 1968: 158).

Wiener's claims about British entrepreneurs have been similarly challenged, not least because the characteristics he ascribes to them were also evident among other national business elites (James, 1990). Few British businesses actually lasted long enough to fall into the hands of third generation owners who, he alleges, were chiefly interested in acquiring quasi-aristocratic life styles. Interestingly, an identical criticism has also been made about the descendants of the *zaibatsu* founders. Their energies, it has been suggested, tended to go into the arts, politics, and social life often at the cost of their business acumen (Morikawa, 1992: 99; Hunter, 1991: 140). More generally, Wiener's work lacks in hard evidence what it possesses in the way of fluent writing. The British retail sector certainly produced a number of dynamic empire-building entrepreneurs at this time, Jesse Boot and Thomas Lipton, for instance. Relatively few sons of businessmen ever received the public school education alleged to have corrupted them, while charges about poor marketing techniques and salesmanship are ill-founded (Berghoff, 1990: 148–67; Nicholas, 1984: 489–506). So, too, are claims that entrepreneurial apathy was to blame for the technological backwardness evident in major industries. Econometric studies have concluded that in preferring older technologies British entrepreneurs generally acted rationally within the restraints imposed by the availability and price of raw materials, and relative factor costs, in particular labour which was both highly skilled and comparatively cheap (McCloskey, 1970: 446–59).

Yet choices about technology and factor utilisation were essentially managerial responses to specific economic circumstances. They should not be confused with entrepreneurship, which is classically defined as the ability to break through institutional restraints, thereby creating new economic paradigms. The hypothesis of entrepreneurial failure might be supported, therefore, on the grounds that industrial investment was hampered by the persistence of a large pool of skilled labour, the small family firm, and the abrogation of control to craft unions (Lazonik, 1991). Here the contrasts with Japan *are* instructive. Only about forty small trade unions existed in Japan in 1914. Contemporary Britain's two million trade unionists on the other hand were most powerfully entrenched in precisely those industries most frequently charged with entrepreneurial failure. Similarly, the persistence of the small scale, family-owned enterprise that was the characteristic of British manufacturing generated a fiercely independent spirit on which attempts to create larger, more efficient enterprises often foundered.

The Japanese economy, too, was still typified by small scale activity but the larger scale *zaibatsu*, particularly the big four of Mitsubishi, Mitsui, Sumitomo and Yasuda, were increasingly important before 1914. Composed of independent companies, their economic and financial links were strengthened by personal or historical ties. Such a cooperative approach was logical in an undeveloped economy in which heavy industry especially was reliant on imported technology and expertise, in which skilled labour was scarce and market mechanisms for supply and distribution rudimentary. It also dovetailed very neatly with certain aspects of Japan's cultural development, in particular Confucianism which imbued Japanese society with a strong preference for agreement and consensus (Morishima, 1982). It was also the case that the concept of the *ie*, or family, extended well beyond immediate blood ties, entailing strong senses of group and vertical loyalty. More generally, it may be that the habit of cooperation had been internalised through centuries of the collective effort necessary for the successful cultivation of rice. At all events, successful cooperation among businessmen was in marked contrast to the stark individualism of the British, although that, too, was the product of previous social development. The early disappearance of the peasantry and the rise of Protestantism, particularly its nonconformist versions, encouraged a vigorous individualism, whether in consumer resistance to mass produced clothing and preference for custom made motor cars, in working-class self help, or in a general tolerance for the eccentric. In 1914 70 per cent of British firms were in family ownership, a far higher proportion than in any other advanced country and one which reflected the persistence of this deeply embedded individualist trait in the British psyche.

Services

Some scholars have sidestepped the issue of British entrepreneurial quality altogether by suggesting that the slowing down of industrial growth before 1914 reflected the fact that manufacturing had only ever been briefly important in a nation whose comparative advantage had always been in commerce and finance (Rubinstein, 1993). Whatever the validity of this particular hypothesis, Britain's merchant fleet provided by far the bulk of the world's carrying services, London was the centre of the world money market, and substantial sums were earned in interest on overseas investments. In terms of employment and the GNP the tertiary sector was of increasing importance. By 1913 public and professional services, transport, and commerce between them occupied some 45 per cent of the employed population and generated rather more than half of the total national income (Crouzet, 1982: 70). Late nineteenth-century changes in distribution also boosted retailing as a source of work, while by 1911 domestic and personal services provided 2.6 million jobs. The growth of domestic service testified to the uneven distribution of wealth in contemporary Britain and also reveals something about the limited range of employment opportunities available, especially for females from rural backgrounds. About 1.5 million people were employed in the professions and public service. The former reflected the growing complexity of society and its consequent need for various types of expertise, while public sector employment grew as both central and local government expanded.

The growth of a service sector was a natural development in a state which had been undergoing the process of industrialisation for a long time. By the same token the tertiary sector in Japan was relatively undeveloped. Estimates of service employment are quite unreliable for the period before 1920 and measures of its income generation even more speculative. The extension of banking, insurance, and transport services certainly implied job creation. Urbanisation and rising living standards, however modest, both created some demand for amenities over and above the basics of food, clothing, and shelter. In addition, the demand for professional services, in education for example, increased. Against this, expansion in service sector employment might have been more apparent than real, simply reflecting limited opportunities in other fields. Also, a mere head count may well exaggerate the extent of change because what was actually happening was a specialising out of functions previously performed but unrecorded because they did not constitute specific occupations. But for what it is worth, one estimate suggests that by 1909 3.6 million (14.3 per cent) out of a total occupied labour force of 25.3 million were engaged in the tertiary sector (Lockwood, 1955: 164).

The system of reproduction

Population

By the turn of the century, demographic transition was well under way in Britain with the high birth and death rates characteristic of pre-industrial societies having evolved to lower levels, depressing the rate of aggregate population growth. Fertility was declining although the precise mechanics of this are by no means clear, particularly as it occurred at varying rates among different social groups. It is easy to exaggerate both the availability of contraceptives and the dissemination of relevant medical and biological knowledge. Explanations couched in terms of the prevailing economic situation are not wholly satisfactory either, since the proportion of illegitimate births, hardly the product of rational economic calculation, also fell. Nor has any convincing single explanation been produced for declining death rates, which were also differentiated according to gender, age, and even location, experience varying between countryside and towns, and between different types of town. Medical advances were limited, although improved water supply and sanitation were of some significance. If dietary improvement was the key, it is puzzling that the death rate should have turned down first among women who, certainly among the working classes, traditionally ate less well than their husbands. Whatever the processes behind these various demographic trends, the outcome by 1914 was a population in which the absolute number of the elderly was rising, while approximately a third was aged under fourteen years.

By 1911 about 80 per cent of the 45 million or so inhabitants of the British Isles lived in urban communities. The heaviest concentrations were in the industrial heartlands (table 1.6). London remained as the major exception, set apart by its several roles as national and imperial capital, world financial centre, and location of the most important entrepot for international trade. Just over half of those employed in the service sector by 1911 and 40 per cent of those engaged in banking, finance, and the professions lived in the south east, although the region had only about 29 per cent of the total population.

Table 1.6 *Population of Britain by regions (million)*

London/Greater London	6.6
SE Lancashire	1.3
West Midlands	1.5
Clydeside	1.3
West Yorkshire	1.0
Merseyside	1.0
Tyneside	0.7

(Waller, 1983: 8)

In the absence of any official modern census before 1920, Japan's population figures are not totally reliable but most estimates converge round about 49.5 million in 1911. Towns were well developed even in the Tokugawa period but Meiji modernisation was inevitably accompanied by some further redistribution of population. But if the direction of migration resembled what was happening in Britain, the orders of magnitude were very different. By 1913 rather more than a quarter of Japanese lived in towns of more than 10,000 inhabitants, while towns of 50,000 citizens contained just over 14 per cent. Despite the steady advance of urbanisation Japan still retained its predominantly rural character in 1914. At 72 per cent, the proportion of people living in the countryside was almost the same as Britain's urban population.

Statistical deficiencies also make it difficult to be certain about the causes of Japan's population growth. As in all industrialising societies, death rates initially turned upwards but started to drift downwards from the early to middle 1880s. The pattern was similar to that occurring in Britain although a death rate estimated at 24.17 per thousand by 1910 was well up on the British figure (Ohbuchi, 1976: 331). Rising demands for labour and some improvement in living standards consequent upon industrialisation may initially have raised the birth rate by bringing down the age of marriage and increasing the proportion of people marrying. Official counts do suggest that an irregularly rising birth rate provided the main impetus to population growth, but this may merely have reflected improvements in registration or a decline in the widespread practice of abortion (Ohbuchi, 1976: 330–2).

Family and women

In both countries the basic unit of social organisation was the family, although direct comparison is complicated by the fact that the Japanese word for family, *ie*, carried with it a meaning much broader than immediate blood relationships and also had connotations of property and reputation. The relationships that in Britain characterised the nuclear or extended family were in Japan extended much more widely, covering all the various groups to which an individual might belong and reaching right up to the emperor, who was regarded as the head of the family that was the nation of Japan. Among the peasantry its strongest manifestation was the village where the natural social cohesion arising from physical proximity was reinforced by a certain amount of self government. The peculiar demands of wet rice cultivation demanded communal and collective action, further cementing the bonds of group loyalty. The fact that many early urban workers retained close links with their rural roots meant that the social structures and mores which developed in the expanding towns were strongly influenced by these traditional concepts. The vertical bonds which linked people in this way, whether as members of the same village, occupation, or religious group, were often stronger than those which, if only informally after 1868, linked them horizontally to those of similar social standing. As for the narrower concept of the family, one aspect of the Meiji effort to modernise Japan was the extolling of the patriarchal warrior family as the model for all, although in the countryside especially more flexible attitudes towards both marriage and inheritance persisted.

In Britain the average size of families fell from six children to three between the 1870s and the 1900s, statistics which again obscure marked differences between social groups. There is no consensus, however, as to whether the nuclear or the extended family was the norm, evidence indicating the existence of both. Statistical indicators certainly suggest that few people actually lived in three-generational households but other evidence reveals that wider networks of kin were very strong and frequently utilised. There has also been disagreement about the British family's function. Suggestions that its traditional economic activities were disappearing, leaving only its social roles as the source of nurture, affection, and legitimate sexual activity, appear to be unfounded. The family unit was still important in business, and among self employed artisans and tenant farmers, while there was also a strong tradition of occupations passing from father to son among both professionals and some skilled workers. Some working-class households were dependent upon income generated by several family members, not just the male head. Such families also relied very heavily on the unpaid domestic work of wives and mothers, something which was also particularly prevalent in rural Japan.

This last point might appear to confirm the notion that prewar Britain and Japan were both highly patriarchal. In Britain employment in domestic service or the sweated industries certainly implied women's subservience, while even in factories their psychological sense of inferiority was reinforced by male attitudes and differential pay. But there is also some evidence that many working-class women accepted this subordinate position quite amicably, with the married ones often trading it off for domestic dominance (Roberts, 1984). Similarly, the fact that the majority of middle- and upper-class women also seem to have accepted a role defined for them by convention, the teaching of the church, and even the exigencies of physiognomy, should not be adduced as evidence of inferiority so much as of difference. Marital relationships were based on affection and mutuality far more commonly than some commentators have allowed, while the notion that middle-class men used their wives for procreation and prostitutes for pleasure, the so-called 'double standard', has been vigorously rebutted (Mason, 1994). Widening educational provision did serve to produce a growing number of educated and articulate middle-class women whose resentment at their perceived inequality ultimately came to focus on their exclusion from the parliamentary franchise. After forty years of peaceful agitation achieved very little, militants opted for more violent tactics through the Women's Social and Political Union. In the process they earned themselves a notoriety and historical attention which their actual numbers and arguably their impact perhaps did not warrant.

In Japan women's subordinate status was actually written in to the Social Code promulgated in 1898 and the Peace Police Law of 1900 barred them from political activity. These measures reflected the historic emphasis on military virtue which had reduced women's basic role to bearing children and looking after men, a position which derived philosophical support from Confucianism. Their duty was defined as one of obedience successively to fathers, husbands, and sons, while their function as panderers to men's pleasures permitted a more open attitude than in Britain towards the keeping of mistresses and prostitution. This tolerance did not extend to wives, however, whose sexual infidelities, as in Britain, were regarded as serious matters. Growing exposure to Western ideas encouraged a few mainly middle-class, educated women to organise largely unsuccessful campaigns to draw public attention to prostitution and poverty. Just before the war the Blue Stocking Society or *Seitosha* was launched. As in Britain, however, far more women were affected by economic change than by intellectual propagandising. The growth of the service sector afforded some new employment opportunities for females as secretaries, teachers, nurses, and clerks, while in the countryside, the mechanisation of textile production provided work for as many as 250,000 women by 1900. Although their economic role, like that of working-class women in Britain, had probably always ensured some degree of independence for peasant women, factory work tended to push them still further into a lifestyle at odds with that demanded by their traditional role and status. Nevertheless, in a society in which status was all important, the vast majority of Japanese women had internalised a value system which ascribed to them a subordinate standing. Japanese women, wrote Clive Holland in 1913, were 'neither rebels nor repines, but accept the position without a murmur' (Holland, 1913: 117).

Social structure and living standards

One of the most obvious features of Edwardian Britain's social landscape was economic inequality. The regional income of the south of England was far above that of the rest of the country, while aggregate unemployment was heaviest in the industrial areas. Even after thirty years of falling food prices, social surveys in York and London suggested that at the turn of the century about a third of the urban population was living on or below the poverty line, which for the first time was defined in terms of income. Thereafter, the rate of improvement in real incomes probably slowed down. Against this must be set the fact that public amenities continued to expand, while parliament introduced a number of measures to deal with some of the causes of poverty identified by the social surveyors. These reforms involved a certain amount of income redistribution. At a time when it hardly fell upon the working classes, direct taxation as a proportion of government revenue rose from about 50 per cent in 1901–5 to 57.8 per cent by 1912–13 (Pollard, 1992: 15).

The other dominant landmark was class, although this should not be taken to imply the existence of overt mutual antagonism (Brown, 1982: 128–64). Nor is it at all clear now where the boundaries lay, given that they were sufficiently flexible to allow a certain degree of mobility. Delineating class according to income tax liability, then payable on annual earnings in excess of £160, gives a working class composed of 5.6 million wage earners, 1.2 million small shopkeepers, and 1.23 million salaried people, most of whom earned less than this threshold. The middle class consisted of 400,000 salaried individuals, 330,000 professionals and some indeterminate proportion of the 580,00 farmers and 622,000 employers. The rest of the employers, along with the landed aristocracy and top professional people, formed the upper income groups from which was also drawn the 2.5 per cent of the total population who owned two thirds of the wealth (Marwick, 1967: 19–21).

Yet even this way of considering class cannot fully capture the complexities and subtleties of British society. It identifies obvious extremes but misses differences at the margins between the classes or the very significant variations which could exist within the broad classifications. The wages of an unskilled worker, averaging between 75p and £1.05 a week facilitated a very different life style from that available to a skilled man, who might earn as much as £2.50 a week. Neither can definitions based on income cater for the observable fact that white collar workers enjoyed a higher social standing than better paid manual workers, such as miners. Class and status were more than purely financial and material categories, involving other considerations which were widely understood but only sometimes institutionalised, as on trains and in the seating arrangements at churches and official functions.

A similarly complex state of affairs prevailed in Japan. The Tokugawa system of formally ascribed status, with its strict codes of behaviour and occupational possibilities for each of its rigidly organised hierarchical groups, was abandoned soon after the Meiji Restoration. The ensuing equalisation of all people, save the royal family and a small nobility, certainly appeared to offer enhanced possibilities of social mobility by removing restrictions on economic behaviour. Yet language and perceptions were much harder to change, while government attempts to instil a sense of continuity and stability at a time of rapid change frequently necessitated the reassertion of old values and concepts. The outcastes in particular continued to be subjected to discrimination and intolerance.

Prewar Japanese society was thus no more amenable than the contemporary British social structure to analysis in simple economic terms because notions of social order and rank were still shot through with other considerations. Contemporaries tended to think in terms of *Joryu Shakai*, literally upstream society, essentially meaning the wealthy but also implying elegance and fashionableness. In the middle were the *Chusan Kaikyu*, a middle income group, usually property owners, but again embracing less tangible traits such as good character, hard work, and a desire to succeed. At the bottom were the *Kaso Shakai*, a term carrying with it overtones of condescension and contempt, and implications of dependence and weakness. Within this latter grouping were subdivisions, including at the very bottom the *Kyumin*, those in extreme deprivation.

Urban incomes were about 1.3 times higher than rural ones but even in the countryside differentials existed, with larger farmers buying up property from smaller ones who could not afford to pay the land tax. While town dwellers probably benefited most from improved social amenities, standards of living deteriorated in the sense that house building did not keep step with inward migration. Major cities rapidly acquired substantial slum districts characterised by endemic poverty. It was generally believed within Japan itself that some 10 per cent of people were poor (Chubachi and Taira, 1976: 407). One prewar survey indicated that slightly under 9 per cent of the population of Hyogo prefecture, which included the major town of Kobe, lived in poverty. Such findings cannot be directly compared with those of Booth and Rowntree since neither their methods nor their definitions were the same. Nor is there much reliable data on the prewar distribution of incomes in Meiji Japan and many calculations are based on related variables. Based on assumptions about rice consumption, Maeda Masana assigned 13.3 per cent of the population to his top or *Joto* category in the 1880s. His intermediate or *Chuto* class made up 29.2 per cent, with the remaining 57.5 per cent classified as inferior, or *Kato*. A government survey in Gifu prefecture, taken at about the same time, suggested that the minimum annual per capita income of the *Joto* was Y46 as against Y23 for the intermediate class.

In the non-primary sector labour's share of the national income actually appears to have fallen from about 80 per cent in 1885 to 65 per cent by 1910. On the other hand, one modern estimate concludes that aggregate real income among the lower social groups rose by some 55 per cent between 1886 and 1912 (Ono and Watanabe, 1976: 371). Whatever happened to income distribution, absolute levels remained very low. Average Japanese consumption was about Y75 a head in 1913, nearly seven times lower than the comparable figure for England (Sheridan, 1993: 92). Small wonder that Clive Holland was moved to observe that even unskilled workers in Britain with their twenty shillings a week wondered how a Japanese could live comfortably on his equivalent of three or four pence a day (Holland, 1913: 147).

The system of power and authority

Formal structures

Unlike Japan Britain had no written constitution formally defining the role of the monarch and the crown's power had gradually diminished over the centuries, although its unseen influence was still considerable and as an institution the monarchy was impregnable. Metaphysical support derived from the sovereign's position as head of the established church as well as from the weight of popular sentiment which had little sympathy for republicanism. Formal, effective power rested in parliament which, like the whole system of power and authority, was heavily biased in favour of the wealthy. By 1900 those without a parliamentary vote included not only women but also more than one in three of adult males, almost all of them from the poorer sections of society. Conversely, some university graduates and the owners of business premises could vote in more than one constituency. Until the passage of the Parliament Act in 1911 the wishes of the lower house elected by even this limited franchise could be thwarted by the unelected House of Lords. Cabinets were drawn almost exclusively from the social elite and it was not until 1905 that any working man acquired cabinet rank. Only after the introduction in 1911 of payment for MPs was there any real prospect of a political career for individuals lacking access to substantial financial resources. Both the Liberal and Conservative Parties drew the majority of their MPs from the business and commercial classes, while relative wealth also shaped the profiles of the two minority parties, the Irish Home Rulers, and the Labour Party.

By 1900 British parliamentary parties were recognisably modern in that they were formally organised and espoused different ideas and principles. Yet if this imparted more of a national flavour to politics, local rather than central government impinged more on the lives of the average citizen. The principle of elected local government had been progressively extended during the nineteenth century and it has even been suggested that prior to 1914 the average Briton was barely aware of the state's activities, beyond the post office and the policeman (Taylor, 1965: 1). Even that is misleading, however. The police were established by central legislation, but forces were locally organised as a safeguard against totalitarianism. For the same reasons the small, centrally funded, standing professional army was subject to civilian control, with many of the infantry regiments raised on a county basis. Education, too, was the responsibility from 1902 of local education committees while the local poor law union remained as the main agency of welfare provision, despite more central intervention after 1906.

In Japan, too, local rather than national horizons remained more important for most people although the state consistently sought to harness local energies to the broader national purpose. Following the Restoration about 300 feudal domains were consolidated into counties and prefectures. General policy objectives were centrally determined in the expectation that considerations of regional honour and compliance with the wishes of the hierarchy would ensure their implementation by local authorities. Targets were centrally set for educational provision, for example, but local government bodies were expected to build the schools. The curriculum was designed in accordance with the ideals and aims set forth in the Imperial Rescript on Education of 1892. Another manifestation of centralisation was the decision to raise a standing conscript army: by 1912 it was a quarter of a million strong.

As for as the structure of central government a written constitution, finalised in 1889, embodied many democratic principles, including a bicameral Diet of 300 paid members, parliamentary parties, cabinet government, secret ballot, and elections. This certainly represented a radical change from what had gone before but its democratic potential was largely circumscribed. First, the role of the emperor was ambivalent. The constitution conferred upon him numerous duties and titular responsibilities but in practice the bodies of which he was nominally head often had different and sometimes competing powers, effectively restricting his role to ratifying ministerial decisions. On the other hand, the spiritual authority deriving from the emperor's status as a living god, was also formally enshrined in the constitution and was capable of being exploited by politicians for undemocratic purposes. Second, the old nobility had been replaced after the Restoration by a small court aristocracy. Membership of the House of Peers in the new Diet could thus be based only partially on the principle of heredity. The numbers were made up by appointment, opening the way for jobbery, the more so since the upper house had constitutional powers equal to those of the lower House of Representatives, and could veto legislation passed up to it. Third, the franchise was limited to males who paid more than Y10 a year in tax, giving an electorate of about 2 per cent of the population. Predictably, the Diet was overwhelmingly agrarian in its composition.

Political parties had emerged by 1900 but they did not represent different ideological positions so much as rival personal groups. Ozaki Yukio observed in 1918 that the basic political concept in the Orient was not that of party but of faction,

> pursuing private and personal interests instead of the interests of the state . . . political parties which should be based and dissolved solely on principle and political views, are really affairs of personal connections and sentiments, the relation between the leader and the members of a party being similar to those which subsisted between a feudal lord and his liegemen. (Tsunoda, de Bary and Keene, 1958: 689–90)

Nor was it constitutional practice for cabinets to be drawn from any majority party; in fact ministers did not even have to be members of the Diet. Appointments were frequently engineered by members of the *genro*, the self perpetuating group of clan leaders who had masterminded the revolution in 1868. They had no formal constitutional position but continued to direct Japan's fortunes in the name of the emperor, frequently resorting to distinctly undemocratic methods. A Social Democratic Party, for instance, was banned on the very day it was formed in 1901, while the later Japan Socialist Party lasted for only a year before it was suppressed in 1907.

By 1900 one of the oligarchs, Hirobumi Ito, had assumed effective leadership of the Seiyukai Party, his chief rival being another of the *genro*, Yamagata Aritomo. As Prime Minister, Yamagata put through the 1899 order allowing the navy and the army to nominate the forces' cabinet ministers from among their own serving senior ranks. His intention was to protect the military from civilian influence, thus ensuring that strategic matters were left to the experts. However, the stipulation that the ministers had to be serving officers meant that they were subject to the relevant chain of military command and could in practice be dismissed only by the Chief of Staff, rather than the prime minister. The most malign effects of this did not become apparent until the 1930s but a harbinger appeared as early as 1912. When the government refused to sanction increased military expenditure, the army minister resigned. The cabinet of chief minister Saionji was forced to follow suit, and a replacement administration was forced out after weeks of manoeuvrings and rioting in the streets, to be replaced by an admiral. Only a corruption scandal impelled his departure in 1914.

Social control

In all societies formal institutions of power and authority are supplemented by less obvious mechanisms of control. It has been commonly argued that education, organised religion, recreation, the press, and even charitable activity, were crucial to the process whereby ruling elites maintained themselves by imposing their own values on the mass of a population. There is no doubt that the Meiji state set out quite deliberately to influence the habits and attitudes of the general population in what was defined by the ruling clique as the national interest. Similarly, governments adopted measures to pre-empt the emergence of social disharmonies of the sort becoming apparent in the advanced industrial nations. Their success has often been attributed to the fact that the Japanese people passively accepted such central direction because they had already internalised many of the values emphasised by the state. Popular quiescence is said to have reflected the strength of the *ie* and prevailing notions of status and hierarchy. In practice, however, there was considerable popular indifference and resentment against some the new regime's edicts, much of it channelled through the Freedom and Peoples' Rights Movement. Other malcontents included those rural inhabitants whose tax burdens increased as a result of the redrawing of administrative boundaries, or who lost valuable labour when military conscription was instituted in 1873 (Waswo, 1996: 22–34). The very fact that it was thought necessary to promulgate a Peace Preservation Law points to the ineffectiveness of social control mechanisms. So, too, does the so-called dangerous thoughts legislation implemented at the turn of the century and giving wide powers to control what were deemed subversive movements.

As for Britain, social control theory has often been used to explain the apparent paradox of a class-based society in which after 1850 there was relatively little sign of serious direct conflict. Leaving aside the moot point as to whether class conflict was ever characteristic of British society, it is by no means self evident that the motives behind private philanthropic endeavour, education and welfare reform, the provision of commercial leisure, or the opinions expressed in the pulpit and the press were invariably self interested in the manner suggested by the advocates of social control theory. Even in those activities where social control motives can be discerned, the intended targets were not always passive ciphers. On the contrary, they frequently adopted a highly calculative attitude towards the various manifestations of social control, imposing their own preferences and values upon them (Thompson, 1981: 189–208; Brown, 1982: 184–9; Donajgrodzki, 1977).

The system of ritual

Britain

By the system of ritual is meant those values and cultural practices to which most individuals subscribe and which bind a society together, along with the institutions which support and sustain those values. Emile Durkheim puts it thus: 'All that societies require in order to hold together is that their members fix their eyes on the same end and come together in a single faith' (Lukes, 1969: 23). However, values are not always easy to tease out, they are not amenable to statistical analysis, they change over time, and they can have different meanings for different people. Generalisations can thus easily distort or mislead. Nevertheless, there is a general consensus that nineteenth-century Britain was held together by collective subscription to a set of principles summed up in the notion of respectability (Thompson, 1988). Professor Perkin has argued that by the middle of the century the 'entrepreneurial ideal' of the commercial middle classes had emerged as the dominant value system (Perkin, 1969). Aspects of respectability such as sobriety, morality, and self help were implicit in this, but his is perhaps a broader definition, extending to a general commitment to capitalism, laisser faire and individualism, and the maintenance of the existing social order with its prescribed roles for labour, capital, and women.

Two institutions in particular provided support and rationalisation for this value system. One was the empire, which served simultaneously as a manifestation and a symbol. The empire had been built, so it was frequently argued, on precisely those virtues of competitive individualism which the ideal enshrined, and in this way contributed to a sense of national identity (Mackenzie, 1986). Even the poorest Briton could take a pride in belonging to the empire on which the sun never set. The other, and probably more vital institution was the church, although it is worth pointing out that religion could still be divisive and that Protestantism, which, with varying degrees of fervour and differing doctrinal emphases, held sway everywhere except in Ireland, was itself internally divided. Even so, Christianity suffused every part of national life in the nineteenth century. Education, philanthropy, and even recreation were frequently set in a religious context. The monarch was head of the Church of England, parliament opened its sessions with prayer, and even for those who were not active members, the church provided the rites of passage from birth to death. Christianity, therefore, was a central prop, buttressing traditional values, providing pomp and spectacle, and endowing official rituals with a metaphysical dimension which everyone understood.

Japan

Japan's national culture was also shaped, albeit much more deliberately, by religious and imperialist or patriotic influences. The cult of the emperor was fostered so successfully that the physically unimpressive and unknown youth who ascended the throne in 1868 was genuinely mourned by the mass of ordinary people when he died in 1912. In terms of religion, Japan was more heterodox than Britain, even though there was a good deal of overlap between the adherents of the main faiths, Buddhism, Confucianism and Shinto, a long-established form of spirit worship which espoused the divinity of the emperor. By the 1890s the Meiji oligarchs had effectively blended Confucianism with Shinto in the interests of the national polity or *kokutai*. As a result religion, in the words of one contemporary, was 'transmuted into an hereditary moral impulse actuating the whole nation' (Holland, 1913: 193). Shinto had no moral code, equating morality with actuality. Behaviour was thus determined pragmatically, reinforcing that aversion to confrontation which so struck Western visitors to Japan. In such a society Christianity, with its strongly prescriptive behavioural codes and its claims to exclusivity, made little headway.

Christian missionaries were briefly important in fostering education, however, although it gradually dawned on Meiji officials that education could be used, not only as a means of modernisation, but also to generate a sense of nationhood. From the 1880s, therefore, centrally controlled school text books and teacher training were both endowed with an imperial, national ethic, disguised as moral culture. In this way imperialism became 'the life-blood and very heart of hearts of Japan' (Holland, 1913: 252). It received an enormous fillip from the successful conduct of the wars against China and Russia. The latter was particularly significant as the first conflict in which an Oriental nation had defeated a European power.

The emotions and responses evoked by the military success against Russia had some resonances with British attitudes at the time of the Boer War although any resemblance was superficial. Japan's triumphs tapped a deeply rooted respect for the military. In part the legacy of *bushido*, the centuries-old code of the *samurai*, it was enshrined in the special political privileges accorded to the armed forces, perpetuated by the inclusion of military drill in educational establishments, and institutionalised in conscription. The

British, conversely, may have enjoyed military spectacle and ceremonial, but militarism as such was not strong. Pacifism had its supporters, often motivated by religious or political convictions. The peacetime standing army was small and the average soldier commanded little respect, save in time of war. Among the lower orders professional soldiering was generally regarded as an occupation of the last resort, while those higher up viewed it as something akin to sport (Brown, 1990: 237–54).

Dissent

A well established and widely accepted set of values, supporting and complementing a strongly centralised structure of formal power and authority, ensured that on the eve of the First World War Japan, like Britain, was a remarkably cohesive society. Nevertheless, tensions were visible. Education may have served its purpose in facilitating the acquisition of Western technical and professional knowledge but inevitably it also produced a more inquisitive and questioning populace. Meiji policy-makers agreed on the need for further modernisation but intellectuals were divided between those who equated that with more Westernisation and those who sought to devise a more distinctively Japanese way forward. From the mid 1890s the latter view began to prevail in the face of mounting evidence that the West had freed itself neither of economic problems nor of social conflict. Before 1914 many Japanese were concerned by mounting evidence that their own society had not entirely avoided the undesirable implications of modernisation. Outbreaks of popular unrest and strikes appeared to threaten the very ethos of national life by challenging existing notions of status and group loyalty. Others detected signs that the effort traditionally exerted on behalf of the group and the nation was being diverted towards personal aggrandisement and acquisitiveness by a hedonistic, younger, post-revolutionary generation. The suicide in 1912 of General Nogi, army commander during the war against Russia, has sometimes been attributed to his despair at what he viewed as the degeneration of traditional national virtues of loyalty and duty.

Such tensions were perhaps inevitable in a society which had been subject to the upheavals inherent in the concerted drive to modern capitalistic development. It was also very likely that a central government always concerned to maintain social consensus would react to outbreaks of popular disorder and expressions of intellectual dissent. Government responses in the years before 1914 included the Peace Police Law, the suppression of socialist parties, a more vigorous attempt to control the press, and attempts to harness the power of organised religion more firmly behind Japanese values. None of this was sufficient to deter anarchists from plotting unsuccessfully against the emperor. The Meiji Emperor in fact died of natural causes in 1912 but the early months of the succeeding Taisho era of Emperor Yoshihito were marked by further signs of political instability, a series of shortlived cabinets falling victim to a potent mixture of military intriguing, street violence, and corruption.

Similarly disturbing currents of unrest were apparent in Britain where the institutions which sustained social values appeared to be on the defensive (Dangerfield, 1961; Stone, 1983: 74–153; Brown, 1995: 1–19). The cohesion and legitimacy of empire were threatened by the rising forces of indigenous nationalism in Ireland, India, Egypt, and white Africa, while its economic rationale was questioned by economists and middle-class intellectuals. Support for formal religion was never as great as contemporaries liked to believe, but measured by recruitment to the ministry and the sale of religious books its hold on society was becoming less secure from the 1880s. Some of the church's social functions were being replaced by professional social services and commercial leisure while the burgeoning press was challenging the pulpit as the main shaper of public opinion. By 1914 attendance at Sunday worship was well down on its 1851 figure. It is irrelevant that for some – perhaps many – church attendance was nothing more than a matter of form. The important point is that even this significance was beginning to wane. At the same time, serious threats to existing social mores appeared to be presented by the militant activities of the suffragettes, the imminence of rebellion or civil war in Ireland, and severe, frequently violent industrial unrest. Beatrice Webb summed up the uncertainties arising from the juxtaposition of these several social movements and trends by suggesting that they all raised the basic issue of whether people were going to be governed as they had been in the past by reason, or by emotion. As it turned out, however, any immediate danger of domestic turmoil was entirely overshadowed by events in central Europe which ushered in the First World War.

2

From Great War to Great Crash: production and reproduction, 1914–c.1930

Introduction

Britain entered the First World War on 4 August 1914. A fortnight or so later Japan joined in on the side of the Entente powers against Germany. British commitment was total, ultimately involving the mobilisation of all her economic and human resources for a conflict costlier and longer than anyone initially anticipated. Japan's military involvement was peripheral, entailing little more than some minor activity against German interests in the Pacific, although she also took the opportunity to extend her influence in China, thereby causing some disquiet in the United States. In the world at large the war unleashed potent forces. Nationalist and Bolshevik ideologies contributed to political instability and economic insularity in the postwar years, technology made rapid strides, governments acquired unprecedented powers of control and influence over their populations, the balance of power and authority shifted as monarchy retreated before the more evident power of the masses, and international diplomacy was driven by a desire to prevent any repetition of war. Above all, disruption of the system of trading complementarities built up over the long nineteenth century radically affected the global economy. In both Britain and Japan, reconstruction and a determination to return to the gold standard were among the most obvious features of the system of production in the 1920s. Socially, it might appear that large scale disruption was caused in Britain by population movements, conscription, state intervention, high casualty rates, and the other characteristics of total war. Yet it is difficult to judge how far the war acted as a catalyst, accelerating trends already apparent in patterns of social organisation and development, and how far it fundamentally altered them. Similar problems arise in the case of Japan where the social effects of the war are not always easily distinguished from those occurring as part of the continuing process of industrialisation, which itself was intimately connected with the war.

The system of production

Agriculture

When hostilities commenced in 1914 virtually three quarters of Britain's imports consisted of raw materials and foodstuffs. Almost four fifths of the cereals, two fifths of the meat, three quarters of the fruit, and all the sugar consumed in Britain were produced abroad. Yet such was the contemporary expectation of a short conflict and such the confidence in the ability of the royal navy to keep open the sea lanes, that for some time the government did not initiate even a voluntary effort to increase domestic food production. Eventually, however, unrestricted German submarine warfare was thought to pose a serious threat to food supplies, while hoarding and panic buying led to rising prices and public discontent. Towards the end of 1916, therefore, a Food Production Department was established with powers to compel farmers to change their cropping patterns in order to increase the amount of land under arable cultivation. Despite the diversion of labour and horses to military uses and scarcities of imported fertilisers and feed stuffs, some three million acres were ploughed up by 1918. The conversion process was further encouraged by the 1917 Corn Production Act, offering guaranteed prices and minimum wages. With the Food Production Department also undertaking the bulk buying of seeds, fertilisers, and machinery, the result was a substantial increase in the calorific value of domestically grown food.

The passage of the Agricultural Act in 1920 appeared to signal a long term commitment both to the principle of intervention and to the policy of encouraging domestic cereal production, but the ending of the postwar boom brought the price of wheat crashing down. Faced with paying out some £20 million a year to honour its guarantees, the government repealed the Corn Production legislation in 1921. Farmers turned away from arable, reverting to meat, vegetables, and fruit, which had a ready access to home markets. However, these particular commodities proved increasingly vulnerable to more efficiently produced and better marketed foreign goods. As a result, and despite some scattered government aid, the most significant measure being the creation of a beet sugar industry, British agriculture in the 1920s generally lapsed into depression. Postwar land sales increased owner occupancy from about a tenth to more than a third of all farms but falling product prices afflicted owners and tenants alike, making it difficult to prosper in the face of high interest payments or relatively stable rents.

Japanese farmers were also struggling in the 1920s, although their problems were potentially far more serious, given the size of the agricultural sector. Even by 1930 the land was still providing employment for about half the population. During the war years output rose, though not so impressively as the figures in table 2.1 suggest, since they have not been adjusted to allow for inflation. Nevertheless, real increases were recorded, and there was a modest growth in the per capita availability of food. In the short term, many farmers did extremely well. Prices reached an all-time high in 1917 but when they doubled again over the following year rioting broke out. Anger was stirred by the huge profits made by the larger farmers and also by the actions of profiteers indulging in forward speculation on rice prices. Casualties were numerous in the 180 or so cities, towns, and villages affected by the unrest and it took troops three weeks to quell the protests.

Table 2.1 *Japan: values of sectoral output (Ymn)*

	1914	1919
Industry	1371	6738
Agriculture	1700	4083

(Lockwood, 1955: 39)

The farmers' prosperity, however, did not long survive the war and in the course of the next decade agriculture became the sick man of the Japanese economy. It is true that, particularly in the later 1920s, there was some diversification into wheat and a wider range of vegetable and fruit production, while poultry farming also expanded. However, these made only marginal contributions to total agricultural output which continued to be dominated by silk and rice. The price of raw silk fell in the postwar slump before recovering sufficiently to register an overall trebling between 1914 and 1929. By the spring of 1929 the export price stood at Y1,420 per *kin* (0.6kg) as against Y800 to Y900 in the prewar period. Yet sericulture was very much a subsidiary activity, providing a secondary income only for about 40 per cent of farming families in 1929. For most farmers rice remained the primary crop, occupying well over half of the nation's cultivatable land. Annual production, however, did not rise much above its prewar level and the price fluctuated considerably. In January 1920 it reached Y55 a *koku* (4.94 bushels) but with the ending of the boom it fell by more than half. For a while, prices were stabilised at a higher level by the provisions of the Rice Act which allowed the Ministry of Agriculture to stockpile at times of low prices and to sell when prices rose. This scheme was undermined after 1927 by a run of good harvests which brought prices down dramatically. Nor did farmers benefit as much as might have been expected from the rising home demand for rice in the 1920s. This was because the government was actively encouraging the cultivation and importation of rice from Formosa and Korea. These imports were equal to between 12 and 14 per cent of domestic production between 1927 and 1929.

The growing volumes of rice imports and silk exports in the 1920s meant in effect that Japanese agriculture was becoming more fully integrated into the world economy than ever before. As a result, internal prices were increasingly influenced by overseas events while Japan's own developing commercialisation meant that such effects were more quickly and thoroughly transmitted throughout the domestic economy. Farmers' costs remained relatively high and attempts to compensate by producing more further depressed crop prices. Consequently, the average rent of a ricefield in the 1920s was 50 per cent above its product value. Japanese farm rents were seven times higher than English levels. The majority of farmers were still small scale tenants who in 1930 occupied almost a half of the country's farmland, as against about a fifth in 1868. The average farm size in the postwar period was one *cho* (2.45 acres) but official estimates reckoned that farms of less than 1.2 *cho* were in deficit and that those smaller than 2.5 *cho* could not sustain an adequate standard of life for their holders.

Although agriculture thus remained of major importance to the Japanese economy, one of the chief effects of the world war was to hasten the process whereby its relative significance declined. The agrarian labour force shrank slightly from 16.4 million in 1910 to 14.3 million by 1920. Over the same period industrial employment rose from 4.1 million to 6.3 million. Not allowing for inflation, the value of agricultural output more than doubled between 1914 and 1919, but that of industry almost quadrupled (table 2.2). As a result, industry's contribution to the GNP by 1919 was 65 per cent larger than agriculture's: in 1914 agriculture's share had outweighed that of industry by about a quarter. The balance continued to shift in this same direction throughout the 1920s. The primary sector contributed slightly more than 30 per cent to the National Income in 1920 but only 17.6 per cent in 1930. Over the same period the contribution of secondary industry rose from 29 to 31.6 per cent (Nakamura, 1994: 4)

Economic growth

Averaging about 1.5 per cent a year through the 1920s, Britain's economic growth was healthier than in the Edwardian years when the high exports of the staples had to some extent disguised their relatively low productivity. In part high growth rates reflected the rising significance in the economy of modern, more technological and thus more highly productive industries. On the other hand, since there was relatively little increase in aggregate capital stock, rising productivity must also have owed something to labour shake-out and its more intensive use in all industries.

While Britain remained a far more important industrial power, the evidence of table 2.2 is that in important respects Japan continued to catch up. Growth rates were considerably higher and productivity was also growing more rapidly than in Britain, although remaining well behind in absolute terms. In 1929 the real GDP per hour worked in Japan was only 31 per cent of that in Britain (Feinstein, 1989; 4). Furthermore, compared with earlier years the Japanese economy performed sluggishly, the average annual growth rate of 3.2 per cent being rather lower than that which had prevailed up to 1920. This was mainly due to the depressed state of agriculture and, though to a lesser extent, of the war-related industries.

Table 2.2 *Britain and Japan: economic indicators, 1913–29*

	Britain		Japan	
	1913	1928	1913	1928
Share of world manufacturing output (%)	13.6	9.9	2.7	3.3
	1913	1929	1913	1929
Share of world manufactured exports (%)	30.2	22.4	2.3	3.9
GDP index	100	100	32.5	51.9
PC GDP index	100	105	100	146

(Bairoch, 1982: 304; Maizels, 1963: 189; Maddison, 1991: 198; Alford, 1996: 151)

Industry

The initial impetus behind Japanese industrial expansion was provided by the war, as the British consul in Osaka explained.

> Not only did Japanese manufacturers find themselves freed from competition in their main market – China – but, owing to the incapacity of England and other regular suppliers . . . they were able to build up a great trade in substitute goods with markets . . . to which they had not previously found entry. (Robertson, 1990: 88)

For example, the expansion of the cotton industry before 1914 had been sufficient to raise its export of piece goods only to the equivalent of about 2 per cent of British exports. Now Britain's military commitments allowed Japan to consolidate a position in the large Indian market, as well as continuing to export to existing outlets in China and the USA. There was also some diversification of cotton products although the old staple types remained dominant. The labour force in cotton spinning rose by 65 per cent between 1914 and 1919. The positive impact of the war on textile manufacture is apparent in table 2.3, which shows an increase of almost 20 per cent in cotton yarn output between 1913 and 1920.

Other industries expanded by supplying to the Allies goods previously obtained from enemy powers. This applied particularly to processed foodstuffs but another minor example was provided by children's toys. For other hitherto relatively undeveloped Japanese manufactures, the war acted as the

Table 2.3 *Japan: industrial outputs*

	1913	1920
Cotton yarn (mn lbs)	607.2	726.8
Raw silk (mn lbs)	30.93	48.23
Coal (mn tons)	21.3	29.2
Finished steel (000 tons)	255	533
Cement (000 tons)	645	1353

(Allen, 1981a: 117)

equivalent of an import tariff. The Unequal Treaties had effectively pre-vented the protection of domestic industry and even their revision early in the twentieth century was not comprehensive. In restricting the flow of foreign goods to Japan, however, war facilitated some degree of import substitution. Woollen goods production benefited from this, for instance, as well as from the increased world demand for military clothing. Similarly, prewar Japan was almost totally reliant upon imported chemicals such as dyestuffs, drugs, and fertilisers. With foreign supplies no longer available, the government established a Chemical Research Laboratory in 1914 and took steps to encourage the dyestuffs and pharmaceutical industries. Indigenous produc-tion began of soda by electrolysis, Bakelite, rayon, and plate glass. The coun-try's first alkali plant, built for the Asahi Glass Company, opened in 1917. Domestic iron, steel, and machine production all grew in the war years as well, partly, as in the case of textile machinery, because they were unobtain-able elsewhere, partly as the knock-on effect of a huge expansion in ship-building. Japanese governments had encouraged construction prior to 1914 but war demand pushed up launchings from 55,000 tons in 1913 to 646,000 by 1919, and the size of Japan's own registered merchant fleet increased by one million gross tons. In the process, the domestic production of metals, re-ciprocal engines, turbines and boilers all benefited. Between 1913 and 1919 the home requirement for iron rose by about half to 751,000 tons, while steel output went up from 924,000 to 1,165,000 tons (Yonekura, 1994: 79). Such increases played their part in boosting the share of industrial output contrib-uted by the modern heavy sector of metals, machinery, and chemicals (table 2.4). Industrial investment multiplied seventeen times during the war, as greatly enhanced profits were ploughed back into further expansion.

After 1920 depression set in as the gradual reappearance of foreign competition deprived Japanese industry of both the protection and stimulus afforded by the war. The breaking of the postwar boom was accompanied by general price deflation. This presented a new situation to the Japanese whose economy, prior to the 1920s, had been in a state of almost constant inflation. Companies had become accustomed to expanding through inflation-oriented asset management, making profits from long term price rises which

Table 2.4 *Japan: shares of real manufacturing output (%)*

	1900	1920
Food products	47.2	30.6
Textiles	25.5	27.8
Metals	1.4	7.8
Machinery	2.9	13.7
Chemicals	9.0	8.9
Others	14.0	11.2

(Francks, 1992: 55)

offset wage increases. The new environment created major problems of adjustment. Comparatively higher production costs, stagnant world demand, and the restrictions imposed on warship building by the Washington naval agreement all put Japanese shipbuilding at a marked competitive disadvantage, for example, while engineering concerns which had expanded to meet the demand for munitions or for textile machinery faced ruination in the postwar slump. Although many firms found their profits wiped out they assumed that the boom would soon return. Thus they resorted to unsound practices, drawing down their reserves, borrowing heavily, overstating their assets, and continuing to pay high dividends. In this uncertain and hazardous climate two responses developed, both of which were consistent long term characteristics of Japanese economic life. One was the collaborative approach taken by private industrialists, best illustrated in the case of textiles. With many yarn traders and exporters on the verge of bankruptcy, the Cotton Spinners' Association came to the rescue, its members agreeing to curtail production and to bear some of the immediate financial losses being incurred by the exporters. The spinning firms and the merchants also worked together to resolve the difficulties caused in the futures market by the drastic drop in yarn prices, the so-called *Sohtokeai* liquidations (Seki, 1956: 27). The spinning concerns took huge losses which they met from the reserves accumulated from wartime profits. These measures not only helped to avert the collapse of a major industry but also paved the way for future growth, encouraging the search for efficiency and strengthening its capital position.

The second response to the postwar depression was an extension of state intervention in the form of more central subsidies to include some branches of chemical production, petrol, and iron and steel, although agriculture was the main beneficiary via the Rice Act. Government also sponsored the establishment of some enterprises on the Asian mainland, including the South Manchuria Railway Company. Tariffs, many of which had been lowered during the war because of shortages, were completely revised in 1926 to give greater protection. Their positive effects were confined to a few industries such as steel, however, although it is likely that improvements in management, training, and technical efficiency were more influential in the long run.

In general the heavy modern industrial sector performed rather better in the 1920s than the aggregate growth figures suggest. Those branches of engineering concerned with prime movers, machinery, textile equipment, bicycles, and scientific instruments all grew, leading to a steep fall from the middle 1920s in imports of items such as railway stock, steam engines, and some types of electrical apparatus. In textiles, rayon became commercially viable in the 1920s. The number of cotton spindles reached 6.65 million by 1929, most of them producing increasing quantities of better quality yarn rather than the lower grades dominant in earlier periods (Allen, 1981a: 112). There was also some technical improvement leading to growing productivity after 1926. Pig iron output by 1929 was almost twice as high as it had been in 1914, steel almost four times higher (Yonekura, 1994: 89, 131). The domestic production of cement tripled over the decade, while coal output rose to thirty four million tons by 1929 and electrical power output tripled. This latter reflected the success of Japan's attempts, initiated during the war, to capitalise on one of its few natural assets, water. The growing availability of hydro-electric power provided the basis for electric furnaces and artificial fertiliser plants. It also freed most consumer goods industries from their reliance on manual labour, facilitating a general shift to mechanisation.

Despite the expansion of the domestic industrial base, Japan remained highly dependent upon imports, particularly for raw materials and technically advanced machinery. By 1930 imports still provided all of the country's aluminium requirements, 85 per cent of iron and steel consumption, 79 per cent of petrol, 93 per cent of lead, 69 per cent of zinc, and 74 per cent of tin. Not surprisingly, the balance of payments slipped into the red after the collapse of the postwar boom (table 2.5). The overall volume of exports may have doubled between 1913 and 1929 and there were certainly annual fluctuations in export values but over the decade as a whole imports persistently outstripped exports. Most Japanese industry remained uncompetitive in international terms. Although the major impetus to economic growth in the decade came from the modern industrial sector, silk and cotton remained by far the most important export commodities, accounting for two thirds of total export values in 1929.

Table 2.5 *Japan: balance of trade (Ymn)*

	Exports	Imports	Difference
1914–19	12065	9190	2875
1920–24	15558	17609	−2051
1925–29	12300	12867	−567

(Nakamura, 1994: 27)

The balance of British industry was shifting too. The heavy sector had traditionally been labour intensive. As the official history of the Ministry of Munitions later put it: in 1914 'no country in the world could show such a high level of workmanship, or so much out-of-date machinery' (Pollard, 1983: 26). It might be thought, therefore, that the diversion of 5.7 million workers into the fighting services would have adversely affected manufacturing, particularly in an economy which was also experiencing restrictions on imports and general shortages of raw material. Certainly some industries such as cotton textiles and railway engineering contracted, while the early uncontrolled voluntary enlistment reduced the mining labour force by a quarter and coal output by 11 per cent. Over the course of the whole war, however, the total industrial workforce declined only slightly from 8.4 million to 8.0 million, while the index of industrial production also fell only marginally, thanks largely to longer working hours, better equipment, improved management, and direct government aid. Mining, for instance, became a highly controlled industry. As in Japan, some sectors were stimulated by the loss of imports. These included the manufacture of scientific instruments, ball bearings, and chemical products previously imported from Germany. Strategic industries, such as aircraft and vehicles, also boomed, with employment in the former rising from 60,000 to 347,000 (Ackrill, 1987: 100). Among the older industries shipbuilding expanded enormously, especially after merchant losses began to mount significantly from the end of 1916. Steel-making capacity was extended by 50 per cent and output rose from 7.7 million tons to 9.5 million over the war years.

The cessation of hostilities in November 1918 ushered in a boom on the back of pent-up consumer demand and postwar restocking. Both steel and coal did particularly well because in the main their major European competitors were still out of action. Shipbuilding also prospered with production reaching a postwar peak of two million tons in 1920. Heavy investment occurred in cotton in anticipation of continued rising demand. Once the boom broke in the spring of 1920, however, it gradually became apparent that the international economic environment which had favoured Britain's staple industries in the prewar period, had changed fundamentally. Throughout the 1920s and despite some productivity improvements, the major industries were characterised by low growth rates, failing exports, and high unemployment.

In coal the major problem was an imbalance between supply and demand. The scarcity of British coal on the international market encouraged the exploitation of new overseas resources. World supplies were thus increased but demand grew only sluggishly throughout the 1920s, at about 0.7 per cent a year as against the annual 4.0 per cent of the prewar years (Supple, 1988: 567). The general stagnation of world trade affected the demand for bunker coal and encouraged the search for fuel economies. Nor was there any compensatory increase in domestic demand, for electricity was gradually replacing coal as a source of heat and power in homes and factories alike. Productivity gains arising from technological improvement and organisational restructuring were modest, constrained by the fact that in 1924 three quarters of the industry's workforce was employed by almost 470 firms in about 1,400 mines. Attempts to shed labour and to force down wages produced serious industrial unrest, culminating in the General Strike of 1926. In the much more competitive international market for coal which existed in the 1920s all coal-exporting nations experienced difficulty. The British industry was disproportionately affected because traditionally it exported a greater proportion of its output than its competitors.

International competition and the loss of export markets were also major problems for the cotton industry, where substantial investment resulted in over capitalisation when the postwar boom ended. Former customers had developed their own industries, while some long standing markets, notably India, were colonised by the Japanese. Initially, Japan's success was attributed to lower wage costs but these were nothing new. The critical productivity advantage which the Japanese came to enjoy in the 1920s lay more in superior organisation, investment in new technologies, and different work habits. Outputs of Britain's major cotton products never recovered in the 1920s (table 2.6). It was significant in this respect that a survey conducted in 1930 found that between 65 and 70 per cent of Lancashire textile plant was more than twenty years old, and competitiveness was further undermined by the lack of any wholesale move towards the vertical integration of firms and processes.

Table 2.6 *British cotton goods output*

	Yarn (mn lbs)	Piece goods (mn sq yds)
1912	1963	8050
1924	1395	6046
1930	1048	3500

(Allen, 1961: 219)

Shipbuilding was even more depressed, although it remained relatively competitive: at least between 1927 and 1930 it built 41 per cent of the world's new motor vessels and 65 per cent of new steam ships (Ackrill, 1987: 89). However, aggregate output was well down in the 1920s with fluctuating output falling as low as 646,000 tons in 1926. The second half of the decade was more prosperous, but even then launchings between 1927 and 1930 averaged only about three quarters of the prewar total. Although many yards had switched to modern, electric power, work organisation remained inefficient while war-induced expansion left the industry with an excess capacity of between 30 and 40 per cent. Again, the major difficulty was the international imbalance between supply and demand in which the British industry, because it was highly geared to exports, was bound to suffer disproportionately. On the supply side, world capacity doubled between 1913 and 1921. Demand, conversely, was depressed by the stagnation of world trade, the increased efficiency of shipping in terms of faster speeds and greater carrying capacities, a contraction in domestic warship construction (ostensibly a commitment to world peace, more pragmatically a cut in government expenditure), and the growing foreign practice of subsidising shipbuilding industries for strategic reasons.

Lower demand from shipbuilders had adverse implications for the iron and steel industry, adding to the problems it already faced because of the expansion in world capacity, especially for pig iron. For obvious reasons, productive capability had increased markedly during the war, but thereafter the industry operated at between a third and a half of its optimum capacity. A general international preference for steel put Britain at a disadvantage since her specialisms had always been in wrought and cast iron. Even some change from acid to basic steel made little difference, as the bulk of continental steel was already of this type and foreign producers were often subsidised by their governments. Furthermore, British costs were comparatively high because this industry, like the other staples, was inefficiently organised and over-stocked with obsolete plant.

To some extent, however, the difficulties facing the British steel industry were eased by rising demand from the car and aircraft makers, symptomatic perhaps of the fact that Britain's industrial structure, like that of contemporary Japan, was changing. Relatively young industries such as cars, aeroplanes, chemicals, artificial fibres, rayon, electrical engineering, and rubber all developed significantly in the 1920s. By 1929 the output of motor vehicles, for example, was 239,000 as against 73,000 in 1919. Motor cycle production between 1923 and 1929 went up from 80,000 to 146,000. Rayon yarn output increased almost ten fold between 1920 and 1930. Yet while such manufactures were growing healthily, they were still relatively insignificant to the national economy as a whole. It is true that between 1907 and 1924 their share of total output almost doubled but this still left their aggregate contribution at about 12.5 per cent. A similar caution is required when considering the proportion of resources taken by these industries, sometimes inaccurately designated as 'new', for the achievements of specific industries can be misleading. For example, against a background in which total industrial employment declined slightly from 8.9 million in 1920 to 8.1 million in 1929, employment in vehicle manufacture rose by 59 per cent, in electrical engineering by 15 per cent, and in silk and rayon by 113 per cent. Even so, the new industries employed only 10.9 per cent of the workforce in 1920 and only 14.9 per cent by 1929 (Aldcroft, 1970: 180). Notwithstanding their problems, therefore, the old staples continued to absorb the bulk of resources and to provide significant numbers of jobs.

The gradual restructuring of the industrial economy in Britain was apparent, however, in the foreign trade figures, for the newer industries were geared towards the domestic rather than overseas market. Given the general export difficulties of the old staples, it was not surprising that in the course of the 1920s exports became less important to Britain's economy. In 1914 they represented 23.2 per cent of the net national income, imports about 31 per cent. By 1929 these figures had fallen respectively to 17.6 and 26.7 per cent. On trend exports rose slowly, but even in their best year, 1929, reached only about four fifths of the prewar level. Britain's share of world exports, 13.9 per cent in 1913, was 10.8 per cent in 1929, and its share of manufactured exports fell over the same period from 29.9 to 23.6 per cent (Aldcroft, 1970: 245–7). In 1913 about 27 per cent of GNP was traded, a proportion which was down to 22 per cent by 1929.

Industrial organisation

Changing industrial structures in the 1920s were accompanied by important developments in business organisation, as larger scale enterprises became more prominent in both economies. During the First World War the total number of business corporations in Japan increased from 17,000 to 26,000 and the number of firms with capitalisations over Y5 million increased from 62 to 368 (Morikawa, 1992: 123). That cotton was one of the country's few internationally competitive industries in the 1920s owed much to the use of modern technology and vertical integration, which consolidated 56 per cent of spindles under the control of seven large firms. Major companies were organised in the powerful Federation of Spinners. Although over half the total Japanese labour force still worked in units employing less than five individuals, a tendency towards larger scale units of production was also evident (table 2.7). In pottery more than half the workforce by 1931 was still employed in units of less than five employees, generally making traditional table ware for the domestic market. But the demand for porcelain and electrical insulators also produced a heavy sector of some twenty large factories employing 6,000 workers between them. Similarly in silk, the majority of

Table 2.7 *Japan: manufacturing plant size (%)*

| | Number of workers | | |
	5–49	50–499	500+
1909	45.7	33.6	20.7
1914	40.0	34.9	25.1
1919	33.9	34.6	31.5
1930	37.0	37.4	25.6

(Minami, 1986: 318).

businesses remained small scale but giants such as Katakura and Gunze did emerge. In wool, handloom weaving almost entirely disappeared and while small and medium firms remained typical in the production of serges and worsted material, the rest of the industry was increasingly in the hands of large vertically integrated firms.

Larger scale industrial organisation was more characteristic, however, of the modern heavy industrial sector where it had been encouraged by wartime developments. The Nagasaki Shipbuilding Company had 15,631 workers in 1918 as against 6,371 in 1910: the labour force at the Shibaura Engineering Works went up from 1,297 in 1911 to over 4,000 by 1917. The proportion of engineering firms employing more than 500 workers rose from 36 per cent in 1909 to more than 55 per cent by 1919 (Okayama, 1983: 162). In 1914 heavy machinery, metals, and chemicals accounted for not more than a fifth of all the enterprises employing more than 500. Yet by 1930 more than a third of the largest 200 firms were in machinery, primary metals, transport equipment, and chemicals. The biggest of all were in those shipyards which were supported by their own steel facilities, such as the Kawasaki and Mitsubishi works (Abe and Fitzgerald, 1995: 3).

The trend towards larger scale operations was most obvious amongst the *zaibatsu*, the family-owned, industrial-financial conglomerates which had most benefited from the Meiji sell-off of state enterprises. During the war firms such as Okura, Asano, Furukawa, and Fujita all seized the opportunity to extend their activities. The main beneficiaries of the war boom, however, were the big four, Yasuda, Mitsui, Sumitomo, and Mitsubishi, all of which diversified, the latter three especially into heavy industry. The 1920s saw their influence in the Japanese economy rising, as they brought together financial, supply, and marketing contacts, especially now in steel, shipbuilding, and chemicals where market infrastructures were not yet very fully developed. The big four were distinguished by their size and the range of their interests and it has been suggested that by 1930 Mitsui and Mitsubishi were 'probably the largest business empires in the world' (Abe and Fitzgerald, 1995: 119). By that time Mitsui had 150 enterprises, Mitsubishi about 200, strategically interrelated but operationally separate. Mitsui's subsidiaries included many of the best performing firms in Japan. Its mining company produced 14 per cent of total coal output, and its trust company was Japan's largest. In controlling over 15 per cent of the country's exports and 14 per cent of imports, Mitsui Bussan highlighted the importance of the *zaibatsu* mercantile activities, most of which also expanded in the 1920s. These organisations offered access to raw materials, overseas market entry, credit facilities, linguistic skills, and returns to scale in distribution. Such advantages enabled the *zaibatsu* to weather more easily than other business concerns the postwar economic depression, further enhancing their dominance in the economy.

As in Japan, the contribution of small firms to British employment and output remained important in the postwar decade, but the larger scale enterprises similarly grew in significance. Big business was most common in newer industries, where market and technical factors favoured a larger scale of operation, especially in the second half of the decade. This produced some high concentration ratios. In their respective industries the three largest firms produced net about 84 per cent of rayon and dyestuffs, 75 per cent of photographic apparatus, 73 per cent of rubber tyres and tubes, and 48 per cent of electrical machinery. Artificial fibre was dominated by Courtaulds and British Celanese, while in chemicals the merger of four main companies in 1926 produced ICI, responsible for about a third of national chemical output. Almost a half of all motor car production in the 1920s came from Ford, Austin, and Nuffield. Overall, the country's largest hundred companies increased their share of total output from 17 to 26 per cent between 1919 and 1930. The distribution of the workforce mirrored these developments to the extent that by 1935 more than three quarters of all those working in factories with more than 100 employees were concentrated into 10 per cent of the largest plants. Larger units also emerged in the old staples but concentration ratios remained comparatively low. In shipbuilding it was just over a quarter. In iron and steel smelting and rolling, the proportion was about a fifth. Many staple manufacturers simply sought protection against economic difficulty in the restrictive practices developed by trade associations, bodies encouraged by government during the war as a way of gaining control over production. Although experience varied between industries, it is doubtful if such arrangements were ultimately beneficial since they tended to protect the inefficient and delay the elimination of excess capacity.

It is sometimes implied that in the 1920s Japanese business enjoyed an advantage over its British counterpart in that it had easier access to capital. Older writers stressed the advantages derived by the *zaibatsu* from their banking activities, which benefited enormously from the limited extent of public share ownership in Japan and the general national preference for saving in the banks. Firms outside *zaibatsu* control, it was suggested, often found it difficult to get investment funds on equal terms. Capital was thus directed to the heavy industrial sector which the *zaibatsu* dominated, and they exploited their oligopolistic position to ensure the most efficient use of technological imports and foreign exchange. Care has to be taken lest too much is read into this, either in terms of contrasts with the rest of Japanese industry or with British industrial finance. The *zaibatsu* kept a tight control over the use of their banks' funds by subsidiaries and none lent heavily within their respective groups. As closed family businesses with no obligation to pay dividends to outside shareholders, they were able to utilise accumulated profit as capital. As for the comparison with Britain, while there was no significant increase in the size of the capital stock in the 1920s, there is no real evidence to suggest that industrial reorganisation and development were hampered by any scarcity of capital. On the contrary, contraction in the international economy gave some commercial banks an added incentive to take a greater interest than hitherto in the domestic economy. Individual institutions certainly helped firms at times of particular difficulty, as when the Bank of England acquired a controlling interest in Armstrong Whitworth. Similarly, the Bankers Industrial Development Corporation put up a quarter of a £6 million capital fund intended to help finance industrial rationalisation. More generally, however, the relatively small part played by British banks in industrial finance reflected a lack of demand as much as a lack of willingness on the banks' part.

More significant differences between Britain and Japan in the development of postwar business were to be found in organisational structures, the quality of management, and labour strategy. To take the first of these, it has sometimes been suggested that the persistence of the family-owned company in Britain inhibited change and growth. Yet family firms also remained important in Japan, suggesting that it was not so much the pattern of ownership as the attitudes that went with it which were significant. Holding companies were a common structural device in both countries but in Japan the *zaibatsu* facilitated informal cooperation between all the various subsidiaries, thereby allowing the family to retain overall control of very diversified activities. British holding companies tended to be federations of several different firms, each anxious to promote its own interests. Strategy may have been coordinated between them but all too often in a purely defensive way to control output, prices, and wages.

Even more important, perhaps, Japanese firms generally invested far more heavily in highly paid managers than their British counterparts. Although the original *zaibatsu* family members retained positions of influence and expected loyalty from their employees, strategic decisions were increasingly the responsibility of the salaried managers. By 1930 top level control tended to be a cooperative effort between the family and the professional managers, although in practice the latter had more influence because they had more skill. This distinguished them from family-owned companies in Britain, where the senior posts tended still to be monopolised by family members, patronage and family interest generally taking precedence over other considerations. Private family interest thus got in the way of rational decision-taking which was usually subordinated to the preservation of the family fortune.

Along with this went a much more systematic approach to the matter of management training in Japan, where the major firms had always sought to recruit managers from the top universities. Even in 1920, 45 per cent of Japan's business leaders were graduates as against a mere 19 per cent in the United Kingdom, a gap which did not narrow during the postwar decade (Wilson, 1995: 81). Although there was an upsurge of British interest in the notion of management as a profession and some firms launched ambitious in-house training programmes, in the older industries the contrasts with

Japan remained. One survey indicated that in the 1920s 44 per cent of Japan's top 200 industrial leaders were university graduates, while a quarter had been educated in high schools or professional schools (UNESCO, 1971: 146). At the end of the decade Arno Pearse compared British textile managers very unfavourably with those in Japan, where, he wrote, managers were selected 'for their knowledge of commerce and aptitude for reorganisation . . . most of them also have had a technical training' (Pearse, 1929: 26).

Another very important difference lay in attitudes to labour management. During the war and subsequent boom, Japanese employers tried to offset problems of labour supply and industrial unrest by raising wages and improving working conditions. In textiles, for instance, the need to draw in labour from the countryside had resulted in the extension of what the Japanese termed paternalism. The pioneer of this approach, Muto Sanji, provided welfare benefits to his workers in the form of medical facilities, educational opportunities, and subsidised accommodation. By 1928, 52 per cent of Japanese factories had dormitories for their workers (Harada, 1928: 121). Muto's aim was to ensure that relations between capital and labour remained those of the 'friends interested in each others' welfare' (Muto, 1919: iii). In this sense his strategy might be seen as a continuation of the prewar determination to prevent the sort of conflict associated with industrialisation in the West.

In heavy industry, employers had been trying well before 1914 to gain control of their workforces from the *oyakata* or sub-contractors. During the war prices rose faster than wages, causing general discontent but also exacerbating existing high rates of labour turnover among scarce skilled workers. With a growing industrial labour force showing signs of flirting with socialism and trade unionism, a number of firms opted for what might be termed an incorporationist labour strategy, designed to minimise labour turnover and to meet the problem of scarce skills by the provision of training. This involved keeping out union activists by providing internal consultation mechanisms, training schools to provide appropriately qualified workers, and the offer of relatively high wages and secure employment to selected key employees. Although the postwar depression weakened labour's bargaining position, the highly competitive international climate led many of the modern firms to develop these employment and wage systems as a way of guaranteeing supplies of skilled labour and protecting their investment in its training. As a result, wage differentials between large modern firms and smaller scale, traditional ones, became even more pronounced than they had been before 1914, since smaller firms lacked the resources to compete on equal terms. This became a self perpetuating process. Companies with the best workers achieved the highest levels of productivity: they could then afford to hire and train the best workers, thus reinforcing higher productivity. In experimenting with such approaches to employees, Japanese firms were undoubtedly able to capitalise on social values such as status, loyalty,

and group solidarity but the system's features were not culturally determined: they arose primarily out of the economic circumstances of the 1920s
(Gordon, 1985; Sugiyama, 1995: 120–40).

The employment systems emerging in significant sectors of Japanese business gave its management a flexibility and control which was lacking in
British industry. In Britain the imperatives of the war effort had boosted
national wage bargaining, a process much encouraged by the state. The exigencies of wartime demand had also produced a growing emphasis on piece
work payment. As a result, much production was locked into outmoded processes, and postwar unemployment gave employers no incentive to progress
beyond craft-intensive methods by introducing more physical capital or
training. It was easier, when required, to intensify work rather than develop
human capital. Training incentives were reduced by the appearance of mass
unemployment Furthermore, craftsman-dominated workshop production
obviated any need for the extension of management functions and hierar-
chies. Few British firms in the staple industries created the sort of specialised
labour management departments set up, for example, by Kawasaki,
Sumitomo Shipbuilding, or Osaka Steel.

Government policy

To some extent the failure of British business in the 1920s to modify itself to
the same extent as was happening in contemporary Japan, reflected the fact
that it was not under the same sort of pressure from the state. In the postwar
period Japanese governments took a number of steps designed to enhance
industrial competitiveness. Tariffs have already been mentioned but also of
long term significance were measures to encourage quality control, cooperation between manufacturers, and rationalisation. Until 1925 industrial policy was the responsibility of the Ministry of Agriculture and Commerce but
in that year the growing importance of industry was formally acknowledged
in the creation of a new Ministry of Commerce and Industry. From the outset
it sought to foster domestic enterprise by reducing unnecessary internal
competition, encouraging scientific management, standardisation, and
economies of scale. For example, prefectural authorities were given power to
supervise the fishing industry and to establish fishery guilds to control the
quality of exports. A law of 1925 provided for the extension of voluntary
bodies to maintain quality standards. Some had compulsory powers of
inspection. Smaller firms were encouraged to pool their export activities. In
some specified export industries manufacturers were encouraged to form
guilds whose tasks included the monitoring of product quality, cooperative
use of equipment and collective sales and purchasing arrangements. By 1930
there were over a hundred such organisations. Combined with the organisational changes occurring in manufacturing, such measures helped to lay the
foundation for export success in the 1930s. In the shorter term, however,

export values did not rise dramatically as most modern industry was not yet internationally competitive.

British governments were not nearly so directive as far as industry was concerned, playing only a small part in its rationalisation. Some of the most enthusiastic rationalisers, it is true, had been actively involved in the administration of the war economy and after 1918 continued to interact with former political colleagues. This may suggest that the rationalisation movement had its roots in the war but, on the whole, change in British industry occurred without much coherent, formal intervention on the part of the state. As part of a general desire to return to prewar normality, the mechanisms of economic control built up during the war were dismantled very promptly after 1918. The government rapidly divested itself of responsibility for the mines and the railways, for example, handing both back to their private owners. The Conservatives flirted mildly with the idea of tariffs in 1923 but the idea was rejected by the electorate. Although there was some support behind the scenes for rationalisation in the staple industries, governments were otherwise generally content to devise relief or limited public works schemes to cater for the human casualties of a changing industrial structure.

In one respect, however, it has often been argued that government policy was positively damaging in its implications for British industry. The decision to return to the gold standard in 1925 at the prewar parity, it has been claimed, put a further burden on the country's export industries by overvaluing sterling. During the war income from overseas was severely curtailed as investments were liquidated, destroyed, or in the case of assets in Russia, confiscated. At the same time, distortions in supply and demand produced rising prices, while government had also to support the huge expenditures incurred by the Allies in sustaining the war. As a result, money supply could no longer be constrained by gold holdings and, although it was not formally acknowledged until March 1919, Britain effectively abandoned the gold standard.

By 1920 prices stood 150 per cent above their 1914 levels and Britain owed almost $4,000 million to the United States. Given that the immediate postwar years were also characterised by trading difficulties and the financial instability arising from the unresolved problems of inter-Allied war debts and German reparations payments, returning to the gold standard had obvious appeal. It appeared to offer the best way of restoring Britain's somewhat diminished international financial standing by signalling a determination to prevent further inflation. It was also a symbol of the prewar normality to which everyone aspired, whether motivated by economic orthodoxy or, as has been suggested of the City of London financiers, naked self interest (Pollard, 1970: 9–16, 22–5). It thus became a priority to return to the gold standard and considerations of national prestige determined that it should be at the old prewar rate, one pound sterling to 4.86 dollars. Beginning with the budget of April 1920, government set about creating the prerequisite conditions, most important of which was to bring British prices back into line with those of her major competitors. Heedless of the impact on employment or on the general level of economic activity, the bank rate was raised in the hope of attracting foreign funds in order to push up the exchange rate. Efforts to reduce public expenditure were hampered by the size of the government's own debts and the higher welfare outlays incurred on pensions and unemployment relief. Nevertheless, in the short term the budget was balanced, wholesale prices fell, short term debt reduced, and the money supply restricted. In April 1925 Winston Churchill announced that Britain intended to return to the gold standard at the prewar exchange rate. It was argued at the time that this represented an overvaluation of some 10 per cent, although much higher figures have been suggested more recently (Redmond, 1984: 520–32).

Yet the impact of returning to gold at the old rate is questionable. The sterling–dollar exchange rate was irrelevant to the price competitiveness of British goods going to the sterling area of the empire which accounted for almost a half of British trade in this period. A lower rate would also have reduced the income from invisibles which alone kept the current account in credit during the 1920s (except in 1926 when there was a deficit of £15 million). It is quite clear, too, that had Britain returned to gold at a lower rate, other countries would have quickly readjusted their own exchange rates downwards, thereby nullifying any British advantage (Alford, 1996: 128–35). This was exactly what happened in 1931 when Britain quit the gold standard.

In Japan monetary policy was also dominated by the determination to revert to the gold standard. With internal demand sacrificed to the export market Japan's 1914 debt of Y1.1 billion was transformed into a surplus of Y7.2 billion by 1920. However, scarcities of resources had also produced galloping inflation and while prices had fallen during the postwar depression, they got further out of international line as a result of the massive Kanto earthquake in September 1923. More than a hundred thousand people died in Tokyo and Yokahama. Millions were left homeless and over half the buildings in the two cities were destroyed. Reconstruction cost millions of yen, with the government importing substantial quantities of heavy machinery for the purpose. The resultant increase in public expenditure and rehousing programmes fuelled a construction and property boom. The net result was a further significant rise in the wholesale price index. With the British clearly intent on restoring the link between gold and sterling the Japanese government felt obliged to take some tentative steps in the same direction.

New taxes were imposed in order to raise government revenue and dampen consumer demand. Reducing levels of government expenditure was more difficult, however. The upsurge of democratic ideas in the decade had resulted in some diminution of central control over the governors of local regions, effectively reducing the state's ability to restrict local authority expenditure – and this at the very time when the reconstruction of a devastated Tokyo was encouraging provincial cities to modernise their own provisions of buildings and services. Deflation was not popular either with the army or the *zaibatsu*, but in any case the unsophisticated banking structure made it difficult for the Bank of Japan to control credit policy. Furthermore, Japanese banking was inherently unstable, for although it was dominated by five major concerns, the very large numbers of smaller enterprises were not subject to any inspection to guarantee protection for their depositors. The system finally gave way under the strain in 1927 when the Bank of Taiwan closed its doors, no longer able to support its huge loans, equivalent to a quarter of Japan's national budget, to Suzuki Shoten. In the ensuing financial panic loans from the Bank of Japan increased by almost 300 per cent and the amount of currency in circulation rose by about half. After a three week period of compulsory closure, more than thirty banks, including the official repository for the Imperial Household Ministry, failed to reopen. The overall result, however, was positive. The national financial structure was consolidated, the number of institutions considerably reduced, and both stability and central control strengthened by a rigorously implemented banking act.

Fostered by the gradual adjustment in the value of the yen, this was sufficient to produce a significant upturn in industrial output. By 1929 a buoyant overseas market for silk and cotton in the USA and India respectively, and the tentative recovery of world trade which boosted the Japanese merchant marine, between them helped carry the balance of payments back into the black for the first time in a decade. With the economic indicators thus generally encouraging, and all the major Western nations already back on it, the Japanese returned to the gold standard in January 1930 at prewar parity – just in time to be swamped by the economic hurricane that had been brewing in the USA since the previous autumn. It was, as Muto Sanji observed, akin to 'opening a window in the middle of a typhoon' (Nakamura, 1994: 39).

The system of reproduction

Population

Although by 1931 the population of England and Wales was just short of forty million, an increase of about a quarter since 1901, the annual rate of growth was only half of what it had been immediately before 1914. The war involved an unprecedented degree of personal mobility as men were called into the forces and workers of both sexes moved to areas of high paying war industry. About 40 per cent of the population continued to live in the seven major prewar conurbations, but the settlement pattern began to change in the 1920s, with the most rapid population increase occurring in the south east and midlands, the areas most associated with the newer industries. The Greater London area expanded with the development of suburbs such as Hendon and Wembley, while there was also some reduction in the number of people living in smaller provincial towns.

If the war disrupted the distribution of population, the same could not be said of demographic trends. In the short term, the absence of men on active service during the war and their return after it produced first a fall and then a surge in the number of births. However, the most striking feature of the 1920s was the falling birth rate, a long term prewar trend. By 1931 less than a quarter of the population was aged fourteen or under, as against about a third in 1901 (Halsey, 1972; 33). In 1900 a quarter of the country's married women were in childbirth each year. By 1930 it was only one in eight. On average, couples marrying in the second half of the 1920s produced 2.2 children as against the five to six common in mid-Victorian times.

There is no evidence that this was caused by a rise in the age at which women married. Nor, contrary to popular myth, did the high casualty rates of the war have any significant aggregate effect on female marriage prospects. Certainly the human losses were unprecedented, the highest estimates suggesting that about 723,000 were killed – 15 per cent of all the men aged between fifteen and twenty nine in 1911. But although there were many individuals whose nuptial plans perished on the battlefields, aggregate female and male marriage rates turned upwards quite sharply after the war, most noticeably among those aged between twenty and twenty four. Statistically, the proportion of married women over the age of fifteen was greater in 1921 and in 1931 than it had been in 1911. It may be that this occurred because the war curtailed emigration opportunities, while postwar welfare inducements and restrictions on entry imposed by some overseas countries weakened both the push and the pull factors behind emigration. Whatever the cause, the number of emigrants certainly declined in the postwar period.

The postwar marriage pattern also throws doubt on the notion of the 'missing generation' to which contemporaries so often referred and to which historians have attributed variously the allegedly low quality of British political leadership or the failures of interwar colonial policy. In fact, the proportion of men aged between twenty and thirty nine was only marginally lower in 1931 than in 1901, the respective figures being 31.42 and 31.66 per cent. In 1931 about 55 per cent of British males were aged between twenty and fifty nine, actually higher by over 5 per cent than the equivalent figure in 1901. The statistical evidence, in other words, does not support the hypothesis of a missing generation.

If the missing generation cannot be blamed for falling birth rates, what other explanations can be offered? Almost certainly, familiarity with mechanical means of contraception became more widespread as a result of the war while qualitative improvements also enhanced the reliability of sheaths and diaphragms. It is possible, too, that the ethical obstacles to the use of artificial means of birth control, particularly those rooted in religious scruples, may have lost some of their force. Over 40 per cent of women marrying between 1910 and 1919 used contraception, as against 16 per cent of those marrying in the previous decade. Among women marrying in the 1920s the proportion rose to 59 per cent (Winter, 1986: 271). Contraception of whatever type, however, was merely a means to an end. In the 1920s married couples were choosing to have fewer children, a decision apparently governed by the calculation that large families inevitably entailed some sacrifice of the expanding opportunities for material improvement. Similar considerations had already resulted in falling fertility among higher income groups even before the war when middle-class families typically were smaller than those of the working classes. After 1918 birth rates among these higher social groups remained the lowest but the sharpest falls in fertility were recorded amongst those previously associated with the highest rates. By 1930 only about a tenth of all families had more than five children, although between 1900 and 1919 the proportion had been more than a quarter.

In Japan similar demographic trends were evident, though arising from different causes and through different mechanisms. Throughout the 1920s population grew by some 700,000 people a year, a cumulative increase of 15 per cent which took the total to 64 million by 1930. This gave rise to some concern in a country where settlement was so densely concentrated in the central eastern region. 'Our island home is small', warned a leading Japanese banker in 1926. 'It is over populated, and the mentality of its inhabitants is in danger of atrophy merely though lack of space for its proper development' (Nish, 1987: 140). With hindsight it can be seen that 1920 represented' a peak in the birth rate which gradually fell thereafter. This had relatively little to do with any spread of contraceptive knowledge, since the Ministry of Home Affairs generally discouraged discussion of the subject. The major causes of falling birth rates were a decline in the ratio of married women, especially those under the age of twenty five, and the rising average age of marriage from the mid-1920s onwards. These developments were closely related to the increasing levels of industrialisation and urbanisation. The expansion of industry both during and after the war drew more people into the towns. Kobe, Nagoya, Kyoto, and Yokahama expanded considerably although Osaka with 2.4 million residents and Tokyo with 2.0 million in 1930 remained the major cities (Trewartha, 1945; 183). About 18 per cent of the population was classified as urban in 1920, 32.9 per cent by 1935 (Mosk, 1983; 77). The trend to smaller families was most apparent in these non-agricultural areas where there were greater opportunities for wives to seek employment outside the home and where the use of child labour was discouraged. By 1935 the gross reproduction rate in industrial prefectures was 2.02 as against 2.69 in the agricultural prefectures (Ohbuchi, 1976: 343).

Women

It is possible that in both countries declining birth rates were connected with changes in the economic and social position of women, although the nature of any such connection is not immediately obvious. Nor is it clear how far the war was directly responsible for such changes as occurred. In Britain, military enlistment and the expansion of strategic industries certainly left substantial gaps in the labour force. The statistics are treacherous but one estimate suggests that almost 250,000 women entered government docks, factories, and arsenals, while another 624,000 went into the metal trades (Braybon, 1995: 150). But these figures represented less of a radical departure than an extension of an existing trend. Immediately before the war women made up 58 per cent of the labour force in the textile industry, 68 per cent in clothing, 35 per cent in food, and 36 per cent in the paper industry (Braybon, 1995: 148). Although the new recruits certainly made a significant contribution to the war effort, they filled only about a third of the newly created vacancies in industry. Rather more went into non-industrial sectors, 430,000 into finance and commerce, 200,000 to local and national government, 100,000 into transport and 110,000 to other services. Overall, however, only about a third of these women were new adult entrants to the labour market, the rest simply transferring from other occupations or coming directly from school.

Furthermore, the status of the new female industrial workers often did not equate with that of the men they had replaced. The level of job mechanisation was frequently higher, pay rates inferior, supervisors invariably male, and it was generally made quite clear that employment was only for the duration. Many of the jobs which did survive male demobilisation disappeared in the subsequent depression and thus the war did not fundamentally alter the gender division of labour in British industry. Similarly in the white collar sector, where in 1918 56 per cent of civil servants were women, by 1928 the proportion was down to 25 per cent and 65 per cent of the male employees were ex-servicemen (Zimmeck, 1988: 88–120). Although the absolute number of women in the workforce increased from about 5.7 million in 1921 to almost 6.3 million in 1931, this represented only a small proportional change, from 29.5 per cent to 29.8 per cent. This was barely an advance on the 1901 figure of 29.1 per cent (Briggs, 1981: 358). According to the 1921 census, only commercial occupations had been permanently colonised by women, a process already apparent before 1914, and the postwar status, pay, and conditions of service for such women still remained inferior to those of men.

Overall, then, it appears that despite women's contribution to the war effort and the slight widening of their job opportunities after it was over, their position changed only slightly and attitudes towards them remained substantially unchanged (Braybon, 1981). Yet the war probably did have a positive impact on middle-class women's self awareness. Even lower down the social scale, in so far as more women than ever before had experienced work, trade union membership, and a degree of financial independence, albeit at lower wages than men, there was probably some weakening of the notion that the sexes were physically designed and providentially intended to occupy different social and economic spheres. Rising incomes and the greater awareness of contraceptive possibilities offered a potential door of escape – for those who wanted one – from the hold of domesticity, while the war cast others into the unanticipated role of widow or spinster.

Some broad recognition of these changes was apparent in the granting of a limited parliamentary vote in 1918, followed by franchise equality with men in 1928, the removal of some legal restrictions against women entering the professions, and some further liberalisation of the laws concerning divorce and child custody. The significance of the Sex Disqualification (Removal) Act in 1919 was less certain, however, since both private and public institutions, including the civil service, continued to impose a marriage bar on women. Oral evidence suggests that women themselves believed that the war worked to broaden their social and economic horizons. For contemporaries, perhaps the most obvious symptoms of change, even amongst working-class women, were more tangible – short hair, lighter clothing (made possible by the development of new fabrics) often styled to obscure the main features of feminine physique, and freer social relations between the sexes.

Some of the most public manifestations of this freedom provoked occasional outbursts of moral outrage in the British press. Similar occurrences in Japan – for instance, the sight of a *moga* (the Japanese contraction of the English term 'modern girl') in Tokyo's fashionable Ginza – induced far more profound and widespread disapproval from the majority of conservative-minded Japanese who remained wedded to traditional views of gender. A few, usually educated middle-class women, tried to challenge conventional belief. The New Women's Association, for example, was founded in 1920 by a former member of the now defunct Blue Stocking Society, and although successful in securing the repeal of the ban on women attending public meetings, the organisation lasted only two years. The Women's Suffrage League, set up in 1924, lasted until 1940 but achieved almost nothing. Neither organisation could throw off the weight of historical tradition. Told that 'times have changed. No one of us present day Japanese women will be happy if she is ignored intellectually and expelled from being her husband's mental companion', one Japanese traditionalist replied that he had 'never heard of a single man so despicable as to confide his ambition to his woman' (Livingston, Moore and Oldfather, 1976: I, 283). Nor were such attitudes found only among men. The few advocates of the female cause were hugely outnumbered by the mass support given to organisations such as the Patriotic Women's Association (1901) and the later National Defence Women's Association (1932), both of which emphasised womanly duties rather than female rights. Although war-induced economic change had entailed considerable social adjustments, Japanese women still generally remained subject to male legal and economic control, their inferior status still perpetuated in the civil code.

Female employment in the tertiary sector grew between the two world wars by some 70 per cent. Gradually, too, the barriers against women in medicine and the law were overcome, with the number of nurses rising by 60 per cent between 1925 and 1930 (Osaka City University Research Institute of Economics, 1989: 135). Women also became increasingly important at the kindergarten and elementary level where the total number of teachers increased by an eighth between 1925 and 1930 alone (Osaka City University Institute of Economics, 1989: 131). Yet it is unclear how far these occupational trends were a direct result of the war which, in one respect at least, actually reduced women's significance. In heavy industry the gender ratio, three to two in women's favour in 1914, was more or less equal by 1919. Overall, however, there was a marginal increase in the number of industrial women, although their inferior status and lower wages were further reinforced by their tendency to quit when they got married. Married women, who worked in large numbers, were generally confined to the low paying farming or retail sectors. Their subordinate role was implicit in the fact that even in agriculture they worked longer hours then men, at considerable cost to their health (Saito, 1996: 130–51).

Social structure and living standards

Broadly speaking, the war served to flatten the social pyramid of Edwardian Britain somewhat, in the process slightly blurring some of the lines of demarcation. The landed interest was hard hit by the steady escalation of land taxes and death duties. A lot of land was sold off in the postwar years, mainly because rents had not kept pace with rising values and landowners decided to cash in on their holdings. As much as 8,000,000 acres may have changed hands between 1918 and 1921 alone. Fortunes could be acquired now in other ways and while business and commerce provided more of them, A. L. Bowley and J. C. Stamp calculated that whereas in 1911 those with annual incomes of more than £5,000 received 8 per cent of national income, they received only 5.5 per cent in 1924 (Bowley and Stamp, 1938: 57–9).

The war's impact on wealth distribution was equally modest. It has been calculated that in 1911–13 the top 1 per cent of the population owned 69 per cent of all the wealth. While their share was down to 60 per cent by 1924, this redistribution affected only the top 5 per cent or so of wealth holders (Stevenson, 1984: 330). Even in the mid-1930s less than 0.5 per cent of the country's property owners held 55.6 per cent of the capital, almost unchanged from 1911–13 (Pollard, 1983: 188). Interestingly, the number of domestic servants actually increased between 1911 and 1931, although the larger establishments maintained fewer, confirming perhaps the marginally broader diffusion of wealth at the top end of society.

In the short term, middle-class living standards deteriorated as wartime inflation drove up prices. This affected both those on fixed incomes and also the large numbers of non-manual workers whose salaries were pegged at 1914 levels for the duration, although their differentials were quickly restored once peace came. About a third of the total cost of the war, put at some £11,325 million, was raised by increasing taxation which affected the middle and upper classes disproportionately since, initially at least, more of their incomes were in the taxable brackets. By 1920, however, changes in the thresholds and rising incomes had brought six times as many people into the tax net than in 1914. One cause of this was the growth of the salariat consequent upon the expansion of management in large scale businesses, the extension of government bureaucracy, the steady progress of the professions, and the slightly wider range of female occupations. These all helped to raise the salaried proportion of the occupied population from 12 to 22 per cent between 1911 and 1921, and the share of salaries in the net national income from 11.3 per cent in 1913 to 17.9 per cent in 1921 (Halsey, 1972: 83). Furthermore, those at the bottom end of the salary range did rather better than those at the top, resulting in a greater degree of equality within the middle class.

Over the same period, the share of wages in the net national income also rose, from 38.5 per cent to 43.5 per cent, and wage earners also helped to swell the number of tax payers, further blurring one prewar division between the working and middle classes. The course of wages during the war is difficult to chart and widely differing results can be obtained depending on the underlying assumptions. The cost of living rose for all social groups and manual wage rates did not keep up, certainly before 1917. On the other hand, families' real incomes were boosted by changes in consumption patterns, the pegging of rents, and the increased earning opportunities afforded by full employment and overtime. The transfer from low to better paid jobs worked in the same direction, while the differentials between unskilled and skilled narrowed considerably in most industries, although it has been suggested that the reverse was true in shipbuilding, iron, and steel (Reid, 1986) Other differentials also got out of line. Before the war the average annual wage of a railway clerk was £76, considerably less than that of a coal-face worker's average of £112. By 1924 the railway clerk's average income was, at £221 a year, about £40 greater than that of the miner (Burnett, 1969: 299–301).

Postwar unemployment may have restored some of the differentials and prewar average per capita incomes were not regained until 1924. Generalisations are thus risky but it is likely that those at the bottom of the social ladder came out of the war with their material well-being enhanced. Certainly there was a reduction of about 36 per cent in the number of people in the care of the poor law between 1910 and 1920 (Burnett, 1969: 383). The war saw off the chronic poverty associated in the prewar years with casual labour. After it was over, working-class living standards also benefited to some extent from growing state welfare provision. It is true that the much vaunted land fit for heroes failed to materialise, victim according to different interpretations, of administrative inadequacies, hard-nosed business opposition, Treasury tightness, or simple lack of political will (Morgan, 1979; Abrams, 1963; Johnson, 1968). Nevertheless, while health and education languished, some genuinely innovative steps were taken in the provision of public housing, the further extension of legal minimum wage legislation in 1919, and in unemployment relief, based now on the principle of work or maintenance. The broadening of the old age pension scheme in 1925 also helped to remove the threat of total destitution although if it was the only source of an individual's income, its recipients were left, along with children, some inhabitants of inner cities, and the chronically unemployed, as those most likely to fall below the poverty line.

A survey of five provincial cities published in 1925, suggested that only 3.5 per cent of their working-class populations were in poverty, considerably fewer than in 1901. The authors attributed this mainly to higher wages and falling family size (Bowley and Hogg, 1925). Social observers in the 1920s noted, too, the virtual disappearance of the ragged and barefooted children common in the big cities of Edwardian Britain, while in terms of its nutritional value, food consumption was not so disparate between rich and poor as it had previously been. Although subsequent investigations from the second half of the decade suggest that statistical measures of improvement could be misleading because they did not allow for the income effects of unemployment, it appears that by 1930 Britons were considerably better off than their grandparents had been.

Attempts to chart changes in Japanese living standards by looking at wage data are complicated by the fact that the discussion of income levels has become entangled with a theoretical debate about the role of labour in the process of industrialisation. The classic view holds that historically a surplus rural labour supply, produced by the steady commercialisation of agriculture, held down costs of production, at the same time enhancing profits and capital accumulation. One interpretation is that this situation persisted well into the 1920s, implying that the Japanese people as a whole gained very little from the country's involvement in the war. While the expansion of domestic agriculture certainly led to a substantial percentage increase in the per capita food supply, it is countered that this was not distributed evenly. The wealthy, it is said, were the main beneficiaries of the wartime increase in national income, most of which was absorbed by rents, dividends, interest and corporate savings. The rest went into the country's huge overseas surpluses or helped to swell gross domestic capital formation from Y816 million in 1910 to Y1,394 million in 1918. Population growth of 6 per cent absorbed some of the increased output of consumer goods and generally the index of aggregate real wages, according to Uyeda's index, remained fairly static throughout the war. Rising demand, fuelled by the expansion in money supply sanctioned by the Bank of Japan, generated inflationary pressures which bore particularly heavily on particular groups of workers, while the downward pressure on living standards was increased by an influx of people moving to urban centres in search of employment. Indeed, it has been suggested that during the war the gap between the poor and the comfortably off in Japan grew wider than at any time since the Restoration, and certainly there was much contemporary resentment directed against those seen as war profiteers, discontent which flared up in the rice riots of 1918.

The alternative interpretation is that during the war the Japanese labour market became highly competitive, and that by 1920 it had passed the stage at which wages were set at subsistence levels. Only this view is consistent with the view that labour derived long term benefits from the war. The share of national income going to unskilled workers rose, real income increased significantly, and consumption rose. Labour's new found self confidence was expressed in wider patterns of consumption, more political activity, greater job mobility, and a growing number of strikes. It is also noted that from the 1920s onwards there was a substantial decline in infant mortality and a gradual rise in the height of primary school children, further indications of rising prosperity. In this version of the past, rural change in Japan did not create a surplus supply of landless wage earners, while the rice riots were symptoms of frustrated expectations, not of absolute deprivation.

Whatever the effects of the war on living standards – and it can be pointed out that the incidence of tuberculosis, already very high by Western standards, peaked during the war in large factories – the pattern of nominal wages was fairly standard during the 1920s (Hunter, 1992: 22). Rising until 1921–22 they generally fell until the end of the decade (Ohkawa and Shinohara, 1979: 390). But this pattern disguises significant differences over time between and within regions, occupations, and genders. In agriculture the wages of annual contract workers went up 40 per cent between 1917 and 1927 whereas daily wages peaked in 1920 before declining slowly until 1929 (Napier, 1982: 345). Overall farm household income fell by a fifth between 1925 and 1929 (Nakamura, 1994: 42). It is also clear that as the ratio of agricultural to industrial productivity diminished over the 1920s, so the real income differential between urban and rural areas widened, although it had been stable until 1915. Even the implications of this are not altogether clear, however, since the functional distinction between town and countryside was not everywhere as clear-cut as it was in Britain. Some proportion of industrial activity, notably silk production, was still located in rural areas and even as late as 1938 one survey revealed that about a quarter of farm households were substantially, and another third partially, reliant on non-agricultural forms of income (Fukutake, 1995: 323).

Average manufacturing wages turned down after 1921, and more sharply after 1923 before settling at a lower level than the postwar peak. However, male wages followed a more volatile pattern than those of women, being higher in 1928 than in 1922. In Japan as a whole, women's wages fell from Y0.96 to Y0.91 a day between 1926 and 1930, while those of men rose from Y2.35 to Y2.55. But over the same period the average daily male wage in Osaka and Tokyo drifted down from Y2.30 and Y2.31 respectively to Y2.08 (Osaka City University Research Institute of Economics, 1989: 259). Even amongst men, significant differences existed. Traditional artisans kept up with factory workers between 1914 and 1924 but then fell behind as rationalisation and labour scarcities held wage levels higher in the factory sector. Among factory workers themselves there were also wide disparities, symptomatic of the dualism increasingly evident in the Japanese economy. If employers in the heavy modern sector sought to offset labour scarcities and industrial unrest during the war and subsequent boom by providing better wages and employment conditions, smaller firms could not compete. The welfare benefits of increasing industrialisation were thus distributed with increasing inequality. Wage differentials between large and small scale enterprises, already apparent before 1914, became more pronounced. By 1932 operatives' wages in the smallest industrial plants (measured in terms of capital) were about 60 per cent of those paid in the very largest plants, although in 1909 they had been about 80 per cent (Yasuba, 1976: 258). The provision of benefits in kind for other industries such as textiles, further widened the real income gap between different groups of workers. The welfare package provided by Osaka's Kanegafuchi Spinning Company, for example, was calculated to be worth an extra Y14 a month to each worker (Pearse, 1929: 99).

Allowing for all these variations between the experiences of different occupational groups, combining the available information on prices and wages into a real income index gives the results set out in table 2.8. The general impression, therefore, is of uneven improvement for all groups. Even for the less well off, there were some benefits to be derived from the extension of welfare provision. Legislative attempts were made to improve

Table 2.8 *Japan: real income indices*

	Real manufacturing wages		Real agricultural income
	Male	Female	
1914	100	100	100
1918	88	79	99
1922	143	145	106
1926	154	151	100
1930	164	157	119

(Nakamura, 1983: 146)

working conditions across the board. The first major step was taken in the form of a Factory Act in 1911 although employer opposition effectively delayed its implementation until 1916. The formation of the International Labour Organisation in 1919 exposed the gap between conditions in Japan and those elsewhere. In 1921 the basis was laid for a national system of employment exchanges. A measure of health insurance for all factory and mining workers was instituted in 1922. Two years later steps were taken to curb some of the worst abuses of contract labour while in the following year the government offered to put up half the operating costs of unemployment relief schemes to be established for casual workers in six major cities. The Factory Act was further extended in 1926.

None of this is to deny that in British terms the Japanese people had low incomes, poorer facilities, and a lower standard of living, or that relative poverty still persisted. It was mainly the best paid workers who benefited from the improving urban amenities, many of which were inspired by the rebuilding of Tokyo on Western lines after the Great Earthquake. Stable factory workers had more to spend on clothing, health, sanitation, and education, while rural and casual workers still spent a higher proportion of income on food and less on rent even where their incomes were similar. In 1919 the average household income of a Tokyo factory worker was 40 per cent larger than that of the poor. Using information from a 1920 survey, some writers have suggested that around 8 or 9 per cent of Tokyo's population could be classified as poor (Chubachi and Taira, 1976: 401). Nevertheless, at constant 1934–36 prices the index of income shows that even the Tokyo poor became slightly better off between 1920 and 1929, confirming perhaps that their absolute if not their relative position was improving very slightly (Chubachi and Taira, 1976: 407). Applying Maeda's original classification scheme to the whole country for 1930 suggests that 17.7 per cent of households or 14.7 per cent of the whole population, were in poverty. This certainly represented an improvement on the situation in the 1880s.

3

And back again: production and reproduction *c.*1930–*c.*1945.

Introduction

In both Britain and Japan the 1930s have a dismal historical reputation. The *kurai tanima* or 'dark valley' of the 1930s has often been portrayed as a major stage in Japan's descent into political extremism and military disaster. At the same time Marxist interpretations in particular have stressed the persistence of low living standards and material deprivation. British perspectives on the decade have usually been similarly coloured by impressions of widespread economic hardship followed by the misery of the Second World War. George Orwell's *Down and Out in Paris and London* and *The Road to Wigan Pier*, or Ellen Wilkinson's *The Town That Was Murdered* all provided graphic contemporary accounts of ordinary British lives and communities battered by the aftermath of the First World War, the 1929 crash, economic depression, and mass unemployment. The relative prosperity of the long boom after 1945 served to underline even more emphatically the apparent futility and waste of the 1930s, captured in such appropriately indignant titles as C. Brook, *Devil's Decade*, C. Graves, *The Bad Old Days*, and R. E. Blythe, *The Age of Illusion*. However, both countries did rather better in comparative economic terms than such language might suggest.

The system of production

The crash: Britain

The recovery which followed Britain's return to gold in 1925 was relatively weak and from 1928 declining world prices adversely affected the ability of primary producers to buy manufactured exports from Britain. Deflationary tendencies already apparent in the domestic economy were exacerbated by events in the United States where the boom of the 1920s climaxed in a welter of frenetic speculation and the dramatic collapse of the stock market in October 1929. These internal difficulties in the world's most important trading and lending nation soon communicated themselves to the international economy in the form of a major slump.

The immediate effects on Britain were three fold. First, there was a downward turn in most of the important economic indices, although this contraction was modest compared with what was happening elsewhere. The 11.4 per cent reduction in industrial output, for example, compared favourably with the 41 per cent drop experienced by German industry. Real GNP went down by slightly more than 5 per cent as against about 30 per cent in the United States. Second, there was a sharp increase in unemployment. By 1932 the official count stood at three million although the actual number was probably considerably higher, as many individuals simply failed to register. The aggregate figure also obscures the concentration of job layoffs in the heavy industries geared to the export markets. In the depression's worst year, 1932, unemployment averaged 60 per cent in shipbuilding, 48 per cent in iron and steel, and 31 per cent in cotton. Finally, the balance of payments deteriorated as world trade contracted. Between 1929 and 1932 the volume of British exports fell by over a third and this was accompanied by a fall in the income from invisibles. As a result, the 1928 surplus of £104 million became a deficit of £114 million three years later. Against this background, European liquidity problems helped to spark off a financial crisis in Britain in the summer of 1931.

America's own banking system proved remarkably fragile in the aftermath of the crash with about 2,000 institutions failing altogether. As American investments were withdrawn from Europe so the crisis of banking confidence spread. First the Austrian, then the German, and finally the British banks came under severe strain as liquidity conscious investors sought to secure funds. In Britain this pressure coincided with the publication of the May Report on government expenditure. It suggested that the country was heading for a massive budget deficit, largely because of the rising burden of unemployment relief. The predictable outcome was a further weakening of foreign confidence in the British economy. Gold poured out of London and Ramsay MacDonald's Labour Government resigned, torn between a mind wedded to the economic orthodoxy of a balanced budget and a heart which rebelled against the conventional remedy of public expenditure cuts.

MacDonald survived as leader of a new National Government until he was replaced by Stanley Baldwin in 1935. By this time recovery was well under way. Indeed, for Britain the depression turned out to be relatively mild with the economy picking up again from 1933. There was no significant failure of domestic business to threaten banking stability and, as the world's largest importer of foodstuffs and raw materials, Britain gained enormously from the fall in their price after 1928. Despite regional blackspots associated with the old export staples, unemployment fell steadily from 15 per cent of the labour force in 1932 to slightly more than 8 per cent by 1938. In one sense, the persistence of unemployment was a positive indicator, reflecting some productivity gains, as hourly per capita output grew at 2.1 per cent annually. Industrial production also rose, at 2.8 per cent a year. These figures were impressive in international terms and also when compared with Britain's own past record. The productivity increase, for instance, was three and half times higher than that recorded for the period from 1900 to 1913.

Economic recovery: Britain

The extent to which recovery was the result of spontaneous economic forces or of deliberate government action has long been a matter of contention among economic historians. The various policy options adopted to meet the crisis were at best of little more than marginally positive significance. The most immediate step was the breaking of the link between sterling and gold in 1931. In theory this should have reduced the price of exports and made imports dearer. But its impact was muted by the fact that half a dozen Latin American countries as well as Australia, New Zealand, and Canada had already abandoned gold while others, including Japan, soon followed the British example. All prices thus spiralled downwards, albeit at different rates, reflecting the perceived strengths of national currencies. The volume of Britain's imports certainly fell, by some 44 per cent, but although export volumes (except in the case of coal) picked up after 1934, by 1937 they were still 35 per cent below the 1913 level and 20 per cent lower that of 1929. On the other hand, abandoning gold did halt the run on the pound while the ensuing fall in the exchange rate restored the appeal of sterling to financiers.

It is by no means easy to distinguish between the effects of leaving the gold standard and the impact of import tariffs, the introduction of which marked the effective end of Britain's long standing adherence to free trade. In April 1932 the Import Duties Act imposed a 20 per cent ad valorem duty on all imports except those on a free list, mainly food and raw materials. In the same year the Ottawa Agreements sanctioned an imperial preference scheme which resulted in some increase in the proportion of British exports going to the empire and a rather larger increase in the empire's contribution to Britain's imports. By the time the duty on iron and steel imports was increased to 33.3 per cent in 1933, about three quarters of all imports were dutiable as against only 17 per cent in 1930.

The effectiveness of these measures, however, was mixed. Industries such as cotton, chemicals, and clothing may have enjoyed higher effective protection than that implied by the nominal rates, although this proposition has been challenged (Capie, 1978: 399–409: Kitson, Solomon and Weale, 1991: 328–38). More certainly, protection raised costs for shipbuilders, car makers, and builders, all of whom needed substantial amounts of light and heavy metals. In addition, foreign producers and governments frequently retaliated by dumping goods on the British market or imposing duties on imported British products. The main beneficiaries of tariffs, therefore, were industries whose primary market was the domestic one. The most thorough modern analysis suggests that on balance the costs of tariffs in terms of lost employment and higher internal production costs outweighed the advantages and hindered recovery (Capie, 1983). It is also worth pointing out that tariffs did not really come into effect until the economy was already exhibiting signs of recovery.

Tariffs were certainly of little utility to the old export staples. As far as they were concerned, government policy became more interventionist than in the past but it was concerned mainly with encouraging reorganisation which, because it relied on the agreement of the businessmen concerned, was frequently of little economic benefit. Some rationalisation occurred under the auspices of measures such as the 1936 Cotton Spinning Industry Act, while a Coal Mines Reorganisation Commission was initiated in 1930. The Treasury-sponsored Bankers' Industrial Development Company (1930) helped set up National Shipbuilders' Security Ltd to buy and dismantle redundant yards. But surplus capacity and uneconomic pits remained in the coal industry. Despite substantial reductions, the cotton industry in 1939 still had 25 per cent excess capacity in spinning and 38 per cent in weaving. Although the threat from Japanese competition had finally been acknowledged, effective response was hampered by the unwillingness of a fragmented industry to lay aside self interest and act collectively. Members of the British Iron and Steel Federation, another body sponsored by the government in order to promote rationalisation, were equally blinkered, interested only in maintaining the tariff to protect prices. Not surprisingly, a league table based on the interwar growth rates of twenty one British industries shows five of the bottom six places occupied by iron and steel, textiles, mining, mechanical engineering, and shipbuilding (Aldcroft, 1970: 121).

Monetary policy was also reversed in an attempt to see off the depression. By 1932 the bank rate was down to 2 per cent as the government sought to reduce the cost of its own borrowing. It has often been argued that low interest rates were beneficial both to industrial and domestic borrowers but care must be taken lest their influence on recovery be exaggerated. For one thing, the volume of bank lending did not pick up significantly until 1936, well after recovery began. In any case, the bulk of industrial investment had always come from re-invested profits rather than from bank borrowings and the prospect of profit was probably as important to investors (and thus to industrial growth) as the availability of low interest loans. With profits rising after 1932, businessmen felt sufficiently confident and financially secure to reinvest.

It cannot be assumed, either, that the house building boom, often identified as a key mechanism in recovery, was induced solely by the possibility of cheap mortgages. Three million new houses were built in the 1930s and with interest at 4.5 per cent, considerably lower than the rate prevailing in the 1920s, credit terms for builders and purchasers alike were undoubtedly more attractive. But other influences such as changing consumer behaviour were equally important in boosting the demand for houses. For technical reasons, construction costs were falling and the development of urban transport encouraged building outside of city centres on land that was relatively cheap. Although two thirds of new houses were built for sale to private buyers, the cost of mortgages was not relevant to the occupiers of rented public housing, the construction of which was encouraged by the progressive erosion of rent controls.

The final aspect of government response to the depression concerned the level of public expenditure. This has attracted considerable scholarly attention because in 1936 J. M. Keynes, the most influential economist of the mid-twentieth century, published his *General Theory of Employment, Interest and Money*. He argued that by increasing its own expenditure a government could lead the way out of depression, even if the enhanced outlays resulted in financial deficits. It has since been suggested that the adoption of such policies brought countries such as the United States, Germany, and Japan out of depression. In fact, American policy was deflationary while increases in German and Japanese public expenditure were intended chiefly for rearmament, not consumption as Keynes had proposed. But while there were some precedents for the sort of approach he advocated in the form of relief works in the 1920s and also in early Labour Party thinking about unemployment, Keynesian ideas did not evoke much immediate enthusiasm in Britain (Brown, 1971: 68–84). They cut right across the prevailing consensus in favour of balanced budgets. Although Treasury thinking in the 1930s was less rigid than was sometimes suggested, the relatively speedy recovery of the economy and the evident resilience of the banking system reinforced an underlying conviction that public expenditure could increase only at the expense of private investment. This orthodox view was stoutly defended by academic and Treasury economists equally as distinguished as Keynes was to become. Thus even the government's main legislative attempt to provide work for the unemployed, the Special Areas Act of 1934, involved the Treasury in sanctioning only very modest expenditures, less than £10,000,000 by the end of 1938.

Such caution was possible because no effective pressure was being applied for more radical measures. Lloyd George had hinted at deficit financing in the Liberal manifesto of 1929 but by this time both he and his party were spent forces. Oswald Mosley also flirted with the idea but any future he had was wasted when he resigned from the Labour Government and was side-tracked into fascism. Even if government had been more strongly pressed to increase spending, it is doubtful if deficit financing would have worked. The level of government expenditure still represented far too small a proportion of the British GNP – about 8 per cent in 1938 – to allow of outlays sufficient to stimulate demand on the scale required. One estimate suggests that to reduce unemployment significantly government expenditure would have required an increase of some 70 per cent, a figure in the realm of political and historical fantasy (Howson, 1981; 265–85).

If anything, government budgetary policy probably served to delay recovery since, initially at least, it involved retrenchment. Budgets became increasingly deflationary as the depression deepened between 1929 and 1932. From 1932 until 1934 central government spending fell heavily, while local government expenditure remained fairly static. Initial measures to stem the financial crisis of 1931 included reducing the salaries of public servants and the levels of unemployment benefit. Naval shipbuilding was also axed, further depressing the shipbuilding industry. In 1934, however, income tax rates were eased and the salary cuts restored. From the following year overall expenditure started to rise again. Only at the very end of the decade, however, did government spending exceed its income and then only under the duress of the growing urgency of rearmament which had been gathering momentum since 1935. Although defence expenditure created a million new jobs in heavy industry, it is generally agreed that loan-financed defence expenditure did little more than modify the normal cyclical downturn in the economy which occurred in 1938–39 (Thomas, 1983: 570–1). Whatever the aggregate multiplier effects of defence spending, its direct impact was partial. Aircraft and shipbuilding certainly benefited as, more generally, did iron and steel. With output rising by over three million tons between 1935 and 1937, the steel industry began to operate at full capacity for the first time since the end of the First World War.

What then of an alternative hypothesis which assigns the primary role in the recovery process to the influence of a development block comprised of the so-called 'new' industries? These, it has been suggested, were closely connected with each other as well as sharing common features. They used electricity rather than steam, utilising modern factory layouts and production methods to turn out goods often manufactured from new types of materials. Generally, they had important linkages into other parts of the economy and were characterised by large enterprises located away from the older industrial centres. Thus the chemical industry was transformed under large scale corporations such as ICI and Lever Brothers while artificial fibre was dominated by Courtaulds and British Celanese. In electrical engineering the establishment of the Central Electricity Board in 1926 initiated a process of productivity improvement. Demand grew from new factories situated away from the coal fields and also from domestic consumers, as most of the new houses constructed between the wars were wired for electricity. These new households also pushed up the demand for electrical products such as vacuum cleaners and radios. Altogether, the number of electricity consumers rose from 750,000 in 1920 to 9,000,000 in 1938, the workforce doubled between 1924 and 1937, and the price of electricity was more than halved.

Paramount among this group of new industries was vehicle manufacture. With the labour force doubling between 1918 and 1938, output reached 500,000 vehicles by 1937. Rationalisation reduced the four hundred firms of the Edwardian period to thirty three. Six of these accounted for 90 per cent of output, with the big three of Nuffield, Ford, and Austin responsible for two thirds of the total. Geographically concentrated in a triangle linking Oxford, Coventry, and Birmingham, the car plants required not only glass, metals, rubber, and instruments, but also created forward linkages in the form of service stations, for example.

To these components of the development block, it is conventional to add building. Its output rose by a third between 1932 and 1935 alone, and the three million new houses built in the 1930s more than offset the removals from the housing stock of some of the worst of the surviving nineteenth-century slums. In a labour intensive industry, it was not surprising that this expansion should have been accompanied by a 50 per cent increase in the size of the workforce. More important still, the building boom stimulated the demand for bricks, timber, electrical wiring, glass, and paint, as well as for associated products such as furniture, wall paper, and domestic textiles. Furthermore, there was an obvious link between the urban development implied by such construction and the need for transport, whether in the form of buses, cars, or motor bikes.

But the notion of the development block has not been without its critics (Alford, 1981: 308–32). For one thing, its very definition has been questioned. None of its component industries was new in the sense that they had just come into being, most developing out of earlier activities. Courtaulds, for instance, was well established long before it shifted into the production of artificial fibres, while William Morris's automobile empire developed out of his Oxford bicycle business. The whole hypothesis in fact rests on a tautology, defining as 'new' those industries with the highest growth rates, thus inevitably 'proving' that they led the recovery (Alford, 1981: 317). Nor was there anything unique about the alleged linkages between the various new industries, for there were equally significant connections between the old and the new. The steel industry benefited greatly from the expansion of the automobile sector, as, by extension, did coal.

Furthermore, while some of the 'new' industries expanded considerably in the 1930s, their overall contribution to total output still remained smaller than that of the old staples. One calculation suggests that in 1930 they were responsible for 15.9 per cent of net industrial output, a proportion which rose to 21 per cent by 1935. Over the same period the share contributed by the staple industries declined but at 27.8 per cent, it was still larger than that of the 'new' industries (Buxton, 1980: 549). If structural change was behind recovery in the 1930s then the 'new' industries could be expected to have exhibited growth rates significantly higher than those apparent in the 1920s. Certainly these were high when measured against the very low but unrepresentative yardstick of 1932: taking the less disturbed year of 1924 as the baseline, however, suggests that there was little discernible difference in their performance between the two decades.

It is also important to note that while the 'new' industries may be high up in any league table based on output growth or employment, rather different rankings appear if other measures are used. There is no evidence to suggest that capital shifted significantly towards them, levels of capital formation in all manufacturing industry remaining generally low in this period. Nor was there anything particularly outstanding about their productivity, although it certainly rose in the aggregate, the result in part of the growing scale of manufacturing enterprise. By 1935 over half of Britain's industrial workers were located in units employing more than 500 people, and such plants were most heavily concentrated in the new industries. On the other hand, the growing size of production units meant that for an increasing number of manual workers the work place became increasingly impersonal, leading to an instrumental view of work which may well have restricted productivity growth.

Finally, it is by no means certain that modern forms of production and corporate organisation were always accompanied by improved managerial performance. In the electricity industry, for example, more efficient generation was not matched by improvements in distribution. In the mid-1930s over six hundred different undertakings were distributing a mixture of direct and alternating current at nineteen principal voltages. Again, ICI had to write off some £20 million invested in a fertiliser plant at Billingham, and the firm was not particularly quick either to exploit the new plastics which its scientists developed. Similar shortcomings were apparent at the Imperial Tobacco Company and also at Courtaulds whose Australian and East Asian markets were increasingly being captured by the Japanese. Motor manufacturers showed little real interest in overseas expansion, an FBI report commenting in 1934 that they had 'lagged behind their American competitors in this respect' (Davenport-Hines and Jones, 1989: 231). Britain's six leading producers took advantage of the protected home market to indulge in the inefficient luxury of turning out 350,000 cars a year based on about forty different engine types. By comparison, the three leading American firms made ten times as many vehicles but used substantially fewer engine variants. Similar inefficiencies in indigenous electrical engineering allowed American radios and vacuum cleaners to maintain relatively high sales in Britain, even after the imposition of tariffs. Amateurish sales techniques did not help British businessmen either, for in general they still viewed advertising simply as a way of keeping goods in the public eye, rather than as a means of exploiting knowledge about potential customers' tastes.

To argue that these 'new' industries were by themselves the dynamic behind British recovery in the 1930s is really to place too much faith in the ability of supply to generate its own demand. In the main, they all prospered on the back of a buoyant domestic demand, the result of three influences which provided the major impetus to recovery. First, aggregate demand was affected by some slight redistribution of income away from the relatively wealthy towards the poor, achieved through the dual mechanisms of taxation and welfare payments: in this respect at least government policy, albeit perhaps unconsciously, contributed to recovery. More important was the fact that wage rates for those in work could not be forced down indefinitely, partly because of the enduring strength of trade unionism, partly because the existence of unemployment benefit provided a floor below which no employer could set wage levels. Finally, and most important of all, the terms of trade shifted in Britain's favour after 1928, resulting in cheaper foodstuffs. Even those, such as the unemployed, whose incomes were more or less fixed, were relatively better off since their money went further. For those in work, the falling real price of necessities released extra purchasing power, facilitating the acquisition of greater quantities and wider varieties of goods and services.

Whatever the causes of recovery, overall growth between 1929 and 1938 compared very favourably with past experience. Net national income grew more rapidly than in the previous three decades. Equally striking was the 25 per cent increase in industrial output between 1929 and 1937. But even these figures pale into insignificance beside Japan's achievements: an increase – though still of course from a much lower base line – of 71 per cent in industrial production, a significant expansion of overseas trade, and an annual average growth rate in GDP of almost 5 per cent (table 3.1).

Table 3.1 *Britain and Japan: per capita GDP index*

	UK	Japan
1913	100	100
1929	105	146
1932	98	141
1937	119	167

(Alford, 1996: 151).

The crash: Japan

Japan's economic equilibrium was severely disturbed by the events of 1929–31. It was unfortunate that the long term objective of returning to the gold standard was realised in January 1930, just as the world economy was turning down. Going back to gold would in any case have required some reduction in Japanese prices which were still too high to maintain the old parity against the dollar. They were pushed even further out of line by the dramatic fall in world prices which followed the Wall Street Crash, and the ensuing internal deflationary pressures were accordingly severe. Over the twelve months following the gold restoration, the aggregate price level tumbled by some 20 per cent, with silk prices falling even more steeply by 50 per cent.

The implications for trade were immense and matters were exacerbated by the imposition of the Smoot-Hawley Tariff which raised the average price of Japanese goods going to America by 23 per cent. Total exports in 1930 were down by more than a quarter. The value of silk exports, whose main market was in America, was almost halved. Since raw silk had accounted for 40 per cent of total exports in 1929, trade deficits accumulated rapidly. As in Britain, gold flowed out to pay off the debts and speculation against the yen mounted. Britain's abandonment of gold in September 1931 further exposed Japan to re-invigorated British competition in both textiles and the carrying trades, while sterling depreciation further increased pressure on the yen. Initially, the government responded with orthodox measures, encouraging saving and further industrial rationalisation, reducing the level of military expenditures, and seeking to dampen speculation by imposing a tight money policy and high interest rates. This merely made matters worse, however, and there followed a sequence of events which almost exactly parallelled those in Britain. By the end of 1931, Japan's gold reserves stood at less than half their 1929 level, some Y700 million having been converted into dollars in anticipation of a decision to quit gold. In December the Minseito Government resigned and was replaced by a new cabinet headed by Inukai Tsuyoshi. Japan immediately quit the gold standard. There the similarities with Britain ended, however, for now economic policy became the responsibility of a veteran banker and politician, Takahashi Korekiyo.

In some ways Takahashi's own early writings had anticipated the investment multiplier elements of Keynesian theory. When he allowed the yen to float down it settled about 60 per cent lower against the dollar by 1933. The resulting lower prices facilitated both increased exports and some import substitution at home. Lower interest rates made borrowing easier and boosted the stock market. Note issue by the Bank of Japan increased by about Y500 million between 1931 and 1936 as reflation became the order of the day, government expenditure rising to Y1.9 billion in 1932 and Y2.2 billion in the following year. Altogether, government expenditure grew by almost a half between 1930–31 and 1937–38. This expansion was financed almost entirely by loans and helped to create virtually full employment without incurring inflation since, initially at least, it merely absorbed hitherto untapped resources.

Yet the economy had sustained a severe shock. Unemployment peaked in 1932 at 6.8 per cent of the workforce, perhaps a million individuals, although this was probably rather fewer than is often alleged (Blumenthal, 1987: 69–71). Farmers, particularly those producing silk, were especially hard hit. In the longer term the number of households involved in sericulture declined from 2.2 million in 1929 to 1.7 million by 1938. Over the same period cocoon output fell by more than a quarter (Waswo, 1989: 125). These statistics hint at the immense economic burden under which Japan's rural communities struggled in the early 1930s. General farm income had already been adversely affected by a succession of good rice harvests in the late 1920s, culminating with a bumper crop in 1929. In addition, silk prices had been sliding down throughout the second half of the decade to the progressive discomfort of those many farmers who relied on silk as a secondary crop. In the year after the 1929 crash, 59 per cent of owner cultivator households and 74 per cent of tenant farmers made losses. Further disaster struck over the course of 1931 in the form of another 33 per cent drop in silk prices. At the same time, rice and cotton prices slipped, reducing the total value of agricultural production by more than 40 per cent and restricting the opportunity for rural families to supplement their earnings by working in cotton factories.

The net result was a fall in farm income of about a third. As almost half of the population was engaged in agriculture, this implied a huge drop in purchasing power, especially on the middle sized farms which were more dependent than the smaller units upon the market (Matsuo, 1989: 1–23). Since the economies of rural villages depended substantially on credit, they faced collapse as farmers found themselves unable to meet their obligations. Everywhere there were indications of rural hardship. Lighting was cut off, teachers' salaries went unpaid, and in 1932 famines occurred in several prefectures. The *Japan Times* for 7 June 1932 noted the desperate measures taken by some communities in the face of starvation.

> The impoverished communities of Nagano, Iwate and Niigata are selling their young girls into prostitution, eating *warabe* (bracken) where such a delicacy is still obtainable, cooking bean-cake ordinarily used as a fertiliser with various kinds of grass for their regular food. (Utley, 1936: 142)

It is against this background of rural depression and yen devaluation that aggregate economic performance has to be set.

Economic recovery: Japan

Japan's recovery, like Britain's, was both swift and substantial. Overall GDP grew at 4.9 per cent a year between 1930 and 1938, compared with rates of 3.7 per cent between 1904 and 1919, and 2.4 per cent between 1910 and 1930. The main impetus came from manufacturing and trade. The index of industrial production may have slipped somewhat from 100 in 1929 to 95 in 1930 and 92 in 1931, but on a corresponding scale American industrial output in the same three years was indexed respectively at 100, 83, and 68. After 1931 manufacturing output grew almost 9 per cent a year, virtually double the 1920s level, and by 1938 it was contributing almost twice as much as agriculture to the net domestic product (Francks, 1992: 54).

Equally noteworthy was the continuing change in the composition of Japanese industrial output. Some relatively new industries appeared, although their importance did not match that claimed for their equivalents in Britain. The greater availability of electrical power facilitated the development of aluminium smelting, Toshiba produced radio parts and records, and celluloid toy manufacture also developed. The main newcomers, however, were aircraft and motor vehicles, where Toyota and Nissan emerged as important producers. Artificial fibres and cotton both expanded, although the relative significance of the textile sector shrank, due mainly to absolute decline in the silk industry. By 1936 the heavy industries, chemicals and arms manufacture, between them accounted for more than half the country's industrial output for the first time. Power generation increased substantially, and the output of mining rose by a third between 1930 and 1936. Pig iron production almost doubled while raw steel output did double. There was a significant increase in the manufacture of explosives, sulphuric acid, dyestuffs, and paint. Commercial and military demand so stimulated shipbuilding that by 1937 Japan possessed a powerful navy and the world's third largest merchant fleet with 4.5 million tons. In the course of the decade she became more self sufficient in machinery, major chemical products, and power plant.

On the other hand, considerable quantities of raw and semi-manufactured materials were still being imported. In 1936 overseas sources provided 20 per cent of rice and bean requirements, 35 per cent of fats and oils, 90 per cent of superphosphate fertiliser, all her raw cotton, wool, and rubber, and significant proportions of strategic metals. Although self sufficiency in steel output had been achieved by 1932, non-integrated producers relied heavily on imported iron, since Japan produced only 70 per cent of its own requirements (Yonekura, 1994: 157). By and large, the main export industries still depended significantly upon imported raw materials. This was true of cotton, which came in from the United States, and wool imported from Australia. Export success, in other words, also sucked in imports, the volume of which increased by a third between 1930 and 1936, with raw materials accounting for about two thirds of the total.

Changes in the balance of industry were reflected in the occupational structure. Textiles employed 55 per cent of the factory labour force in 1929, but only 37 per cent eight years later. In the same period the proportions engaged in the metals, chemicals, and engineering sectors grew from less than 25 per cent to 43 per cent. By 1940 non-agricultural employments occupied more than half of a workforce totalling 32.48 million people. Of these, nearly ten million were engaged in mining, transport, communications, and manufacturing (Nakamura, 1994: 105). If the majority of manufacturing workers were still employed in small scale plants, there was a substantial increase, especially after 1933, in the proportion working in factories of more than 500 people. The tendency to dualism which had emerged in the 1920s was strengthened in the following decade.

Industrial expansion went hand in hand with a substantial growth of overseas trade, particularly in light consumer products. Although exports fell in the short term from Y3.3 billion in 1929 to Y2.2 billion in 1931, by 1934 they exceeded the 1925 level. In a period of falling prices and contracting demand, Japan was able to penetrate still deeper into markets once dominated by what were now comparatively high cost producers such as Britain. Freed of the burdensome link with gold, the value of exports more than doubled between 1930 and 1936 and through the 1930s as a whole their volume grew by three-quarters. Japan was responsible for about 4 per cent of total world exports and rather more of world manufactured exports (table 3.2). These were notable achievements, given that they occurred over a very short period of time in an environment of depression and protectionism. Although textiles, which had once made up three quarters of exports, now accounted for rather less than 60 per cent, most of this was due to the waning of silk. Rayon, wool, and particularly cotton, grew vigorously, so much so that by 1936 Japan had become the world's leading exporter of cotton piece goods. Bicycles, toys, rubber tyres, celluloid, metals, and machinery also began to make significant contributions to exports. Unlike silk, however, such goods competed directly with those of other industrial producers. Together with the growth of Japan's economic interests in China, Indonesia, and Malaya, this provoked some alarm in the West where reactions included the imposition of tariffs and quotas on Japanese goods. 'The Japanese competition bogey', observed one English industrialist, 'has got everybody scared stiff.' He added that 'a war of self defence is something which everybody must be prepared to face' (Robertson, 1990: 978–8). He meant an economic war but the defensive response of the West to Japan's export success provoked an equally understandable resentment within Japan. The reply was in kind, entailing the imposition of discriminatory tariffs in favour of imperial imports. There is little doubt that the deterioration of international trade relations provided further justification for Japan's growing conviction that the only way to safeguard essential raw materials and markets was to secure its own economically self sufficient empire.

Table 3.2 *Britain and Japan: shares of world manufactured exports (%)*

	1913	1937
United Kingdom	22.4	20.9
Japan	3.9	6.9

(Maizels, 1963: 189)

Such thinking perhaps gained further impetus from the fact that the American market was becoming less significant to Japan. In 1926 it had absorbed by itself 42 per cent of Japanese exports, but by 1936 the diminution of the demand for silk reduced the overall proportion of exports going to the USA to only 22 per cent. As a result, Japan's trading surplus with the United States turned into a deficit. The reverse was true, however, of Asia and India which, along with Europe, now became Japan's major markets. Positive balances were established with all these areas and sales to Japanese colonies in Formosa and Korea also grew markedly. Korea, Formosa, and Manchuria were taking 38 per cent of Japan's exports by 1937 as against about 16 per cent in 1916 (Wilkinson, 1990: 165).

Business organisation

Some explanations of Japanese export expansion emphasise the role of yen devaluation and the availability of cheap labour. The latter was nothing new, but the falling value of the yen did have an effect. In cotton cloth, for instance, 60 per cent of the production cost lay in the purchase price of the raw material. As the value of the yen fell, so the cost of imported raw cotton rose. The export drive can therefore be seen as an attempt to offset the rising import bill by selling more overseas. This could be best achieved by reducing domestic manufacturing costs and improving labour productivity. Recent work thus tends to place more emphasis on the contribution of the organisational forms of Japanese manufacturing and the role of appropriate strategies in marketing, technology and labour. To give just one example, it has been argued that there were at least as many, if not more, engineers working in Japanese as in British industry by the middle 1930s (Uchida, 1991: 132). In short, Japan's export success derived mainly from the superior productivity and efficiency indicated in table 3.1. By the mid-1930s the Lancashire cotton masters accepted that the comparative advantage in cotton goods manufacturing had passed to the Japanese. The introduction of the High Draft Spinning System improved labour productivity by more than 40 per cent between 1929 and 1934. In weaving labour efficiency was boosted by the wider utilisation of automatic looms. Both developments represented a significant shift towards capital intensive technology. In spinning nominal average wage costs fell by almost a third between 1930 and 1936, although at the same time the low paying small mills and spinning firms were disappearing (Sugihara, 1989: 156).

Productivity gains were also recorded in the heavy industrial sector. The average capacity of blast furnaces doubled between 1929 and 1936, as larger, modern, and more fuel efficient furnaces were installed. Raw steel productivity increased by a quarter in the first half of the 1930s alone. In coal the increased utilisation of mechanical conveyors increased output per man-shift, while foreign observers who had noted technical defects in Japanese engineering as recently as the 1920s testified to significant improvements in the following decade. Aggregate output per worker in industry rose both absolutely and also relatively to agriculture. Allowing for population growth, the average domestic product per worker in Japan increased by almost 80 per cent between the wars, mainly in the 1930s (Patrick, 1971: 216). As might be expected, the gains were lower in smaller firms than in the larger enterprises which were able to pay higher wages to workers made more productive through heavy capital investment. All told, investment in Japan grew during the 1930s at a massive 11 per cent a year, as against 1.23 per cent in 1919–30 (Francks 1992: 54). The average lending rate imposed by the commercial banks fell, though not so far as the Bank of Japan's discount rate which went down by about half between 1931 and 1936 when it reached 3.29 per cent. In fact, however, long term industrial borrowing from financial institutions actually declined, high levels of profit providing the main source of large scale fixed investment funds for the heavy industries.

The evidence confirms a considerable widening of the productivity differential between large and small scale enterprises after 1933 (Morishima, 1982: 113). The bigger firms were hit later by the depression and recovered more quickly than the smaller ones. This underlines the contribution of industrial structure and organisation to recovery. By 1937 the *zaibatsu* controlled between them over a quarter of the country's mining operations and more than a third of its shipbuilding. They also had a substantial grip on the major sources of capital, holding 61 per cent of the insurance business and about a fifth of banking activity. Mitsui alone held 7.7 per cent of all Japan's industrial capital, Mitsubishi 5.5. per cent, and each controlled more than 100 different enterprises (Hunter, 1989: 125). Mitsui subsidiaries, for instance, included the Mitsui Bank, the Mitsui Trust, Mitsui Life Insurance, Mitsui Busan Kaisha or general trading organisation, and Tokyo Menka, the country's largest cotton importing company. Other interests included mines, a warehouse business, iron and steel works, chemical and dye-works, paper, rayon and celluloid factories, cotton mills, power companies, and a huge department store. Their commercial transactions in 1930 alone exceeded the Japanese state revenue. Furthermore, although overtly competitors, the various *zaibatsu* interests were often closely connected. Sumitomo was allied by marriage or adoption to Mitsubishi and Mitsui, and both worked together to help establish the Japan Iron Company in 1934. The integrated nature of the *zaibatsu* enterprises, combined with their influence in the Diet and the bureaucracy, made them a far more potent force in the Japanese economy than the 'new' industries allegedly responsible for British recovery in the 1930s.

Industrial change in Britain did not produce organisations with such interlinked or wide ranging interests. Indeed, the outcome and often the underlying motive of British merger activity was frequently defensive, aimed at price maintenance rather than efficiency improvements. Five main structural developments occurred between the wars: leading companies became much larger in terms of their value; they more closely resembled their American counterparts; there were more multi-unit enterprises; concentration levels rose; and trade associations exerted a firm hold on pricing and market sharing (Wilson, 1995: 175). More negatively, however, much British business remained uncompetitive as the persistence of family ownership continued to act as a brake on organisational innovation. To some small extent, perhaps, this can be blamed on government. Although the abandonment of gold in 1931 certainly opened the way for a more managed economy by increasing the autonomy of domestic economic policy, the state's main interest lay in fiscal affairs, the exchange rate, capital flows, and tariffs. Little attempt was made to take advantage of the opportunity for more comprehensive intervention afforded by tariffs, which thus remained primarily as protective devices for specific industries. In so far as government interfered at all in industry its main concern was in the depressed regions and motivated by political rather than economic considerations. National industrial policy thus remained incoherent and ad hoc, stressing price maintenance rather than efficiency and constantly foundering on the rocks of entrepreneurial independence. Furthermore, what might appear as government intervention, the action of the Bank of England in helping to establish the Lancashire Steel Corporation, guaranteeing the Lancashire Cotton Corporation, and putting up some of the nominal capital for the Bankers' Industrial Development Company, were in fact attempts by the Governor, Montagu Norman, to pre-empt direct central initiatives in industrial finance (Tolliday, 1987: 197–210).

State intervention in Japanese industry on the other hand was far more purposeful and directive, perhaps because of the closer links between government and business. As one commentator has it, this was a period of gestation in the evolution 'of a genuine Japanese institutional invention, the industrial policy of the developmental state' (Johnson, 1982: 115). In Manchuria state capitalism was established as the norm. Under the region's economic construction programme, one company was set up to develop each main industry in accordance with government targets. In 1927 the Ministry of Commerce and Industry (MCI) established a sort of think tank which developed strategies for the rationalisation and control of industry. A Resources Bureau was created to collect comprehensive data on the nation's economic activity and a law of 1929 required all factories to provide information about their financial and productive capacities. The Industrial Rationalisation Bureau was charged with making a range of industries more efficient by standardising their output and introducing cooperative selling. The bureau also administered the Major Industries Control Law of 1931 which gave MCI the power to authorise legally enforceable cartel agreements drawn up with the consent of two thirds of the enterprises in any industry. Cartels, it was reckoned, would enable firms to regulate production and increase profitability. Participants were obliged to report frequently to the Ministry about their investment plans and other matters. Twenty six cartels were established in major industries and many mergers followed. The result was a further incentive to efficiency whereas in Britain manufacturing trade associations, which had some 1,300 members by 1944, were used simply to guarantee prices and market quotas (Wilson, 1995: 155–6).

Although Japan's strategic enterprises were left mainly in private hands, thereby further consolidating the power of the *zaibatsu* in the modern heavy sector, they were subject to increasing state intervention. In steel, for example, where production was still not internationally cost competitive, tariffs helped to keep the domestic price competitive, while the Ministry of Commerce encouraged effective rationalisation by assisting with the establishment of the Japan Iron Company, a merger between the Yawata ironworks and leading private firms. A law of 1934 sought to bring the oil industry under government control in return for tax and other financial benefits. Over the next four years government intervened legislatively in the automobile, artificial oil, steel, machine tool, and aircraft industries. A scrap and build plan for shipping gave the merchant marine a number of fast new ships. In 1936 another scheme made the production of more than 3,000 automobiles a year subject to the issue of a licence from MCI. Successful applicants received tax breaks and import duty exemptions but in return they, too, had to submit their investment plans to MCI and agree to produce military vehicles. Since only firms with a majority of Japanese ownership were eligible to apply, this effectively broke the dominance of the American car makers in Japan and allowed new firms such as Nissan to develop. Combined with controls governing manufacturers' and export guilds, such measures provided the government with a powerful means of directing the economy.

Nissan was one of a number of industrial conglomerates whose standing grew in the 1930s to challenge that of the older *zaibatsu*. Sometimes called the 'new *zaibatsu*', these organisations generally lacked the defining *zaibatsu* characteristic of family ownership and control. Although they benefited from the popular anti-*zaibatsu* sentiment which both left and right fostered for their own political ends during the depression, the newcomers lacked the financial power of the older-established enterprises. They were thus more dependent on government patronage and received rights of development in Manchuria from whence the older enterprises were excluded. The connection between the new industrial conglomerates and the state became still stronger after the outbreak of full scale war against China. By 1938 Nissan was smaller only than Mitsui and Mitsubishi.

In so far as government thus sought to direct and coordinate industrial activity in particular directions, it was of some importance in promoting Japan's growth and recovery during the 1930s. Military expenditure, however, has perhaps been overemphasised as a causal factor in this process.

Certainly between 1931 and 1941 it outpaced the growth of national expenditure by about a fifth but a more significant acceleration occurred in the second half of the decade (Yonekura, 1994; 157). Growing involvement in Manchuria pushed up defence spending between 1930 and 1936 but the military still generated only a relatively small proportion of aggregate demand. Since government spending was financed in the main from borrowing rather than from demand-depressing taxation, economic progress, at least in the first half the decade, depended, though to a lesser extent than in Britain, on thriving private demand as much as on government expenditure. For example, only about a tenth of total steel demand was generated by military and other government requirements, the bulk of it being destined for civilian projects. Domestic demand also picked up as farm income began to recover. Although still well down on 1925 levels, agricultural prices by 1936 were some 30 per cent up on the 1931 figures. Similarly agricultural production remained lower than in 1925 though rising by 77 per cent between 1931 and 1936. Albeit modestly, farm household expenditure thus rose, not only on consumer goods but also on farm inputs such as fertiliser, a major product of the chemical industry. Government policy was also influential here. Measures included amendments to the 1921 Rice Law and efforts to reduce the burden of farm debt. The Ministry of Agriculture and Forestry launched a rehabilitation programme to encourage cooperative buying, selling, and credit provision, while an extensive public works programme in the countryside provided special grants for infrastructure investments.

Defence expenditure did assume growing significance mainly after 1936, when the assassination of Takahashi removed a finance minister who had sought to minimise the claims of the armed forces on his expansionary spending policies. Heavy industry, particularly steel, automobiles, and shipbuilding, was increasingly stimulated by military demand and the onset of war against China in 1937 led to a more rapid and progressive distortion of the economy. Government borrowing almost quadrupled between 1937 and 1941 when it reached Y2,406 million. By 1940, 17 per cent of national output was directly or indirectly serving military expansion.

The Second World War

Whatever the respective roles of the market and government activity in stimulating recovery in prewar Britain and Japan, the outbreak of world war heralded far reaching extensions of intervention in economic and social life. Planning against the eventuality of a second global conflict had been underway in Britain almost since the end of the first, although the tempo accelerated from the middle 1930s. Provision was made for the stockpiling of strategic materials while a shadow factory scheme was prepared to ensure adequate industrial production. Systems devised for raw material control and food rationing rested on the lessons learned in 1914–18. So, too, did manpower planning with its provision for safeguarding labour supplies to strategic sectors, and coordinating military and civilian requirements. The necessary administrative structure came effectively into place. A small war cabinet was responsible for broad decision-making, implementation being left to various ministries, including new ones such as Supply, Shipping and Food, created especially for the emergency. Universities provided a fruitful source of the technical experts, particularly economists and statisticians, on whose work planning ultimately rested.

Britain's intention of running the war economy according to financial restraints was soon abandoned in the light of the initially precarious military situation, seen in the retreat from France, the close run Battle of Britain, and the surrender of all her European allies. Churchill's appointment as premier in 1940 ushered in planning governed chiefly by the availability of physical resources and Britain shifted decisively to a centrally managed economy in which the state allocated resources, determined production priorities, and controlled prices. Government expenditure, which in the last full year of peace had amounted only to some 8 per cent of GDP, reached 50 per cent by 1943.

Strangely, the transformation to a war economy in Japan was rather less well managed although the transition was less obvious or abrupt because she had been militarily engaged on the Asian mainland for some time. The Major Industries Control Law was passed as early as 1931, the year in which the Kwantung Army engineered the Mukden incident and used it as a pretext for invading and annexing Manchuria. Subsequent measures taken to assist recovery from the depression had, as indicated above, given the government a substantial degree of leverage over economic activity and this was extended in the light of the developing military situation. By 1936 the army's five year plan for the further expansion of heavy industry had pushed the balance of payments into the red, compelling the imposition of import controls as the only way of meeting the required targets. The outbreak of full scale war in 1937 necessitated further intervention, otherwise imports would have been sucked in to satisfy the army's demands for emergency spending of Y2.5 billion. In September 1937 legislation was rushed through to control the disposition of labour. The measures also allowed the military to expropriate facilities and plant, dictate what was to be produced, and impose quotas and controls on prices, materials and capital flows. The outbreak of war in Europe in September 1939 led to freezes on prices and wages and the introduction of rationing. Nevertheless, most government intervention operated only indirectly through the Industrial Control Associations, notionally subject to the Cabinet Planning Board but in reality still functioning primarily in their own private interests.

All wartime planning, of course, was subject to the vagaries of the strategic situation. Both Britain and Japan relied heavily on imports whose security could not be guaranteed: as major combatants, both also had to transfer massive financial and labour resources to munitions production while simultaneously raising the strength of their respective armed forces. After the fall of France, Britain stood alone in Europe against Germany. With Western Europe either occupied or neutral, and a pared-down navy hard pressed to defend the trade routes, the immediate problem was one of simple survival. Agriculture had been declining in importance since the late nineteenth century and its condition had not been improved by the fall in world food prices after 1928. The sector's contribution to the GNP fell by 30 per cent between the wars. Even though the 1930s had produced some government assistance in the form of subsidies, the establishment of marketing boards, and inducements to small holders, Britain remained heavily dependent upon imports for vital food stuffs. Overseas sources still provided well over four fifths of British butter, wheat flour, and sugar consumption. With shipping space urgently required for munitions and other strategic materials and the sea lanes threatened by the lurking menace of U-boats, the need for greater self reliance was obvious. Furthermore, the availability of food was important for civilian morale, itself a significant consideration in sustaining the war effort, even though there was more widespread anticipation and acceptance of war in 1939 than there had been in 1914.

Industry's problems were legion. Resources had to be diverted as quickly and as efficiently as possible away from consumer goods to war production. This had to be achieved under the disruptions caused by the German air onslaught which was sustained with varying degrees of intensity throughout the war, and with priorities that changed, not according to the normal workings of the market, but in accordance with strategic requirements. The immediate need in 1940, for example, was for fighter aircraft, but the longer term requirement was for tanks and bombers. Production was hampered also by recurrent shortages of raw and semi-manufactured materials. As a result of prewar neglect, the light metal alloys so vital to aircraft production were in short supply. Some resourceful collecting of scrap helped here, with even the royal household's saucepans finding their way into fighter planes. In most instances, however, scarcities were caused by the disruption of established trade patterns. Before the war a fifth of British imports by value were from Europe and pretty well all had been cut off by 1941. Supplies of rubber were lost when the Japanese occupied Malaya and it took time to develop synthetic substitutes. Even when alternative sources could be found, delivery was by no means certain in the face of the U-boat campaign which intensified through 1941 and 1942. German attacks were incessant and at the height of the Battle of the Atlantic between February and April 1941 1.6 million tons of British shipping was sunk. Britain's shipping losses during the war amounted to some eleven million gross tons. Even when the much needed imports did get through, they still had to be paid for at a time when inflation was pushing up their prices and when exports were being curtailed in the interests of war production. The expansion of industry itself helped to pay some of the cost, but most of the necessary money was found by running down civilian consumption and overseas assets, by borrowing from the empire, and partly by the American provision of lend-lease. By the end of the conflict Britain's cumulative current account deficit stood at over £10 billion.

Finally, there was the problem of labour supply. Industrial production had to be increased and restructured while at the same time competing for valuable manpower with the massively inflated armed forces. The problems were exacerbated in certain key industries, notably shipbuilding and engineering, by the shortage of skills, a legacy of long term unemployment in the depressed areas. It was neither an easy nor a quick task to restore dormant work disciplines to older men who had not worked for years or to younger men who had worked only fitfully, victims of a system which laid them off as soon as apprenticeships were complete. Yet the process was accomplished sufficiently effectively to cast doubt on the view that long term unemployment in the 1930s had rendered some individuals permanently unfit for work.

On the whole, Britain coped extremely well with these substantial obstacles to the effective running of the wartime economy. Food supply was secured by a combination of careful import planning, agricultural improvement, and economy. Every effort was made to ensure that food imports represented the maximum nutritional value against the shipping space they occupied. The area of farm land under cultivation was substantially increased through a programme of subsidised reclamation, drainage, and ditching. The numbers of resource-consuming farm livestock were reduced and by 1941 some four million acres had been ploughed under in order to grow crops. Guaranteed prices were introduced as an incentive to production, while agricultural wages were raised to encourage labour to remain on the land, where its efforts were supplemented by those of the Women's Land Army. Rising levels of mechanisation, particularly tractors whose numbers increased from 60,000 in 1939 to 190,000 by 1945, and the more intensive application of fertilisers, pushed up farm productivity by between 10 and 15 per cent. These measures were accompanied by others designed to encourage civilian economies in the use of food and the utilisation of food substitutes, most memorably perhaps, powdered egg.

For reasons of public morale Churchill rejected scientists' suggestions for the introduction of a basic uniform diet, and while there were obvious shortages and hardships during the war – civilian consumption as a proportion of the GDP fell from 79 to 52 per cent – wartime rationing never included bread, potatoes, or alcohol. Food prices were subsidised, and the use of a points system ensured equality of treatment for all, while preserving some limited element of consumer choice. Inevitably there were gaps in the system and a black market developed, but generally the population was persuaded that equity was being applied. More importantly, nutritional levels were maintained and inflation minimised. The prices of essential items rose by about half between 1938 and 1945, compared with a doubling in the first war. Wages also increased by about 50 per cent as against 79 per cent between 1913 and 1918 (Glynn and Booth, 1996: 152). At work, employers were pressed to provide better facilities while, more generally, people were chivvied along, as in the First World War, by the prospect of postwar social reform.

Although imports, particularly of vehicles, aircraft, and munitions, remained essential, industrial output was expanded significantly. Export industries such as cotton were contracted, while others were diverted to production for the home market. Consumer industries were run down under a scheme which left production to nucleus factories, allowing the transfer of resources to more important commodities. Lines Brothers Ltd, for example, the major British producer of toys, manufactured munitions. Strategic heavy industries expanded spectacularly in terms of workers and output, often under the impetus of substantial injections of public money to facilitate the greater use of mass production techniques. The aircraft producers, who in 1938 had turned out less than 3,000 planes between them, built 26,000 in 1943. Increases in tank production were even more impressive, rising from 419 vehicles to 7,476 in the same period. The most obvious indicator of industrial expansion was the soaring GDP, which rose from £5,500 million in 1938 to reach a peak of more than £7,000 million in 1943 before settling at a slightly lower level for the rest of the war.

The successful allocation of human resources was central to these achievements. In May 1940 the Ministry of Labour acquired unprecedented powers governing the occupation, location, and remuneration of the workforce. This draconian measure was tempered by government support for improvements in working conditions and the provision of wage incentives. The state's new powers were in any case deployed infrequently and sensitively by Ernest Bevin, a man whose contribution to the war effort was in many ways as important as Churchill's own. As leader of one of the country's biggest unions, the Transport and General Workers, he was trusted by the workers as one of their own, although he could do little to prevent an increase in the number of strikes during the war, despite the fact that they were officially illegal under an order of 1940. What was achieved, however, was the necessary reorganisation of the workforce. Male conscription put almost a quarter of the working population under arms. By 1945, the size of the prewar military establishment had been multiplied by a factor of ten, with 437,000 women and 4.7 million men serving in the forces. At home, employment in strategic industries expanded – in shipbuilding by about 50 per cent, in engineering by 65 per cent, and in marine engineering by 34 per cent. In part, this was achieved by the categorisation and prioritising of civilian occupations which facilitated the transfer of labour to war industries. More importantly, however, the total size of the workforce was much larger – at its peak by three million people – than it had been before the war. The extra workers were secured by the final mopping up of the unemployed whose numbers were down to less than 100,000 by 1942, and by the substantial recruitment of women. With shortages of manpower becoming severe, single women between the ages of twenty and thirty were conscripted late in 1941 and given the choice of serving in the auxiliary services or industry. Overall, the number of women in the workforce rose by about half. Their numbers in engineering and the civil service increased respectively by 34 and almost 50 per cent, while 204,000 women were working on the land by 1945.

The military fortunes of the Japanese in the early days of the war were quite the opposite of Britain's. Following the success of the surprise pre-emptive strike against the Americans at Pearl Harbour in December 1941, they swept through South East Asia on a seemingly irresistible tide of victory. In the short term, neither the ill-prepared Americans nor the hard-pressed, badly trained, and poorly led British appeared able to halt battle hardened troops supported by an economy which had been geared to war for some years. In a short space of time, their armies occupied Malaya, Singapore, Hong Kong, the Philippines, Burma, and the Dutch East Indies. They threatened India and their airforce bombed northern Australia.

Early appearances were deceptive, however. Like Britain, Japan's precautionary economic planning against the eventuality of war had a long pedigree. An Armaments Industry Mobilization Law had been passed in 1918 while the statistical work of the Bureau of Resources had also been undertaken with military needs in mind. Yet neither this, a longer and earlier experience of action, nor the progress towards economic modernisation over the previous two decades, could save Japan from defeat in a long war against the United States, let alone the anti-Axis alliance. Even without allowing for the adverse effects of inter-service rivalries, conflicts within the high command, or America's success in breaking Japan's communications codes, the limitations of Japan's resources and of her planning mechanisms made defeat inevitable. The Americans took time to mobilise but after the Battle of Midway in June 1942 when four Japanese aircraft carriers were sunk, the pendulum swung as Japan's underlying economic frailties were exposed.

Chief among these was the shortage of basic resources, which had played no little part in the decision to take on the Americans in the first place. Various considerations had prompted territorial expansion in the 1930s, including pan-Asianism and the search for living space for a growing population. Most important of all, however, was Japan's high level of import dependence and the degree to which it had been increased by the continued expansion of modern heavy industry. Of the country's aggregate consumption of metals in 1936, for instance, home production was responsible for less than 9 per cent of lead, 39 per cent of zinc, 29 per cent of tin, 70 per cent of manganese, and about 50 per cent of aluminium (Trewartha, 1945: 113). This dependence on others was reinforced by the protectionism which clouded world trade in the 1930s, causing autarky to appear as an attractive proposition for Japan. Yet the aggressive territorialism inherent in such a strategy, coupled with the continued activities of 1.5 million Japanese troops engaged on the Chinese mainland, greatly alarmed the United States in particular. In September 1940 Japan took advantage of the war in Europe by occupying the northern half of French Indo-China, thereby gaining access to airfields for use against China. America promptly placed an embargo on the export to Japan of specialist metals and other strategic materials. Opinion in Japan was divided about the wisdom of further antagonising the United States but in July 1941 the Japanese responded to German requests for assistance against the USSR by moving into the southern half of French Indo-China. The Americans promptly halted oil exports to Japan. This was potentially crippling since Japan produced only about 11 per cent of her own oil and relied on America for about three quarters of her requirements (Trewartha, 1945: 97). Japanese calculations suggested that oil reserves in October 1941 were sufficient to support the forces for about two years, after which they would effectively be immobilised and by which time also America would be much better prepared for any conflict. With defeat a certainty if the onset of hostilities was delayed, the advocates of immediate war prevailed over more cautious elements. Reckoning that oil, food, and raw material supplies could be sufficiently sustained so long as shipping losses did not exceed a million tons a year, the Japanese, after some hesitation, decided to strike first by launching the attack on Pearl Harbour. Thereafter, conquest provided her with access to many of the essential raw materials which she required, including bauxite and tin, as well as oil from the Dutch East Indies and rubber from Malaya.

But continuity of supply could not be guaranteed. Initially the Japanese were welcomed in many of the newly conquered countries as liberators from Western colonialism. But their inability to maintain living standards in the occupied territories soon combined with the cruelties of the secret police and the army to alienate civilian populations and foster resistance movements. This placed a further strain on limited and overstretched military resources, and also provoked internal unrest in supplying areas, sometimes interrupting the flow of materials to Japan itself.

More importantly, the long sea lanes on which the extended Japanese empire depended ultimately became indefensible. The imperial navy was slow to organise a convoy system and the shipbuilding industry could not provide sufficient escort vessels to deal with what has been called the 'most effective submarine campaign in the history of warfare' (Smith, 1995: 30). Although Japan's shipbuilders exceeded all expectations by building 1.03 million tons in 1943 and 1.74 million tons in 1944, shipping losses were much heavier than anticipated. Over two million tons went down in 1943, a figure which doubled in the following year. By 1945 less than a quarter of the prewar merchant fleet was still afloat (Nakamura, 1994: 113). Raw material shortages mounted inexorably. The scarcity of oil in particular hampered

both the civilian and military effort, although both aircraft and warship production kept up remarkably well. The production of aircraft units and warships in 1944, for instance, was respectively four and two times that of 1941
(Nakamura, 1994: 118).

Fuel shortages, however, made it increasingly difficult to mount an effective defence against the ever growing weight of American airpower, further
adding to the problems against which an under-resourced industry already
struggled. By November 1944 the Americans had driven the Japanese from
their recently acquired conquests and were sufficiently close to launch air
raids upon their homelands. Thereafter Japan's industrial capacity, half
starved by the scarcity of resources, was effectively bludgeoned into submis-
sion by air attacks far more intensive than anything the Germans managed
against Britain. The dispersion of small scale factories throughout residential areas made it all but impossible to distinguish between industrial and
civilian targets, particularly in Tokyo where there were many such plants
producing weapons against the anticipated land invasion. In March 1945
the city was bombed so heavily that an estimated 100,000 people were
killed, more than died in air raids in Britain over six years of war.
Ultimately, the Americans took to giving advance warning of raids, partly to
save life, partly to impede the Japanese industrial machine by increasing the
rate of absenteeism. By June 1945 40 per cent of Japan's most important
cities had been gutted, Tokyo so much so that it was removed from the list
of targets.

Worse was to come, however. In April Okinawa, the first of the Japanese
home islands, was invaded. Both sides suffered heavy casualties as the
Japanese revealed how fanatically their homeland would be defended.
Coupled with the still considerable strength of Japan's ground forces, this
tenacity was sufficient to persuade the Allies to abandon a full scale invasion
in favour of dropping atom bombs on Hiroshima and Nagasaki. In hindsight
it is easy to question the morality of unleashing such terrible forces but even
after the first explosion there were many Japanese who wished to continue
the struggle. Similarly, when the emperor intervened to announce Japan's
surrender with the understatement of all time – 'the war situation has not
necessarily gone to our advantage' – some of his officers tried unsuccessfully
to prevent his broadcast and then committed suicide in front of the imperial
palace.

The sustained intensity of the American onslaught on Japan pointed up in
very stark terms the disparities which existed between the industrial capacities of the combatants in the Pacific War. Even had raw material shortages
not been rife, the structure of the Japanese economy was still not comparable
with that of either Britain or the United States. Even at its peak, for instance,
Japan's armaments production was only a tenth of that of America: vehicle
production was relatively small, and poorer coal stocks were mined exhaus-
tively and wastefully. American steel output in 1941–42 was seven million

tons a month, not much smaller than Japan's entire annual output of eight million tons (Trewartha, 1945: 291). Such inequalities became even more pronounced as Japan's raw material supplies were progressively cut off. Nor was Japan's economy yet supported by comparable levels of technical and scientific expertise. Despite some extension of higher education – 40 universities and 184 colleges in 1928 became respectively 45 and 342 by 1945, for example – the country's capacity for independent technical progress was still relatively limited. Mitsubishi was certainly capable of designing the Zero fighter which was faster and more manoeuvrable than any American plane until 1943, but on the other hand, it was British inventiveness which came up with radar, penicillin, and jet propulsion, as well as helping to develop atomic weapons.

Above all, of course, compared with Britain and America, Japan had a far larger proportion of resources tied up in an agriculture which was still backward and unable to support the war economy indefinitely. About 16 per cent of the land area was under cultivation compared with 22.5 per cent of Britain's and the latter's productivity advantage was evident from the fact that each farm worker looked after seven or eight times as much land as a Japanese equivalent. As imports were reduced, so the need for self sufficiency became more urgent. Yet highly labour intensive agriculture was progressively denuded of its strongest and ablest workers as they were conscripted into the armed forces or to war work. At the same time, supplies of farm machinery dwindled while the chemicals used in fertiliser manufacture were increasingly diverted to explosives. Intensive cultivation merely exhausted the land and by 1945 domestic agricultural output was down to a third of its prewar levels. Distribution was constantly disrupted by civilian evacuation into the countryside and by frequent confiscations on behalf of a military establishment desperate for food. By July 1945 meat and fish supplies were respectively 20 and 30 per cent of their 1941 levels. The official ration of 1,500 calories a day was below the minimum physical efficiency requirement but many Japanese had even less than that, reduced, with official encouragement, to eating leaves and weeds. This in turn had further adverse effects on industrial productivity which was already threatened by problems of labour supply.

Over the war as a whole, as table 3.3 indicates, Japan's total working population declined. The increased demand associated with war required some redistribution of the industrial labour force but the scope for such readjustment was limited by the fact that in 1940 almost 90 per cent of employees in the large manufacturing enterprises and 61 per cent of those in medium sized enterprises were already working in the strategically vital heavy and chemical sectors. The problem was further exacerbated by the army's insistence on the sanctity of the draft which made it impossible to organise an appropriate exemption policy of the sort adopted in Britain. Indiscriminate conscription caused the proportion of skilled workers engaged in productive work to fall from 34 per cent in 1941 to 22 per cent by 1945 (Gordon, 1985: 247). The iron and steel sector lost a third of its skilled manpower in 1942 alone, with disastrous consequences for output. Measured in tons per worker it fell 60 per cent between 1941 and 1944 (Gordon, 1985: 283).

Table 3.3 *Employment in Japan*

	Oct 1940	Nov 1944	May 1945
Working population (millions)	32.48	29.72	27.64
		Distribution (%)	
Agriculture	44.3	47.2	50.6
Mining/manufacture/ transport/communication	30.7	33.7	30.8
Commerce	15.4	6.8	5.7
Government	9.6	12.2	12.8

(Nakamura, 1994: 105)

In the absence of any substantial reserve of unemployed industrial workers on which to draw, residents of the Japanese countryside and the colonies provided supplementary sources of labour, and some prisoners of war were set to work in the mines. The former were often reluctant recruits and required training. So, too, did the unmarried women who were also drafted into industry on a large scale. Although about two fifths of the economically active population in prewar Japan had been female they were largely confined to low status work, often in the service sector. They may not have been reluctant to work but both relative lack of appropriate skills and poor nutrition took their toll of efficiency. By 1944 virtually the whole population had been mobilised, including even children of middle school age and above.

The other approach to finding labour for strategic production was to divert it from the consumption industries, which were ruthlessly reduced, as military expenditure soared to a peak outlay of Y33 billion in 1943. By 1945 the output of cotton and wool textiles was running at about 1 or 2 per cent, soap at 4 per cent, of prewar levels (Nakamura, 1994: 120). Although some 42 per cent of national income (Y17 billion out of Y40 billion) was allotted to civilian consumption in 1941–42, it accounted for only Y11 billion out of Y65 billion (18.5 per cent) by 1944–45 (Bisson, 1945b: 55–9). This was a far higher reduction of net national product consumption than in Britain where it dropped from 78 per cent in 1938 to 51 per cent by 1944. By 1944 real wages in Japan were a third down on their 1939 level (Gordon, 1985: 52): in Britain they were actually 21 per cent higher. Not surprisingly, there is some evidence to suggest that morale was a problem among Japan's civilian workforce. Although legislation compelled employers to provide welfare, dining, health, and recreational facilities, workers resisted attempts to increase the working day above eleven or twelve hours. Absenteeism was a serious problem even before American air raids intensified and government attempts to tighten controls made matters worse. As early as 1941 a Home Ministry survey reported that 'the impact of controls seems to be considerable. They can create a feeling of oppression, of government high-handedness, leading to discontents, complaints, work-place tensions, lower morale and productivity' (Gordon, 1985: 317).

It is a natural enough assumption that the contrasting outcomes of the Second World War for Japan and Britain depended, in part at least, on their respective abilities to run their war economies. On the whole, Britain did this more successfully than Japan. In many ways the British appeared more flexible, more innovative, and more resourceful than either the Germans or the Japanese with whom they were subsequently compared so unfavourably. Despite the higher levels of economic intervention and control customary in Japan, government failed to adjust sufficiently rapidly to the requirements of modern total warfare. Strategic economic planning lacked overall coordination, partly because the prime minister lacked effective power and partly because responsibility was divided among various economic ministries. It was thus difficult to establish priorities in the early stages of the war. In the main the various ministries responsible for key sectors functioned quite independently of each other. Not until 1943 were regional administrative councils established to eliminate wasteful duplication between central and prefectural government effort. Most damaging of all, perhaps, there was no central coordination of raw material allocation. Indeed, government as such did not formally control it at all. The Major Industries Association Ordinance, promulgated in September 1941 and establishing the Industrial Control Associations, may have vested existing private cartels with official powers over material, labour, and capital supplies but it effectively left production in the hands of the cartels. As a consequence, different industries competed against each other for resources, with the result that production was not shaped by conformity to any strategic considerations, depending rather on the interplay of what were essentially private, profit-driven interests. By 1942 shortfalls in the output of vital commodities pointed to the defects of this system and ultimately led to the establishment of a Ministry of Munitions to coordinate industrial production. This made little difference, however. The problems of industrial production were by this time becoming insuperable, and there was still ambiguity about control of the new ministry. Formally, it was headed by politicians but real executive power was in the hands of a veteran Mitsui executive. Nor did it do much towards reconciling the conflicting claims of civilian and military interests for materials. A further dimension to these disputes was provided by the fierce internecine rivalries which existed between the various branches of the armed forces, each of which functioned as a separate entity, even to the extent of possessing independent air arms, while the army actually built its own submarines. As the war dragged on, so these various levels of competition for dwindling resources and finance affected major military decisions and their implementation (Bisson, 1945a).

Yet if British economic planning was apparently more successful, it was by no means perfect. Inevitably there were mistakes, just as there were on the battlefields, and the whole bureaucratic edifice might never have materialised at all had Dunkirk or the Battle of Britain turned out differently, as so easily might have been the case. Equally, anything more than sheer survival depended on the support of both the Soviet Union and the United States. Although Britain diverted some of her own scarce military output to the Soviets, Russia acted as a vast sponge, drawing in German effort and resources at terrible human and physical cost to itself. Only the entry of the United States into the conflict made possible the reconquest of Europe, while the lend-lease programme was vital to Britain both in providing scarce materials and avoiding an even more severe balance of trade crisis. Altogether some $21 billion of goods reached Britain, about a third of it in the form of highly nutritious foodstuffs.

It has also been argued that the war economy was characterised by poor management, lack of technical expertise, inefficient utilisation of labour, and confrontational industrial relations (Barnett, 1986). It has been pointed out, for example, that it took 13,000 hours to build the frame of a Mark V Spitfire, whereas the comparable German Messerschmitt 109 was built in only 4,000 (Barnett, 1986: 148). British industry lacked the skill and expertise to manufacture radar and radio which, as a result, had to be made in the United States. Similarly, Britain acquired more than half its tanks, almost a fifth of its aircraft, and just under 30 per cent of its military vehicles from America under the lend-lease programme. In this sense, too, it might plausibly be argued that Britain emerged on the winning side primarily because America was its ally.

By the same token, it can be suggested that Japan was defeated mainly because America was the enemy. No matter how efficient a planning system had been devised, no nation at Japan's stage of economic development could have sustained a long war against the industrial might of the United States and its allies. How was it, pondered a Japanese diplomat, 'that Japan, a poor country, had the temerity to wage war against the combination of so many powerful nations . . . The contest was unequal from the first' (Horsley and Buckley, 1990: 10). That Japan sustained her war effort for so long might be advanced as an argument for the *success* of her economic planning, although this must have owed much as well to the spirit of the people who were every bit as determined (or resigned) as Londoners during the Blitz. It was this fortitude which enabled the population to cope with air raids and growing material deprivation. Although standards of living had never been high in absolute terms, such improvements as had been registered before the war were lost as civilian consumption was ruthlessly squeezed. On the battlefields it was the strength of the nationalistic ethos rather than any overwhelming military might which lay behind Japan's early successes: the British armies which surrendered to the Japanese in the Far East were often larger than their conquerors. Above all, it was this spirit which lay behind the fanaticism of the *Kamikaze* pilots and the defence of Okinawa. It was the Americans' appreciation of this fact which brought down the atom bombs on the Japanese, completing the virtual destruction of half a century's economic progress.

The system of reproduction

Standard of living: Japan

That progress had given Japan the highest standards of living in Asia during the 1930s, and even facilitated some small degree of catching up with the West, although the evidence is not always unambiguous or consistent. It is difficult, therefore, to substantiate the older view that Japanese imperialism in this decade rested on the deliberate and progressive impoverishment of the people, although that was certainly their condition by the time the war ended in 1945.

This is not to suggest of course that prewar Japan was without its poor. Using Maeda's measures and definitions, 17.8 per cent of households could be classified as poor in 1930, which translated into 14.7 per cent of the total population. Most of the poor tended to be outside the modern industrial system altogether, quite mobile, sometimes taking work which verged on the illegal and which was generally irregular and often at the mercy of the weather. In 1934 about a fifth of the Tokyo poor were unskilled day labourers, almost 11 per cent were self employed craftsmen and 8 per cent were waste collectors. Their absolute income rose over time but the depression widened the relative gap between them and the rest of the workforce. At constant 1934–36 prices, Tokyo ghetto incomes in 1934 stood at 92 as against 128 in 1929, their lowest at any time since 1912 (Chubachi and Taira, 1976: 407).

At the opposite end of the scale were some 180,000 families which between them received 22 per cent of total household income in 1930. This included at the very pinnacle of the social pyramid, about 1,800 well off *zaibatsu* aristocrats and landlords who alone enjoyed about 10 per cent of aggregate family income. All incomes above Y1,200 a year were taxable. There were only 569,046 tax-payers in 1931, but they included individuals such as Baron Iwasaki Hisaya of Mitsubishi who paid tax on an income of Y2.3 million in the financial year 1935–36 when average national income per head was Y165. Such levels of personal wealth help in part to explain why political extremists found it relatively easy to stir up popular resentment against the *zaibatsu* families in the early years of the decade.

The vast majority of the population of course fell between the extremes, but experience and standards were very varied. Immediately below the giants of the income spectrum was a small middle class, estimated at about 1.8 million families and whose numbers increased in line with the expansion of the service sector. At constant prices, the output of the commercial sector rose by about 40 per cent between 1929 and 1939 with administrative and professional services growing respectively by about 18 and 48 per cent (Ohkawa and Shinohara, 1979: 314). Within this group incomes ranged quite widely. A 1931 salaries comparison between a university faculty and a prefectural office revealed a median range between the equivalent of £60 and £120 a year. This was not high by British standards where the contemporary dividing line between middle- and working-class incomes was conventionally set at about £250 a year, but as a whole the middle income group in Japan absorbed 30 per cent of all family income.

The remaining half of household income was shared by the majority of the population, 10.6 million of the nation's 12.6 million families. That group, too, was characterised by wide internal disparities. One of the most marked remained between the rural majority and the urban minority, although migration from the countryside to the cities continued to such an extent that by 1935 over 30 per cent of the population lived in cities of more than 100,000 inhabitants (McCune, 1942: 164–5). Although rural communities were beginning to recover from the worst effects of the depression by the middle 1930s, the ratio of agricultural productivity to manufacturing productivity fell from 44.8 per cent in 1919 to 22.8 per cent in 1938. Real income differentials between urban and rural areas thus increased by the end of the 1930s, a development mirrored in a consumption gap considerably wider in 1938 than it had been in 1914 (Ono and Watanabe, 1976: 367). It was in the cities that patterns of social life become most modernised and Westernised, to the evident resentment of rural leaders.

> It is a well known fact that the countryside has been made subordinate to the city in Japan's industrialisation to date. All laws have protected commerce and manufacturing and exploited rural villages; the burden of taxes, too, has been made heavy on rural areas and light in cities . . . for the manufacturers the countryside has become a place where raw materials can be bought cheaply and finished goods sold dear. (Waswo, 1989: 133–4)

It was not surprising that by British standards all wages within Japanese industry remained low, for in 1934 the average ratio of factory wages to net product was only 27 per cent as against 44 per cent in the United Kingdom. It was also true that because of technological advance, labour demand did not always keep pace with industrial output, putting some downward pressure on wages. Nevertheless, the further development of dualism within the Japanese economy brought continued advantages to skilled workers in the heavy industries, mainly in the form of better wages, greater job security, and fringe benefits such as high interest savings schemes or social and sporting facilities. Particularly during the depression years, differentials within Japanese industry widened. In the heavy industries real wages actually rose, even through the worst years, 1929 to 1933, because money wages fell less than prices. For the unskilled, however, which included the large numbers of women engaged in agriculture and textiles, real wages dropped in these years by a fifth. By 1936 wages in light industry and cotton spinning were 70 per cent of their 1929 level. All workers in the traditional small scale sector did less well than those in the modern heavy industries. By the early 1930s operatives in the smallest manufacturing enterprises earned about 60 per cent of those employed in the largest plants (Yasuba, 1976: 258).

Notwithstanding all these qualifications and variations, the statistical evidence points to overall improvement in living standards for many Japanese. An index based on 1914 shows real wages climbing to reach 174 in the first half of the 1930s. Even though they fell back slightly after 1935 to 166, they remained considerably higher than the 155 attained in the second half of the 1920s. A similar picture emerges from a wide-ranging contemporary survey of Japan's industry. In 1936 almost 2.6 million workers in 90,602 factories had to work an average of 7.9 hours in order to earn one yen. By 1939 3.7 million people in 137,422 enterprises could earn that sum by working only for 5.9 hours (Trewartha, 1945: 264). The rising liquidity of banks catering primarily for small depositors also suggests some modest income improvement, and some regional redistribution appears to have occurred as well, with provincial banks gaining at the expense of metropolitan institutions in Tokyo and Osaka. Per capita food intakes, which had risen in the 1920s, at least kept pace with rising population thereafter, and by the second half of the 1930s large scale famines and epidemics had all but disappeared. Between 1925 and 1935 the proportion of personal expenditure devoted to food fell from 57 per cent to 50 per cent (table 3.4). Together, food and

Table 3.4 *Japan: personal consumption expenditures (1934–36 prices Ymn)*

	1925	1930	1935
Food	6,037.2	6,162.3	6,494.9
Clothing	813.3	1,113.1	1,678.2
Housing	1,377.9	1,416.8	1,506.6
Fuel and light	435.5	507.8	556.3
Medical and personal	354.6	474.8	869.5
Transport	311.9	364.3	418.3
Communication	45.1	66.0	86.6
Social	401.9	386.5	341.5
Education and recreation	831.3	876.5	1,042.0
Aggregate expenditure	10,608.7	11,368.1	12,993.9

(Ohkawa and Shinohara, 1979: 344)

clothing absorbed about 63 per cent of expenditure (more than half as much again as the British level) in the average household, but as personal per capita spending rose, so more was available for housing, education, and recreation (table 3.5). The improvement was also reflected in demographic trends. Overall mortality rates were far lower than those characteristic of other Asian countries, and in some particulars even compared favourably with parts of Europe such as France and Spain. A Japanese boy born in 1935 could expect to live ten years longer than his grandfather born in the 1880s.

Table 3.5 *Japan: selected per capita expenditures (Yen per head)*

	1925	1930	1935
Total	177.7	176.2	187.5
Food	101.1	95.5	93.7
Clothing	13.7	17.3	24.2
Education and recreation	13.9	13.6	15.0

(Ohkawa and Shinohara, 1979: 344)

Qualitative indicators also pointed to improvements although of course they were by no means unequivocal or straightforward, as the evidence on working conditions reveals. In the mines, for example, conditions remained particularly bad, Baroness Ishimoto suggesting that there was little to differentiate between the life of a pig and that of a miner, thirty of whom died in accidents for every million tons of coal raised: the comparable figure in Britain was ten. She also described women working the mines in conditions which had been banned in England in the mid-nineteenth century (Livingston, Moore and Oldfather, 1976: I, 315) Even in industries such as textiles, where conditions were rather better, not all Western observers were convinced. Helen Mears was certainly not pursuaded by her tour of the Tokyo mills belonging to Dai Nippon, one of Japan's main cotton companies. She noted afterwards that Japanese businessmen had

> travelled enough in the West to observe conditions that convince them that Western management's express concern for labor is a game. They try to play it; they have learned the rules; they can issue statements and prepare reports expressing the sentiments they feel are expected of them, but . . . the hypocrisy is too apparent. (Livingston, Moore and Oldfather, 1976: I, 315)

Freda Utley took a similarly jaundiced view, although she was undoubtedly influenced by her pro-Marxist anti-Japanese sympathies (Utley, 1931). Such evidence has to be set against the more positive assessments provided by Arno Pearse, who dismissed Utley's views as 'absurd', while Ferdnand Maurette of the ILO wrote with enormous enthusiasm about working conditions, like Pearse stressing the importance of the welfare benefits provided by

employers, particularly in textiles and parts of the modern, large scale industrial sector (Pearse, 1929: 91; Maurette, 1934).

Yet such benefits were generally beyond the reach of most of the small
scale producers who continued to provide the bulk of jobs in Japanese manufacturing. This was partially offset by the fact that the Japanese state took a
more active and systematic part in the provision of social welfare than is
often appreciated. In general, Japan's policy-makers did acknowledge a
governmental responsibility for welfare. It was believed, however, that this
was best served by providing an appropriate legislative framework and then
fostering economic growth, thereby providing individuals and institutions
with the financial means to deal with social emergencies. It was not automatically considered to be the duty of the state itself to provide the actual social
care, although it did sometimes do so. It is true that of an increased state
expenditure reaching almost Y1,000 million between 1930 and 1936 only
14 per cent went to social welfare, compared with 62 per cent on the armed
forces and 17 per cent for debt servicing. On the other hand, responsibility
for welfare provision was widely devolved. The complex structure is best
understood from some examples. The Retirement Fund Law required all
firms with more than fifty workers (such firms employed almost two thirds of
the industrial workforce) to set up funds for retirement or severance pay. The
importance of this was that at the time only about half of all companies had
such schemes in operation. Similarly, Health Insurance legislation in 1922
provided protection for those manufacturing workers not already covered
by their employers' own arrangements. Health insurance was extended in
1938 to farmers and the self employed. Other government initiatives
included an Industrial Injuries Assistance Act in 1931, Seamen's Social
Insurance in 1940, and Employees' Pension legislation the following year. To
this should be added the various welfare functions carried out by municipalities. As early as 1920, for instance, Osaka established a department of social
welfare, whose amenities included housing, public baths, labour exchanges,
day nurseries, maternity care, and boarding house provision (Osaka
Municipal Office, 1920).

Of course, provision remained patchy, particularly in terms of medical services. Although there was one doctor to every 10,000 people, most lived in
the cities, leaving the countryside sparsely provided for. Protection against
poverty was rather better organised in that the relief system established in
1874 still provided public assistance to the chronically ill and all those under
the age of thirteen or over seventy who lacked income. It was administered at
local level and by 1928 twenty major municipalities and all the prefectures
had welfare commissions. However, as the relief scales operative in 1930
were still those of 1870 it is doubtful, even after some adjustments in 1932, if
it did much more than keep applicants alive, and it certainly did little to
redistribute income and wealth. Compared with contemporary Britain, the
most striking gap appeared to be in the provision of measures to deal with

unemployment, although this was never as serious a problem as it was in Britain. Official estimates in eight large towns in 1932 put the unemployment figure at 500,000 which was translated into a national total of two million, probably too high. In any case, given Japan's economic structure, it was always possible for some proportion of the urban unemployed to return to their families in the rural villages. For the casual workers among those who remained, the state encouraged the major cities to establish voluntary unemployment insurance schemes, even to the extent of putting up some of the necessary finance. Although some were thwarted by determined opposition from employers, individual municipalities did provide some protection for their own citizens (Hiratu, 1936: 48–81).

On balance, then, the evidence seems to suggest that average living standards, both quantitative and qualitative, were rising in Japan in the 1930s. Even so, for most people the level of improvement was hardly commensurate with an annual growth rate in the GDP of almost 5 per cent. This raises the question of why standards did not improve even more significantly, or, to put it in a slightly different way, what happened to the bulk of the increased national income generated during the decade if it did not benefit the mass of the people in the form of higher consumption levels.

One important explanation relates to the changing terms of trade which compelled Japan to export more in order to pay for her imports. In the exact reverse of British experience, Japan's imports became more expensive relative to exports. Between 1930 and 1936 the average export price dropped by 5 per cent while import prices rose by 29 per cent. This extra cost absorbed about a fifth of the gain in real national product attributable to export expansion. Between 1934 and 1938 Japan lost a billion yen a year of real income because she could no longer import goods at the prices prevailing in 1930 (Lockwood, 1955: 171).

Another contributory factor was that some of the rise in per capita income represented the goods and services which were required for urbanisation and industrialisation but which did not actually increase real consumption. Food and raw materials had to travel further, cities expanded, markets became more elaborately organised, and the size of the state sector increased. All these developments generated new jobs and income in the national accounts but certainly as far as consumption is concerned, they are more properly reckoned as costs rather than gains.

Demographic factors also acted as a brake on more extensive improvements in living standards. Although the rate of population growth slowed down, total numbers rose from 63 million to 71 million between 1929 and 1937, making for an overall increase of some 29 per cent between 1920 and 1940. In the course of the 1930s anxieties were expressed about the possible implications of overpopulation, but the nascent birth control movement was suppressed by the military-dominated government for fear that it might weaken military and economic potential at a time of growing international tension. Inevitably, therefore, rising population absorbed some part of the growing national income. It also added to the problems of urban over-crowding, and in this sense also adversely affected the standard of living. In 1932 the average household size in Japan was 5.1 persons and by 1940 the population density was 500 per square mile. However, if this latter figure is recalculated in terms of cultivated land only, then population density was more than 3,000 per square mile, the highest on earth and about a third higher than contemporary Britain (Trewartha, 1945: 139). In this context it is significant that despite the relative improvements in life expectancy noted above, the League of Nations *Statistical Year-book* for 1933 recorded an absolute mortality rate among Japanese infants almost twice as high as that in Britain. A Home Office survey also reported in 1936 that as many as 120,000 Japanese were dying every year from tuberculosis (Utley, 1936: 185).

There is no doubt, either, that from the middle of the 1930s the growing influence of the military distorted the pattern of economic activity so that the income benefits which might have been expected to accrue from high levels of economic growth were reduced. Production was gradually directed away from consumers' towards producers' goods for the armed forces: once the nation's resources were fully utilised by 1937 this could continue only at the absolute expense of domestic civilian consumption, as the previous section indicated. Even before this stage was reached, however, more tangible improvements in living standards were probably limited by traditional pat-terns of expenditure and habits, particularly a notably high propensity for saving and investment rather than consumption. It is significant that even in boom years as much as 15 per cent of annual net product was invested in plant and construction, while savings in small financial institutions grew faster than in the banks.

Standard of living: Britain

Private philanthropy, charitable activity, and voluntary social service all con-tinued to flourish in the Britain of the depression. Similarly, the local author-ities continued to shoulder responsibility for the actual provision of some services, particularly education and housing. Nevertheless, the Great War, the greater influence of collectivist sentiment, and the sheer scale of postwar unemployment, served to accelerate the process, already evident in the Edwardian period, whereby the state itself assumed a greater responsibility for social provision. This was symbolised in the formal abolition of the poor law system at the end of the 1920s and in the absorption of the old Local Government Board into a new Ministry of Health. The growing significance of the state's role was evident in that fact that total public expenditure on welfare by 1935 had reached £382.4 million or almost 10 per cent of the national income, compared with a 1924 outlay of 5.8 per cent (Mowatt,

1955: 497). Pensions were increased and put on a new contributory basis in 1925. The extension of health insurance raised the number of those covered from 13 million in 1914 to about 20 million by 1939. By this time some 3.2 million children were receiving free or cheap school milk. Immunisation programmes against diphtheria and other infantile diseases were implemented, while medical inspection become a regular feature of school life. Above all, the state bore the brunt of providing relief for the unemployed, 43 per cent of whom were still eligible to receive unemployment benefit in 1936. Another 37 per cent were in receipt of the dole, and the remainder were dependent on public assistance. The combined impact of these measures was such that by 1939, it has been suggested, 'the welfare state was standing, but still incomplete and in scaffolding (Mowatt, 1955: 495).

Welfare benefits, modest though they were by later standards, certainly played a part in raising aggregate living standards in interwar Britain. At the very least, it is likely that the existence of unemployment relief provided a floor below which wages could not sink. Contemporary observers were virtually unanimous in their view that poverty caused by low income was much less common after the First World War than before it. In turn, this may help to identify another influence which protected living standards during the depression years, namely the enhanced share of the national income going to labour (table 3.6). This reflected the generally low levels of profitability during the period, rising industrial productivity, and the ability of organised labour to retain the wage improvements secured during the war years, notwithstanding the decline in the number of trade unionists. On the other hand, it is clear that in the 1920s at least, the major beneficiaries of this trend were those in receipt of salaries, rather than wages. Furthermore, in industries such as iron and steel, textiles, building, engineering, and mining, indices of weekly wage rates show that not until the very end of the 1930s, if then, did rates recover to match the pre-depression levels (Mitchell and Deane, 1971: 351).

Table 3.6 *Britain: distribution of national income (average decade %)*

	Wages/salaries	Rents	Profits
1905–14	47.2	10.8	42.0
1930–39	62.0	8.7	29.2

(Deane and Cole, 1962: 247)

More important, therefore, in raising British living standards, was the advantageous shift in the terms of trade after 1928 which pushed down the price of imported food significantly. As a result, real wages by 1938 were about 10 per cent higher than they had been in 1929, and even those on fixed incomes benefited, as the evidence of rising consumption suggest. In real terms average per capita consumption rose by almost a quarter between 1910–13 and 1936–39. Greater quantities of meat, fresh vegetables, poultry, tea, and dairy produce were all consumed and George Orwell even went so far as to suggest that the availability of cheap luxuries, among which he listed fish and chips, tinned salmon, and cut price chocolate, prevented revolution (Orwell, 1962: 80–1). Certainly the range of available foodstuffs broadened as a result of new retail methods and improvements in food technology. Nestle introduced instant coffee in 1929, for instance, and brand names such as Kelloggs and Heinz became standard purchases for an increasing number of Britons.

Nor was rising consumption confined solely to food. By 1937 only about 37 per cent of the average working-class budget went on comestibles as against approximately 60 per cent in 1914. Some of the saving was directed to leisure, whose commercial manifestations were an important feature of economic and social life in the 1930s. On average four people out of every ten attended the cinema each week, popular dancing flourished, professional football matches attracted huge crowds, and the pools and betting prospered, holding out as they did the prospect of a quick way to wealth. The number of radio licences per thousand families rose from almost thirty in 1929 to just over sixty eight by 1938: motor car ownership almost doubled over the same period to more than two million, while the 500,000 rented telephones in use in 1930 had grown to more than 1.1 million by 1938 (Bowden, 1994: 246). Between the 1920s and 1938 the number of wage earners legally entitled to a paid week's holiday doubled to three million, a figure raised as a result of legislation in 1939 to about eleven million. Even before this, about fifteen million people were taking an annual week's holiday, though this included only about a third of wage earners on weekly incomes of less than £4.00 (Mowatt, 1955: 502). Nevertheless, overall demand was sufficient to encourage the development of appropriate commercial responses. The first of Billy Butlin's holiday camps was opened at Skegness in 1937.

Equally important though less measurable contributions to better living standards were made by measures to improve air quality and make fuller provision of parks. A Public Health Act in 1936 extended controls over slaughterhouses and food adulteration, while most water supply was municipalised by 1939. Above all, the three million or so houses constructed in the 1930s represented a substantial qualitative improvement upon the slums which, in part at least, they replaced. Rowntree's survey of York in 1936 found 11.7 per cent of the population living in slums compared with 26 per cent in his 1899 survey. Inside sanitary facilities and electric power were now more common, while the falling birth rate further contributed to a reduction in overcrowding. By 1931 the average English and Welsh household contained only 3.7 persons as against 4.4 in 1911.

This reduction in the size of the average family made its own contribution to sustaining living standards during the 1930s, as did a second demographic trend. Overall, the British population rose only sluggishly, a modest fall in the death rate coinciding with a more substantial fall in births. By 1939 the rate of natural increase was half the level it had been just after the end of the First World War. The outcome was a declining dependency ratio within the population. Between the wars the number of those who both produced and consumed increased by 27 per cent: a lesser increase of 18 per cent occurred in the number of those who merely consumed.

Between them, state welfare provision, rising real incomes, more and healthier food, a better general and individual environment, and demographic patterns contributed significantly to improvements in aggregate standards of living. The fruits of progress became evident in 1939 when 70 per cent of army conscripts were given the top physical rating. Although not strictly comparable with the 30 per cent similarly assessed in 1914, since they were volunteers and not a true sample of the entire male population, the figures did indicate the general trend. So, too, did the increase between 1910 and 1938 in life expectancy, which rose for women from 55 to 66 and for men from 52 to 61. Infant mortality fell from 110 per thousand live births in 1910 to only 61 per thousand by 1940. Tuberculosis, which killed 51,000 people in England and Wales in 1910, claimed only 27,000 victims in 1940. This was the disease most sensitive to the general physical state of the populace, and the figures confirm that the most important causes of improvement lay in better diets and environments. Certainly, medical advance made relatively little contribution, being largely confined to the development of salves for sexually transmitted diseases and insulin for diabetics. For the rest, hospital provision remained erratic and access to doctors was still governed largely by income and geography.

As in Japan, however, the aggregate and average statistics concealed significant differences of experience determined by considerations of class, family structure, location, occupation, age, and gender. Although an official survey of 1938 showed that the average family income was twice its 1914 level, this concealed enormous variations. At the very top were the few who earned more than £2,000 year and took 11.7 per cent of the nation's total pre-tax income. Earners at this level were relatively immune from the economic fluctuations of the thirties. Professional incomes also kept well ahead of prices, with the average salary of a doctor rising two and a half times, that of a barrister slightly more than twice between 1913/14 and 1935/37. Most salaried workers also did well, despite the pay cuts imposed on some of them during the crisis of 1931. Their 71 per cent average rise in income enabled them to enjoy a certain level of affluence. The geographical distribution of such prosperity was very skewed, however. Well over a third of the nation's middle-class families (defined according to income) lived in London and the south east: they were the main beneficiaries of cheaper mortgages and better housing. They were the major purchasers of the small family cars which in the form of the £100 required in 1931 to purchase a Ford or an Austin 7 represented about a third of the average British salary. It was their children who by and large accounted for the increased numbers attending public school and it was they who sustained an expansion in the number of domestic servants, though now more commonly in the form of a daily Mrs Mop rather than a resident Jeeves.

Although salaries were usually accompanied by better working conditions, regular increases, pensions, and greater job security, they actually rose more slowly in the 1930s than aggregate money wages, 71 per cent against 103 per cent. Yet for the bulk of the population, almost 90 per cent of whom earned less than £150 a year with a significant proportion on less than £120, higher personal expenditure was restricted perhaps to greater quantities and varieties of foodstuffs and other basic necessities, possibly supplemented by the luxury of a radio. With an average industrial weekly wage for men and boys of less than £3.00, print workers earning almost £4.00 were relatively prosperous. They were certainly better off than farm workers on about £2.00. The largest category of low paid workers consisted of juveniles and women, the latter's average wage being about half that of men.

Notwithstanding such variations, by the standards of the late nineteenth century poverty levels declined significantly. The *New Survey of London Life and Labour* calculated that a tenth of Londoners lived in poverty in 1934. By applying his 1899 standard to York in 1936 Rowntree calculated that only 6.8 per cent were still in primary poverty. However, use of an updated standard based on an estimate of human needs increased the proportion to 18 per cent or a third of the working-class population. Judged by a similar criterion, 37 per cent of working class people in Bristol and about 30 per cent of those on Merseyside were still in poverty. For the individual, this meant clothes purchased at jumble sales, inadequate diets, infant and adult mortality rates far higher than the average, and little access to entertainment, save perhaps a cheap cinema seat or the warmth and relative brightness of a free municipal library reading room. Even there, however, officious librarians sometimes censored the racing pages of the daily papers in order to discourage gambling, which for many represented the only hope of escape from a life that was still largely dreary and uninviting. Significantly, in the best-known contemporary novel of working-class life, Walter Greenwood's *Love on the Dole* (1933), the heroine secures her family by becoming the mistress of the local bookmaker.

Relative deprivation was most common among three groups in particular. Because large families placed heavy demands upon income, they tended to be among the strugglers and in the interwar years the number of children in poverty actually increased. Rowntree reckoned that a man with three dependent children needed the equivalent of £2.68 a week, although a working miner in South Wales could expect to take home only £2.25 while unemployment insurance gave £1.80 and the dole £1.75 per week. Poor children were joined, secondly, by some proportion of the old. Neither increases in the amount of pension nor reductions in the upper qualifying age were sufficient to save from poverty those elderly members of society who lacked other forms of income. As a result, about one in ten of all applicants for public assistance were over the age of sixty five. Finally, there were the unemployed. The figures are not absolutely reliable but the conventional assertion of 10 per cent unemployment throughout the 1930s translates into 1.2 million workers, each with two dependants. However, high turnover rates of unemployment suggest that at one time or another as many as twelve million individuals may have been affected (Glynn and Booth, 1996: 88). In many cases their plight was worsened by the fact that they were highly concentrated in the regions dominated by the old staple industries. The reliance of whole communities upon a single industry was cruelly exposed when the depression caused its contraction or closure. When the town's ironworks shut down, J. B. Priestley likened Stockton to a theatre kept open solely for the sale of drinks in the bars and chocolates in the corridors (Priestley, 1934: 342). Government attempts to encourage movement out of the depressed areas were generally unsuccessful, although South Wales lost about 6 per cent of its population, much of it to the burgeoning car factories of Oxford and the south midlands. On the whole, however, the unemployed were reluctant to leave communities which they knew, the more so because even in the more prosperous regions of the country there were few realistic alternative employment opportunities. Some indication of the hardship suffered by the unemployed in the early 1930s is perhaps provided by the fact that when the Labour Government abolished the seeking work test the number of applicants for relief more than doubled in two months.

Growing levels of expenditure on unemployment relief helped to trigger off the financial crisis of 1931 and it was all too predictable that with the retrenchers firmly in power the ensuing economy measures would affect the unemployed. In the short term, the National Government reduced benefits by 10 per cent, tightened the regulations governing entitlements in such a way as to exclude many married women, and applied the hated means test to almost a million people. As the economy picked up, rationalisation of the system resulted in better levels of provision but administrative quirks still left many recipients at the mercy of condescending and bureaucratic officials. In any case, life on the dole was more than just a matter of income. In the depressed regions especially, whole generations were born, grew up, and married without ever working at all. Apart from the sheer waste of human potential, the price was exacted in terms of marital strain and breakdown, emotional stress, and, in the opinion of some, a loss of work discipline. Little of this got into the record, yet it cannot be ignored. Equally, however, neither can the fact that in the 1930s the vast majority of the labour force continued to work. Herein lies the apparent paradox between the statistical record of aggregate improvement and the popular portrayal of Britain on the dole.

4

Power and ritual,
1914–c.1940

Introduction

In a characteristically tendentious aside A. J. P. Taylor has remarked that the First World War 'left few permanent marks on British society' (Taylor, 1965: 163). Certainly the evidence assessed in previous chapters suggests that on the whole the war tended to accelerate or redirect existing economic and social patterns rather than to create new ones. This was also true of the power and ritual systems. Although change did occur the national structure of politics remained broadly intact. Similarly, while individual lives, beliefs, and attitudes were disrupted, the war, for all its magnitude, did not fundamentally impinge on rituals and values.

Japan was not a major combatant, but the pace of economic modernisation was certainly boosted by the war, which pulled the country more fully into the world economy. The resulting social tensions and stresses did not accord at all with the establishment preference for harmony although for a while it appeared that these could be contained within the existing political framework. In the longer term, however, Japan's fledgling democracy proved less resistant than Britain's more mature power structure to the political extremism stirred up by economic dislocation after the 1929 crash. Nationalists and extremists found it relatively easy to exploit aspects of the ritual system which in themselves were not inherently all that different from those in other countries. Yet it is misleading to overdraw the contrast between the 1920s as a period of prosperity and hope as against the descent into fascism and military rule during the 1930s. There were important intellectual and institutional continuities between the two decades. Furthermore, to pose the question of 'what went wrong' is to portray the 1930s as something of a diversion from the steady progress of modernisation initiated in the nineteenth century. In turn, this implies that there is only a single normative path of economic and social development for a newly industrialising nation, culminating inevitably in a modern social democracy. This is a highly deterministic view of history and it ignores the reality that for many contemporary Japanese it was the experiment with democracy in the 1920s which was the aberration, its subsequent demise representing a welcome return to a more familiar, ordered tradition.

The system of power

Britain

It has been suggested that one of Prime Minister Asquith's major achievements was to take Britain into the First World War as a united country (Cassar, 1994). In fact, this was not particularly difficult, since opposition to involvement was confined to a few pacifists, some members of the labour movement, and two or three minor government ministers. The initial popularity of the conflict was apparent from the packed recruiting stations which facilitated the waging of total war for almost two years on a voluntary basis. Despite declining enthusiasm, the product of the unexpected duration and intensity of the struggle, the broad pattern of power and authority remained intact, although there were signs of stress. By the end of the war isolated incidents of unrest were occurring among British troops in Europe. In Ireland, Easter 1916 saw an ill-fated nationalist rising. Otherwise, the outbreak of the war prompted the cessation of suffragette militancy and industrial unrest also died down although this proved only a temporary respite. As workers flooded into the munitions centres, swamping the supply of accommodation, so rents shot up. Scarcities and hoarding caused food prices to rocket and the general price index rose by a third in the first twelve months of the war. Civilian discontent grew in some major cities, particularly Glasgow, the key engineering centre at the heart of what became known as Red Clydeside. Although rationing was eventually introduced, resentment was further roused by evidence of war profiteering. On the shop floor, trade union reluctance to abandon traditional working practices in the interests of the war effort was eventually overcome in the Treasury Agreement of 1915. Yet militance continued to grow, fed by a general weariness at the length of the war and its costs, both human and material. At 5.6 million, the number of working days lost through industrial action in 1917 was almost two and a half times the figure for 1916 (Mitchell and Deane, 1971: 72). In the hope of pacifying the malcontents the government established the Ministry of Reconstruction in 1917 as an earnest of its intent to provide tangible rewards for the deprivations suffered during the war.

Nevertheless, the essential soundness of the nation's political structure was confirmed when Britain escaped the worst excesses of the upheavals which swept across the Continent once hostilities ended. Noting in his diary that thrones and empires were tottering all over Europe, John Burns, the former

Liberal minister, added rhetorically 'when will Britain, the mother of them all, throw over the sterility of Kings, the chloroform of courts, the snobbery of palaces? England is gassed by convention and held back by regality' (John Burns Diary, 28 October 1918. B.L. Add MSS 56340). These were somewhat unlikely sentiments from a man who had enjoyed excellent personal relationships with both Edward VII and George V, but they did underline the enduring strength of the British monarchy and of the empire over which it ruled.

This is not to say, however, that the power structure was completely unaffected by the war. One significant development lay in the loss of Ireland, although the principle of change had been accepted (except by Ulster Unionists) before the war with the passage of the Home Rule Bill in 1914. That the postwar settlement had to go much further by granting independence rather than home rule to twenty six of Ireland's thirty two counties probably owed less to the abortive and ill-supported Easter Rising than to the British government's heavy handed and repressive response. The execution of the leading rebels thoroughly alienated Irish public opinion and swung it decisively behind Sinn Fein. Encouraged by its overwhelming success in the general election of 1918 the party formed an independent, republican government, in effect simply disregarding the British. At this point, the IRA took up arms all over Ireland. The unduly aggressive activities of the auxiliary crown forces, the Black and Tans, further antagonised the Irish. Just under 1,500 died on both sides before 'the troubles' ended. A treaty proposing the establishment of a twenty six county Irish Free State was approved by the British in December 1921 and by the Irish Dail the following January.

Another obvious change occurred in the political and social roles of Britain's traditional landed elite. During the war, the pressures on food production had pushed up farm prices, thereby raising rents. The rise was insufficient, however, to offset the growing tax burden on landed wealth. This incentive to dispose of property was strengthened by both a buoyant land market and the attractive, more flexible alternative of holding wealth in government bonds and securities. Larger estates survived rather better than smaller ones but between 1918 and 1922 about a quarter of Britain's cultivated land area changed hands, in most cases passing into the possession of former tenant farmers. As individuals, members of the landed class continued to be active in national politics, Bonar Law's cabinet of 1922 containing three viscounts, two marquises, a duke, and an earl, for example. But the landed interest ceased to function as an identifiable entity, progressively abandoning its traditional involvement in county politics and public duties in the postwar years (Thompson, 1990: 1–24).

It is sometimes suggested, too, that the war represented a significant stage in the general historical march towards collectivism. According to the occupational census, 321,000 people were working in public administration in 1911: ten years later the figure stood at 464,000, an increase of about 45 per cent (Mitchell and Deane, 1971: 60). As the war progressed, censorship, rationing, control of strategic industries, conscription, and planning for postwar reconstruction all represented further encroachments by the state on individual and private freedoms. By 1917, however, concern was being expressed at the rising levels of public expenditure such intervention entailed, and this helped to ensure that once the war ended there was a determined push to restore the freer prewar regime. State-controlled industries were returned to their owners, rationing was ended, and many of the planned social reforms perished on the altar of orthodox economics. Nevertheless, it could be argued that the war was significant to the progress of collectivisation in three ways. First, it familiarised citizens with the idea of intervention. Second, it brought into prominence the Labour Party and saw the creation in 1920 of the Communist Party of Great Britain (CPGB), inspired by the Russian Revolution and formed from an amalgam of left wing malcontents and ideologues. Both parties were committed to the principle of the directive state. Finally, the war indicated what government could achieve, given the necessary political will. In this analysis, the triumph of collectivism over laisser faire is often identified with the replacement of Asquith by Lloyd George as Prime Minister in 1916.

It is difficult, however, to square this interpretation precisely with developments both before and after the war. Asquith's own prewar Liberal administrations had taken some significant, albeit rather ad hoc steps along the road away from laisser faire, mainly in the form of welfare legislation. Prior to 1914 the levels of intervention eventually necessitated by the war may have been unthinkable, but the evidence of the interwar years does not indicate that the war brought about any wholesale ideological conversion to collectivism, certainly not within the system of power and authority. The CPGB utterly failed to secure any foothold in the national political system and its importance remained largely symbolic as the first major political party in Britain to ground a revolutionary strategy in industrial conflict. As for Labour most members of the prewar party had had a vague commitment to state intervention but in practice there had been little to choose between their policies and those of the Liberals with whom they formed, in effect, a progressive alliance (Brown, 1985). During the war itself the Labour Party shifted to the right. By 1918 only three of its MPs were sponsored by the left wing Independent Labour Party while the socialist societies lost the right to elect their own representatives to the party executive. Even the adoption of the new constitution in 1918 was more rhetoric than reality. At most, clause four, committing the party to state control of the means of production, exchange, and distribution, signified the demise of the prewar alliance with the Liberals. It was not translated into a comprehensive political programme, as the record of the two interwar Labour administrations indicated.

In fact, interwar parliamentary politics were dominated by the

Conservatives, in part at least because Irish independence and partition removed some seventy anti-Conservative MPs from Westminster, leaving a rump of Ulster Unionists who provided an inbuilt parliamentary advantage for the Conservatives. Party prospects were also enhanced by organisational improvement, involving the training of agents and female organisers. By contrast, Liberal constituency organisation gradually crumbled and although the party's parliamentary vote did rise throughout the 1920s, effectively it was Labour which emerged after 1918 as the main anti-Conservative force within the power structure, making steady progress at both municipal and parliamentary level, invariably at Liberal expense.

This was one of the decisive shifts of early twentieth-century politics and there is an extensive debate on the extent to which it was a direct outcome of the war and how far it would have happened anyway (Brown, 1974; Laybourn, 1995: 208–26). Some argue that the growing identity between party and social class in the prewar period was bound to lead to Labour's triumph (McKibbin, 1974). Against this, however, Labour's local election successes prior to 1914 were not accompanied by any significant parliamentary progress after the initial breakthrough in 1906. Most of the forty or so Labour MPs held their seats because the Liberals had allowed them a free run against Conservative opponents in selected constituencies. Philip Snowden, Labour MP for Blackburn, admitted quite candidly in 1913 that the evaporation of Liberal goodwill would also herald the disappearance of his party in the House of Commons (*Labour Leader*, 26 June 1913). This suggests that it was the war which turned the situation decisively in Labour's favour.

Certainly, divisions over how best to conduct the struggle finally split the Liberal Party between Asquith and Lloyd George. Although eventually re-united, the party never regained its prewar confidence. Labour's wartime division was less severe and, because it centred on the issue of whether to fight at all, was more readily healed once peace returned. More importantly, perhaps, Labour MPs participated in wartime coalition administrations, thus establishing an effective riposte to the jibe that they lacked any real experience of government. Party organisation also became much more professional under the guiding hand of Arthur Henderson. He created a strong central organisation, complemented by comprehensive regional and local structures based on the trade unions. Labour was thus an immediate beneficiary of rising trade union membership.

It seems likely that some trade unionists, soured by Liberal handling of prewar strikes and the equally heavy handed attitude of the Liberal-led Coalition during the unrest following the war, transferred their allegiance to Labour. A similar process may have occurred among working-class Irish voters in England who were alienated by the Liberals' association with the suppression of the Easter Rising and the later activities of the Black and Tans. It has also been suggested that the rather philosophical, even cerebral, approach to politics adopted by the Liberals was best suited to a restricted electorate of the sort functional before the war. If this is true, then the extension of the franchise in 1918 almost certainly contributed to their subsequent decline.

Whatever the merits of this particular argument, the Franchise Act of 1918 represented in its own right another important development in the system of power and authority, although again one with prewar origins. Even before 1914 it was widely accepted that some degree of reform would be necessary, but the degree of sacrifice entailed during the fighting removed any lingering justification for a restricted male electorate. Accordingly, therefore, the legislation enfranchised all adult men over the age of twenty one. Its other main provision was to give the vote to women over the age of thirty, although it remains a moot point as to how far this was the inevitable outcome of years of patient campaigning, suffragette violence, or part of wider emancipatory processes arising out of, or predating, the war. Voting equality with men came in 1928 and the following year Margaret Bondfield became the first of her sex to hold cabinet office. By this time women formed slightly more than half the electorate, a situation which both main parties had taken into account in overhauling their organisations. The evidence suggests that women tended to a slight preference for the Conservatives, although as a group they derived few tangible benefits from their new electoral importance, and certainly did not gain significant access to the national systems of power and authority. The first female took her seat in the House of Commons in 1919 but women were never more than an extremely tiny minority of MPs.

With the obvious exception of the Irish imbroglio, these changes in the postwar institutions of power and authority occurred relatively peaceably. In one sphere, however, the war appeared to enhance the potential for confrontation. Relations between capital and labour had been severely strained immediately before 1914. Initially, there was a marked reduction in the severity and incidence of strike activity. Government intervention secured the suspension of many restrictive union practices for the duration, absorbed businessmen into central administration, and encouraged cooperation between workers and employers through the establishment of Joint Industrial Councils, of which twenty six were operative and a further fourteen planned by 1918 (Wrigley, 1976; Wrigley, 1982; Wrigley, 1987). Yet these developments took place against a background of chronic and rising industrial unrest, and the hope that they were paving the way for a more consensual approach evaporated pretty rapidly once peace returned. In engineering particularly the enhanced bargaining power conferred upon labour by the demands of war brought local shop stewards to prominence. Their general antipathy towards the Whitley Councils and centralised labour relations was made more significant by the fact that their influence was often greater than that of full time national officials. In the first full year of peace, industrial action cost Britain 35 million days (seven times the 1918 figure) and in 1921 a national mining strike carried the figure to 85 million. Although issues of recognition and working conditions were sometimes involved, the strikes more usually arose out of wage disputes.

Apart from the upward pressures put on the cost of living during the postwar boom, skilled workers wished to restore differentials eroded during the war, while the unskilled naturally wished to preserve their relative gains. At the same time the disruptive potential of industrial confrontations had been considerably increased by organisational developments. By 1920, there were twice as many trade union members, some eight million, as there had been in 1914. Mergers and amalgamations were producing larger, more powerful unions such as the Transport and General Workers' (1922) and the Amalgamated Engineers' (1921), while the TUC had been restructured along more professional lines. The employers, too, were better organised through the Federation of British Industry (1916) and the British Employers' Federation (1919). This probably served to reinforce the contemporary popular suspicion that many employers had done rather well out of the war. The resulting sense of grievance was heightened once the postwar boom broke. Strikes increasingly arose out of employers' efforts to push down wages or to introduce more intensive forms of work, using the Bedaux system of time and motion study. When Sir Eric Geddes, himself a businessman, axed many of the promised social reforms as part of postwar government retrenchment, the railwaymen's leader, J. H. Thomas, observed that unrest was the product of a sense of betrayal, the 'frustration of agelong expectations accelerated by the developments of the war' (Charles, 1973: 31).

Government, however, put a more sinister interpretation on events. The background of European upheaval, the attempts of Russia's Bolshevik Government to export its revolution, the foundation of the CPGB, and evidence of discontent in the army even before demobilisation returned to civilian life thousands of men with military training, all fed a suspicion that behind industrial militancy lay forces with revolutionary intent or potential. Such fears were intensified when in 1920 London dockers refused to load the *Jolly George* with arms intended for Poles fighting against the Bolsheviks in the Ukraine. The dockers' stand was endorsed nationally by both the TUC and the Labour Party, and in the provinces by three or four hundred local Councils of Action organised to oppose British interference in Russian affairs. Although the government continued to encourage industrial arbitration and conciliation, it also armed itself with emergency powers.

As deflation cooled the strike fever and rising unemployment threatened job security, so unrest died down after 1921, but there was to be a major reprise in the form of the General Strike in 1926. The export difficulties encountered by the coal industry led to persistent disputes between the miners and their employers which government could hardly ignore, given the size of the mining labour force and the significance of coal in the economy. One threatened strike was averted by the provision of a short term wage subsidy, but in June 1926 the miners struck with the backing of the TUC, which ultimately called out about 2,500,000 workers in support. For nine days silence prevailed in the manufacturing districts before the TUC leaders, fearful that they would not be able to maintain control for much longer, accepted an offer of mediation and called off their action.

At the time it suited the right wing press and Conservative ministers to present the strike as a revolutionary threat. It was portrayed as all of a piece with the *Jolly George* incident, with the (forged) Zinoviev telegram which purported to suggest that the Labour Party was the creature of Moscow, and with an (unsuccessful) government attempt to prosecute a communist charged with incitement to mutiny. Such an interpretation of the General Strike also found favour with the left for whom it represented the moment at which the British revolution should have happened. But if anyone wanted a show-down in 1926 it was the government rather than the TUC, which was totally unprepared and called the stoppage off as soon as it could. It is probably more realistic, therefore, to see the events of 1926 not as the abortive harbinger of a new social order, but rather as the final dramatic climax of the unrest which had flared up after 1909 and been only partially quenched during the war. The suggestion that it was a revolution manqué was ridiculed by Beatrice Webb, who likened it rather to a series of compulsory bank holidays (Mackenzie, 1978: 262). For the miners it was nothing of the sort and under considerable hardship they remained on strike for a further nine months, bequeathing a legacy of considerably bitterness to succeeding generations of mining communities.

The General Strike was followed by a quieter period in industrial relations. A Trade Disputes Act in 1927 outlawed sympathetic strikes and a new mood of accommodation was apparent in the talks held between Sir Alfred Mond of ICI and Ben Turner of the TUC. Thereafter rising unemployment, most severe in the heavy industries where union density was highest, took its toll of trade union membership and militancy alike. The total number of trade unionists tumbled from 5.2 million in 1926, bottoming out in 1933 at 4.4 million before recovering to more than 6.0 million by 1938, the highest figure since 1921. Textiles replaced coal as the major locus of unrest, but the weavers' strike of 1932 was the last national stoppage of the interwar period. In the 1930s industrial unrest never reached the heady levels of the immediate postwar years, the number of lost working days creeping only once above three million after 1932.

The legislation of 1927 embodied an attack on trade union freedoms which served to unite the industrial and political wings of the labour movement around the objective of electing a Labour Government. This appears to confirm what has sometimes been called the pendulum theory of working-class activity, which posits an undulation over time between an industrial and political emphasis. In fact, the hypothesis fits quite neatly the twenty years or so following 1900, but less well thereafter. The Labour administration of 1929–31 actually overlapped with a minor upsurge of unrest, while the rule of National Governments headed by Conservatives after 1935 coincided with reduced levels of strike activity.

The dominance of National/Conservative administrations in the 1930s was accompanied, initially at least, by a collapse in the Labour vote. The record of by-elections after 1929 suggested that the party was heading for defeat in the next election anyway, but the split in the cabinet and MacDonald's defection to the National Government led to a far heavier reversal than anticipated. Labour was reduced to a mere fifty two seats in 1931. In the main, this was a result of the first-past-the-post electoral system in which small swings of votes produced major changes in seat numbers. Four out of every ten seats captured by Labour in 1929 had been won on a minority vote. After the debacle of 1931 the party recovered quite well, especially at the municipal level where control of the London County Council was secured in 1934. Nationally, too, there was a swing of 9 per cent in Labour's favour in 1935, although this still left parliamentary seat numbers well short of the 1929 total.

Labour support was concentrated most heavily in the industrial heartlands, notwithstanding the fact that its inability to help the unemployed while in office was compounded by a conspicuous failure in opposition to champion their cause. Perhaps this did not matter too much since the efforts of extremist groups and parties to exploit unemployment reaped little long term political gain. Reductions in benefits and the introduction of means testing provoked violent protest in some areas, and temporarily boosted membership of the communist-led National Unemployed Workers' Movement (NUWM) to 37,000. Government was sufficiently concerned to infiltrate the organisation and at one stage serious consideration was given to banning the NUWM's hunger marches. Yet even at its peak membership represented only 1.5 per cent of the officially registered unemployed. For all their rhetoric about destroying capitalism, the communists did their best and most successful work in handling individual cases within the existing social system. Even where they did succeed in establishing a more significant presence within local political structures, this was often despite rather than because of their political beliefs (Macintyre, 1980).

If anything, right wing extremism appeared to represent a more serious threat. In high places, Oswald Mosley's British Union of Fascists (BUF) had some tacit support, sometimes more overt as in the case of Lord Rothermere. In the late 1930s the BUF was planning to fight almost thirty constituencies in Yorkshire and Lancashire. By this time, however, such popular appeal as it enjoyed had been eroded by a ban on political uniforms and marches, and also by growing trade union hostility as international fascism increasingly revealed its repressive nature. Relatively rapid recovery from depression and rising living standards both prevented fascism from securing any powerbase among the middle classes (Pugh, 1982: 280). For all that he was one of the few politicians with a positive programme for tackling unemployment and for all his undoubted talents as a public orator, Mosley failed to persuade many of the unemployed to follow him. Nor, given the structure of the British economy by this time, could he exploit a depressed rural proletariat which in other countries, including Japan, provided much of the support for right wing extremism

Like the British people as a whole, the unemployed generally proved resistant to political extremism of any sort in the 1930s, and they displayed a remarkable degree of resignation to their plight. The cultural bedrock of working-class life remained largely intact, despite the economic and social disturbances associated with war and the postwar years. Richard Hoggart claimed that in the 1930s there was 'a premium on the taking of pleasures now, discouraging planning for some future goal, or in the light of some ideal' (Hoggart, 1965: 132–3). For most people, the pub, sport, family, and gambling remained far more central to existence than any idealist struggle to change the system under which they lived. Orwell illustrated the point well when he noted that Hitler's reoccupation of the Rhineland passed almost unremarked in the working-class districts of Britain. By contrast, the suggestion that advance publication of football fixture lists be abandoned, thereby threatening the pools which had ten million clients by 1938, 'flung all Yorkshire into a storm of fury' (Orwell, 1962: 80). He further attributed the relative passivity of the unemployed to the availability of cheap foodstuffs and luxuries, and to the essentially law-abiding nature of the British proletariat (Orwell, 1962: 80–1). There was something quintessentially British about the action of the sailors who mutinied at Invergordon in 1931 against pay cuts, all the while protesting their loyalty to the King and asserting their willingness to accept reductions which they considered reasonable.

On the other hand, neither rising living standards nor a respect for law and order probably stronger than that prevailing in Britain, were sufficient to save contemporary Japan from political extremism. The contrast with Japan is similarly instructive when considering W. G. Runciman's explanations of British quiescence. He has posited that resentment was not a function of deprivation *per se*, but rather of the individual's assessment of his or her position relative to others with whom comparison was habitually made (Runciman, 1966). This implies that protest was muted because the regional concentration of unemployment in Britain did not foster the development of any overwhelming sense of anger against the system. On the other hand, comparative economic hardship in the Japanese countryside *was* responsible for unrest in the 1920s and simmering rural resentment was successfully exploited by the opponents of democracy in the 1930s.

Japan

For Japan as for Britain, price dislocations, food shortages, profiteering, and the wage distortions arising from new and urgent patterns of demand, inevitably meant that during the First World War domestic unrest was generated among producers and consumers alike. Before 1914 trade union development had been limited, hampered by low incomes, the dispersion of the workforce among small plants, the predominance of women in the factory sector (60 per cent of the 900,000 factory workers in 1915 were female), and ideological factionalism among leaders. Only about forty unions existed in 1911 and industrial action was correspondingly rare. Although the authorities were alarmed by increasing evidence of industrial unrest, slightly more than 100 strikes occurred between 1903 and 1907, compared with over 2,000 in Britain over the same period. In stimulating the rapid expansion of the industrial base, however, the war also nurtured the first significant flowerings of a European style national trade union movement. In 1919, by which time the number of unions had reached almost 200, about 500 strikes occurred.

Japanese trade unionists used the language of workers' rights and class struggle familiar to their counterparts in Britain, but it has been argued that even before the war their main objective was to translate traditional notions of the employment relationship into the industrial context. This effort was intensified when the war produced rapid economic expansion. The traditional employment relationship had always been viewed as existing between status unequals in which benevolence was required from the one party in return for loyalty and obedience from the other. In this interpretation, the extension of factory paternalism in the 1920s is seen as the outcome of this dynamic between employers and workers, not just a managerial reflex response to unrest. In other words, industrial unrest in postwar Japan was not merely the product of specific economic circumstances but reflected longer term ambitions on the part of workers (Smith, 1988: 236–70). Government response included a decision to sponsor the *Kyochokai*, a group of scholars, civil servants, and employers set up to research labour problems and to encourage industrial harmony. Suzuki Bunji, leader of the country's main labour organisation, attended the inaugural meeting of the ILO as an official representative. Legislation was passed encouraging the establishment of works councils and by 1929 about 112 such bodies had been created, a quarter of them in the Osaka-Hyogo-Kyoto region (Totten, 1967: 203–44).

A much tougher line was taken, however, with the other main outbreak of discontent arising from wartime dislocation. In the countryside, the huge profits secured by some of the larger farmers provoked resentment. Even more alarming from the authorities' point of view, however, was the impact of escalating food prices. By 1917 they were almost double their prewar level, although average wages were only about a quarter higher. The following summer protest spread from a small village on the Sea of Japan to engulf the entire country in a spate of arson, looting, and confrontation. After several weeks the most serious threat to stability since 1868 was finally quelled by the imposition of martial law and the arrest of some 25,000 people, about a quarter of whom were convicted. After the immediate furore had some-what abated, Prime Minister Terauchi Masatake resigned.

His departure presaged the end of fifty years of dominance in Japan's power and authority system by men from the Satsuma and Choshu clans, who had engineered the Meiji Restoration. The new premier, Hara Kei, was the first drawn from outside this circle of oligarchs who had effectively governed the country since the 1860s. As the first prime minister holding a seat in the lower house and heading a cabinet drawn principally from the majority party in the Diet, he acquired the epithet of the Great Commoner. His elevation thus appeared to confirm the view that Japan was moving inexorably towards a Western style democracy, entailing popular participation in government, constitutional rights, the absence of class distinction, free choice of work, and equality between the sexes. The deaths of Okuma and Yamagata early in 1922 removed two more of the *genro* and by 1924 only Saionji was left of the old ruling clique. This finally ended the divorce of political leadership from the decision-making process, a separation clearly inimical to the development of democratic government. It also left open the way for the emergence of larger, more complex leadership strata made up of groups with different experiences and often with competing aspirations.

Against this background, the Diet was increasingly perceived, especially by liberal social thinkers, as the key institution through which such conflicts and differences could be mediated, just as in the Western parliamentary democracies. In 1919 the small electorate was more than doubled when the tax qualification for voters was lowered. Even more far reaching was the legislation of 1925 which gave the vote to men over the age of twenty five, although those in receipt of public or private assistance on the grounds of poverty were excluded, as were all women. The number of voters was thereby raised from about 3.0 million to 12.5 million, including for the first time the majority of city dwellers. This helped to enhance the status of political parties in the power system. Apart from one short break, the two largest – Seiyukai, and what was consolidated in 1927 under the name of Minseito – monopolised the premiership in the 1920s.

Another symptom of the democratic tendencies developing in the Taisho era from 1912 was the proliferation of small left wing bodies. Eager to capitalise on the more important role that party now appeared to be assuming in the whole structure of power, they in fact failed to establish a very effective political presence. In part this was a function of their numerical weakness. They showed little interest in the problems of the rural masses, while the limited development of industry denied them the opportunity of securing a power base in an industrial proletariat, even after the extension of the franchise. Intermittent economic upheaval in the interwar years tended to make industrial workers an unstable group and by 1930 they still made up only about a fifth of the total labour force. Even at their peak, therefore, Japanese trade unions could claim the support of only about 8 per cent of industrial workers and some of those belonged to company unions, established by employers as part of the attempt to attract and retain scarce skills in the 1920s. To the extent that such unions catered for skilled workers, the trade union movement was deprived of its own natural leadership. Furthermore, while employer interest in labour welfare may have been intended to minimise the appeal of independent trade unionism and its socialist leanings, it is also true, as suggested above, that workers themselves held to notions of loyalty and obedience at variance with orthodox socialist theories. Although the industrial labour force did expand significantly from the mid-1930s, by that time the military-dominated government was promoting 'patriotic unions'. In 1940 these were brought together in the five million strong Greater Japan Industrial Patriotic Society and independent unions were officially abolished.

The weakness of the left was also a result of defective leadership. It tended to be somewhat elitist, drawn mainly from the expanding higher education system. Between 1918 and 1928, the number of Japan's universities increased from five to forty and over the same period the total number of students also rose from 65,000 to 166,000 (Marshall, 1982: 279). In the 1920s government attempts to retain strict control over this expansion were ineffective. The universities became hotbeds of Marxism. At the same time, the growing influence of the Diet and the burgeoning bureaucracy served to isolate and diminish the influence of academics who had once carried considerable political weight, especially on matters relating to social policy and education. From such disaffected groups the left derived its main leadership, but this assorted collection of liberal intellectuals and middle-class socialists was largely set apart by background, life style, and skills from such organised labour movements as did exist. Six years of compulsory schooling with a centrally determined curriculum left the mass of the people with a generally conservative and backward outlook, whereas the university-trained radicals had broader, more forward looking and often more Westernised attitudes.

Nor did the Japanese left prove any more resistant to factionalism than its Western counterparts, syndicalists, socialists, and Marxists directing much of their ideological energy against each other. The *Yuaikai*, the moderate friendly society founded in 1912 by Bunji Suzuki, was highjacked by radicals who transformed it into the General Federation of Labour or *Sodomei*. It became a major vehicle for the spread of socialist ideals, trade unionism, and the advocacy of industrial action but recurrent schisms reduced it by 1923 to being the most cautious of the left wing groups. On the far left, the effectiveness of the newly founded Communist Party was similarly restricted by internal divisions.

Communism also had to contend with the added burden of being legally proscribed and any explanation of the left's failure to make more headway during the 1920s must take into account government repression. Assisted by the fact that the police service was organised on a national rather than a local basis, governments found it relatively easy to clamp down on movements deemed to be subversive. Already alarmed by the incidence of the rice riots, authority was deeply suspicious of the syndicalist sympathies which it detected in some postwar strikes. Attempts to institute a a system of workers' control during a strike at Kawasaki's Kobe dockyards in 1921 were forcibly broken up by troops and the union activists arrested. A year or so later the leaders of the Communist Party were rounded up by the Special Police Branch amid allegations which had some mild resonance with the Zinoviev affair in Britain. Even the democratising tendency of the 1925 franchise legislation was tempered by the passing of the Peace Preservation Law, a deliberately vague measure designed to facilitate the control of ideas designated as subversive to the Japanese state. It was used to justify the arrest of radical student leaders in 1926, for example. In 1928, when the first election under the wider franchise was held, the legislation was toughened by Imperial Ordinance and heavier penalties were imposed for plotting against the constitution and political system. Over the following twelve months or so, over a thousand communists were arrested and then discredited at public trials. A special bureau established by the Home Office was charged with dealing with radical movements and examining overseas methods of communist suppression. Although it proved difficult to prevent the continued circulation of communist literature, state oversight of the commercial press was important in depriving dissenters of vital publicity.

Towards the end of the 1920s there also a noticeable hardening in the government's attitude towards rural radicalism. Even before 1914 unrest in the countryside had been officially monitored, particularly the appearance and activities of liberal, even socialist-influenced tenants' unions. With farmers facing severe economic pressure following the collapse of the postwar boom, the number of such unions increased. More than three quarters of the 408 candidates put up for the 1925 local assembly elections by the Japan Farmers' Federation were successful. Just as government sought to foster industrial peace by legislating for industrial councils, so its initial response to agrarian movements included efforts to persuade landlords to be more conciliatory. Thus the Tenancy Conciliation Law in 1924 was followed two years later by an ineffective measure to encourage individual ownership. By 1927 the number of tenants' unions had grown to almost 4,000 and their combined membership of 365,332 represented almost 10 per cent of all tenant farmers. Three years later the number of tenant disputes was running at about 5,000 a year.

Three quarters of the disputes occurred in about two fifths of the nation's forty seven prefectures, running in an almost continuous belt around Osaka (Smethurst, 1986; Waswo, 1977). These were the better off, technically most advanced, and most industrialised parts of the countryside, where landlords showed a greater tendency to neglect their farming in favour of non-agrarian interests and where the limits of output increases with existing technologies forced farmers to challenge rent levels. This suggests perhaps that the actions taken by the movement were less a revolutionary threat brought about by endemic poverty than an expression of frustrated rural expectations and short term economic difficulty. Bureaucrats viewed the activities of the tenants' unions with suspicion, blaming them on exogenous influences such as the Russian Revolution, the earlier rice riots, the example of industrial strikes, or the unwelcome influence of the Taisho democracy movement. In the 1930s an Economic Rehabilitation Programme was established to provide funding for cooperative selling and buying by village committees. Such committees were once thought to have become effective agencies of central government, preparing the way for totalitarianism. Recent research, however, suggests that the leaders of these organisations tended to be the same commercially minded farmers whose frustrations were thought to be undermining traditional communities. Perhaps this was why ultimately a more repressive line prevailed. The rural radical movement was progressively undermined by arrests and suppression as part of the general clampdown on left wing subversion.

There is no doubt that protest movements, whether agrarian, industrial, or merely intellectual, were symptomatic of a growing Japanese interest in democracy. It is no coincidence that unrest occurred just as the first generation of those who had been the recipients of mass education reached adulthood during and immediately after the war. To some of the now better informed and better mentally equipped Japanese, patriotic sentiment which proclaimed the emperor's benevolence hardly seemed to equate with the evidence of their own eyes. Furthermore, the repressive responses of the authorities to social unrest meant that progress towards a more liberal political regime in the 1920s was more tentative than references to Taisho democracy might suggest. Indeed, the accession of the Showa Emperor Hirohito in 1926 appeared to coincide with a further hardening of anti-liberal sentiment, a development which Japan's parliamentary institutions were ill-equipped to resist. The influential Privy Council and the upper house of the Diet both remained centres of reaction. In the lower house, the two dominant parties were not at all ideologically distinctive, both being broadly opposed to radical change and interested mainly in foreign rather than domestic issues: both were reluctant to widen the franchise for fear that their position in the Diet would be weakened. This was partly why the granting of universal male suffrage was accompanied by the safeguard of the Peace Preservation Law. Hara, despite his Great Commoner tag and even his assassination by an ultranationalist in 1921, was distrustful of the burgeoning labour movement and opposed the extension of voting rights.

More important, perhaps, the restricted franchise operative before 1925 had made it unnecessary for the main parties to cultivate any mass following during the first two decades of the century. Instead, they developed alternative sources of support among those groups to which the constitution, either by design or neglect, allowed particular influence. These included the bureaucracy, the forces, the *genro*, the nobility, and big business. Such relationships were frequently oiled with cash and in 1916 a Western observer, Walter McLaren, suggested that few party politicians had made such large fortunes out of bribery as Japanese cabinet ministers (Livingston, Moore and Oldfather, 1976: I, 237). There was some public sympathy for Hara's killer because not only members of the Diet but also three members of his cabinet had been involved in corruption scandals. During the 1920s big business especially used its financial power as a political lever. Kato Takaaki, Prime Minister in a coalition cabinet from 1924, had connections with Mitsubishi, for example, while Mitsui had links with Seiyukai Party figures (Roberts, 1973: 209–10). Apart from the obvious threat to democratic principles posed by such relationships, the undue political influence of the *zaibatsu* helped to sustain the notion that power was intimately connected with the existing hierarchy.

Such a state of affairs could serve only to undermine the credentials of the Diet, already inherently flawed by the constitutional independence of the armed forces. Both the army and navy grew increasingly discontented during 1920s, distrustful of democracy, fearful of socialism, and alarmed both by intellectual anti-militarism and, externally, by the menace of the Soviet Union. Convinced that Japan was under threat both at home and abroad, they watched with growing resentment as civilian politicians reduced the military budget by more than 50 per cent between 1919 and 1926 alone and pursued conciliatory policies towards both the United States and China. Their annoyance was exacerbated in the late 1920s when Chinese government moves against independent war-lords brought conflict with Japanese interests in Guandong Province. There was a strategic dimension, too, to the tension between the army and the democratic politicians. During the 1920s the belief grew that the cause of Germany's defeat in 1918 had been primarily economic rather than military. Japan's military leaders increasingly inclined to the view that their own success in any future war would hinge on the ability of the army to control all the resources of the economy.

Army suspicions of democratic government were also shared by some civil servants. From the early years of the twentieth century there had developed a cadre of bureaucrats disturbed by what they saw as the unruliness of contemporary society. Determined to preempt what they saw as the undesirable social results of Western style development, they sought alternatives to both laisser faire and socialism. They worked to integrate village institutions into the administrative structure, creating local voluntary organisations to promote social solidarity, shoring up local elites, and drafting legislation to deal with the emerging industrial labour force. By 1918 many of these bureaucrats had risen to influential posts and their experiences in the 1920s fostered further doubts about the ability of parliamentary government to maintain harmony and to reconcile conflict. At the same time, the relative shortage of senior posts led many of them to cultivate outside contacts in order to have a second career when they retired from the civil service (Silberman and Harootunian, 1974: 183–216). Like the soldiers, administrators enjoyed a status and respect in Japan higher than that of the politicians. Their recruitment through a system of competitive examination meant that not only were they drawn from the intellectual elite in a society which historically had equated education with merit and status, but, unlike the politicians, they were untainted by corruption (Smith, 1988: 156–72). Because the *samurai* had been converted into administrators during the long Tokugawa peace, the civil service was regarded as the repository of the essential *samurai* value of selflessness. In the summer of 1934, by which time army influence in government was growing rapidly, a Cabinet Investigative Bureau was set up as a forum for reformist army officers and like-minded bureaucrats. Civil servants within the Ministry of Commerce and Industry were particularly anxious to harness the industrial cartels, established during the great depression, as instruments of state rather than private business. In these ways connections between the civil service, the armed forces, and the worlds of business and politics were forged, gradually weaving together individuals who, for various reasons, were suspicious of democracy, of socialism, and civil dissent.

Thus in the 1920s the inherent weaknesses of the left, economic pressures, and flaws in the democratic structure of the constitution all paved the way for the triumph of totalitarianism in the following decade. The civilian politicians proved unable (and in some cases unwilling) to prevent the growing manifestations of army independence. This was evident as early as 1931 when they failed to reverse the invasion of Manchuria. Emboldened young army radicals increasingly tried to take the law into their own hands. In 1932 they murdered Prime Minister Inukai whose cabinet had been formed with the express intention of controlling army interference in politics. Thereafter, no prewar Japanese government was headed by a party politician and rival groups within the army vied for ultimate control. In 1936 junior officers attempted a coup in Tokyo which was put down only on the express orders of the emperor. The mutineers were drawn from the *Kodo-ha* or Imperial Way faction and somewhat paradoxically their repression by the rival *Tosei-ha* or Control school paved the way for a greater degree of army intervention in government. The new cabinet was headed by a professional diplomat, Hirota Koki, but in effect it was chosen by the Minister of War, General Terauchi.

This seemed to emphasise the growing irrelevance of political parties in the power structure although they did continue for a time to provide the majority of cabinet members and to attract support at general elections. Although policy was not determined exclusively by the army, which always had to compromise with business and bureaucratic interests, party participation in the cabinet was virtually eliminated by 1937 and the army was able to push its nominees quite easily into important posts within the civil administration. In 1940 parties were formally disbanded and their structures incorporated into the Imperial Rule Association. At local level, too, army dominance was soon complete. A plan of 1936 devised by the war and navy ministers to reform local government so as to increase central control was not implemented, but four years later that control was being exercised through more than a million newly established local neighbourhood associations. These were conceived as both administrative units for wartime needs such as rationing, air defence, and fire fighting and also as a means of achieving national political objectives.

There has been disagreement as to whether the gradual ousting of democracy in Japan produced a fascist state in the 1930s. Notwithstanding the events of 1936, there was no seizure of power through concerted military action as happened in Italy, Germany, and Spain (Halliday, 1975). Nor was there any mass political fascist party in Japan. On the other hand, the military's gradual assumption of power did rest partly on its successful exploitation of popular ultranationalist sentiment which fed on contemporary discontents. First among these was a lingering resentment that the First World War peace settlement had somehow cheated Japan of the rewards due to a supporter of the victorious alliance. Ever since the Restoration, Japan had perceived the Far East to be its own legitimate sphere of influence, but the peace treaties contained little concrete recognition of this aspiration. Furthermore, Britain's abrogation of the Anglo-Japanese Treaty after the war represented a rebuff and an additional blow to national pride. In the new atmosphere of international cooperation, formal alliances seemed outmoded and Britain judged Japan was no longer needed as a shield in the Far East against either Russia or Germany. The treaty was also unpopular with the Americans and the Chinese, both of whom regarded it as an undesirable prop for Japanese ambitions in Asia. Even though Japan was given a permanent seat on the Council of the new League of Nations, the Allies refused to incorporate into the Versailles Treaty the principle of racial equality. Resentment against this apparent discrimination was further reinforced by the American decision in the 1920s to close the door to any more Japanese immigrants. Not only did this place them on the same footing as the despised Chinese but it also closed off one possible remedy for the problem of overcrowding. It was remarked at the 1925 Honolulu session of the Institute of Pacific Relations that the 'prevailing opinion seems to be that the pressure of population in Japan can only be relieved by emigration abroad and industrialisation at home' (Nish, 1987: 140).

It also seemed to the Japanese that the Western powers were intent on limiting her economic and political autonomy. The London Naval Treaty of 1930 imposed restrictions on warship building while the progressive erection of trade tariffs by the industrial powers in the 1930s appeared as yet further evidence of a general Western inclination to isolate and discriminate against Japan. In periods of economic difficulty the British and other European nations could always draw upon the resources of their empires, while the Americans and Russians were large enough to be self reliant. Neither was true for Japan, although rapid industrial expansion during the interwar years highlighted the national dependence upon foreign trade to compensate for the lack of an indigenous raw materials base. The imposition of foreign tariffs in the 1930s further reinforced the appeal of overseas expansion and economic autarky, based particularly on the mineral-rich north eastern provinces of China.

The depth of feeling on these issues was considerable. The government was quite unable to redeem the situation created by the army's invasion of Manchuria largely because that action was so popular within Japan, even among some left wing groups. Although both the Social Democratic Party and the breakaway National Labour-Farmers' Party opposed imperialism in principle, they soon drifted towards supporting the army. Shortly after the occupation of Manchuria the left wing social democratic movement split between adherents of the international socialist ideal and those who succumbed to fear of police surveillance or to sheer jingoism. Japanese socialists, like their European predecessors in 1914 proved the truth of John Burns's gloomy adage that national blood was thicker than socialist water (John Burns Diary, 29 October 1914. B.L. Add MSS 46337). Equally popular were the assassinations in 1932 of the premier who had signed the humiliating London naval agreement, and Baron Dan, a leading Mitsui executive. Popular support ensured that would-be assassins and plotters escaped fairly lightly if they were brought to court. Patriotic fervour intensified still more when full scale war broke out against China in 1937. The decisive actions of the army contrasted sharply with the apparent pussyfooting of the democratic politicians and also appeared to save Japan's face in the international arena.

At home the military carefully propagated its image as the champion of ordinary people. By the 1920s the social basis from which its commissioned officers were drawn had become much wider than before 1914. This gave extra credibility to army attacks on the extremes of wealth in Japanese society and its criticism in particular of rich businessmen and powerful politicians. Clever manipulation of public opinion produced an upsurge of feeling against big business in the early 1930s, prompting the *zaibatsu* to engage in philanthropic and charitable activities as a way of redeeming their tarnished public image. Criticism of big business even rallied to the ultranationalist cause some of the socialist groups who shared their antipathy towards private capitalists.

The army similarly presented itself as the protector of the rural masses in the countryside where years of relative official neglect and concurrent official rhetoric about the traditional national virtues embodied in ruralism provided an especially receptive soil. So, too, did the fact that although there were very few substantial landlords in Japan the scarcity of written tenancy agreements left many farmers feeling insecure (Fukutake, 1995). As the majority of recruits were drawn from rural areas it was also relatively easy for the army to exploit the hardships faced by rural society. As one military plotter explained at his trial in 1934, it was not desirable that 'soldiers should be worried about their starving families' (Boyle, 1993: 168). Yet economic discontent alone does not explain the success of the army's appeal in the countryside. It also had a well established influence in agrarian communities, partly through the activities of the many reservists involved in local education, and partly through the redeployment as school instructors of army personnel made redundant by expenditure cutbacks. It has also been argued that the military was always likely to be well received in rural areas where the survival of the landlord system preserved a structure of social relationships particularly amenable to totalitarianism (Dore, 1959). Finally, it cannot be overlooked that the army and its ultranational supporters appealed to values and sentiments deeply entrenched in Japanese society.

The system of ritual

Japan

In seeking to explain what 'went wrong' in interwar Japan, Marxist scholars have suggested that Japanese democracy was enfeebled because the 1868 Restoration had pre-empted a genuinely proletarian revolution, birthing instead a bourgeois bastard. It might equally be argued from a Weberian perspective, however, that what happened in Japan was more akin to what occurred in Edwardian Britain. In both cases a range of new and more liberal social ideas and values were being increasingly espoused at the very time when extraneous political and economic circumstances stimulated strident reiterations of the traditional. Japanese modernisation had inevitably been accompanied by more open discussion of democratic ideas as a new generation asserted individuality more openly and more consciously than before. Even before 1914 authority, fearful of the potential for social disharmony, had increasingly reiterated the importance of the family-state centred on the empire and fathered by the emperor. By developing her relationships with the West, linking her more closely to the international economy, and encouraging the growth of an indigenous labour movement, the war helped to make Japan a more pluralistic society than ever before, reinforcing interest in democratic ideas and values. After 1920 and under the pressure of slowing growth rates, disparities of wealth, and agrarian hardship, so the call was increasingly heard in some sections of Japanese society for a rejection of Western ideas and the reassertion of traditional Japanese values of harmony and unity. More generally, the feeling grew that democracy had not protected these, and opinion turned away from the notion of balancing conflicting interests through the Diet. This process was reinforced by the economic difficulties of the 1930s and the deteriorating international environment.

Although their organisational influence was widespread, extending to a number of secret societies such as the Black Dragon and the Blood Pledge League, ultranationalists were never as ideologically cohesive as is sometimes implied. However, they were united in opposing big business and in denigrating democratic institutions such as the Diet. On the positive side three particular values were increasingly reasserted through the interwar years. One was imperialism. Ultranationalists shared a belief that as the most advanced country in the continent, Japan should take the lead in freeing Asia from Western colonialism. In advocating such policies they were able to capitalise on popular resentment at the West's treatment of Japan and also on the failure of democratic politicians to stand up to Western pressure. Mindful of American sensitivities and Chinese nationalism, the politicians took a cautious attitude towards expansion in the 1920s. In the process they further antagonised the military, already annoyed by defence cuts.

Militarism provided a second source of inspiration for ultranationalism. The transformation of the *samurai* into an administrative bureaucracy under the Tokugawas had carried a military ethos into government while the experience of the *bakufu*, the Tokugawa's system of military government, made the people as a whole more amenable to the notion of authoritarian rule. Martial prowess had always been accorded a special place within the Japanese value system and military virtues had always been stressed in the education curriculum. This process was fostered in the interwar years by the redeployment of army officers in schools. Their presence generally reinforced anti-democratic sentiment and from the 1930s teachers were compelled to devote more time to military training. One Western inhabitant recalled how in his village all children were summoned to partake in ten minutes of military type drill, following instructions being broadcast nationwide by the government (Livingston, Moore and Oldfather, 1976: I, 440).

The prestige of the army was also part of the legacy of Japan's past, boosted by popular memories of relatively recent success against China and Russia, and the military took care to propagate its image as the champion of popular causes. It may well be true, as Ferdnand Maurette implied in 1934, that admiration for the army was not the same as supporting its overseas ambitions. Ultimately, however, that was where the admiration led (Maurette, 1934: 45).

Along with this went a renewed emphasis on Emperor worship, achieved partly through the reassertion of Shintoism in the school curriculum and partly through the purging of those whose ideas threatened to reduce the emperor to a less elevated status. The most prominent casualty was Professor Minobe Tatsukichi. His works were banned in 1935 on the grounds that his view of the emperor as merely a constitutional organ represented an act of lese-majesty. As head of the country and the chief decision-maker, Hirohito might have prevented the growth of army power. However, his position demanded that he act on the advice of counsellors and Saionji, sole survivor of the old clique of ruling advisers, sought to prevent him from becoming embroiled in politics, fearing that it would damage imperial prestige. Although he did sometimes intervene in politics, as at the time of the 1936 coup attempt, Hirohito remained to a significant extent aloof, and certainly remote as far as the mass of the population was concerned. To them he remained divine, a characteristic re-emphasised in the new book on the basic principles of national polity (*kokutai*) issued in 1937 for the use of all schools and colleges. The imperial throne, this asserted, was 'coeval with heaven and earth . . . Japan is a divine country. The heavenly ancestor it was who first laid its foundations, and the Sun Goddess left her descendants sove-reign over it for ever and ever' (Boyle, 1993: 173). The book then went on to criticise Western notions of individualism, democracy, and communism, in this way helping to insulate public opinion against the dangers inherent in an expansionist foreign policy.

Imperialism, emperor worship, and militarism were all deeply rooted within Japanese society which, it has been argued, had a different ethos from Europe. Since the Reformation, European states had been morally neutral, confining themselves to the maintenance of order while leaving the forma-tion of values to the discretion of individuals and groups. That separation had never held true in Japan where the state had always sought to shape indi-vidual values and thought. The definition of good was handed down from on high, meaning that notions of right and wrong were malleable and deter-mined by the state, rather than any external code of moral absolutes (Maruyama, 1963). The concept of the nation as a family, headed by an emperor of divine descent, gave Japanese nationalism a particular exclusiv-ity, rendering it far more potent than the latent xenophobia of the average Briton. Ultranationalists espoused more extreme and aggressive forms of existing ideas and were prepared to be more forceful in pursuing Japan's national interests.

The assertion of such Japanese values and the rejection of Western-inspired alternatives were encapsulated in the work of Kita Ikki, the most outstanding and articulate right wing ideologue in prewar Japan. He argued that Japan was in need of rescue from malign Westernising influences. To achieve this, he believed, it was necessary to remove everything standing between the emperor and his people. Thus he urged capitalists to follow the 1868 example of the feudal lords by returning their wealth to the emperor. The Diet should be abolished, leaving supreme power in the hands of the armed forces responsible to the emperor alone. Yet although Kita's experi-ence of prewar China persuaded him that the army should be the chosen instrument of reform, he excluded the senior ranks on the grounds that they shared in the general corruption which made reform necessary in the first place. A Japan thus re-ordered, he argued, would be able to shake off its inferior international status and then have 'recourse to war to correct the injustices in international territorial boundaries', a policy 'to which people ought to give their unconditional approval'(Morishima, 1982: 149). Such views struck echoes in the hearts of many Japanese, but they were particularly well received by junior officers in the army.

To some degree as well the tension between old and new values was a reflection of the divergent pace of social change within Japan. Higher education and town life were still a minority experience but they encouraged, particularly among the young, the adoption of Westernised life styles. The countryside, however, still home to over half the total population, remained more firmly wedded to the ideas and structures of the past, even though the spread of education and greater individual mobility had certainly increased its level of political consciousness. From a rural perspective, therefore, the towns and much of what they represented appeared to threaten the essential spirit of Japan. It was significant, for example, that the typical member of the ultranationalist Blood Pledge League, responsible for the campaign of political assassination in 1934, came from a rural area and appeared to want a return to the supposed solidarity and social harmony of traditional village life, now disrupted by Westernisation. 'If grass were to grow on the roof of the Mitsokoshi Department Store', said one of the ultranationalists' intellectual mentors, 'Japan would not fall, but if the rain leaked through the roofs of five million Japanese farmers' homes what would become of Japan?' (Boyle, 1993: 168). Significantly, it was from the countryside that the vast bulk of army recruits was drawn and it was there also that popular attitudes and values appeared to have been most outpaced by the advance of Western technology, institutions, and ideas, causing a dangerous imbalance between what actually existed and what people felt should exist. 'There are signs', suggested a British diplomat, 'that . . . the rapidity with which industrialisation was effected renders her economic fabric ill-adapted to stand the strain of social unrest' (Nish, 1987: 137).

Yet there was also a more subtle dimension to these tensions, embracing more than a simple conflict between old and new values. As in the 1880s, there were intellectuals who sought a distinctively Japanese way forward, a middle way between the traditional and the modern. Miki Kiyoshi, for example, a one-time Marxist, argued in the 1930s that the state was the only viable agent of reform because it alone could transcend the interests of individuals and groups. Japan, he asserted, should reorganise itself on the basis of native corporatism whereby the individual was subordinated to the interests of the whole body politic. It was this type of thinking which lay behind the notion of a self sufficient co-prosperity sphere in Asia. But while it was a more sophisticated response to contemporary Japan's difficulties than merely reiterating the traditional values, its outcome was the same: war was envisaged as the creative mechanism for its achievement (Waswo, 1996: 95–9).

If the value and ritual systems within interwar Japan showed some signs of polarisation, similar tendencies evident in Britain before 1914 seemed to have evaporated by the time the war ended. Victory seemed to vindicate existing structures and values. With the exception of Ireland, the ties of empire appeared to have been reinforced by wartime cooperation, while at home the concession of a wider franchise betokened confidence rather than weakness on the part of the state. So, too, did the way in which after 1920, the government prepared for the anticipated show-down with organised labour. It may also be that the war created a greater sense of nationhood which was manifested in many ways: the playing of the national anthem at the end of public entertainments and ceremonies, the observance of Armistice Day, the formation of the British Legion, and the appearance in even the smallest villages of war memorials. These, it has been remarked, 'became the touchstone of one of the things that was held in common by Britons, a shared myth of mud, poppies and puttees' (Smith, 1995: 172). In this way the conflict of 1914–18 made Britons out of people whose identities hitherto had been mainly derived from their immediate localities. As Professor Robbins suggests, England, Wales, and Scotland could be both a three nation and a single nation entity depending on the context, but the long process of forging a British identity reached its apogee around the time of the First World War (Robbins, 1988: 185). Yet if the war was commemorated as an heroic event of national significance, there was a marked reaction against those held responsible for the magnitude of the slaughter. Though less widely or intensely felt, the growth of *anti*-militarist and pacifist sentiment in inter-war Britain was the very reverse of what was happening in Japan.

At the level of the individual the war may have strengthened family ties. One outcome certainly was a fresh emphasis on maternity and child care. For some classes certain trends in leisure activities may also have served to strengthen the family unit, in so far as possession of a motor car or listening to the radio were essentially family-centred activities. On the other hand, war also marked a major disjuncture for many. No one can guess at the psychological effects of the collective burden of grief borne by the widows, parents, and children of about 750,000 war dead, nor at the consequences of the physical and mental scars carried by a further 1.6 million who had been wounded or gassed. 'This war', noted Vera Brittain, 'means such a waste of life even when people don't die' (Brittain, 1933: 220). When the war ended she wrote,

> for the first time I realised with all that full realisation meant, how completely everything that had hitherto made up my life had vanished with Edward and Roland, with Victor and Geoffrey. The War was over: a new age was beginning: but the dead were dead and would never return. (Brittain, 1933: 463)

Not surprisingly, it is sometimes implied that the war had an adverse effect on religious belief, for by the end of the 1920s church attendance was certainly well down on its prewar level. It is also true that after 1918 the churches never again enjoyed the level of political influence they had commonly exerted before. Nevertheless, the conclusions to be drawn from these facts are by no means obvious (Wickham, 1957: 210). The growth rate of church membership had slowed down long before 1914 and in fact membership of all the main churches kept pace with population growth during the 1920s (Currie, Gilbert and Horsley, 1977: 25). What seems to have happened is that the disruption to established social patterns brought about by the war weeded out those for whom church attendance had been mainly a matter of respectable habit. Again, the fact that the war raised profound moral and theological questions which allowed of no easy answers, did not inevitably lead to the destruction of religious faith. In some cases certainly it had precisely the opposite effect. There was an upsurge of popular interest in spiritualism and, in intellectual circles, a renewed interest in Catholicism. 'Atheism tempered by hymns' was a clever but misplaced description of interwar religious life in Britain.

Whatever the institutional hold of Christianity, there is no doubting its continued influence on morality. The number of recorded crimes per hundred thousand of the population rose from 273 in 1921 to 399 ten years later but the major sources of increase were in traffic offences and petty larceny (McClintock and Avison, 1968: 23). Neither could be taken as indicative of any lessening of moral restraint: rather they reflected perhaps the greater opportunities brought about by rising prosperity. Nor can it be argued that the restraints on sexual behaviour imposed by religious belief were seriously weakened by the war. This process was allegedly facilitated by the greater availability of contraception, and made more likely by the breakup of stable communities and the realisation that individual relationships might be abruptly terminated by death. The assumption also derives in part from evocations of the roaring twenties with their liberated women and more sexually explicit dance crazes which so outraged letter-writing clerics. In fact, however, there is little statistical evidence of a more relaxed sexual climate. The actions of a few flappers cannot be taken as representative of the populace at large and indeed the early 1920s witnessed an official campaign against sexual deviance, something which in the popular mind tended to be associated with artistic experimentation. The enduring strength of traditional moralism was illustrated most notably at the time of the abdication crisis in 1936.

As Prince of Wales, Edward VIII simultaneously annoyed establishment figures and endeared himself to ordinary people by his apparent radicalism and sympathy for the worst affected victims of the depression. Stanley Baldwin resolutely resisted attempts by the new king to find a way of marrying the divorced American commoner, Mrs Simpson, while retaining the throne. His own innate sense of duty compelled Edward to abdicate but it pointed to the strength of traditional values that divorce, at least for public figures, was still regarded as unacceptable. In the event, the king's decision did not weaken the monarchy as some had feared.

In fact, few Britons had as much information on the developing constitutional crisis as did Americans and Europeans. British press coverage was remarkably restrained, even though the growing influence of newspapers was one of most significant developments in the system of ritual. Under the entrepreneurial drive of magnates such as Rothermere and Northcliffe, circulations soared. For most people, newspapers became far more influential moulders of mass opinion than the pulpit. Only the *Daily Chronicle*, the *Daily Herald*, and, after 1938, the *Daily Mirror*, were not Conservative in outlook. In this way the press reinforced the conservative, imperial, and pro-establishment outlook being propagated by other new opinion formers, such as cinema, whose potential in this respect had been tapped during the war. Feature films and newsreels alike presented an establishment view of inter-war Britain, monarchist, imperialist, civilised, settled, and united. Analysis of newsreels reveals a heavy emphasis on government achievement and a neglect of opposition opinions. Similarly, BBC radio refused to give air time to supporters of the General Strike in 1926, while Baldwin's easy mastery of the medium may have made an important contribution to the broad appeal of interwar Conservatism.

5

Recovery and the long postwar boom: production and reproduction, 1945–c.1970

Introduction

In the summer of 1945 Britain emerged from the Second World War as a victor nation, Japan as a defeated and occupied one. For Britain the cost of winning and the maintenance of the empire proved rather lower than it had been in the earlier global conflict, at least in human terms. Casualties of some 400,000 included 60,000 civilians killed in air raids. Between a third and a half of the merchant fleet was sunk, capital formation fell to about half of its already low 1938 level, some 10 per cent of prewar national wealth was sacrificed through external disinvestment or bomb damage, about a third of English houses were damaged or destroyed. Japan's defeat naturally incurred far heavier costs. Almost a half of the prewar imperial territory was lost, and if victories in the Far East encouraged colonial independence movements by destroying the myth of white supremacy, the legacy of occupation cruelty hampered the rapid restoration of commercial links. Out of a prewar tonnage exceeding ten million, only a million tons of merchant shipping remained afloat, communications between the main islands were cut, and air raids destroyed 40 per cent of sixty major cities. A quarter of Tokyo's housing and much of its industrial plant were put out of action. All told, about 35 per cent of the national wealth of 1944–45 was lost, although it is worth noting that steel-making capacity remained almost twice what it had been in 1937 and the economy was equipped with two and a half times as many machine tools as before the Pacific War. Human casualties were enormous. Between 1937 and 1945 some 2.7 million people died, including 1.7 million military personnel and an estimated 668,000 victims of air raids. On top of this, the Japanese suffered the incalculable psychological impacts first of two atomic bombs and then of being occupied for the first time in their recorded history. None of modern Japan's military involvements had ever turned out so disastrously.

Within a decade or so, however, both countries had largely recovered and thereafter their situations were transformed. Japanese independence was restored by the Treaty of San Fransisco in 1951 while the return of normality in Britain was symbolised by the final abolition of food rationing in 1954. Thereafter the British economy grew faster than at any time since the Industrial Revolution, ushering in a period of unparalleled prosperity. In Japan, the long postwar boom sustained growth rates so high that the nation was carried rapidly up the international league table of economic performance.

The system of production

Postwar recovery: Japan

Initial recovery in postwar Japan was slow. Under General Douglas MacArthur the occupying authorities (mainly American and hereafter referred to as SCAP, short for Supreme Commander Allied Powers) had to deal immediately with the short term problems arising from wartime dislocation. The dropping of the atomic bombs and the intensity of the allied air raids in the last months of the war had caused wholesale disruption, with an estimated ten million people fleeing to the countryside. Some thirteen million were unemployed, including most of the seven million demobilised soldiers, three million expatriates from the empire, and those thrown out of work by the closure of arms factories. The average Japanese wage at the end of 1945 was the equivalent of thirty US cents a day and real income in 1946 stood at about half the 1936 level. Neglect of water and flood control facilities during the war contributed to widespread flooding in 1946. Since the countryside had been stripped of resources to support the war effort, agricultural productivity had declined and food production was already inadequate even before the rice crop failed in 1945. By 1946 official rations provided only a fifth of the required minimum food intake, necessitating massive imports from the USA. Between 1945 and 1948 the USA provided about $1 billion worth of non-military aid to Japan, mainly to prevent mass starvation and disease. In this situation of agricultural inadequacy and very limited consumer goods production, food became a major trade item on the black market, and in many places barter replaced cash transactions. Prices quickly escalated. Demobilisation and resettlement allowances added further inflationary fuel and the wholesale price index, based on 1934–36, rose from 15 in April 1946 to 197 by March 1949. Consumer prices rose by over 1000 per cent between 1946 and 1949.

Inflation was further stoked up as both the government and the banks poured money into the reconstruction of basic industries at a time when savings were negligible and resources scarce. Although more than half of Japan's factories were still intact, they required conversion to peacetime production, neither an easy nor a quick task. Power was scarce because coal production was down to 500,000 tons a month, more than half of it required in domestic premises. Manufacturing was caught in a vicious circle of dependency. Recovery required raw materials, which could be obtained only from overseas. Yet they could be paid for only by increasing exports, which was difficult in the absence of raw materials. Significant sectors of industry were disrupted by the loss of the prewar territories on which they had relied for resources or markets. Matters were made even worse by uncertainties about the timing and scale of reparations, while the reconstruction of basic industries such as steel and shipbuilding was a sensitive issue, given their military connotations. Finally, new laws establishing labour rights led to the rapid growth of trade unionism and an upsurge of unrest. By 1947 about 46 per cent of industrial workers were unionised and strikes became common as organised labour, often under extreme left wing leaders, challenged management for control of production. All in all, it was hardly surprising that by 1948 production had reached only a third of its 1938 level with trade recovery lagging still further behind.

The liberalisation of labour law was part of a general determination by SCAP to reorganise the Japanese economy on broadly democratic lines in order to prevent it ever again being used by an authoritarian government as an instrument of war. Apart from labour, economic reform centred on two other key areas. First, democratisation was extended to the land. The system of tenancy and landowning was abolished as it was believed to have been a major influence behind the rise of prewar militarism. Roughly four million existing tenants farmers became landowners and by 1950 the amount of land occupied by tenants in Japan had fallen from almost 50 to about 10 per cent. In the absence of alternative employments, the proportion of the working population engaged in agriculture actually increased between 1940 and 1950. The result was the perpetuation of small farms. Even by 1976 three quarters of farms outside Hokkaido were still less than 2.5 acres in size. Nevertheless, inflation allowed the new owners to pay off their debts very quickly, while the relative scarcity of food, coupled with the availability of cheap labour, gave them every prospect of making a decent living. Heavy mechanisation, government subsidies, protection, and the further development of cooperative approaches to marketing and purchasing, though not production, helped to keep up farm income. The index of agricultural output went up from 110 in 1952 to 170 by 1970, and Japan became more or less self sufficient in rice (Allen, 1981b: 75). One wider consequence of the farmers' growing prosperity was that the agrarian market for home goods expanded. At the same time, sufficient labour was released to satisfy industry's rising demand for human resources. These were significant achievements in a political sense, too, because in the opinion of some observers the limited size of the home market and its large, relatively low-income rural component had been important influences in turning Japan towards overseas expansion during the 1930s.

Attempts to reform industrial ownership were also deemed crucial by SCAP to the democratisation of Japan, but were generally less successful. In 1945 ten major *zaibatsu* accounted for slightly more than a third of the total value of the economy, the four largest for about a quarter. The Americans believed, not entirely accurately, that big business had actively encouraged warmongering in the 1930s and they were accordingly resolved to weaken it. In 1947, therefore, anti-monopoly measures identified some 325 businesses for dismemberment. The intention was to terminate family ownership and dissolve the *zaibatsu* holding companies. However, the reforms largely overlooked the financial and banking interests of the monopolies, while official enactments could do little to weaken the informal ties that had bound the *zaibatsu* together. Full implementation of the proposals was in any case resisted not only in Japan but also in the United States, where their anti-capitalist tenor was deemed inappropriate at a time of growing Cold War tension. Ultimately, the holding companies of the big four *zaibatsu* were liquidated and about fifty other companies were dissolved or reorganised. In the long run this probably benefited the Japanese at the expense of their overseas competitors. Henceforth decisions were made in the interests of individual enterprises rather than of the larger business groups with which they were now more loosely associated than before. This encouraged the growth of a powerful, internal competitive dynamic.

Thereafter the plans to reform business were allowed to languish somewhat as part of a general modification of American policy. From 1947 onwards some of the more radical proposals were dropped, private overseas trade was once more permitted, and strong measures were taken on the advice of the special presidential emissary, Joseph Dodge, to stabilise wages and prices in order to control inflation. By 1951 the real income index was rising again and if the national trade balance was still adverse, the deficit was much smaller than it had been. In 1945–46 the value of Japan's imports was almost three times greater than that of her exports: by 1950 exports had increased eight fold against a three fold increase in imports. In part, the softening of SCAP policy reflected the realisation that American tax-payers could not be expected to subsidise an economically emasculated Japan indefinitely. More significant was the consideration that the developing Cold War in the Far East was conferring upon Japan a particular geographical and strategic significance. This became apparent when the Korean War broke out, an event aptly welcomed by Prime Minister Yoshida Shigeru as 'a gift of the gods'. Once again, war played a decisive part in enhancing Japan's economic situation, as the Americans, who formed by far the largest contingent of United Nations forces fighting in Korea, drew heavily upon Japan's vehicle and munitions industries. By the end of 1951 industrial output had passed the prewar level and the balance of payments was back in the black, with war-related material accounting for almost two thirds of exports. Two years later industrial output was 50 per cent up on prewar level and real national income 30 per cent higher. Even after hostilities ended in Korea, Japan continued to supply to America special procurements sufficient to pay for 14 per cent of her imports, a source of foreign income which she would otherwise have lacked.

Postwar recovery: Britain

For Britain, too, the second half of the 1940s was a period of considerable economic difficulty in which the actions of the United States were influential. Certainly there was far less physical destruction to repair than in either Japan or Western Europe. The infrastructure of both the economy and society remained intact although strict controls were required in order to prevent popular expectations of prosperity causing inflation. Trade prospects were favourable. With Germany and Japan effectively removed from the international market and dollars in short supply, Britain was almost the only major non-dollar country still possessed of a significant industrial capacity. As such, she had a unique opportunity to re-establish herself quickly as a major international trader. On the other hand, certain key industries, particularly the railways and mines, were in need of modernisation while raw materials were scarce and expensive. There were acute labour shortages in agriculture, mining and textiles. More generally, the export industries had been so contracted during the war that by 1945 they employed only 2 per cent of the workforce as against 10 per cent in 1939. With exports in 1945 running at about a third of their 1938 level but imports at about 60 per cent, there was a huge current account deficit. The restoration of manufacturing was made all the more urgent by the significant deterioration in the balance of invisible trade. Heavy losses of merchant shipping and the liquidation of overseas assets and gold reserves during the war had considerably reduced the earning potential of the capital account. At the same time an additional debt had appeared on the deficit side of the ledger in the form of the £3.5 billion borrowed from overseas, mainly the empire, in order to help finance the war. These sterling balances were to make their effect felt for many years.

The financial position was worsened by the unexpectedly swift termination of the war in the Pacific and the abrupt cessation of the lend-lease programme. To provide some breathing space for the reconversion of an economy that had been more thoroughly geared to war than that of any other combattant, Britain negotiated a low interest loan from the United States, agreeing in return – albeit reluctantly – to make sterling freely convertible again in 1947. The loan ran out far more quickly than anticipated, partly because Britain continued to import more from America than she could export in return. Although the general current balance of payments account moved back towards the black, the dollar gap remained wide. As a result, when Britain restored sterling convertibility there was a rush to exchange pounds for precious dollars. Such was the outflow of gold and dollar holdings that convertibility was abandoned within five weeks. This suggests that the American insistence upon convertibility represented a wildly unrealistic assessment of Britain's economic strength. On a more positive note, however, Britain was a major beneficiary of the American Marshall Aid plan, which invested some $7.0 billion in European recovery, receiving funds worth 5.2 per cent or 7.5 per cent of the GDP, depending on whether the calculation is made before or after the sterling devaluation of 1949 (Alford, 1996: 191).

The Labour Government, elected in 1945, was less than enthusiastic, however, about one of the underlying motives behind Marshall Aid, America's desire to foster European economic and political integration as a bulwark against Soviet Russia. This ran counter to Labour's intention of maintaining all the military trappings consonant with the status of a major independent power. Such an ambition, however, was expensive. Coupled with the commitment to major domestic programmes of welfare provision and industrial reorganisation, it helped perpetuate the general belief that Britain's financial position was still precarious and sterling overvalued. Speculation against the pound intensified in 1949 when a mild depression in the United States led to some curtailment of imports and the consequent widening of Britain's dollar gap. After some prevarication in the face of American pressure, the government brought the exchange rate down to $2.80, a devaluation of 30 per cent. Such a substantial reduction was intended to end the speculation once and for all, although the very fact of devaluation probably discredited the government. It was also argued by some critics that an upward revaluation might have made more sense, given that it was not difficult to sell goods abroad. Certainly the growth of exports had succeeded in reducing the deficit on visible trade to about £51.0 million by 1950, although there is disagreement as to how far this was the result of general economic recovery and how far the outcome of the government's own highly publicised and orchestrated export drive. The visible trade deficit was more than offset when invisible earnings returned to the black after 1948, although there was something of a hiccup when the Korean War caused resources to be switched away from exports to defence expenditure. This provoked another short term financial crisis which not only carried away substantial amounts of reserves but also saw off the Labour Government in 1951.

Even so, the general economic indicators looked promising. National Income had grown by about a quarter between 1945 and 1950, by which time Britain accounted for slightly more than a fifth of total world manufactured exports. Exports were greater than those of France and West Germany combined. Two thirds of car output alone went abroad, representing half of the world's total vehicle exports. Industrial production was also up, equal in 1951 to the combined production of France and West Germany. Steel manufacturers produced a record 16.4 million tons in 1952 under the impetus of the Korean War and about 45 per cent of world shipping tonnage was being built in British yards.

Economic growth

By the early 1950s, therefore, Britain had largely left behind the most immediate effects of the war. For the next twenty years or so, along with most of the industrial world, she experienced something of a golden age of economic progress. Unemployment and inflation were low, productivity rose, and per capita GDP rose steadily, by about 40 per cent between 1950 and 1966 compared with 29 per cent in the interwar period. Industrial output went up 3.7 per cent annually between 1948 and 1960 as against the yearly 3.1 per cent increase achieved between the wars, and the 1.6 per cent recorded between 1877 and 1913 (Pollard, 1992: 229). In historical terms, therefore, these were healthy statistics. By the mid-1960s, however, it was becoming apparent that Britain's golden age rested less on any inherent improvement in her own competitiveness than on two external influences over which she had no control: continuous expansion of international trade and favourable terms of trade which made imports cheap relative to exports. Compared with other industrial nations Britain's economy was lagging. In the first half of the 1960s annual per capita GDP growth of 2.2 per cent was less than half the EEC average and although it pulled ahead very slightly in the second half it was well behind again by 1969. An annual increase in total output of 2.6 per cent in the 1950s and 2.7 per cent in the 1960s compared poorly with the Western average of 4.2 per cent and 4.8 per cent respectively in the same two decades. Although productivity increased at an impressively healthy rate of 4.3 per cent a year, in manufacturing it remained absolutely lower than that of many of her competitors – by 50 per cent in the case of America. In 1966 the new Professor of Economics in the University of Cambridge, Nicholas Kaldor, took Britain's comparatively slow growth rate as the theme of his inaugural lecture because it was, he believed, 'one of the basic economic facts which has increasingly entered into national consciousness' (Kaldor, 1966: 1).

In the main, Kaldor measured British performance against that of Western Europe and the United States although he described Japan's record as 'outstanding', a verdict fully justified by statistical indicators (Kaldor, 1966: 2). By 1957 Japanese exports were still slightly short of prewar levels but the foreign trade account was almost balanced, industrial production was already two and a half times, the GNP 50 per cent, and per capita national income 10 per cent higher than before the war. Overall, manufacturing output grew at 14 per cent a year between 1953 and 1971, with annual machinery output rising even faster at 19.6 per cent. National income more than tripled, between 1959 and 1971. Overseas trade regained its prewar level in 1963. All of this was happened without any noticeable inflation. The wholesale price index was stable between 1952 and 1962 and if it rose in the following ten years by some 12 per cent, that was modest compared with the 40 per cent increase recorded over the same period in Britain.

Other comparative measures were similarly favourable to the Japanese. Average labour productivity improved 10.7 per cent a year as against the 4.3 per cent achieved in the UK. Real GDP per head between 1950 and 1973 increased annually by 8.0 per cent compared with 2.5 per cent in Britain (Maddison, 1991: 50). By 1965 the level of fixed capital formation per head of the Japanese workforce was equal to Britain's. In effect, Japan had achieved in twenty years a level of industrialisation that had taken fifty in Britain. By 1962 *The Economist* was warning that Japan was becoming dangerously competitive 'in a much wider field of industry than most people in Britain at present begin to imagine' (Wilkinson, 1991: 142). Across a whole range of industries Japan was overtaking the former workshop of the world. By 1956 she was the world's largest shipbuilder, a place long occupied by Britain. In the same year only 12,000 private cars were made in Japan. Four years later the figure had risen to 165,000 and by 1967 a million. At that point, productivity in British and Japanese vehicle manufacture was roughly comparable but six years further on the average British worker was producing just 5.1 vehicles a year, far fewer than the 12.2 turned out by a Japanese counterpart (Pollard, 1992: 242). By 1969 Japan was the world's second largest producer of cars, making twice as many as Britain. In motor cycles the story was even more spectacular. It was not until the late 1940s that Honda Soichiro began fitting war surplus engines to bicycles, but within a decade his products had destroyed the once all conquering British motor cycle industry. By 1970 Japanese steel output was four times larger than Britain's. By this date also Japan had overtaken Britain as an exporter of manufactures, her share of the world total having risen to 11.7 per cent from 3.4 per cent in 1950 (Blackaby, 1979: 241). Over the same period Britain's deteriorating competitiveness drove her share down to 10.8 per cent, well down on the 1950 proportion of 25.5. Just how uncompetitive Britain was becoming is apparent from table 5.1, which reveals all too clearly an inability to retain market share, the massive growth of which underlay Japan's export

Table 5.1 *Comparative changes in manufacturing exports (% change attributable to various factors)*

Factors	UK		Japan	
	1950–55	1955–59	1950–55	1955–59
Growth of world market	+38.5	+26.3	+37.8	+26.3
Area/commodity pattern	−6.4	−4.9	−17.1	−4.6
Market share	−29.6	−12.6	+92.7	+46.9

(Alford, 1996: 229)

success. The reasons for both Britain's relative lag and what was popularly described as Japan's economic miracle over the 1950s and 1960s have been debated in a literature whose very extensiveness testifies to the lack of any general consensus about either phenomenon. Discussion has ranged over a number of themes, including the role of government, investment, education, managerial practices and attitudes, industrial relations, and economic structures. Before proceeding to survey the various arguments it is worth making two preliminary points. First, it must be emphasised that in the period between 1950 and *c.*1970 Japan paid a heavy social cost for its economic miracle. Already by the end of the 1950s her trade policy was provoking some minor irritation in the West as only about 20 per cent of her imports were free of tariffs or quotas. Even after some of these were removed, administrative barriers still made it difficult for Western firms to penetrate or set up in the Japanese market. Other critics pointed to the apparent paucity of state welfare provision, emphasising the fact that in the 1950s Japan's annual budget typically allocated almost as much expenditure to agriculture as it did to welfare and health. Japanese governments interfered relatively little in matters of wages, for example, and, despite some improvement, wage differentials between large and small firms remained more marked in Japan than in Britain. Thus in 1951 workers in plants of between five and twenty nine individuals received 38 per cent of the wage of those engaged in units employing more than 500, 62 per cent by 1970. For those in enterprises of thirty to ninety nine workers the increase was smaller, from 56 to 70 per cent (Morishima, 1982: 171). On the other hand, some of these complaints overlooked the fact that historically the Japanese state had never been more than a partial provider of welfare, sharing the burden in partnership with family and employers.

Nor, it was pointed out by the critics, was much attention paid to the physical consequences of industrialisation. Urban expansion proceeded largely unfettered by planning requirements, and land prices, especially around Tokyo, soared. A survey of 1970 concluded that social capital in Japan in terms of houses, property, and public amenities was barely half that of Britain. Furthermore, Japan was arguably the most polluted country in the world by the late 1960s, the combined result of a high concentration of people and industry in the eastern central area, reliance on coal and oil for energy, and the single minded prioritising of economic growth. Chemical smog in the cities was a serious health hazard, nearly all fresh surface water was impure while the Inland Sea between Honshu and Shikoku was among the most contaminated stretches of water in the world. However, the dearth of investigative journalism and an unwillingness to rock the collective social boat kept the worst of these abuses from the public until the late 1960s when it become widely known in Japan that discharges of methyl mercury had been poisoning the sea south of Kyushu ever since 1953. The Basic Law for Environmental Pollution Control in 1967 failed in practice to oblige either government or industry to prevent pollution. Only after a series of successful lawsuits against companies was this legislation tightened up.

Second, it should be borne in mind that the measure of Japan's remarkable relative progress was generally defined in terms of manufacturing productivity. In the service sector, Britain remained far ahead in the level of its financial expertise and importance. The same was true of distribution which appeared to the outsider to function almost as a form of supplementary welfare relief, so labour intensive was it. Retail outlets remained small and independent retailers far more common than in Britain where between 1950 and 1971 the multiples raised their share of trade from 22 to 39 per cent. The disappearance of Britain's small shops was further hastened after 1964 by the abolition of resale price maintenance.

Britain also outperformed Japan in the primary sector. The SCAP land reforms had been designed to destroy tenancy rather than encourage economic efficiency. As a result Japan was saddled with too many farm households relative to land supply. Although heavy investment certainly raised productivity levels, the persistence of very small farm units made it economically inefficient. Technically and organisationally Japanese farming remained behind that of Britain, where agriculture revived after 1945. With no increase in the cultivated land area and a falling labour force, British farm output increased by 2.5 per cent a year between 1951 and 1973, thanks largely to significant but declining subsidies which generally funded the more intensive application of science to farming rather than supporting increases in capital stocks. Taking the full range of economic activities into account, therefore, gives a rather different picture of the productivity differential between Britain and Japan. Table 5.2 shows that while the Japanese were catching up, they still lagged a good way behind Britain in 1973.

Table 5.2 *Real GDP per hour worked*

	1950	1960	1973
UK	100	100	100
Japan	24	33	62

(Crafts, 1991: 263)

Occupational structure

Even this perspective, important though it is, cannot offset the fact that in manufacturing industry, productivity, and thus, conventionally, economic growth, Britain lagged far behind Japan. In looking for an explanation, Kaldor fastened on the idea that growth potential was determined by a country's ability to transfer labour from the low productivity sectors into high productivity manufacturing: the greater the capacity for labour transfer the greater the potential for growth. This analysis appears to equate well with the situation in Japan, where the 1950s did see massive shifts of labour from agriculture to the manufacturing sector. About half the labour force was still engaged on the land in the middle 1950s, but that proportion was down to 15 per cent by the early 1970s. Even that remained considerably higher than in Britain. Because the British agricultural sector was already quite small, Kaldor suggested that growth was hampered by having too large a proportion of the workforce in the non-productive tertiary sector. However, an attempt by the Labour Government to apply his hypothesis by forcing labour out of the service sector through a pay-roll tax did not work. This perhaps confirmed the suspicions of Kaldor's critics that he had revealed only a correlation between low growth rates and occupational structure rather than a causal relationship.

This did not deter two Oxford economists, R. Bacon and W. Eltis, from coming up with a similar sort of explanation for British decline, particularly after 1960, couched in terms of de-industrialisation (Bacon and Eltis, 1976). They argued that the proportion of workers in Britain's manufacturing industry was shrinking, as both labour and capital were increasingly absorbed by activities such as national and local government which did not actually produce a marketable output. Furthermore, the competition for labour between manufacturing and services was blamed for sustaining a wage-price spiral damaging to industrial productivity. It was also argued that the growing public sector necessitated heavy taxation which added further to the burdens on both industry and the employees in it. This, they concluded, lowered corporate profits, thereby reducing the availability of investment capital and simultaneously encouraging wage demands from over-taxed workers.

This diagnosis had a superficial appeal and prompted some misconceived corrective measures. In hindsight it has been found wanting as an explanation for slow growth, not least because the pattern of occupational distribution apparent in Britain was common to all advanced countries. More specifically, it cannot seriously be maintained that labour was being attracted from industry. Although the *proportion* of the workforce engaged in manufacturing was certainly falling, the *number* of workers actually increased until 1966, after which both the absolute numbers and the proportion declined, the latter reaching 32 per cent by 1973. By that date 55 per cent of the workforce was to be found in the service sector. It was also the case that the majority of the new jobs appearing in the service sectors were taken by women, not erstwhile industrial men. Other critics of the hypothesis observed that the British tax burden was not unduly high by international standards, further pointing out that tax cutting by the Tories in the course of the 1950s failed to improve economic performance. Finally, little evidence was produced to support the view that industry was deprived of investment capital in the way posited by Bacon and Eltis. The major constraint on investment appears to have been low demand, rather than any shortage of available funds.

Investment

In turn, this must cast doubt on the oft-made assertion that British industry was starved of investment capital by the indifferent attitude of the banks towards the needs of manufacturers. The very antiquity of this criticism implies a degree of sustained incompetence and short-sightedness on the part of British bankers beyond the realm of plausibility. Various official investigations by the Radcliffe Committee (1959), the Prices and Incomes Board (1967), and the Bolton Committee (1971), suggested that it was no more valid in the postwar period than it had been when it first surfaced in the late nineteenth century. British banks had plenty of liquid assets to lend, particularly as capital exports were restricted in the postwar years, while institutions such as the Industrial and Commercial Finance Corporation had been set up precisely to provide industrial capital. The reality was that British industry still relied mainly for its investment funds, as it had traditionally done, on retained profits rather than bank loans. Thus comparisons with the very active role played by the banks in Japan were misconceived. The situation there in 1945 compelled the banks to become the major suppliers of capital and each of the major industrial groups which subsequently emerged was organised around a bank. Furthermore, the banks found it easy (as did the postal savings system) to channel private savings into industry. In part this was because the equity market was relatively small, and partly because government policy encouraged private thrift by taxing consumer interest payments rather than, as in Britain, the interest on savings. This reinforced the high saving propensity evident among the Japanese. The average family was saving a tenth of its income in the 1950s and a fifth in the 1960s. There is some disagreement as to whether this was the cultural legacy of *samurai* frugality and Confucian ethics or whether, more mundanely, it reflected the nature of welfare arrangements which compelled the individual to make private arrangements for the costs of education and other social needs (Sato, 1987: 153–4).

It is true, of course, that Japan's economic miracle was accompanied by prodigious levels of investment. As a percentage of the GNP, gross investment averaged 28.8 per cent between 1955 and 1964, considerably higher than the UK average of 15.8 per cent (Williams, 1971: 169). At its peak in the years between 1954 and 1973 Japan's investment in new industrial facilities rose as high as 36 per cent of GNP. Yet Britain's own rate of capital formation from the 1950s to the 1970s was unprecedentedly high in terms of its own past levels and not until the 1960s did general investment levels get seriously out of line with her international competitors. Research and development (R and D) expenditure remained substantial until the 1970s.

In any case, it is generally accepted that there is no straightforward link between investment volumes and rates of economic growth. Not all countries with high levels of investment grew rapidly in the 1950s and 1960s. Britain's problem was not so much one of investment volumes as of efficiency, for it did not secure the high returns achieved in Japan and elsewhere.

One possible explanation for low returns on investment in Britain is that too much went into the public sector which between 1951 and 1966 accounted for between 37 and 58 per cent of the total (Williams, 1971: 167). Inter-country comparisons of national expenditure are fraught with methodological difficulty but one estimate suggests that in 1967 central and local government expenditure in Britain accounted for 39.0 per cent of Gross National Expenditure (GNE) as against only 20.6 per cent for Japan. However, it is worth noting that the British figure was not out of line with those for West Germany and France, respectively 40.0 and 40.9 per cent (Sheridan, 1993: 188). Here again, however, the problem may have been one of efficiency rather than volume. In so far as some proportion of British public investment went into monopolistic nationalised industries, it is often argued that returns were bound to be lower since such enterprises lacked any competitive incentive to improve efficiency and productivity. Equally important, less than a third of R and D expenditure was funded by private industry as against 63 per cent by government, most of this going into defence projects which had relatively little commercial spin-off. For example, Britain had the lead in jet engine technology in 1945 and continued to pour money into expensive aircraft development, even though the domestic markets, both military and civilian, were far too small to sustain realistic competition with the Americans. Investment in defence projects may have been justified in terms of Britain's continuing great power status, but it was not generally profitable in economic terms.

Japan had no such burdensome pretensions and one counterfactual estimate suggests that had Japan spent 6 or 7 per cent of its GNP on defence in the 1950s and 1960s then growth rates would have been about 2 per cent a year lower (Patrick and Rosovsky, 1976: 45). But this would have left growth rates at about 8 per cent, still way ahead of Britain. As it was, the national police reserve established during the Korean War subsequently expanded into a small Self Defence Force of 250,000 personnel but military expenditures always remained relatively insignificant. Most R and D expenditure was therefore undertaken by private firms and went into civilian projects, taxation was accordingly lower than in other countries, and Japan was able to modernise most of the industrial base by the late 1950s. Furthermore, as an extensive importer of foreign technology, most of Japan's R and D budget went into development rather than expensive basic research. Consequently the production of modern vehicles, chemicals, and machinery was cheaper and more efficient than in Britain.

Human capital

A similar discrepancy was apparent in the pattern of investment in human resources. The quality of the Japanese labour force improved rapidly in these years. Only 38 per cent of the population had been educated beyond middle school in 1955 but that had increased to 91 by 1975. In Britain there was some delay in implementing the raising of the school leaving age to fifteen as laid down in the Butler Education Act of 1944 and even by 1961 only about 5 per cent of boys and just over 3 per cent of girls stayed on at school after the age of sixteen (Halsey, 1972: 175). Too much should not be made of this contrast, however. Evidence gathered by the Japan Management Association in 1972 indicated that the extensive and rapid recruitment of rural labour presented Japanese industrialists with the sort of training and disciplinary problems encountered by early nineteenth-century factory masters in Britain (White, 1985: 264). More important, perhaps, was the contrast in the type of education being provided. The British system was strongly academic in emphasis. The 1944 Education Act envisaged three tiers of secondary level provision, represented by grammar, technical, and secondary modern schools. The technical schools never really caught on, however, because they were expensive to equip and because middle-class parents attributed a higher status to the more academically orientated grammar schools. The result was that by 1960 there were only 260 of them and most disappeared when comprehensive secondary schooling was introduced in the next decade. This reorganisation, however, did little to bridge the gap between average British school children and their international counterparts, because it failed to address underlying weaknesses of curriculum, teacher training, or the suspicious and even contemptuous attitude towards education which existed in parts of British society.

At the tertiary level, a higher proportion of the relevant age cohort attended university in Japan than in Britain, although the majority attended private institutions which were plagued by financial shortages, large classes, and a lack of direct contact with staff. The highly selective, state-funded British universities were far more effective in getting students through the system and in providing a high quality training. On the negative side, they were widely criticised for exhibiting the same academic bias as the grammar schools. Britain spent heavily on training scientists rather than technicians and engineers, and even then relatively few of them were employed in private civilian industry. Even the elevation of the colleges of advanced technology into universities and the upgrading of other institutions into polytechnics failed to alter the balance. Neither was able to recruit the required number of students from the schools and thus drifted towards the arts and social sciences. By 1974 15 per cent of the 174,000 undergraduates at English and Welsh universities were studying engineering and almost a quarter pure science. The respective proportions of Japan's 1.59 million students were

21 and 3 per cent. While the British engineering industry in particular constantly complained of scarcities of skill, an adequate supply of highly trained technicians enabled Japan to capitalise on the vast expenditures she incurred in importing foreign technology – $218 million between 1956 and 1960, and a staggering $2.0 billion in the 1960s. Britain's attempts to keep up were feeble. The Ministry of Technology, created in 1964 by the Labour Government to encourage technical progress, was not even charged with addressing the matter of educational investment. It remained little more than an ill-fitting jigsaw of small and specialist bodies, plagued by internal frictions and lack of any clear policy. It generally made a mockery of Prime Minister Harold Wilson's vision of forging a modern Britain in the white heat of technology.

Industrial relations

Even when British investment did go into productive industry and technology rather than defence, there were other influences at work lowering its returns. One of the most frequently identified was the trade union movement whose activities and attitudes were freely blamed for Britain's lagging performance. But although Britain's labour relations were often compared, invariably unfavourably, with the situation in Japan, the contrast was by no means clear cut. It was certainly not simply a matter of a worse strike record, for until the 1960s at least Japan's workers were more militant than Britain's (table 5.3). Under the influence of the SCAP reforms, unionism in Japan grew rapidly to embrace about 40 per cent of the total labour force by the mid-1950s, not far short of the 44.5 per cent of contemporary British workers who were unionised. The Japanese movement lacked cohesion in that its leadership was divided between communist and socialist labour federations but the late 1940s saw a rash of strikes in key industries, largely in response to continuing material deprivation. Although SCAP intervened to preempt a projected general strike in 1947, it was not until the defeat of the national carworkers' union in 1953 by Nissan that the initial burst of postwar unrest began to diminish. It by no means disappeared, however, as was evident from a bitter three month steel strike in 1959 and an equally acrimonious ten month stoppage at Mitsui's Miike Mine in the following year. However, the declining trend of stoppages is evident from the figures in table 5.3. During the 1950s reorganisation within the union movement led to the creation of

Table 5.3 *Number of working days lost through strikes per 1000 employees*

	1955–59	1960–64	1965–69
Japan	254	177	107
UK	220	146	175

(Koike, 1987: 292)

the Japanese Workers' Federation (*Domei*). Numerically smaller than the more radical *Sohyo* which by 1968 had 4.2 million members, mainly in the public sector, *Domei* followed moderate policies akin to the British labourist tradition, although, unlike the British TUC, it was not formally aligned with any political party.

Behind the decline of industrial unrest lay the gradual consolidation of company unionism and the further evolution of what became known as the Japanese employment system. These had their origins in the years around the First World War, as large companies tried to shield their workforces from left wing influences and secure skilled labour in a period of scarcity. Throughout the interwar years Japanese governments had sought, though not always successfully, to provide an environment conducive to harmonious industrial relationships, efforts which were intensified during the Second World War. Regulations issued under the remit of the National Mobilization Law covered such matters as minimum and age-linked wages, family allowances, the compulsory provision of dining and health facilities and encouragements to systematic labour recruitment and training. It was during the war, too, that the practice of the annual or semi-annual pay increase became more widespread. All of these elements contributed to the Japanese employment system but only after a period of postwar unrest in which the management vision of labour relations (seniority wages with management discretion, guaranteed employment for some workers, and weak unions) triumphed over labour's aspirations for a livelihood wage determined by age, seniority and family structure, contractually guaranteed jobs for all, and equal union participation via works councils.

The resulting employment system and the dominance of company unionism have often been identified as playing an important role in Japan's economic success. In particular the provision of significant fringe benefits, and the resort to an internal labour market based on seniority and merit-related pay systems and employment for life, created flexible attitudes to change and cemented the interests of employees and firms together. As the system applied only to certain core workers within each firm, managers could control labour costs by utilising temporary employees in times of expansion, while permanent workers had every incentive to raise productivity in order to enhance their own merit payments. The downside of all this was that in the late 1950s core workers made up only about a third of the industrial labour force. Temporary male workers and those who worked in small firms were excluded, as were virtually all women, even though they made up about 40 per cent of the workforce at that time.

Others have offered anthropological or cultural explanations for the success of Japan's employment system, arguing that as the influence of the *ie* declined, so large corporations replaced it as the source of the individual's status and identity (Nakane, 1970). In providing the security and hierarchical structures traditionally associated with the family house, so the company became the primary group to which individual loyalty was committed. This is said to explain why Japanese employees worked so hard for their companies. Whatever the origins of its employment system, there is no doubt that industry did not exhibit the polarisation between employees and employers that characterised significant parts of British industry (Koike, 1987: 289–329). It is significant in this context that some of the most successful British industrial enterprises, ICI and Unilever, for example, followed labour management strategies which incorporated some aspects of the postwar Japanese system.

Another feature of Japanese labour relations was that bargaining was conducted between each company and its own employees, with wages generally determined according to internal criteria rather than the market. This was altogether more systematic and cohesive than the ramshackle and overlapping bargaining structures which were identified by the Donovan Commission in 1968 as providing considerable scope for friction in British industrial relations (Royal Commission on Trade Unions, 1968). Trade unionism had emerged much earlier than in Japan, and during industrialisation the labour process was dominated by norms and customs derived from inherited craft conditions. This led to the emergence of multi-unionism in many major industries. Wage bargaining, generally conducted nationally between employers' and workers' organisations, was thus a protracted and potentially disruptive affair, with wages fixed according to external market signals but reflecting craft differentials. During both world wars the unions secured the perpetuation of their work practices and traditional procedures as the price of their support. Yet these were often incompatible with the demands of mass production, while the persistence of craft organisation allowed small groups to disrupt whole factories or industries, particularly in the key engineering sector. This potential was further strengthened by the postwar commitment to full employment which enabled the unions to raise the spectre of labour shortages. Workplace bargaining also conferred considerable power on shop floor officials, especially in the engineering and automobile sectors. In this situation frequent short stoppages, arising from demarcation disputes, restrictive practices, delays in technological innovation, and high manning levels were the price employers paid for industrial peace. The longer term outcomes included falling productivity, deteriorating product quality, poor delivery rates, uncompetitive prices, and ultimately the loss of markets. One study concluded that restrictive practices were responsible for the inefficient use of labour in fourteen out of twenty three cases examined (Pratten and Atkinson, 1976: 574). The net result in one industry, motor vehicles, was that by 1973 a Japanese worker produced almost two and half times as many cars per year as an equivalent British worker.

Such practices were probably more significant than actual strikes in lowering return rates on investment. This at least was the conclusion drawn by later researchers. As much as a half of rising industrial productivity in the

1980s was attributed to the falling costs of unionisation (*Economist*, 14 September 1996: 23–4). Similarly, table 5.3 shows that Britain's strike record was actually better than Japan's until the mid-1960s. It is true that certain sectors were notoriously strike prone and also performed particularly badly from the mid-1950s, although this by no means proves the existence of a causal relationship between performance and strikes. Britain's aggregate strike record during the 1950s and 1960s, however, was not unduly bad in international terms. Between 1946 and 1973 the net total of stoppages was 1,261 a year, involving 835,000 workers in the loss of 3.9 million working days (Durcan, McCarthy and Redman, 1983: 172).

From the mid-1960s strikes did become a more serious problem in Britain, in part because the unions had by then abandoned the notion that there were any natural constraints on wages (Phelps Brown, 1975: 3–24). Wage rates, which had risen on average by 4 per cent between 1955 and 1965, rose by an average of 9 per cent between 1965 and 1974. Despite the election of a Labour Government in 1964 and the consequent passage of pro-union legislation, attempts to incorporate trade unionists into the process of national economic planning and to impose pay restraint repeatedly failed. The TUC proved unable to command the support or control the actions of its constituent members, while the fragmented nature of wage bargaining militated against incomes policies, as did the lack of credible sanctions against those who failed to comply (Richardson, 1991: 417–42). The final irony came in 1969 when the Labour Government's plan for trade union reform, *In Place of Strife*, was unceremoniously ditched when the unions rejected it out of hand.

Management

By the end of the 1960s British labour relations were certainly more troubled than those of Japan. Yet if trade unions were the villains, resembling the pre-war Japanese army in that they were too powerful and apparently uncontrollable, management must also bear part of the blame. Significantly, management failure was blamed for the inefficient deployment of labour in twenty one of the twenty three case studies referred to above. For years, British managers connived at overmanning, hoarded labour, and even subcontracted its management to the workers themselves in the form of the gang system found for example in steel, shipbuilding, and the docks. In cotton it was management rather than the unions who were reluctant to extend shift working in the late 1940s and 1950s, on the grounds that labour supply was sufficient to keep the industry working at full capacity (Singleton, 1991). Unable or unwilling to break free of the legacy of the past when labour had always been the cheapest factor of production, British industrial managers appeared oblivious to the efficiency costs of their labour policies. Trade unionists were suspicious of industrial training on the grounds that it posed a threat to their control of labour supply, but employers, with a few notable exceptions, were equally reluctant to take up training. Fearing that expensively trained workers would be constantly tempted to move to higher paid jobs in other firms, they frequently left training to an apprenticeship system which generally imparted low levels of skill and perpetuated a defensive trade mentality. This was perhaps a natural enough response at a time of full employment but the postwar British economy suffered from a chronic lack of skilled workers, even when unemployment began to rise. It also affords an interesting contrast with Japan, where from the 1920s management had seen training and worker welfare as instrumental in securing company loyalty, a policy which was quite widely adopted in the 1950s.

Nor was poor handling of labour the only aspect of British management open to criticism. Although again there were some obvious exceptions, there was a general reluctance to innovate. In the main, private industry remained old-fashioned and backward looking, missing modernisation opportunities in the quest for quick profits, though to be fair it was encouraged in this direction in the immediate postwar period by the government's emphasis on exports. Although the Platt Mission concluded in 1944 that equipment in the British cotton industry was out of date and the industry insufficiently integrated, manufacturers ignored government attempts to encourage both modernisation and reorganisation. In opting for immediate profits by expanding their labour forces they did exactly what a Board of Trade Working Party Report warned against in 1945.

> One thing that must be done is that the unique opportunity of the short transition period of intensive demand should be used by the industry to get itself into shape to pay higher wages to meet the difficult competitive conditions which lie ahead. The one thing that must be avoided is the enjoyment of this period as a fool's paradise of easy profits. (Miles, 1968: 37)

The employers also rejected proposals for concerted action on the grounds that this represented an interference with management prerogative. A similar managerial conservatism was also apparent in another leading industry, shipbuilding. A visit to the Clyde in the mid-1950s prompted the head of Mitsubishi's Nagasaki shipyard to comment that 'what the British did they did very well, but in a completely traditional way' (Horsley and Buckley, 1990: 61). A decade or so later the Geddes Report made the same point, complaining that the British industry was stuck with outdated equipment, poor sites, high factor costs, and inflexible approaches to the changing market. It was calculated in 1961 that 60 per cent of the buildings and 38 per cent of the plant and machinery in British manufacturing and building dated from before 1948: Japan had completely modernised its industrial base by 1957 (Daly, Hitchens and Wagner, 1985: 48–61).

Another very obvious manifestation of this conservatism was the slowness with which business structures changed in Britain. True, the decline of family controlled business was a major postwar trend and small businesses (defined as less than 200 employees) certainly became less important, their numbers falling from 136,000 in 1935 to 60,000 in 1963 and their contribution to net manufacturing output dropping from 35 to 16 per cent. Large enterprises became correspondingly more significant. The biggest 100 firms were responsible for 22 per cent of net manufacturing output in 1949 but about 40 per cent by 1970. They had an average of 20,300 workers in 1958 but 31,189 in 1972. By 1973 the top three firms in each industry accounted for 42 per cent of production as against only 29 per cent in 1951. Yet it was not until the 1960s that modern forms of organisation began to make much progress and by 1970, only a third of British firms were structured on the multidivisional basis often identified by business theorists as conducive to economic success (Chandler, 1990; Channon, 1973: 238).

On the other hand, it is worth entering the caveat that in the United States, where the multidivisional structure was most fully developed, economic growth was not particularly impressive by international standards in these years. Equally, the merger activities which produced higher levels of industrial concentration in Britain were rarely accompanied by significant increases in the rate of growth of output. Larger corporate size was not often matched by larger plant size, indicating that the main motivation was ownership and control rather than the increased economies of scale in production. This has been appropriately described as a form of 'corporate conspicuous consumption'(Alford, 1988: 63). Even when the Labour Government set up the Industrial Reorganisation Corporation in 1966 to provide official state encouragement for mergers, the results were not always very happy. The establishment of the British Leyland Motor Corporation in 1968 brought together some of the best known names in British motor manufacture but did not produce much rationalisation of production.

It has sometimes been suggested that the state sector provided the best example of the failure of reorganisation to achieve economic improvement. There is little doubt that the postwar Labour Government's nationalisation programme was a rather haphazard affair, bringing into public ownership the utilities and the Bank of England but only coal and iron and steel of the major productive industries. Strugglers such as cotton and shipbuilding were left in private hands, though in view of their prewar difficulties each might have been regarded as prime candidates for nationalisation. So, too, might the vehicle industry, a veritable hotchpotch of small and large producers but whose importance to the postwar export drive ensured that it escaped the reorganisation inherent in a shift to public ownership. Emerging as it did from a complex interplay of economic, political, historical, and even quasi moral arguments, the whole nationalisation exercise lacked coherence (Millward and Singleton, 1995). Critics subsequently suggested that under public ownership the lack of financial accountability discouraged restructuring while fostering inefficiencies and overmanning. For all that it was denationalised in 1952 and then renationalised in 1967, iron and steel underwent little fundamental change. By international standards its production units remained middle sized and output was raised in the main by extending existing plant, rather than scrapping and rebuilding. Old fashioned plant with lower degrees of mechanisation and smaller furnaces left it with relatively low productivity. Against this, however, is the evidence that over a long term perspective, the nationalised industries actually performed rather better than manufacturing industry. Total factor productivity grew at 2.2 per cent a year between 1951 and 1985 as against a 1.1 per cent growth for manufacturing, although the latter figure was adversely affected by the economic difficulties of the 1970s (Alford, 1996: 266).

All of this perhaps reflected a general British reluctance to consider management as a profession requiring particular technical skills. While it is tempting to blame government for the fact that Britain did not acquire its first business schools until the 1960s, employer indifference and suspicion also played a part. In general, managers were as inadequately trained as were the directors of manufacturing industry. In 1966 over a half of industrial company directors lacked any higher education experience, still less management qualifications. Not surprisingly, when Lord Stokes was appointed to oversee the 1968 merger of the British Motor Corporation and Leyland he discovered 'management . . . overmanned in practically every area . . . short of management skills in lots of areas . . . relying on a combination of hunch and whim to plan and price its products, which . . . appears naive and amateurish' (Pollard, 1992: 245). In this he was merely reiterating the findings of a Brookings Institution study which castigated British management for its low overall quality, lack of professionalism, and the excessive influence of old boy networks. Whether it originated in the public schools of late Victorian England or not, the cult of the amateur remained strong in Britain right through into the postwar years. The 1971 liquidation of the toy manufacturers, Lines Brothers, a blue chip company, was widely attributed to the fact that too much reliance had been placed upon family members rather than on appropriately trained professional managers (Brown, 1996: 185–6).

The Lines' experience seemed to reflect a management style vastly different from that common in Japan where there was a long tradition of favouring able managers rather than family members. In the postwar years Japanese companies competed with each other for the best graduates from the top universities and then invested heavily in inculcating them with high levels of technical skill, ensuring their loyalty by rewarding them with contracts embodying the lifetime employment and seniority pay systems. Yet it is by no means certain that the implied causal relationship was all one way, running from better trained managers to higher productivity. Seniority wages and lifetime employment contracts were sustainable primarily *because* the economy was growing rapidly and because a high proportion of the workforce was young and thus cheap. The Japanese themselves began to question the viability of this employment system when the economy slowed down in the 1980s and the age profile of the workforce had changed. Furthermore, these features were limited to certain groups within the workforce. It is also significant that as Japanese companies expanded their operations into other countries they did not necessarily introduce these features of management into their overseas plants, yet still they managed to achieve higher levels of productivity.

In turn, this has prompted the view that the superiority of Japanese manufacturing industry lay as much its distinctive production practices as in its managerial organisation. In particular the concept of continuous, statistical quality control was taken far more seriously than anywhere else, not least because the country's almost total reliance on imported raw materials meant that waste could not be tolerated. Just in Time (JIT) production, pioneered by Toyota from 1956, further increased efficiency by minimising the amount of capital tied up in warehousing and stocks. In some sectors, mainly engineering, a similar principle governed relationships between main producers and subcontractors who were tied together in long standing relationships, thereby providing both parties with security and ensuring flexibility. This system had expanded considerably during the war and after it was over the number of subcontractors, as a proportion of all small and medium sized firms, grew steadily, accounting for 58 per cent by 1971 (Aoki, 1987: 283). Total quality control was learned from the American, W. E. Deming, who became something of a management guru in Japan in the 1950s, while Toyota's JIT system was based on practices used by the Ford motor company at its Baton Rouge plant. This suggests perhaps that Japan's willingness to borrow and adapt ideas was at least as important to economic success as innate cultural influences.

Japanese industrial production techniques were certainly facilitated by changes in the structure of business enterprise which, in contrast to British experience, appeared to increase efficiency. SCAP's attempts to reform the *zaibatsu* may not have been thoroughly accomplished but the way was opened for other dynamic entrepreneurs such as Yataro Nishiyama of Kawasaki Steel and Honda Soichiro, the automotive engineer. Business was strengthened and made more aggressively competitive. Nor did reform prevent the reappearance of powerful industrial groupings, the *Keiretsu*, arguably more efficient than the old, family-dominated groups they replaced. Six major corporations emerged – Mitsui, Mitsubishi, Sumitomo, Dai-ichi Kangyo, Sanwa, and Fuji. All acquired banking and financial institutions, ultimately spreading their manufacturing activities very widely. Each was able to design, develop, manufacture, and sell commodities using its own resources and materials from within the group. Unlike major British enterprises, they were under no pressure to maintain constantly high profit levels in order to ward off hostile take-over bids. Mutual shareholdings within and across groups meant that only about a quarter of their shares were ever traded on the stock market in the 1960s. This may have been a new development but it rested on traditional principles of trust, obligation, and cooperation. It certainly distinguished these sectors of Japanese business from British companies, even those in which family control had similarly diminished and where interlocking directorships were common. The wider basis of shareholding in Britain compelled British firms to be profit conscious. Indeed, in terms of the measures traditionally used in Britain to assess corporate success, returns to capital, and annual profitability, Japanese companies did not perform particularly well in these years. Nevertheless, given their structure the *Keiretsu* and other large scale independents such as Hitachi and Masushita could take a long term perspective, concentrating on market share and penetration rather than the annual balance sheet. With government encouragement, they targeted specific Western technologies and acquired production licences. Complemented by the permanent relationships between manufacturers and sub contractors characteristic of other parts of the industrial economy, mainly engineering and motor vehicles, the whole added up to an integrated industrial effort far in advance of anything achieved in Britain.

Government

The involvement of Japan's government in encouraging industry has often given rise to the view that economic success was attributable to the proactive role of the state. Certainly economic policy was largely consistent throughout these years in its prioritising of growth and industrial development. This may have derived partly from the only briefly disturbed postwar dominance of the Liberal and Democratic parties which coalesced into the Liberal Democratic Party in 1955. Too much should not be made of any contrast with Britain in respect of political continuity, however. Although the Labour Government was replaced in 1951 by the Conservatives, who held office for thirteen years before giving way to another Labour administration in 1964, there was not much significant difference between them in economic policies or priorities. The removal of postwar controls was begun in the late 1940s by Labour and completed in the early 1950s by the Tories. Thereafter, it has been argued, there emerged a broad consensus known as Butskellism, a term derived from marrying the name of the sometime Conservative Chancellor, R. A. Butler, with that of the Labour leader, Hugh Gaitskell. Although this interpretation has been challenged, almost the only ideologically motivated policy reversal initiated by the Conservatives after 1951 was the denationalisation of the steel industry. Even the changes associated with the more overtly interventionist approach of the 1964 Labour Government were more rhetorical than real, complementing rather than fundamentally redirecting existing policies. Despite fierce criticism of the stop–go economic cycles produced by Conservative priorities, Labour governments were unable to do much to change the pattern, ultimately resorting to the devaluation of sterling in 1967. While this continuity reflected, for at least part of the time, a genuine political consensus, it is also possible that British civil servants, mindful of the possibility that government might change every five years, promoted only policies they believed both parties would accept, i.e. continuity at the lowest common denominator.

The dominant motif of economic policy in these years was Keynesian demand management, with both parties deploying broadly the same set of tools – variations in the public sector borrowing requirement, interest rates, and taxation – in pursuance of four broad aims, full employment, stable prices, balance of payments equilibrium, and (mainly towards the end of the period) higher levels of economic growth. Thanks to Keynes, the first of these appeared to have a sound basis in economic theory, while history gave it a pragmatic rationale. For most West European countries, the experience of deprivation and mass unemployment in the 1930s had been eclipsed by the memories of invasion and/or occupation in the course of the Second World War. This was not true of Britain. Even though the 1930s had brought aggregate material improvements, economic priorities in the postwar years were strongly influenced by the determination to avoid any reappearance of mass unemployment. Nor was the pursuit of this goal unsuccessful, although this might have had as much to do with the expectations created by the policy's advocacy as to its actual implementation. National unemployment in the 1940s averaged 2.0 per cent of the workforce. It was only half a percentage point higher in the following decade, although, as indicated above, the costs of this included overmanning, labour hoarding, and lower productivity. In the course of the 1950s regional blackspots did begin to reappear, usually in the areas ravaged by job losses in the 1930s and where the same staple industries were still struggling as international competition became fiercer – Northern Ireland, Scotland, Wales, and the north of England. By 1964 unemployment in these regions was respectively 6.6, 3.6, 2.6, and 3.3 per cent (Glynn and Booth, 1996: 284). Government encouraged industrial relocation by means of concessions and incentives. Between 1945 and 1964 firms moving to designated areas created 345,000 jobs but by the 1960s regional policy was costing £166.0 million a year as against only £5.3 million in 1950. Businesses were often persuaded or permitted to relocate for socio-political reasons rather than economic ones, thereby actually adding to the burden of uncompetitiveness. From 1964 national unemployment began to rise more sharply, partly because some of the new Labour Government's measures such as compulsory redundancy payments and the introduction of a pay-roll tax encouraged employers to stop hoarding labour, partly because British firms were proving increasingly uncompetitive in the face of the growing foreign challenge.

Full employment, however, was not easily compatible with price stability. The cost of living index went up by 50 per cent between 1942 and 1960, faster than anywhere in Western Europe except France. It is generally accepted that the main impetus behind this was the strong bargaining position conferred upon organised labour by the commitment to full employment and the consequent wage-price spiral. But as we have seen, wage increases were not matched by equivalent productivity gains, further reducing British competitiveness, especially as the spiral tightened from the middle 1960s.

Given the fixed exchange rate, rising prices inevitably meant that imports were sucked in while exports became overpriced in overseas markets. Consequently, Britain's share of world manufactured exports fell dramatically in these years. The result was a deteriorating trade balance, prompting fears about the exchange rate, speculation, and recurrent balance of payments crises. Although the volume of British exports increased by about a quarter between 1950 and 1963, and by a further 40 per cent from 1963 until 1970, this represented a lower rate of expansion than that achieved by other countries. In part this was because 43 per cent of exports at the end of the 1950s were still going to slow growing markets in the sterling area, reflecting not only dollar shortages and the strength of imperial sentiment but also postwar European dislocation. More seriously, however, slow export expansion reflected the declining price competitiveness of British manufacturing. At the same time, the growing liberalisation of trade, which involved the ending of quotas, encouraged the growth of imports, particularly from the late 1950s. The current account was in deficit in 1951, 1955, 1960, 1964, 1965, 1967, and 1968, although from the perspective of the 1990s the sums seem modest. Consequently the Treasury frequently initiated short term measures to correct deficits in the balance of payments, whose vulnerability was heightened by the persistence of the sterling balance problem and the diminishing proportional significance of invisible overseas earnings.

There is some debate about the impact of the resulting stop–go policies, whereby the economy was alternately deflated and inflated, on occasion as in 1959 quite deliberately for short term electoral advantage. On the one hand, it is argued that such policies were inimical to investment and thus reduced the scope for productivity gains, thereby damaging Britain's position in the world market. On the other, it is difficult to see how the removal of the sterling burden would have contributed to any improvement in industrial efficiency. Certainly no long term improvement was evident after the 1967 devaluation. It can also be pointed out that other national economies were not precluded from combining high growth rates with periodic squeezes. The balance of payments was the major constraint on unlimited growth in Japan, for example, and remedial action involving short term deflation and the imposition of credit restrictions produced stop–go cycles in 1954, 1957, 1961, and 1963. However, Japanese industry proved far more responsive than Britain's to such policies. The SCAP reforms had reduced private wealth so drastically in Japan that the banks had been left as virtually the only sources of capital. In the early 1950s they provided 60 per cent of industrial investment and this remained the case into the 1970s. Since the banks were always short of liquid funds they depended on borrowing from the Bank of Japan. During Japan's frequent postwar balance of payments crises, the Bank of Japan curbed its lending, thus compelling the commercial banks to follow suit. In turn, industry responded immediately in terms of prices and costs because internal competition was so fierce. In Britain this did not happen and stop–go produced economic retardation because costs and prices were so rigid.

British economic policy then was characterised in these years by the pursuit of several different objectives which, because they could not all be realised simultaneously, resulted in recurrent short term changes of priority, though certainly until the mid-1960s maximisation of employment was generally top of the list. At the very least, the resulting uncertainty was not conducive to growth or to long term business decision-making. The situation in Japan was quite different. The sole priority throughout this period was to achieve economic independence by maximising growth through industrial development. To this end the government initially targeted heavy industries such as shipbuilding, coal, steel, power, fertilisers, and chemicals. Investment and growth targets were set, incentives provided to industrialists, and the home market kept as closed as possible to outsiders. Shipbuilding so prospered from government orders to make up the wartime losses that by 1956 Japan was the world's largest producer. Although at the end of war all the equipment of Yawata Steel was designated for reparations it never in fact left Japan. Instead it became the basis of Nippon Steel. Still small and inefficient by international standards, the industry was then encouraged by concessions and tax exemptions from the Ministries of Finance and of International Trade and Industry to relocate at deep-water sites so that ores could be more cheaply imported and processed more efficiently. In the early 1950s the scientific instruments sector, cameras, sewing machines, and then from the mid-1950s electronics, clocks, televisions, and precision instruments were also singled out for preferential government treatment. By this time coal, originally brought back to life by American money and Japanese tax revenues, was being allowed to contract in favour of oil. Other older industries were similarly induced to run down. They included textiles, ceramics, woodwork, food and drink, which together with coal, still employed about half of Japan's industrial workers in the mid-1950s. As a result, Japan's industrial structure was radically changed over a relatively short period of time, with the importance of the machinery sector, including electrical goods, rising sharply (table 5.4).

Economic planning was aided by the provision of a comprehensive bank of all the statistical material gathered by government agencies, a prewar practice now more powerfully sanctioned by the Statistics Act of 1947. Also important was the role and high status afforded to economists within the bureaucracy, following the publication in 1947 of *A Report on the Actual Conditions of the Economy*. The 1955 *Five Year Plan for Economic Self Sufficiency* was followed in 1960 by the announcement of the *Income Doubling Plan*, postulating an average annual growth rate of 7.2 per cent for the decade 1961–71. As the boom, which in 1950s had been led by consumer durables, now spread as well to the service sector, especially leisure, this target was revised to 8.1 per cent. Even this proved unduly cautious since the economy grew at a staggering annual rate of 12.7 per cent from 1967 to 1971. Instrumental in this was the 1962 *National Development Plan* aimed at developing heavy industry along the Pacific coast. By 1970 the four designated industrial areas of Kanto, Tokai, Kinki, and the Seto Inland Sea were responsible for about 90 per cent of all industrial output. Between the mid-1950s and the mid-1970s industry's contribution to the GNP rose from 25 to 45 per cent while its share of the labour force went up to 36 per cent.

Table 5.4 *Japan: industrial structure, 1954–77*

	% of total manufacturing output (value added)		% employment	
	1954	1972	1954	1972
Textiles	13.1	6.2	18.5	9.8
Paper	4.0	2.9	3.1	2.7
Chemicals	16.5	11.5	8.3	6.7
Metals	10.6	9.0	6.3	5.8
Machinery	14.5	23.8	13.6	22.5

(Allen, 1981b: 104–5)

The success of these various schemes has encouraged the view that government planning was the key element in Japanese growth. Particular stress has been placed on the contribution of the main planning agency, the Ministry of Industry and International Trade (MITI), though few would go as far as one American admirer who judged its achievements to be on a par with the development of the atom bomb and the moon landings (Johnson, 1982: 240–1). Nevertheless, such accolades do contrast vividly with the criticism usually meted out to the apparently less successful interventions of the Treasury, the main influence on British economic policy. MITI's function was first to identify the particular sectors to be promoted. These were then protected by means of import controls, encouraged through subsidies and preferential taxation, and developed by means of low interest capital loans from the Japan Development Bank, or the Import Export Bank. 'It was up to us', noted one MITI official, 'to allocate resources, capital and foreign technology and we made sure that all these were concentrated in several selected and preferred industries' (Horsley and Buckley, 1990: 45). The task was facilitated by the fact that relatively few companies controlled the *Keiretsu*, each of which was centred around a bank, the primary source of investment capital in Japan. Identification of targets was supported by administrative guidance. This often carried with it the veiled threat of sanctions if it was ignored, prompting the comment of one Western observer that administrative guidance was 'Japanese for unwritten orders', although it must be emphasised that the bureaucrats had no legal powers of enforcement (Johnson, 1982: 265). The guidance was intended as a part of a dynamic process in which a long term perspective was always operative, allowing the economy to adjust smoothly to changes in the comparative advantages of particular industries.

It has been countered that MITI merely added industries to its target list as soon as they showed themselves to be internationally competitive. In other words, policy followed rather than led private performance. This, for example, is the thrust of Yonekura's study of the steel industry, in which it is suggested that MITI's role was no more than 'indirect and intermediate' (Yonekura, 1994: 281). Government had learned during the war that no matter how hard it drove the industry, it was impossible to raise productivity or output without the spontaneous and motivated willingness on the part of the firms themselves. As Professor Shinohara has observed, all the administrative guidance in the world would have availed nothing had it not been for the dynamism and responses of Japanese industrialists (Allen, 1981b: 101).

Others have noted that attempts to guide the postwar economy often met with resistance. Toyota, for example, insisted on its freedom to manufacture diesel trucks despite advice from MITI that this was already satisfactorily done by Isuzu. Similarly, MITI bureaucrats were unable to prevent the establishment in 1969 of a joint venture between Chrysler and Mitsubishi Heavy Industries. Both examples underlined the fact that government depended upon the cooperation of businessmen. Yet if attempts to target specific industries were not uniformly successful, the state did perform the role of a reactive broker, in providing the infrastructure and encouraging technical borrowing from abroad (Calder, 1973). At the very least, the consistent enunciation of a commitment to growth provided a confidence booster for private capitalists.

This might help to explain the failure of most British attempts to provide similar administrative guidance. Advice to nationalised industries on investment policy or to private industry on plant location never worked very effectively because there was no persistent consensus, as there was in Japan, about economic priorities. In Japan, the critical factor was the 'commitment of all major institutions – companies, government, trade unions, and banks to long term industrial success' (Eltis, Fraser and Ricketts, 1992: 22). In Britain, the Treasury had different priorities, the unions supported planning unless it impinged upon free collective bargaining, while industrialists were generally suspicious of government. Lip service was paid to industrial efficiency but other considerations usually took precedence. Furthermore, the financial structure of private British manufacturing meant that far more attention had to be paid than in Japan to the demands of share holders for annual profits.

The ability of MITI to influence business decision-making was enhanced by an interplay of personnel between the political parties, the civil service, and the trade unions, particularly through the *Keidanren*, the main institutional representative of big business. Retired bureaucrats entered political life so commonly that between 1959 and 1989 they occupied 30 per cent of seats in the Diet and 50 per cent of cabinet posts (Eccleston, 1995). Similarly, in the 1950s a number of former top ranking MITI officials gravitated towards the steel industry which had been given such a key role in fostering industrial recovery. The resulting symbiosis between politicians, bureaucrats, and business leaders, often cemented by a common education in the University of Tokyo's law faculty, has led to explanations of Japan's economic miracle in terms of 'Japan Incorporated'. In some of its most extreme forms this explanation verges on conspiracy theory in which democracy and the normal working of the market were allegedly stifled in the interests of growth and global success (Wolf, 1984). Such interpretations have less to do with economic reality than with long standing and deep seated Western suspicions of Oriental despotism. More moderately, it has been suggested that successful planning grew out of

> intimate, effective team-work between corporate executives and government officials at every level. United by a group spirit that make the Japanese behave like a tight-knit family, businessmen and bureaucrats cooperate to promote continuing growth. (Livingston, Moore and Oldfather, 1976: II, 435)

Of course, retired British civil servants and politicians also frequently found their way into company boardrooms, and they also often shared a common, usually public school and Oxbridge, educational background with their fellow directors. In most cases, however, such transfers might more properly be regarded as a form of pension enhancement, whereas Japanese bureaucrats, who tended to retire much younger at about fifty, still had useful working lives before them. Again, with the exception of personnel links between the Ministry of Defence and armaments manufacturers, the transfer was as likely to involve a financial as a manufacturing institution. Finally, it is likely that all the British took with them were the values and priorities imbibed from a Treasury-dominated civil service. The Treasury had a powerful influence on the training and recruitment of all civil servants but was strongly criticised in a 1968 report for failing to devise new training methods or to encourage a more professional approach towards economic management.

The Treasury's approach to economic policy has attracted a great deal of criticism, an unfavourable contrast with the praise usually lavished upon

MITI (Hobsbawm, 1969; Glynn and Sutcliffe, 1972). Emphasising macroeconomics and the theoretical problems associated with aggregate demand, it was largely indifferent to industry or growth, and encountered little serious resistance to its priorities from politicians. Treasury obsession with sterling and the balance of payments, both of which appeared to afford an opportunity to regain the central role in economic planning which had been lost during the war, is also said to have worked against the best interests of industry. The Treasury, it has been claimed, was unduly influenced by financial interests whose health depended upon sterling, and its conservatism ensured the failure of Labour's experiments with French forms of indicative planning (Pollard, 1981). The National Economic Development Council (NEDC, 1962), the Department of Economic Affairs (DEA, 1964) and the Prices and Incomes Board (PIB, 1965) can all be seen in this light. None succeeded in their missions to set broad economic targets, partly because neither employers nor unions could control their constituencies but also, significantly, because of the attitude of the Treasury. Indeed, the DEA was established precisely to reduce Treasury power but it was disbanded because it never gained any control of policy instruments.

Yet if the Treasury has been criticised for adopting policies which were often inimical to manufacturing industry, this is a criticism of its choice of priorities rather than a failure to deliver them. It is also a criticism easily made in hindsight, since the true cost became evident only in the rather changed international environment of the 1970s. Although symptoms of underlying problems were already apparent and growth was comparatively low, economic performance did not deteriorate significantly in terms of output and productivity growth until after 1973. Furthermore, the pursuit of full employment was reasonably successful, certainly until the mid-1960s. In addition, the balance of payments, which had been in the red on the visible side for decades, was generally held in the black by the value of invisibles. These Treasury targets were met while maintaining military forces consonant with great power aspirations, dismantling an empire, and sustaining one of the highest standards of living in the world. It might be concluded, therefore, that Treasury planning was not so much unsuccessful as wrongly, if understandably, directed.

Social attitudes

The distinguished British economist, Alec Cairncross, himself intimately involved in postwar economic planning, has written that 'growth policy seems to rest on social and political values at least as much as on economic variables' (Cairncross, 1971: 220). The most influential exposition of this sort of view in a British context has been advanced by Professor Wiener. Although his particular hypothesis has been effectively demolished on methodological and historical grounds, this does not automatically exclude explanations of postwar performance couched in terms of social attitudes. In the words of an EC document, Britain was affected by European-wide changes in which the Protestant work ethic was 'substantially eroded by egalitarianism, social compassion, environmentalism, state intervention, and a widespread belief that working hard and making money was anti-social' (Wilkinson, 1990: 215–16). In some ways these were the exact reverse of the values espoused both officially and privately in postwar Japan, where the average citizen's willingness to work hard at the cost of family and free time, became legendary. Professor Morishima attributes this primarily to the long term cultural legacy of Confucian ethics and the Japanese emphasis on harmony and consensus, an explanation not easily reconciled with other evidence suggesting that historically the Japanese were not always as diligent as they later appeared to have become. At the end of the nineteenth century, for example, Osaka shipyard workers were notorious for keeping irregular hours and wishing 'to work and play as they please' (Gordon, 1985: 28). During the Second World War absenteeism in industry was running at 20 per cent even before the air raids intensified and nothing could get workers to do more than eleven or twelve hours a day (Gordon, 1985: 314). It would be dangerous to generalise on the basis of a few isolated examples, but it seems that, whatever the influence of a culturally derived commitment to harmony and group loyalty on Japan's economic miracle, SCAP reforms and the effects of the Second World War had removed some of the earlier obstacles to their successful functioning in the economic sphere.

It has been suggested that this process operated at two levels (Waswo, 1996: 110). Defeat and occupation shattered the long held view that Japan's national spirit (*Yamato Damashi*) would always triumph over material disadvantage. The general response to defeat was shame rather than guilt. At one level, therefore, a commitment to economic growth became a way of redeeming the national pride forfeited through the loss of empire and military failure. At the individual level there was a determination to secure the future as expressed in 1945 by a young naval officer, Nakasone Yasohiro: 'I stood vacantly amid the ruins of Tokyo . . . As I looked around me, I swore to resurrect my homeland from the ashes of defeat' (Horsley and Buckley, 1990: 172). Such responses might be interpreted as reflections of that desire to catch up with the West which had driven Japan ever since the Restoration, but there is no doubt that this ambition was sharpened and given new focus by the experience of defeat. It gave a new dynamic and direction to economic structures and policies inherited in many cases from the past, such as the utilisation of overseas technology, the system of labour management, the role of government in economic planning, and the concept of time as a social rather than a private entity. Accordingly, the Japanese were more open to change than they had previously been, an attitude on which SCAP built. Although some of the politicians originally designated as war criminals ultimately made their way back into influential positions, one effect of SCAP's business purges was to open the way for a new generation of highly motivated entrepreneurs. Similarly, with little wealth available for it to claim in the immediate postwar years, organised labour came to appreciate that its best hopes of improving living standards lay in supporting industrialists' efforts to raise productivity.

In Britain it is probably true that in 1945 most people looked forward and embraced Beveridge's vision of a comprehensive welfare state, to which the Labour Government gave legislative substance. This was in marked contrast to 1918 when promises of a land fit for heroes were rapidly forgotten in the rush to restore the world of 1914. Even in 1945 there was probably less of a consensus for change than has sometimes been suggested (Addison, 1975). There were high level disagreements about the extent and desirability of the proposed reforms, with professional medical interests being particularly resistant to the notion of a state health service. Manufacturing industry remained largely unaffected, while educational reform did not have the radical impact which some of its advocates wished. Overall, victory probably encouraged an underlying view that the present way of doing things was best. Those who shaped postwar policies and determined priorities were also heavily influenced by their experiences of the 1920s and 1930s, while the lack of any fundamental disruption removed the need for any major institutional restructuring whether of government, business, labour, or the professions. The British did not consider it necessary to devote nearly as much of their share of Marshall Aid to industrial redevelopment as did the French and Germans, for instance. At the same time, the exigencies of the economic situation strengthened the position of organised labour and allowed industrialists to indulge in short term profit taking rather than in long term restructuring. In this way the effect of the war was to confirm the short termism which had been endemic in British industry since the nineteenth century, with employers reluctant to exert authority over security-minded employees (Coleman and Macleod, 1986: 588–611). It took both the Germans and the Japanese some ten years to rebuild their industrial infrastructures after the war. Starting from a much more favourable position in 1945 Britain could have done the same much more quickly. The real cost of the failure to do so did not emerge, however, until the 1970s.

The system of reproduction

Occupations

As table 5.5 indicates, the significance of agricultural labour continued to diminish in postwar Britain, reflecting both a continued dependence on imports and the growth of productivity achieved through greater capital inputs and substantial state subsidies. Industrial employment also declined, albeit modestly before 1970, with a corresponding expansion of services, mainly distribution, finance, and government. At first sight these trends appear to lend some support to the hypothesis of de-industrialisation, but the underlying pattern was in fact replicated in every advanced industrial country, including Japan, where there was also a dramatic expansion in tertiary employment, particularly from the late 1960s. This reflected rising expenditure on education and leisure, as well as the growing corporate demand for information technology, finance, and insurance. By 1970 the proportion of tertiary sector workers was only slightly smaller than in Britain. At the same time industrial employment also increased by about two thirds as labour was released from both agriculture and mining. In 1950 about half of those leaving middle and high schools went to work on the land. By 1960 the proportion was only 10 per cent and five years later it had halved again. This was facilitated by increased mechanisation, while the small size of the average Japanese farm allowed much of the work to be undertaken by retired people. Heavy government support maintained the viability of small scale farming but by 1970 only 15 per cent of farm households were full time.

Table 5.5 *Britain and Japan: occupational structure, 1950–70 (% of total workforce)*

	1950			1970	
	UK	Japan		UK	Japan
Agriculture	4.9	48.3		3.2	17.4
Industry	49.4	21.9		44.8	35.1
Services	45.7	29.8		52.0	47.5

(JISEA 1995: 20)

Demography

In both countries changing occupational patterns were accompanied by general increases in the total number of inhabitants. By 1971 the United Kingdom was home to 55.5 million, significantly fewer now than the 100 million or so in Japan. Britain received substantial influxes of foreigners in the postwar years, the customary flow of Irish, displaced Europeans, and then West Indians, Indians, and Africans from the Commonwealth. Their arrival was generally offset in aggregate terms by significant emigration. Only in 1951 and again between 1959 and 1963 was there a net in-migration. The major cause of rising population, therefore, was the excess of births over deaths. In the 1930s birth rates had been lower than replacement levels but, in common with most of Europe, they picked up immediately after the war ended. Apart from a sharp decline between 1947 and 1952 the

upward trend continued, owing something to the falling age of first marriage, and to the sense of security created by full employment and state financial help in the form of the Family Allowance scheme payable from 1946. Yet
the typical British family got smaller as more married women were drawn
into the labour market. This was due less to wider awareness and use of
improved contraceptive techniques than to changing choices about the desirable size of a family.

In Japan fertility had begun to decline in the interwar period, although the
inevitable postwar baby boom saw the largest ever recorded increases –
about 2.7 million births each year between 1947 and 1949. Even so, wartime
population losses were so heavy that in 1950 there were 2.3 million fewer
men and 534, 000 fewer women than projections based on the 1940 population figures anticipated. Both the removal of the ban on contraceptives in
1949 and amendments to the law allowing abortion only for economic reasons influenced the subsequent dramatic decline in the birth rate. At a stable
but low level, the birth rate was sufficient to expand the population at
slightly more than 1 per cent a year. It is also possible that the formal abolition of the *ie* had some impact on the traditional Japanese view of children as
an investment against old age. This should not be pushed too far, however,
since traditions do not wither immediately at the behest of legislators and
respect for age and seniority remained powerful sentiments. A more important influence on decisions about family size probably emanated from
changing settlement patterns. The disproportionately high migration of individuals in the child-bearing age groups from the countryside to the cities
ensured that the rural birth rate fell. Although the majority of Japanese still
lived in the countryside in 1950, the situation was reversed by 1970. The
number of cities more than doubled while the proportion of people living in
them grew to more than 70 per cent. Increased urbanisation in the densely
packed eastern seaboard meant space was at a premium and housing accordingly expensive. Coupled with the long term demands made on the parental
purse by the costs of education, this was sufficient to ensure that two children became the norm in the typical city family.

Falling family size played a part in reducing the relative important of
young people. In Britain the proportion of people under fourteen rose very
slightly, from 22 per cent of the population in 1951 to 23.7 per cent in 1971,
but this was still well down on the 32 per cent of 1901. In Japan too, there
was a similarly significant drop in the proportion of inhabitants under the
age of fourteen, although over a shorter time span. The figure dropped from
35.4 per cent in 1950 to 23.9 per cent in 1970 (Waswo, 1996: 133).

In both countries this was accompanied by increased adolescent independence and assertiveness. Although local studies have identified the emergence of a youth culture in prewar Britain, postwar youth had greater
purchasing power (Fowler, 1995). In real terms teenage earnings were 50 per
cent above their prewar level, the outcome of labour shortages and the full

employment policy (Abercrombie and Warde, 1988: 424). With the ending of postwar controls advertising began to play on adolescent fears. Foundation garments for twelve year olds appeared, as did special films geared to teenage interests. Among the major beneficiaries were the fashion and popular music industries, as transistor radios, record players, and distinctive clothing became the icons of the newly affluent young adults. The definition of the teenage years became ever more elastic but one casualty was childhood, which was relentlessly narrowed down. Boy scouts were balloted on whether to replace their traditional shorts with long trousers, BBC radio ended the long running 'Children's Hour' programme, and according to one 1959 survey, the bulk of girls expected to be in a steady relationship by the time they were fifteen.

In the 1950s at least, such manifestations of teenage independence were very rare in Japan but one harbinger, albeit as yet fairly restrained, lay in attitudes to marriage. The tradition of the arranged marriage had been pretty universal in the Meiji period and remained so through the Taisho and early Showa years. Research published in 1958 showed that the majority of Japanese still believed that parents should be consulted in the choice of partners while go-betweens were still widely deployed. It was clear, too, that despite changes in the family since 1945, its traditional function of nurturing the young and maintaining the old remained strongly entrenched (Chiye, 1962). Nevertheless, the principle of marriage between mutually consenting individuals was written into the new 1947 constitution and nuptial relationships based on the notion of romantic love did become marginally more popular as Western influence spread during and after the Occupation.

The other end of the demographic spectrum was occupied by an increasing proportion of older people. In 1951 11 per cent of the population of England and Wales was over sixty five. Twenty years later this had risen to 13.3, the result of better standards of living, medical breakthroughs in the form of new drugs, and the more systematic provision of health care through the welfare state. Such influences reduced the level of infant mortality and raised life expectancy. The outcome was an increase in the dependency ratio, fewer workers now having to support more dependants. This placed a burden on tax-payers and on the health and social services as the demand grew for home helps, meals on wheels, and hospital geriatric units. Such pressures were probably intensified by some relative weakening of family ties.

Japan's demographic contours were assuming similar shape. The 5 per cent of the population over sixty five in 1950 grew to 8 per cent by 1975. On the other hand, its implications were as yet less marked than in Britain. The formal abolition of the *ie* as a legal entity did not immediately serve to weaken the traditional importance of the family in Japanese society. This, and the general veneration for age, ensured that the rising numbers of old people in Japan were supported in the main by their own kin. Something like a third of retired Japanese lived with their children and in 1963 there were only 690 institutions for the elderly in the whole country (Bethel, 1992: 127).

Women

The strength of the family as a social unit in postwar Japan was both a product and a symptom of the survival of the powerful ideology of domesticity. Although Japanese women feared, not without some justification, sexual abuse by the occupying forces, 20,000 of them had married American servicemen by 1955, and such liaisons did provide public displays of deference to women that were very unJapanese. Part of the social reform programme initiated by SCAP was designed to promote women's position.

> With regard to choice of spouse, property rights, inheritance, choice of domicile, divorce and other matters pertaining to marriage and the family, laws shall be enacted from the stand-point of individual dignity and the essential equality of the sexes. (Hendry, 1987: 27)

The abolition of the *ie* ended the institutional and legal supremacy of male household heads. It was also intended to elevate the status of women and there were some indications that they responded positively to their new circumstances. There was an increase in the number of divorces initiated by women, for example. In the 1950s new women's pressure groups appeared and legislation controlling licensed prostitution was passed in 1956. By 1949 51 per cent of employed women were in trade unions. More than two thirds of females voted in the general election of 1946 and by 1968 more women than men habitually turned out to vote in elections.

But the *ie* and the concepts that went with it had been fundamental to Japan's social organisation for centuries and their legacy could not be dispelled overnight. Historically, the domestic role of the woman in Japan was derived from the structure of the senior warrior families in the Tokugawa period. Even if this ideal had become somewhat diluted by the advent of factory women after the Meiji Restoration, its hold on Japanese society was immensely strong. Despite their exercise of the vote, postwar women's political organisations remained feeble and few of their number reached the top levels of political life. The women's movement, such as it was, remained divided and weak, certainly when compared with the Japan Mothers' Convention (1955) and the Housewives' Federation (1958) which mobilised women as consumers far more effectively than they ever were for direct political purposes. Once wartime pressures were removed, they resumed their subordinate position in the labour market where the establishment of the Women's and Minor's Bureau of the Ministry of Labour in 1947 changed little. In the first postwar decade jobs were relatively scarce and priority was given to men. Even when the economic miracle raised the demand for labour, the pattern of female employment was still influenced by the strength of the domestic ideology. Participation in the workforce conformed to the classic 'M' shape, high among women aged between fifteen and the middle twenties, then declining as marriage and child rearing took over. A second, though lower peak occurred among those re-entering the labour market in their mid-thirties. At all levels, however, their wages were generally significantly lower than those of men.

The high status of the housewife, who lacked the downtrodden image increasingly fostered in the West, was reinforced by the education system. Junior school girls studied cooking and sewing and in the 1960s home economics was made mandatory for girls in senior high schools. Higher education was little different, with female graduates actually less likely to enter the labour market than nongraduates – only 6 per cent of women entering the job market in 1965 were graduates. Tertiary education was widely seen as a means of acquiring a highly educated and thus a well paid husband. Indeed, the high demands made on the successful salaryman by his employer rested on the assumption that his wife would devote herself full-time to running the domestic side of his life. More generally, the Japanese did not interpret sexual equality as implying equal rights on Western lines. As one Japanese scholar pointed out in 1967, the traditional notion of the individual in Japan involved a variety of social obligations but had no place for any concept of rights (Hendry, 1987: 206). Thus gender equality for the Japanese meant that each sex should be equal in its ability to fulfil its respective family role.

Like the Japanese, British women found their economic significance much increased by the shortage of labour during and after the war, although most of those who joined the labour force had been in it previously. By 1951 some 6.5 million females were working, a figure that continued to rise thereafter. Even more significant was the growth in the number of part timers from a base of 779,000 in 1951 well into the millions by the start of the 1970s. Women made up 34.6 per cent of the British workforce by 1971, operating over a wider range of jobs than ever before. Paradoxically, this coincided with a rise in the proportion of women marrying and a fall in the age of first marriage, both of which might have been expected to reduce their participation in the labour market.

The explanation lay in the fact that lower ages of marriage combined with longer life expectancy and smaller family size to give women potentially longer working lives. In the late nineteenth century about a third of the average woman's life span was taken up in child bearing and nursing; by the mid-twentieth century the proportion was only about 5 per cent. New domestic labour saving technology worked in the same direction, while among those for whom work was not an absolute economic necessity, the spread of consumerism provided an alternative incentive. So, eventually, did the 1970 Equal Pay Act, the principle of which had been broadly agreed since 1946. It was rushed through by a Labour Government under pressure from women's organisations and a more general concern about the waste of resources implied by the failure to offer women equal rewards for work. But old habits died hard. Average pay for women remained well below that for men while women also remained under-represented in some occupations, particularly the professions. Nor did they make much more political progress than the Japanese, despite their rather earlier start. The first female life peer was not created until 1958 and between 1945 and 1970 there were never more than two dozen women MPs in the House of Commons. Thus although there were differences between social classes and it may have been more openly resented by women themselves, the domestic ideology remained quite strong in Britain as well, despite the sometimes rancorous denials of female emancipationists.

Standards of living

Aggregate living standards rose to unprecedented heights during the long postwar boom. During the war material deprivation in Japan was far worse than anything experienced in Britain, although popular expectations were certainly more modest, conditioned as they were by lower prewar living standards. Calorific intakes fell to dangerously low levels in the last months of the war and the results were recalled later by the wife of a diplomat:

> We had no energy beyond that needed to prepare our rice and keep our house and ourselves clean. My fingernails were almost gone, and I had to bandage my fingers to keep blood from getting on everything I touched . . . all our spare time was taken up in searching for food, or for people who had food to sell. (Livingston, Moore and Oldfather, 1976: I, 471)

Nor was much expected of the American occupiers, especially as there existed a widespread view among the victors that the Japanese should not be permitted living standards higher than those of the nations Japan had invaded during the war. In fact, American policy turned out to be far more humane than anticipated. Japan received higher priority in relief funding for food and medical aid than most of the countries it had occupied. Mass immunisation programmes were initiated as a precaution against disease and almost half the population was protected against tuberculosis. Average life expectancy rose from forty seven in 1946 to sixty three by the time the American occupation ended. Although rural amenities were often still fairly rudimentary most of the shattered cities had been rebuilt by this time too. One civilian returning to Tokyo in the mid-1950s marvelled at the progress. 'What rapid reconstruction and what prosperity! . . . The city seems indeed a new creation' (Maraini, 1960: 38).

In the short term, however, the situation was desperate. The annual inflation rate reached 365 per cent in 1945 and city dwellers poured into the countryside, desperately bartering goods for food. Scavenging in US army garbage dumps became routine while black market commerce became so ubiquitous that the death from malnutrition of a prominent Tokyo judge in 1947 was allegedly caused by his principled refusal to buy anything through it. Various attempts to reduce the annual inflation rate were moderately successful but it was still running at 165 per cent in 1948. It was at this point that American policy changed in the light of the developing Cold War. Along with the financial measures effected by Joseph Dodge, the Korean War finally dealt with inflation and put the economy back on a firm footing.

From the early 1950s there were significant, widespread, and sustained improvements in average living standards, although direct state welfare and public amenity provision remained well behind British standards. Average real wages in manufacturing went up 400 per cent between 1950 and 1975. At constant prices personal consumption expenditure rose from Y6,305 billion in 1952 to Y13,792 billion in 1962 and Y23,944 billion in 1971 (Ohkawa and Shinohara, 1979: 262). In per capita terms such expenditure more than doubled between 1960 and 1970. One important measure of improvement was changing dietary patterns. Per capita consumption of rice fell and by the early 1970s it accounted for less than a third of agricultural output. There was a compensatory increase in the output of market garden and animal products (table 5.6). Between 1950 and 1980 whisky consumption went up 5,500 per cent with the greatest increases occurring in the 1960s. *Sake* drinking rose more or less continuously until 1975 (Smith, 1992: 147).

Table 5.6 *Numbers of livestock in Japan (000)*

	1960	1970
Milch cows	824	1,804
Beef cattle	2,340	1,787
Pigs	1,918	6,335
Hens	52,153	223,532

(Allen, 1981b: 80)

A second mark of prosperity was provided by the falling share of household expenditure devoted to food, down from 37 per cent in 1966 to 33 per cent by 1974. Along with this went improvements in domestic living arrangements. Modest though they were by Western standards, the mass housing estates which appeared in the cities represented significant advances on what had gone before. Displayed inside these new residences was an ever widening range of consumer goods. Fridges and vacuum cleaners were still comparatively rare but by 1957 washing machines, the production of which had risen eight fold between 1953 and 1956, were common. In 1954 only 1 per cent of households owned a television but the proportion was up to 50 per cent by 1960. Four years later, 90 per cent owned a tv and more than half had fridges and washing machines. In the countryside, inflation had rapidly wiped out most of the debts farmers had run up in acquiring land as part of the postwar land settlement. Thereafter rising domestic demand, coupled with extensive government subsidisation and protection against imported foodstuffs, ensured that most rural inhabitants enjoyed rising standards of living. This was particularly so for the 85 per cent or so of farmers who by 1970 were essentially part timers. The condition of the other 15 per cent of full timers was more variable, however, only about half of them running economically viable farms. The others, often elderly couples, were struggling to keep up, exceptions to the general prosperity.

Poverty is always a difficult concept to discuss in a Japanese context, partly because of its unique social connotations and partly because it received little official publicity. That it existed cannot be disputed but it appears to have declined both relatively and absolutely. Applying Maeda's 1930s classification of social structure to the definition of poverty used by the Welfare Ministry, i.e. the guaranteed minimum level of living figure, suggests that the proportion of the population in poverty fell by more than 50 per cent between 1930 and 1968 (table 5.7).

Table 5.7 *Maeda's social structure of Japan (%)*

	1930	1968
Superior	10.6	4.6
Intermediate	24.6	43.6
Inferior	47.1	43.1
Poor	17.7	8.7

(Chubachi and Taira, 1976: 431)

The impact of the economic miracle on living standards emerged even more emphatically from an official survey which described 15.6 per cent of Japan's households as poor in 1960 but only 6.3 per cent in 1967, prompting the conclusion that the country was on the way to the 'dissolution of poverty' (Smith, 1992: 147). This owed relatively little to the redistributive effects of state welfare. Until the late 1950s the only help available for the poorest segment of the population was Public Assistance (Livelihood Protection) enacted in laws of 1946 and 1950 and half of total state welfare expenditure went on it. Yet the rate of economic growth was so high that relatively few people qualified for it. In 1965 social security benefits provided only 1.2 per cent of all household income in Japan, although less well off families, those earning under Y200,000 a year, derived 12.8 per cent of their income from this source (Ono and Watanabe, 1976: 376).

A similar pattern of improvement was apparent in Britain although the ending of the war did not bring about any overnight transformation. One contemporary later recalled that

> we still bathed in water that wouldn't come over your knees unless you flattened them; we still wore clothes with the ugly 'Utility' half moons on the label. Chewing carrots for sweets . . . we wondered at stories of chocolate cigars and real pineapple that didn't come out of tins. (Cooper, 1964: 35)

Fear of a repetition of the price increases of 1918–20 was strong, given the inflationary potential of pent-up consumer demand, accumulated wartime savings supplemented by demobilisation allowances, and widespread material shortages. In 1946, the sheer magnitude of economic reconversion combined with world food shortages to compel the government to ration bread, a step which had been avoided during the war itself. A particularly virulent winter in 1947 left a snow-blanketed nation shivering with inadequate coal supplies before flooding 600,000 acres of arable land and taking a dreadful toll of farm livestock, thus further adding to the general sense of frustration that victory appeared to have brought few tangible rewards. Potatoes were rationed at the end of the year and by 1948 general ration allowances were lower than they had been during the war itself: even supplies of dried egg ran out. Alcohol and cigarettes became prime targets for criminals while spivs appeared in every town hawking scarce goods. In the main, however, they were never able to take advantage of commodity shortages to the same extent as their equivalents in other countries, and Britain was spared the emergence of any serious black market (Smithies, 1984: 85–110). On the other hand, wage rates did not keep pace with the rising cost of living and real incomes were maintained mainly by overtime payments and the upgrading of workers. Gradually, however, supplies and outputs improved and as sufficient stocks were built up, so controls were gradually relaxed. Bread came off ration in 1948, petrol, clothing, furniture, and soap by 1950. By 1954 only 11 per cent of consumer expenditure in Britain was still subject to direct controls.

By this time, too, the benefits of the welfare state were becoming evident, although the system was not as radical as has sometimes been claimed. Britain already possessed quite an advanced range of welfare services, not all of Beveridge's proposals for eliminating the giants of want, disease, squalor, idleness, and ignorance were implemented, while his fundamental purpose was not the redistribution of wealth but the state supplementation of private provision against the major causes of deprivation. The attack on squalor was initially hampered by shortages of material and labour which restricted the progress of the building programme. By 1951 there remained a crude shortfall of 729,000 houses although this was largely remedied by the construction of seven million new ones between 1953 and 1972. Their quality was also much improved. The General Household Survey of 1972 showed that 88 per cent had bathrooms as against 62 per cent in 1951, 96 per cent had toilets (80 per cent), and 34 per cent central heating. Ignorance was tackled through the Butler Education Act of 1944 which raised the school leaving age, ended fee paying, and created a three tiered system of secondary schooling. As for want, family allowances were paid from 1946, while by 1949 a million individuals were receiving national assistance. The lynch pin of the system was the National Health Service established in 1948.

From the 1950s the aggregate statistical indicators of living standards all moved in the same direction. By 1972 the annual death rate was almost three times lower than it had been fifty years earlier and diseases of affluence began to replace those of deprivation as the major killers in Britain. Infant mortality declined to the extent that a boy born at the beginning of the 1970s had a life expectancy of 69.6 years as against 44.1 in the 1890s. Based on 1970 as 100, the average weekly earnings index rose steadily from 65.3 in 1950 to 83.8 by 1960. Though it fell back somewhat after the mid-1960s, real domestic per capita income rose at about 2.0 per cent a year throughout this period. Patterns of consumer spending changed accordingly. The share of expenditure allocated to food fell (table 5.8) and within it there was considerable substitution of superior for inferior foodstuffs. Most notably, the per capita consumption of meat, eggs, butter, vegetables, and fruit all increased, matched by declining intakes of margarine, potatoes, and wheat products. Translated into current money values, the rising proportion of expenditure on cars, reflected in the final figure in table 5.8, meant an increase from £90.0 million in 1950 to £910 million in 1964. In 1950 there was a car for every twenty one people in Britain: by 1979 one for every 4.7. The number of owner occupiers doubled between 1951 and 1972 and in all homes, consumer durables accumulated steadily. By 1964 90 per cent – the same proportion as in Japan – had tv as against a mere 0.2 per cent in 1947. Another indicator of improvement, not apparent in table 5.8, was the huge increase in spending on leisure activity. Britons spent £380 million on holidays in 1951 but £1,448 million in 1971, with the number of passports issued more than doubling between 1951 and 1966 (Benson, 1995: 86).

Table 5.8 *Distribution of British consumer expenditure (% shares based on current prices)*

	1950	1965
Food	29.1	26.0
Housing and maintenance	8.6	11.1
Household goods	5.0	4.1
Radio: electrical	1.9	2.4
Motor and fuel	1.9	7.6

(Pollard, 1992: 276)

Not everyone shared to the same degree in this consumption bonanza, for relative poverty still survived even if the official standard of poverty – an income below the level of National Assistance of £8.52 a week – implied that in 1966 only 2.6 million people (5 per cent of the population) were poor. However, since this represented what government was prepared to pay rather than a measure of what people were actually thought to need, it was widely argued that the National Assistance measure was too low. In this context it is worth noting that in 1971 4.7 million people (about 9.4 per cent of the population) were receiving supplementary benefit.

Class

In 1963 a Ministry of Labour survey suggested that British consumption patterns varied not according to class but according to family size and composition. Certainly it was now difficult to distinguish the social classes by their dress as was possible at the turn of the century. Recreational activities also appeared to be transcending traditional class barriers, particularly among the postwar generation, as Harry Hopkins described in 1963.

> While 'Dad' might persist in the old firmly working class pursuits like pigeon racing, darts or the dogs, or in things rooted in regional cultures, like the cultivation of pot-leeks on the Tyne or hound-trailing in the north-west, his children grew up into leisure occupations that were classless, international, and embraced the whole proliferating mid-century world of the hobbyists . . . people were brought together by dedication to chrysanthemum-growing or weight-lifting or bag-piping, in which class was transcended by common possession of the deeper secrets of judo, the spirit of folk-dancing or the Greater Truth of Hi-Fi. (Hopkins, 1963: 431)

Radio and television, the latter accounting for almost a quarter of all leisure activity in the 1960s, were equally important in this process. The apparent decline in the class basis of postwar politics, seen in falling popular support for the Labour Party, three Conservative election victories in the 1950s, and the emergence of the Butskellite consensus, also appeared to point in the same direction.

So, too, did widening educational opportunity. In 1921, 66 per cent of 12–14 year olds were at school but only 3.2 per cent of the 16–18 year olds. By 1968 the respective proportions were 100 and 30 per cent. It could also be observed that by 1971 the occupational structure was more balanced and differentiated than in 1900. It now comprised of three comparably sized blocks, each containing between a fifth and a quarter of the total workforce – the semi-skilled manual, the skilled manual, and clerical and sales workers. These three central blocks were flanked beneath by the unskilled, and above by professional, technical, administrative, managerial, and supervisory workers. So pervasive were these trends towards social reorganisation that they were interpreted by some sociologists as heralding the decline of traditional class distinctions and, more particularly, the transformation of the working class into part of the middle class through a process of embourgeoisement.

Some have argued that this was the logical outcome of the blurring of class barriers which had occurred during the Second World War. Certainly neither bombs nor bullets were socially discriminating in their effects, inner city evacuees provided many a comfortable middle-class family with a first and shocking exposure to the realities of urban working-class existence, and Churchill's inspirational leadership provided a sense of national purpose and unity. Similarly, the construction of the welfare state appeared to vindicate the theory of the Military Participation Ratio (MPR) – that the greater the degree of popular participation in a war, the greater the degree of equality, particularly in welfare provision, that will be conceded afterwards (Andreski, 1954). On the other hand, wage differentials between the working and middle classes did not change much during the war and most Britons asked in 1948 about their social position unhesitatingly assigned themselves to one or other of the traditional classes, prompting one authority to conclude that the war certainly did not abolish class (Marwick, 1982: 48). Nor did the social legislation of the Labour Government, for the evidence is that it was the middle rather than the working classes who derived most benefit from it. Widening educational opportunity had some limited impact on social mobility in the postwar period, but the majority of sons, of whatever class, continued to find work in the same occupational category as their fathers.

The embourgeoisement hypothesis can be criticised under four broad headings. First it ignored gender. In the 1970s three fifths of men were still classified as manual workers, three fifths of women as non-manual. In so far as class had historically been determined by the occupation of the male head of the family, this suggests that there had been little significant change. Second, it was by no means certain that, with the exception of food and drink, consumption patterns were converging. The professional and managerial classes devoted far more time and money to leisure, for example (Young and Wilmott, 1973: 212–26). More important, perhaps, by treating people only as consumers, the thesis ignored the very obvious differences which existed between the conditions under which individuals earned their ability to consume. If the incomes of manual and salaried workers were converging, the former earned theirs for longer hours of usually more physically demanding work. There also remained marked differences between white and blue collar workers in terms of job security, fringe benefits, long term prospects, and even work clothing. Class gradations were still institutionalised in the work place, with segregated catering or car parking facilities. As Professor Perkin has observed:

Managers and workers come from opposite sides of the tracks, from different social backgrounds and educational experiences, speak with different accents, have different expectations . . . and feel themselves locked into different slots in the social framework. (Perkin, 1989: 514)

Third, embourgeoisement theory ignored issues of what might be called social acceptance. With the possible exception of the young, it was not clear how far individuals from different classes accepted each other as equals in either informal or formal situations. House ownership and higher education remained more typical of the middle classes, even though workers' aspirations were starting to change. A 1962 survey indicated that 82 per cent of manual workers wanted their children to go into higher education compared with 88 per cent of middle-class parents (Sanderson, 1994: 383). In practice, however, the proportion of students from the manual working class entering universities in the early 1960s was still only 3.1 per cent. Far from becoming a vehicle of embourgeoisement, the educational system created under the Butler Act actually appears to have worked in the opposite direction. Only a fifth of all children went to grammar schools and a twentieth to technical schools. Even by the 1950s very few working-class children got to grammar schools which were in any case very unevenly distributed through the country. The Labour Party's shift to a comprehensive system from 1964, an idea which had been mooted since the 1938 Spens report, came too late to have much impact on the putative process of embourgeoisement.

Finally, the persistence of significant inequalities in the distribution of wealth and income hardly supported the idea of socio-economic convergence. Thus it has been remarked that 'disparities . . . certainly did not narrow significantly, from the early 1950s to the early 1970s under governments of either political shade' (Westergaard and Resler, 1975: 118). Such shifts of wealth as did occur in the 1960s took place mainly amongst the top wealth owners and its overall distribution remained uneven, albeit around a rising average (table 5.9). However, such calculations are fraught with statistical and technical problems. A slightly different picture emerges from a longer perspective, although again the redistribution remained fundamentally skewed (table 5.10). Income inequalities also remained higher than might be thought consistent with a process of embourgeoisement, though they became less marked, in part due to welfare legislation. In the 1950s welfare expenditure accounted for 16 per cent of the GDP, a proportion which rose

Table 5.9 *Great Britain: distribution of personal wealth, 1960–70 (%)*

Wealth-holders	1960	1970
Top 1 per cent	28.4	20.7
Top 10 per cent	63.1	51.9
Bottom 80 per cent	23.8	33.6

(Halsey, 1978: 38)

to 26 per cent by the mid-1970s. The redistributive effects of this expenditure, coupled with the direct taxation system, are difficult to calculate but 4.7 million people were receiving Supplementary Benefit alone in 1971. Across a range of incomes the general effect was to benefit families and pensioners at the expense of the single and childless. More particularly, those at the very bottom benefited significantly. In 1974 welfare and tax provision almost tripled the money available to the lowest decile of income earners from £4.67 a week to £13.31.

Table 5.10 *Great Britain: distribution of personal wealth, 1950–76 (%)*

Wealth-holders	1950	1976
Top 1 per cent	47.2	21.0
Top 10 per cent	74.3	50.0
Top 25 per cent		71.0

(Lowe, 1994: 368; Halsey, 1978: 38)

For a variety of reasons then, embourgeoisement seems to be an inappropriate description of British society before the 1970s. The idea was attacked by a succession of economists and sociologists who did not accept that class distinctions had been eradicated merely by the spread of consumerism. In some ways the hypothesis appeared more applicable to contemporary Japanese experience, although matters are complicated by the preeminence of vertical social relationships. Largely irrespective of income, the ethos of the group, of insider and outsider, was still the dominant social construct, securing the primary loyalty of, and giving identity to, its individual members. It was evident everywhere – in patterns of leisure activity, in the cooperative activities of farmers, in the business federations such as Japan Chamber of Commerce for Small Businesses and the *Keidanren*, and in the conscious attempts made by universities to recruit staff from among their own graduates. Similarly, status was a function of age or ability, rather than merely of income, heredity, or wealth.

This said, all the evidence suggests that Japan was well on the way to becoming one of the most middle-class societies in the world, at least – and this is an important caveat – in the eyes of its own people and their aspirations. Public opinion surveys carried out by the Prime Minister's office in 1959 and again in 1969 produced the self assessment of status outlined in table 5.11. Nearly 90 per cent of Japanese believed themselves to be middle class or, to use the older terminology, *churyu*, mid-stream. By this, however, they tended to mean not so much actual membership of any objective middle class as enjoyment of its life style, an aspiration encouraged by fifteen years of continually rising incomes. It is also significant that polls taken in Tokyo in 1961 revealed no expectation on the part of respondents that they would move down the social scale – all expected to advance at least one step upwards. In the early 1970s the extent of mobility from manual to non-manual occupations between the generations in Japan was very similar to that of Britain, around 30 per cent. Britain had a considerably higher rate of descent from the non-manual to manual category, however, 36 per cent as against 28 per cent in Japan (Morishima, 1982: 182). Nor was Japan marked by many of the other surviving badges of class still so apparent in Britain. In the work situation, distinctions between white and blue collar workers were minimal. Fringe benefits tended to vary according to the size of the firm, rather than between different groups of workers within an individual company. Although ethnological and other studies have revealed the existence of significant subgroups defined by taste and consumption within the middle class, it is generally true that in cultural terms Japan was more homogeneous than Britain. In part this was a function of an education system far less divisive, both socially and educationally, than that introduced in Britain by the 1944 legislation. Central monitoring of the curriculum ensured that every child studied the same things on the same day. High culture was correspondingly pervasive in Japan, not confined to small elite, while mass culture was correspondingly refined, despite a marked popular penchant for violence and sex. TV provided a uniform diet of programmes, in the process ironing out some of the contrasts between rural and urban areas which had been common in prewar Japan.

Table 5.11 *Japanese social structure (%)*

	1959	1969
Upper	0	1
Upper mainstream	3	7
Middle mainstream	37	52
Lower mainstream	32	30
No differentiation	17	8
Unclear	11	3

(Chubachi and Taira, 1976: 432)

Perhaps the most obvious symptom of embourgeoisement in Japan was a significant *narrowing* of income differentials and the consequent reduction of poverty. The emphasis is required because this should not be taken to imply the total absence of great individual wealth, of relative poverty, or of any income differentials at all. As far as the first is concerned, war and the SCAP reforms between them effectively eliminated some of the top echelons of wealth, while the progressive tax system and high inheritance tax made it more difficult thereafter to accumulate and transmit wealth. Similarly, Japan's small, relatively uniform geography meant that were no significantly underprivileged regional groups and such localised pockets of relative back-wardness as did survive were generally addressed by the various economic plans produced in these years. The outcome was that one of the greatest pre-war income differentials, that between agricultural and non-agricultural households, was considerably reduced, although a small proportion of farm-ers failed to keep up. So, too, did the *burakamin*, although Japan lacked any sizeable immigrant group of the sort so often disproportionately represented among the poor in the West. Even the Koreans, for all the civil discrimination against them, were economically quite successful.

Given the greater variety of occupations and the operation of the seniority wage system, it was not surprising that income inequalities were greater in urban than in agricultural areas. The persistence of the dual economy worked in the same direction. Only the existence of large numbers of work-ers, often female, who could be laid off at will and provided with minimal fringe benefits, enabled the large employers to sustain the characteristic Japanese employment system for the privileged. One scholar has suggested that wage differentials between large and small scale enterprises were larger in 1960 than they had been at the beginning of the century (Yasuba, 1976: 252). All these caveats notwithstanding, income inequality in Japan nar-rowed quite rapidly, especially after 1960, and its spread was lower than in almost every other industrial country in the world.

6

Realignments:
production and reproduction,
1971–1995

Introduction

Explanations of Japan's rapid growth in the 1950s and 1960s must not overlook the generally prosperous international economic climate, for it was as favourable as it had been in the early period of industrialisation (Nakamura, 1994). Heavily dependent upon foreign trade, Japan derived enormous benefit from the stability of the dollar–yen exchange rate which, taking no account of relative price movements, remained fixed until 1971 at the 1949 level of $1:Y360. Japan was thus well placed to benefit from the liberalisation of world trade after 1945, not least in the freedom with which foreign technology could be imported. Initially, the legacy of anti-Japanese feeling engendered by the war was slow to dissipate. When American pressure secured Japanese entry to the General Agreement on Tariffs and Trade (GATT) in 1955, several countries refused to grant Japan most favoured nation status and imposed restrictions on imports. However, from the mid-1960s, after Japan was admitted to the Organization for Economic Co-operation and Development (OECD), official attitudes moderated and became more open. With world trade expanding steadily, other nations did not quickly perceive any serious threat to their own economies.

Favourable terms of trade enabled Britain also to benefit from growing international commerce, although as former colonial territories gained their independence, so the pattern of trade gradually began to shift. Efforts to negotiate entry to the Common Market were rebuffed until 1973 but Britain played a leading role in establishing the European Free Trade Area in 1957. Accordingly, the proportion of exports going to the Continent rose from 27 to 37 per cent between 1958 and 1969, mainly at the expense of the older imperial markets whose share declined over the same period from 42 to 29 per cent (Williams, 1971: 175). Absolute volumes of exports continued to increase, while their value went up by more than a third between 1960 and

1967 alone. This, however, largely masked underlying weaknesses, the most serious of which was the declining international competitiveness of the manufacturing sector.

At the beginning of the 1970s the long postwar boom collapsed under the weight of two events. In August 1971 the strains of the Vietnam War and internal problems in the American economy led President Nixon to suspend dollar convertibility. This effectively terminated the 1944 Bretton Woods agreement which had underpinned international monetary stability by fixing the convertibility rate between the dollar and gold. Two years later war broke out in the Middle East between Israel and her Arab neighbours. In an attempt to weaken Western support for Israel the Organisation of Petroleum Exporting Countries (OPEC) increased the price of crude oil by two thirds and reduced exports. The result was a massive and sudden increase in the costs of manufacturing and transport throughout the world.

For Japan, the readjustments necessitated by these events were further complicated by growing domestic concern about the high social costs of the economic miracle. But if growth rates after 1971 were much lower than in the previous two decades they continued to be outstanding in international terms, and at the end of the 1980s Japan replaced America as the world's largest creditor nation, the position held a century earlier by Great Britain. By 1978 Japanese firms occupied the top six places in an international league table based on annual company turnovers. The top wholly-owned British company was ICI in twenty first place (Nakase, 1981: 86). Japan, conceded *The Times* in 1980, had now become 'the world's leading industrialised nation', on the way overtaking Britain in terms of per capita GNP (*The Times*, 21 July 1980). This appeared as yet another symptom of the economic and social malaise which beset Britain in the course of the 1970s. Rampant inflation, industrial unrest, declining growth rates, and an accumulating balance of payments deficit all contributed to the abandonment of Keynesian demand management and fuelled a debate about national decline. So, too, in a different way, did entry to the Common Market in 1973. Long term visions of European unity appeared to threaten national autonomy, although that was probably inevitable anyway, given the emergence of a genuinely world economy in the last quarter of the twentieth century. In tone the plethora of influential writing on the theme of national decline was reminiscent of that being published a century earlier. The general message was aptly summed up in the view that 'things in some very real sense are going badly in Britain and need to be changed' (Coates and Hillard, 1986: x). However, diagnosis was easier than remedy. After the ignominious Winter of Discontent in 1979, a new Conservative Government came to power, intent on reversing what it saw as the incoming tide of national decay.

The system of production

The troubled 1970s: Japan

The American decision to suspend dollar convertibility in 1971 was accompanied by the imposition of a 10 per cent import surcharge. By this time the American market absorbed 31.0 per cent of Japan's exports (it had taken 27 per cent in 1960) and it was only to be expected that the Japanese should wish the yen to retain its prevailing value against the American currency. Reluctantly, however, they were persuaded in December 1971 to readjust the rate to $1:Y308. As the yen continued to appreciate, the Japanese government tried to cushion the domestic economy by pumping money into it. This strengthened the inflationary tendency apparent since the mid-1960s when the policy of balanced budgets was abandoned. Attempts to cover deficits by issuing bonds added a further inflationary impetus because they competed with private industry for savings. Tanaka Kakuei's 1972 blueprint for remodelling the economy also turned out to be inflationary. *Building a New Japan* was designed to encourage industrial diversification by linking every part of the country through a system of bullet train lines, national highways, bridges, and tunnels. At the same time, the growing national wealth was to be redistributed through a modernisation of the welfare system, while simultaneously addressing the now serious problems of pollution. However, speculative attempts to anticipate the effects of these radical proposals, especially on land prices, merely added to inflation which in 1973 was running at 15.7 per cent. It was at this point, with national confidence further shaken by Tanaka's arrest on bribery charges, that the oil crisis broke.

When OPEC imposed its export embargo, Japan had forty five days' supply in the distribution system and a mere four days' worth in reserve. Oil supplied three quarters of her annual energy needs, 85 per cent of it originating in the Middle East. The impact of OPEC's action was all the more emphatic in that the winter of 1973 was exceptionally cold in Japan. An ambivalently worded statement of support for the Arab position secured the lifting of the export ban in March 1974, but heavy reliance on oil left Japan very vulnerable to its escalating price. Misplaced government price controls merely distorted the market and in 1974 the national rate of inflation touched 31.6 per cent. In the same year GNP actually contracted for the first time since the war, company profits fell on average by 80 per cent, and a third of publicly listed firms went into the red. Unemployment reached 1.1 million and a further 400,000 were laid off, although they did not appear in the official statistics. Registered bankruptcies in 1974 reached 11,000, a postwar record, but rose even higher in succeeding years.

Tanaka's proposals tempted the Economic Planning Agency to forecast a growth rate of 9 per cent, only 2 per cent lower than the 1961–70 average, but it was never likely that the high levels of the previous two decades could be sustained during the 1970s. Some of the underlying influences behind

Japan's economic miracle were already losing their force. In particular, the narrowing of the technical gap with the West raised the prospect of diminishing returns on imported technology, the cost of which was in any case getting higher as Japan neared the frontiers of technical knowledge. There was also a growing popular demand that the environmental problems associated with unchecked economic growth should be addressed. Following the revelations about the poisoning of the Minamata Village waters and severe asthmatic outbreaks among workers in petrochemical installations in the early 1970s, pollution became the second or third most regularly discussed topic in the Japanese press, and an official survey indicated that some 60 per cent of the population wanted more effective government action. MITI largely succeeded in emasculating the 1967 Pollution Countermeasures Basic Law, which set standards for air, water, noise, vibration, subsidence, and offensive odours, but in turn the Ministry was itself effectively undermined by the so-called Pollution Diet at the end of 1970. The establishment of an Environmental Agency with cabinet standing and the passage of fourteen anti-pollution laws was indicative of the new mood in Japan and signalled the end of unrestrained industrial development.

The international events of 1971–73 also acted to retard growth rates. Investment rates fell from a peak of 37.3 per cent of GNP between 1965–70 to 31.1 per cent in 1976–78. Savings did not drop comparably and they were partly absorbed by a government anxious to bridge the gap between rising public expenditure and fairly stable tax revenues. Taking up surplus saving enabled the government to fund increased outlays without unduly stimulating inflation, even though the budget deficit by 1980 was estimated to be 40 per cent of expenditure. By this date the growth rate had recovered slightly but in aggregate the economy grew between 1974 and 1979 at barely half the rate achieved between 1967 and 1971. This was a miserable achievement in terms of Japan's immediate past although by foreign standards it remained remarkably good and certainly better than that of Britain (table 6.1). Given the international context and the problems experienced elsewhere, there was probably some justification for Prime Minister Fukuda's claim that Japan's

Table 6.1 *Comparative annual growth indicators: Britain and Japan (%)*

	1973–79		1979–88	
	Britain	Japan	Britain	Japan
GDP	1.5	3.6	2.3	4.1
GDP per employee	1.3	2.9	2.0	3.0
Manufacturing output	−0.7	3.6	0.6	6.8
Manufacturing output per employee	0.6	5.0	4.0	5.8

(OECD, 1990: 48–52)

performance in these years also was 'a kind of miracle' (Horsley and Buckley, 1990: 110). It comprised three main elements.

First, there were important structural changes, although in some respects the patterns apparent from the 1950s remained unchanged. Thus tertiary sector employment, which recovered from the oil shock quite quickly, continued to grow while agricultural contraction continued (table 6.2). A record postwar rice crop in 1969 led the government to offer inducements encouraging farmers to diversify or to sell land to larger scale enterprises. But partly because of its centrality in Japanese diet and partly because of the importance of rural support to the Liberal Democrat Government, rice continued to receive heavy subsidies, and diversification was correspondingly slow. Yields per acre compared quite well with those of other countries but yield per worker remained low. By 1984 agriculture accounted for only 3.1 per cent of the GNP.

Table 6.2 *Britain and Japan: occupational structure (%)*

	Primary		Secondary		Tertiary	
	Britain	Japan	Britain	Japan	Britain	Japan
1950	4.9	48.3	49.4	21.9	45.7	29.8
1960		30.2		28.0		41.8
1970	3.2	17.4	44.8	25.1	52.0	47.5
1980		10.4		34.8		54.8
1990		7.2		33.6		59.2
1993	2.2	5.9	26.2	33.7	71.6	59.4

(JISEA, 1995: 20)

In manufacturing textiles were hard hit during the 1970s, as were the heavy industries, such as steel and chemicals. All were affected by competition from newly industrialising countries with lower wage levels. The heavy industries were also largely blamed for environmental pollution. MITI's ability to shape industrial policy was weaker in the 1970s than it had been in the previous two decades. The government's financial difficulties reduced its influence while major firms were now far less dependent than in the past on financial help from the state. It was also apparent that the long standing consensus within MITI on policy priorities was under strain. Differences emerged in the mid-1960s between those who argued that domestic markets should be opened up to international competition and those who wished to continue protecting indigenous industries. There were also internal disagreements about the best way to deal with the social costs of high growth. Nevertheless, MITI took the lessons of the Pollution Diet to heart. From 1971, the selection criteria for industrial expansion were extended to include high income elasticity of demand, high productivity growth, and environmental and labour standards. MITI's budget for dealing with industrial pollution problems was increased from Y274 million in 1970 to Y638 million in 1978. One short term benefit was that as early as 1975 atmospheric concentrations of sulphur dioxide were reduced by half.

In effect, the new thrust of industrial policy was to reduce the importance of heavy manufactures in favour of lower energy consuming, high value added, assembly-based, and knowledge-intensive industries. Sweeping new powers were taken to achieve this, including the upgrading in 1971 and 1978 of the Provisional Measures Law for the Promotion of Specified Electronic and Machine Industries, an act of 1973 to adjust petroleum supply and demand, and the Depressed Industries Law of 1978 which created recession cartels to prune uncompetitive industries such as aluminium. Once again, Japan's response to a difficult economic environment was to plan for the medium and long term and if MITI's direct role was now less significant than in earlier decades, it still exercised important advisory and lobbying functions, particularly on behalf of the fledgling information technology industries (Okimoto, 1989; Warshofsky, 1989). During the 1970s, therefore, the foundations were laid for subsequent national success in electronics, computer, and industrial robotics. Expenditure on computer technology, already worth $168 million in 1972, expanded hugely. Just as Japan's production engineers had benefited from Deeming's insights in the 1950s, so in the 1970s they absorbed equally important lessons from another American expert. As head of Unimation, a leading American robotic firm, Joseph Engelberger had not attracted much interest in his own country, but he drew huge audiences when he lectured in Tokyo in 1967. Two years later Japan's first industrial robot was built under licence by Kawasaki Heavy Industries and by the mid-1980s 250,000 such machines were in service, well over half the world total. Even those outside the lifetime employment system did not feel at all threatened by the introduction of automation since there was a labour shortage and work was easy to find.

The fruits of this industrial restructuring soon became evident from the later 1970s as high quality Japanese electronic goods flooded the world market: this export growth was the second feature of Japan's recovery from the oil crisis. During the first economic miracle overseas markets had been vital in enabling Japan to earn the foreign exchange required for the purchase of raw materials and technology. The main engine of growth, however, had been provided by domestic demand. Its highly competitive nature left Japanese firms sharply honed, ideally placed to benefit from the expansion of the American money supply in the second half of the 1970s. Rising oil prices and deficits on services still kept the overall balance of payments in relatively small surpluses or even in the red between 1973 and 1975 and again in 1979, but the value of exports rose more than five fold between 1970 and 1979. Motor vehicles, the main assembly industry, led the way with 2.5 million units sold overseas in 1976 alone. Shortage of fuel had compelled motor manufacturers to develop more efficient engines while they also had to comply with the world's most stringent emission laws, prompted by the growing national concern with atmospheric pollution. They were thus in a perfect position to meet the growing Western demand for more fuel efficient and environmentally friendly motor vehicles.

Japan's lead in fuel efficient technology was one result of a concerted national campaign to economise on the use of energy, the third element in economic recovery. In the 1960s energy imports had absorbed 35 per cent of the GNP and by the beginning of the 1970s the national energy requirement was growing at 10 per cent a year, sufficient to suggest that by 1980 Japan would account for a fifth of the world's total consumption. In fact, energy use grew very little, the result of a major conservation campaign involving the use of administrative guidance to improve insulation, impose uniform standards, and encourage the use of alternative energy sources, such as liquefied gas, solar power, hydro-electric schemes, and nuclear power. By 1982 twenty four nuclear reactors provided 30 per cent of national electrical needs while conventional power stations reduced their reliance on oil by more than 50 per cent over the decade as a whole. At the same time, it was decided to hold much larger oil reserves than had been the case in 1973, with policy geared to reducing dependence upon the Arabs by cultivating other sources of supply. Consequently, when the price of oil doubled again in 1979 – the second oil shock – Japan suffered nothing like the disruption of 1973–74. A single year of zero growth and 8 per cent inflation was mild compared with what happened elsewhere in the world. By 1980 growth was back at 3.7 per cent.

All in all, Japan's experiences of the oil shocks in the 1970s once again highlighted the responsiveness of her decision-making processes, the ability of policy-makers to choose and implement the right options, and the importance of social arrangements which facilitated cooperative and flexible responses to changing external conditions. As Prime Minister Fukuda later commented:

> The first thing we did, after returning to a state of normality, was to invest in saving energy, and then in labour-saving methods and modernisation. So while the rest of the world was in turmoil and unable to invest, Japan was making new investments across the board. (Horsley and Buckley, 1990: 121)

The troubled 1970s: Britain

Almost the reverse situation prevailed in Britain where changes in the international economic environment ruthlessly exposed frailties in the manufacturing sector. The benefits deriving from the progressive liberalisation of world trade were already diminishing when Britain finally secured entry to the Common Market in 1973. Even without the added burden of rising oil prices, this entailed a transfer of resources likely to have produced some short term structural unemployment. On balance, the annual payments required of EEC members also involved Britain in a net cost which aggravated the increasingly precarious balance of payments position. Traditionally kept down by a highly efficient agriculture and cheap imports from the old imperial territories, domestic food prices rose as a result of the protectionist Common Agricultural Policy with its subsidisation of inefficient European farming.

As a major importer of primary products, Britain was also affected by the ending of dollar convertibility and the growing American budgetary deficit which was exerting such a baleful effect on international price stability. Rising domestic prices thus added to the inflationary pressure already set in motion in Britain by the wage-price spiral and by speculation against sterling. It was further reinforced by an ill-considered expansion of the money supply between 1971 and 1973. Although new international exchange rates were agreed in 1971, they proved impossible to maintain. Sterling was allowed to float from June 1972 and it depreciated by 12.5 per cent, prompting a domestic property boom and further wage demands. Government attempts to restrain inflation by regulating prices and incomes failed to win trade union support. Power workers banned overtime and the miners went on strike. Failing supplies of power and lighting led to the imposition of a three day working week in November 1973.

The economic climate was already unfavourable, therefore, when the oil crisis pushed world wide commodity prices to their highest level since the Korean War, further strengthening the striking miners' hands and plunging Britain into what was probably its most disturbed peace time decade of the century. In February 1974 the Conservative Government was defeated in a general election, a verdict confirmed later in the year when a second election gave Labour a slender overall majority of three. Macro-economic performance proceeded to deteriorate badly (table 6.1). Total manufacturing output actually fell, while real output and productivity grew more slowly than hitherto, GDP growth falling to its lowest rate in the entire postwar period. Inflation and unemployment both rose. The current account, relatively healthy since the 1967 devaluation, deteriorated into consistent deficit between 1973 and 1979. Only the potential of Britain's off-shore oil fields provided any redeeming feature in an otherwise dismal picture.

The best hope of escaping from these problems lay in exporting but, as the last chapter indicated, much of Britain's industrial base was relatively inefficient, greatly constraining the ability to adjust to the harsher international climate. Even before 1973, manufacturing industry had been caught in a vicious circle. Low productivity growth had caused prices and unit labour costs to rise faster in the 1960s than among competitors. Before 1973 Britain's disadvantage in international trade was reflected in a declining share of world exports and a rising propensity to import. As a result, output grew more slowly while competitive weakness reduced the profitability of foreign trade. In turn, this reduced the need to increase capacity while lower profits diminished the supply of investment capital required to raise productivity. Thus the vicious circle was complete. Japan was among those nations locked into precisely the opposite virtuous circle.

It was now, too, that British industry paid the penalty for its unenviable reputation for poor product design, finish, delivery, and service. Between 1967 and 1981 the relative export share declined in nine of the most important commodity categories (Coates, 1994: 12–13). The British share of manufactured exports fell from 10.8 to 8.8. per cent between 1970 and 1981 alone (Pollard, 1992; 301). Even domestic consumers showed a marked preference for imports, drawing them in to such an extent that by 1975 foreign products accounted for 28 per cent of the domestic sales of industrial goods: in 1961 the proportion had been only 11 per cent (Alford, 1996: 252). With prices rising, workers showed a natural reluctance to accept cuts in real wages, thereby denying employers the option of compensating for failing competitiveness by reducing labour costs. The second half of the decade was thus characterised by widespread industrial failure and unrest. Japan's response to the oil crisis was to control inflation by raising interest rates and shrinking the money supply. This worked though it hurt consumers. In Britain, as in many other Western societies, the stress was placed rather on lowering unemployment or reducing its impact by increasing social spending. Either way, the result was that the economy appeared to be uncontrollable, locked into a deadly spiral of industrial inefficiency, rampant inflation, and trade union unwillingness to see either money wages or the social wage (broadly defined as welfare expenditure) reduced.

As the worst effects of the oil price hike began to work through into the domestic economy, the new Labour Government appeared powerless to stop the downward slide. In 1974 and 1975 GDP fell for first time since 1946 and even the 1973 level of output was not regained until 1977. This pattern was repeated when the second oil shock hit, although Britain's own oil supplies by then provided something of a cushion. Output still fell between 1979 and 1981, however, and did not recover until 1983. The result was yet more unemployment. Numerous changes in the basis of measurement make long term direct comparisons difficult but overall there was a six fold increase in the nine years to 1982, by which time 2.7 million people were out of work. The main losses occurred in manufacturing where employment fell by more than 20 per cent between 1979 and 1982 alone as monetary policy was tightened and serious attempts made by a new government to control the growth of public expenditure.

This was a somewhat belated acknowledgement that inflation rather than unemployment was the most pressing economic problem, although the Labour Government had effectively abandoned Keynesian demand management in the mid-1970s. The increase in the retail price index was in double figures for all but two years of the decade (1973 and 1978). In the worst period of all, the summer of 1975, retail prices were rising at the rate of 27 per cent a year. In terms of what it could buy in the domestic market, a 1973 pound was worth a mere 35p by 1980. The inflation inherent in surging world commodity prices had largely worked itself out by 1974 but Britain's inflation rates remained out of line, further worsening the balance of payments position.

Excess domestic demand may have had some upward effect on prices but it is generally agreed that cost-push was a more potent influence. It appears that from the mid-1960s new generations of workers, whose attitudes had been influenced by postwar labour shortages rather than memories of prewar unemployment, became more militant. Britain thus suffered from a wage-price spiral which the oil crisis and government policy exacerbated. In particular, the Conservatives' threshold payment system guaranteeing wage increases as the price index rose, merely built inflation into the economy. From 1974 Labour Governments tried unsuccessfully to contain union demands. The TUC proved unable to deliver either the realistic wage demands or the productivity agreements which were its side of the bargain encapsulated in the Social Contract. In return the government offered the repeal of Conservative trade union legislation, price controls, rent freezes, and pension increases (Wrigley, 1996: 273–92). In 1975 average wages in industrial manufacturing rose by 26.4 per cent, slightly above the rise in retail prices of 26.3 per cent. Average earnings for all employees, however, went up by 27.6 per cent. In the following year failure was even more marked. Retail price rises may have been brought down to 12.9 per cent but the average industrial wage increase was 15.3 per cent, 13.9 per cent for all employees (Peden, 1986: 215). In 1978 both the TUC and the Labour Party Conferences rejected the principle of pay restraint, imparting further energy to labour unrest already boosted by falling real income in 1977, the result of speculation which caused sterling to depreciate against the dollar (table 6.3).

Table 6.3 *Working days lost in Britain, 1971–85 (000)*

1971	13,551
1973	7,197
1975	6,012
1977	10,142
1979	29,474
1981	4,266
1983	3,754
1985	6,402

(Richardson, 1991: 433)

Such speculation was encouraged partly by Britain's mounting balance of payments deficits. There was also a general belief in the international money market that excessive public expenditure was contributing significantly to inflation. In effect, the Bretton Woods monetary system had operated rather like the old gold standard, providing an automatic brake on loan-financed government expenditure. When the system was abandoned this external control also disappeared. As a proportion of GDP the Public Sector Borrowing Requirement (PSBR) trebled between 1972 and 1975 alone, and it continued at high levels throughout the decade, though in fact not much out of line with levels in other advanced countries. Public expenditure had been accelerating under the Conservatives but under Labour it recorded its fastest ever yearly increase, 12.7 per cent between 1973/74 and 1974/75 (Tomlinson, 1990: 285). One cause of this was government determination to plan the economy, using the newly created National Enterprise Board to oversee industrial strategy. At constant prices, state funding for innovation and general industrial support increased by 39 per cent between 1973/74 and 1975/76. Over the same period expenditure on regional subsidies went up by 63 per cent. The largest single financial investment was in British Leyland whose dreadful performance and reputation confirmed that such direct government initiatives could do little to eliminate the root causes of industrial inefficiency, which lay in overmanning, restrictive practices, confused industrial relations procedures, inappropriate company structures, and low quality management. Public expenditures were also boosted by a well-intentioned if misconceived attempt to offset wage controls by maintaining the social wage. Outlays on health and personal social services thus rose, retirement pensions increased faster than inflation, and long term supplementary benefit rates were improved, though the effect was partially minimised by inflation. Rising job losses also increased the numbers eligible for state support.

From 1976 onwards the government began to set annual targets for the aggregate growth of the money supply, although these were not always met. By September 1976 the pound had fallen to $1.64, prompting a request for help from the International Monetary Fund (IMF). The following month, despite a record minimum lending rate of 15 per cent, sterling fell further. In what appeared to be a rerun of 1931, a public expenditure cut was demanded by the IMF for supporting the ailing pound. Cash limits cut real expenditure on welfare by almost 5 per cent in 1977–78. Although it picked up again later on, the unions protested vociferously against falling real incomes and the projected welfare reductions. A day of action – in fact inaction – by public sector workers in 1979 was the most significant industrial stoppage since 1926. As strikes escalated over the Winter of Discontent, refuse piled up in the streets and the dead remained unburied.

The contrast with Japan could hardly have been more vivid. Immediately prior to 1973, the real income of workers' households in Japan had been rising by 4.7 per cent a year. Yet when the government applied the brakes to the money supply in order to control inflation, workers moderated their demands, accepting relatively modest annual wage increases between 1974 and 1976. In the opinion of one senior Japanese civil servant, the heart of Britain's difficulties lay in the intransigence of organised labour. 'The decline of Britain, in my opinion, is basically attributable to the fact that discipline has waned . . . Workers are like undisciplined troops. They stop marching and go to bed' (Wilkinson, 1990: 219). This may have reflected less an objective truth than his own experience of very different attitudes in Japan. It is equally difficult to know what to make of a contemporary survey which found that nearly half of 2,000 British managers believed labour relations to be first rate (Daniel and Millward, 1983: 255). Whatever the actual position, it was somehow symbolic that in 1979 per capita GNP in Britain fell behind that of Japan for the first time.

The 1980s

The new Conservative Government elected in 1979 was determined to allow the discipline of the market to achieve what it believed the state could not, although, as suggested in the previous chapter, Britain's problems had not been caused so much by the fact of state intervention as by its direction. Nevertheless, Mrs Thatcher's administration set about reducing direct state involvement in industry, reforming trade union law to allow greater flexibility in the labour market, and imposing tight money controls. Freedom of action over monetary policy was to prove increasingly difficult, given the constraints imposed by membership of the EEC and the growing mobility of capital, both of which meant that national interest rates tended to move in line with each other. Yet unlike the Heath Government which had been defeated in 1974, the Thatcher cabinet was deterred from pursuing its objectives neither by the practical difficulties of curtailing public expenditure, nor by the prospect of rising unemployment and trade union opposition. Not surprisingly, therefore, most of the standard indicators of economic progress – employment, share of world trade, balance of payments, growth, and standards of living – show that in the years after 1980 Japan continued to outperform Britain.

Table 6.4 shows the contrasting fortunes in terms of unemployment, although such international comparisons are notoriously unreliable. In Japan some of those who lost jobs, mainly the young, the old, and women, simply left the labour force altogether, returning to their families rather than registering as unemployed. British figures are probably more reliable, though not absolutely so. For one thing, the basis of computation was frequently changed in the course of the decade. Students, for example, were barred from registering as unemployed during vacations. For another, it was clear that a large informal or black economy was developing whereby people signed on as unemployed while continuing to work. Nevertheless, the broad trends were clear enough. Unemployment was consistently low in Japan: indeed the ageing of the population and the low birth rate produced serious labour shortages. Britain on the other hand experienced its worst years of sustained unemployment since the 1930s. As then, there were marked variations in its spatial distribution but from the middle of the 1980s regional policy, no longer given the high priority it had received for the previous thirty years, increasingly ignored the problems of heavy industry, being geared rather to innovation, small business, and the regional initiatives of the EEC.

Table 6.4: *Britain and Japan: comparative unemployment rates (% of labour force)*

	Japan	UK
1974–81	2.0	5.7
1982–85	2.6	11.7
1986–89	2.6	9.3
1990	2.1	5.8
1993	2.5	10.4

(Based on Maddison, 1991: 265; JISEA, 1995: 69)

High unemployment reflected the general contraction of manufacturing. This, of course, was a development common to most advanced countries but the growing external deficit indicated that the process was going too far to be consistent with a balanced current account. With government financial and monetary policy encouraging consumer demand from the mid-1980s, imports surged even more, reflecting a dangerous shortage of domestic productive capacity. Furthermore, despite the wholesale elimination of the weakest producers, labour costs per unit of output were still rising, by 20 per cent between 1980 and 1984 alone, for example. By 1990 manufacturing occupied less than 20 per cent of the labour force, down from 35 per cent in 1964. Certainly more people than ever before were actually in work by 1990, but many of the new jobs were inappropriate for those displaced by industrial decline, tending to be low paid, commonly part time, often done by women, and mainly in the service sector.

There were still those on the left in Britain who believed, contrary to the evidence of numerous official inquiries, that such problems were attributable primarily to the failure of the banks to provide industrial investment capital. It was also claimed that the removal of exchange controls in 1979 had attracted institutional money abroad. In fact, this was as mistaken a diagnosis as it had been in earlier periods. Only a tenth of total British investment in this period was directed overseas and in any case the world capital market was by now so integrated that any shortage in Britain would have drawn in foreign funds.

Arguably, one positive by-product of high unemployment was a reduction in industrial militancy, although as tables 6.3 and 6.5 indicate, it was a long hard slog. Fear of unemployment was by no means the only factor at work. It is possible that the defeat of the miners' strike of 1984–85 had a psychological impact on workers' general willingness to strike. Ostensibly about pit closures, the stoppage was engineered by the miners' leaders, apparently for political reasons. The government responded equally toughly, also for political reasons, mindful of the consequences which had followed the previous Conservative capitulation to the miners in 1974. Probably of greater influence on the pattern of industrial action was the continuing process of occupational restructuring away from heavy manufacturing towards the less strike prone and less intensively unionised service sector. Both contributed to a decline of union membership from its 13.2 million peak of 1979 to 10.2 million by 1988. Government legislation, which according to one study was responsible for about a quarter of the drop in union membership, may also have had a role in reducing industrial militancy, although there is no agreement on this point (*Economist*, 14 September 1996: 23–4). Parliamentary acts of 1980, 1982, 1984, and 1988 barred secondary action, made unions liable for damages incurred by strikes, required strike decisions to be supported by secret ballots among union members, and abolished the closed shop, while social security payments for strikers were also reduced. Whatever the reasons, industrial militancy declined. Although the number of workers affected was about the same in both decades, compared with the 1970s the incidence of strikes was halved in the 1980s. However, it was still way ahead of Japan's and this remained an important difference between the two nations.

Table 6.5: *Industrial disputes: total days lost* (000)

	Japan	UK
1980	998	11,964
1985	257	6,402
1990	140	1,093
1992	227	526

(JISEA, 1995: 70)

So, too, did overall growth performance (tables 6.1. and 6.6) as Japan surged to world leadership in many important economic activities. By 1988 the world's top ten banks were all Japanese, while the Nippon Telegraph and Telephone Corporation was the world's most valuable company, worth in theory as much as West Germany. Per capita GDP in 1990 was, at $23,801, considerably higher than the UK's $17,083 (JISEA, 1993: 11). By the early 1990s Japan was spending $725 million a year on computer technology and making a third of the world's cars, steel, and ships, two thirds of its computer chips and consumer electronics. More than half the world's stock of industrial robots and machine tools – 368,054 of them – were to be found in Japanese factories, compared with a paltry 8,189 in Britain. The powerful Japanese economy seemed immune when the world stock market crashed in October 1987. Share prices on the Tokyo exchange faltered briefly but they recovered quickly and rose 120 per cent over the next two years.

Table 6.6: *Japan and UK: annual real growth rates (%)*

	Japan	UK
1983	2.7	3.7
1984	4.3	2.3
1985	5.0	3.8
1986	2.6	4.3
1987	4.1	4.8
1988	6.2	5.0
1989	4.7	2.2
1990	4.8	0.4
1991	4.3	(2.2)
1992	1.1	(0.6)
1993	(0.2)	1.9

(JISEA, 1995: 12–13)

Nevertheless, as in the 1970s, Japanese growth rates in the 1980s were well down on those recorded in the 1950s and 1960s and the collapse of a speculative boom in 1989 pushed the economy into a relative depression. In the first six months of the year the Tokyo stock market lost almost half its value, leaving individuals, banks, and other institutions with reduced assets. The president of Masushita resigned following a massive profit drop, while Nissan lost money for the first time since 1946 and cut its workforce.

Such symptoms of apparent malaise in the early 1990s prompted some speculation as to whether the bubble of success had finally burst, a worrying prospect for the world economy, given the magnitude of Japan's global influence (Woronoff, 1996b). It was suggested that the social consensus on which previous progress had been founded was beginning to break down; others pointed to the difficulties of sustaining improvements in living standards as the financial burdens of increased longevity became evident. High import dependency was also deemed a potential source of weakness, although as far as food was concerned it is worth remembering that late nineteenth-century Britain was in a similar position. Despite agricultural improvements, Japan was still importing 16.1 per cent by value of her food requirements in 1992, over half as much again as the 10.7 per cent then being purchased abroad by the United Kingdom. A similar disparity persisted in terms of energy supplies, as table 6.7 suggests. On the other hand, past experience suggested that Japan would respond appropriately and effectively to these potential problems. In any case, the difficulties of the early 1990s should not be allowed to obscure the realities of Japan's underlying economic strength.

Table 6.7 *Japan and UK: import dependency, 1991 (%)*

	Japan	UK
Coal	94.7	22.4
Oil	99.6	54.9
Gas	96	9.5
Iron ore	100	86.5
Copper	95.3	100
Tin	100	99.2
Bauxite	100	100
Nickel	100	100

(JISEA, 1995: 65)

> The economy has a base of industrial capital that has no equal, quantitatively or qualitatively. Because of its many small businesses, Japan has more entrepreneurs per head of the population than any other big industrial economy. Demography may drive down saving, but each individual's propensity to save testifies to a preoccupation with the future . . . Japan has a well educated labour force. The implicit contract that had provided for wage flexibility in return for greater security of employment may need to be renegotiated but is unlikely to be torn up. Most important, the enterprise networks that are so efficient at promoting specialisation and adaptability, are too valuable to be abandoned. (*Economist*, 6 March 1993: 22)

Japan's depression was, as one British newspaper observed, the kind 'that most Western leaders would give their right arms for – unemployment at just 2.5 per cent, a current account surplus of $117 billion (£80 billion) last year and likely to rise . . . healthy exports and a strong currency' (*Independent on Sunday*, 28 February 1993). Furthermore, over the 1980s as a whole growth rates remained generally higher than those of most industrialised countries, even if now beginning to fall behind those of other expanding Asian economies.

Despite some short term fluctuations, therefore, Japan generally continued to outpace Britain in the 1980s and early 1990s, although the growth gap was certainly not as large as it had been during the thirty years or so after 1945. Inflation in Britain was gradually brought down as the weakest segments of manufacturing were ruthlessly allowed to go to the wall and productivity picked up. Labour productivity in manufacturing increased annually by an average of 4.5 per cent between 1979 and 1988, ahead of most European countries and certainly ahead of Japan where the increase was only 3.3. per cent a year (Hannah, 1994: 344). More generally, improved levels of productivity and the international reputation enjoyed by companies such as Glaxo, ICI, RTZ, Shell, and BP suggest that British industry – in part at least – finally began to shake off some of the legacies of the past. However, lesser improvements in the non-manufacturing sector pulled Total Factor Productivity (TFP) growth in business down to 1.5 per cent a year. This compared with 2.0 per cent in Japan and puts into perspective government apologists' claims that between 1979 and 1988 Britain had experienced an economic miracle of its own.

Some economists have interpreted the narrowing growth gap as an instance of convergence theory in action. This posits that in the initial stages of industrialisation late starters will inevitably outgrow more mature economies (Abramovitz, 1986: 385–406). In this hypothesis there is thus nothing surprising about the contrasting growth records of Britain and Japan during the long postwar boom. However, it is also implied that as original economic leaders are overtaken so they will eventually address impediments to growth, just as those who have caught up are relaxing their efforts. The result should be a narrowing of the gap in relative growth performances. This, it has been claimed, is what happened in the 1980s. To some extent Britain had by that stage accepted its status as a relatively backward country, and was beginning to respond to the advantages which this offered (Feinstein, 1994: 122).

Yet case studies suggest that the learning process was by no means all one way. In steel, for instance, the British increasingly adopted Japanese production practices, while the Japanese moved closer to British forms of corporate organisation (Hasegawa, 1996). Neither was the evidence of real growth rates, particularly after 1988, totally supportive of the convergence hypothesis (table 6.6). The '1990s show', it has been suggested,

> opened just as the 1980s show had opened: the gloomy recession act took up most of the time before the first interval; seat prices had doubled; and everyone was 25 per cent better off than they had been ten years before but fearful of finding they had no job when they came out. (Johnson, 1991: 255)

Furthermore, while the government claimed to have had some success in weakening institutional barriers by reducing trade union power and allowing poorly managed businesses to go to the wall, other critics suggested that the Conservative experiment in freeing the economy from state interference and controlling the money supply was an 'almost unmitigated failure' (Pollard, 1992; 379). Targets for money supply and the PSBR were rarely met, falls in the latter achieved partly by selling off nationalised industries and partly by North Sea oil revenues, which in their best year, 1985, provided more than £12 billion for the national exchequer. In 1990 Britain still had the highest rate of inflation of all the advanced economies, the highest interest rates, high unemployment, and large scale bankruptcies. The picture was not much better by 1993. Inflation may have been brought down to 2 per cent, but unemployment stood at 3.2 million, and was an important contributor to the public sector deficit which exceeded 6 per cent of the GDP.

Above all, nothing had been done to stem the flood of imports as Britain piled up the worst current account deficit in her history, notwithstanding the welcome but purely fortuitous bonus provided by North Sea oil. At its peak oil represented 6.5 per cent of the GDP and it averaged about 5 per cent over the first half of the 1980s. The consequent reduction of imports, combined with some overseas sales of British oil, helped to produce healthy surpluses on the current account between 1980 and 1986. Between 1980 and 1982 there was even a surplus on visible trade. But the off-shore oil fields were not infinite. Estimates at the beginning of 1994 suggested that they would last only for a further six or seven years. Declining oil revenue contributed to the massive deficits which began to accumulate in the second half of the decade. By 1988 the current balance was £14,617 million in the red (Curwen, 1990: 142), further proof of rising import penetration and of Britain's declining share of world exports, which by 1992 was down to 5 per cent.

Japan in the world economy

Japan's balance of payments moved in precisely the opposite direction, reflecting both the relatively closed nature of her home market and the continued success of overseas sales. By 1992 she accounted for some 9 per cent of total world exports. Except in 1973, 1974, and 1979, healthy surpluses on visible trade were sufficient to offset deficits on the invisible account. Trade balances accumulated steadily, multiplying six fold between 1980 and 1992, by which time they stood at $132.4 billion compared with a deficit for Britain of $24.62 billion (JISEA, 1994: 32). The result, however, was a growing volume of complaints from the world community, particularly the United States whose own export difficulties had been increased by an over-valued dollar.

The general tenor of international dissatisfaction was that Japan traded unfairly by protecting her own economic interests. Her foreign aid programme was criticised for taking the form of thinly disguised export subsidies. This was characteristic of most countries' aid programmes but in Japan's case the resentment was magnified because she devoted such a small proportion of her wealth – about 0.2 per cent of GNP in 1975 – to overseas aid. Similarly, it was noted that Japanese participation in international efforts to drive down the value of the dollar had been accompanied by government loans to small firms to tide them over the difficulties caused by the consequential rise in the price of exports.

Another major grievance concerned the difficulties foreigners had in penetrating Japan's own markets. Mounting trade deficits over the 1970s and 1980s had pushed some primary producers to seek increased sales to Japan where they came up against the protection afforded to Japan's farmers. From the Japanese point of view that protection had its own internal logic. It derived partly from the ruling Liberal Democratic Party's dependence on rural votes, and partly from the desire to keep agriculture viable as economic growth drew more and more people away from the land. As for manufactured goods, imports supplied only about 5 per cent of domestic demand between 1970 and 1985. Over the same period the share of aggregate European demand for manufactures met by imports rose from 7 to 13 per cent. In some instances certainly, import penetration was deliberately obstructed by government. Foreigners also complained about the restrictive operations of the *Keiretsu*. Linked by common banking facilities, cross locking directorships, and holdings of stock, as well as by the personal ties arising from shared social or educational backgrounds, these groups exerted enormous influence within the Japanese economy. In the 1980s the big six controlled 650 companies, employed 1.8 million workers, and generated 18 per cent of the country's corporate profits. It was repeatedly claimed that they cooperated to keep foreigners out of the Japan. For instance, before tenders were formally submitted for new building projects, domestic contractors customarily agreed among themselves on the prices and distribution of the work. Overseas firms were not invited to participate in such discussions. Britain encountered similar problems in the telecommunications sector. In the mid-1980s the Japanese government ended the monopoly of Kokusai Denshin Denwa and invited tenders for the supply of telecommunications services, anticipating only domestic applications. Both the government and indigenous companies then put up obstacles when a consortium of the British firm, Cable and Wireless, Pacific Telesis of America, and some Japanese partners put in a bid. Only after representations at prime ministerial level was the Anglo-American consortium allowed in, along with another Japanese enterprise, with the result that telecommunications charges in Japan came down closer to international norms.

The structure of Japan's distribution system also made it difficult for outsiders to establish any secure foothold within the domestic market. Even in the early 1990s considerably more than half of all sales in Japan were handled through the medium of small retail outlets, the so-called 'Mom and Pop' stores. This compared to about 3 per cent in the United States and 5 per cent in Europe. So complex was the distribution system that goods changed hands many times and retailers, selling low volumes, kept prices high. High quality imported goods sold at three to six times the price charged in their country of origin. From the Japanese point of view, the prevalence of such small scale retailing had the social advantages not only of providing employment but also of preserving a sense of local community. Shopkeepers tended to live in or near their premises and took responsibility for civic tasks such as fire fighting, street cleaning, and recycling rubbish. In the 1970s laws were enacted to protect small retailers from larger competitors hoping to benefit from economies of scale. From the point of view of outsiders, however, this appeared as yet another example of the Japanese protecting their own against the threat of more efficient, large scale competition from outside. The failure of the American retail chain, Toys R Us, to establish itself in Japan in the 1980s became a major issue between the two countries, for instance. Added to this was the complaint that the large Japanese trading companies maintained an oligopoly of imports, consistently favouring the particular *Keiretsu* to which they belonged. As a result, it was difficult for foreign retail companies to establish appropriate sales and service networks.

The inability of foreigners to penetrate the internal Japanese market was merely underscored by the apparent ease with which the Japanese could sell their own products abroad. That there was a connection between the two appeared to be confirmed by the fact that time and time again, having kept overseas producers out of their own country, the Japanese proceeded to dominate the world market. One of the most notorious instances of this process involved the semiconductor memory chip. Even though the Americans invented it, attempts by American companies IBM and Texas Instruments to manufacture and sell in Japan were frustrated by MITI. So successful was MITI's programme to encourage a domestic chip industry after 1976 that by 1983 the Japanese had won 70 per cent of the world market.

Yet Western annoyance did not rest on economic considerations alone. Behind the growing resentment still lay a half-articulated belief that the Japanese did not really deserve their economic success because they were essentially copiers, rather than creators. They compensated for a lack of imagination, it was felt, by borrowing ideas and keeping the home market tightly protected. This notion of the Japanese as an uncreative nation of borrowers had a long pedigree. It may have reflected either a general Western perception that truths arrived at by reason are superior to those achieved by intuition, or a simple ignorance of Japan's long heritage of quality achievement in the visual and performing arts. Equally, it seems also to imply that creativity can be understood only in technical or scientific rather than in social or organisational terms. Nevertheless, in the context of technological and economic performance it was a view also shared by some Japanese. 'We suffer a brain drain', said one paper, 'not for any lack of funds, equipment or high standards in individual fields, but for a system that holds down adventurous spirits' (Boyle, 1993: 376). The immediate cause of this comment was the rare award of a Nobel prize to a Japanese scientist, and the country's failure to win many such accolades was frequently adduced as evidence for a lack of native ingenuity. As of 1988, Japan's five prizes were overshadowed by the seventy seven won by British scientists. However, Nobel prizes were not necessarily a good guide to inherent creativity in science and technology since they were usually awarded for seminal breakthroughs at the frontiers of knowledge. It may be more significant that in 1982 Japan, with 7.3 per cent of the total, ranked third in terms of the number of publications in the world's leading scholarly scientific journals. Britain was slightly ahead with 7.9 per cent. Equally revealing, the rate of return from R and D expenditure, measured by the number of patents obtained per scientist and engineer, increased four fold in Japan between 1967 and 1984, years when it was falling everywhere else in the industrialised world. This has been attributed to the dominance of large firms in Japanese technological innovation and to the nature of the advanced training provided for technical personnel. It may have lacked the rigour of the more academic regimes common in the United States and Britain, but because it was geared to the needs of particular firms, it was probably more cost effective (Okimoto and Saxonhouse, 1987: 385–419).

Others point to the fact that while huge sums were spent on importing foreign technology, state expenditure on R and D remained very low in Japan. At 2.15 per cent of the National Income in 1978, Japan's R and D expenditure was actually just behind Britain's 2.29 per cent, but by the early 1990s Japan had pulled well ahead (table 6.8). From the mid-1980s in particular, there was a considerable increase in Japan's financial commitment to long term, basic research in superconductivity, nuclear energy, and bacteriology, three of the leading scientific fields. It is also important to remember that most research in Japan was funded by private industry rather than by government, which accounted for more than a third of British R and D outlays in 1991, much of it of course still devoted to defence projects (table 6.8).

Table 6.8: *R and D expenditures: Japan and UK*

	% of national income	% funded publicly
	Japan	
1975	2.11	27.5
1985	3.13	19.4
1992	3.55	18.0
	UK	
1991	2.80	34.2

(JISEA, 1994: 25)

Yet it may be questioned as to whether technical creativity *by itself* is essential for industrial success at all. The Japanese captured the international microchip market mainly because they produced a much higher quality article than their competitors. The USA was the world's leading maker in 1973, but within ten years the Japanese had almost three quarters of the world market and only two of America's top six producers were still in business. The reason was made clear in 1979 when Hewlett Packard revealed that the chips it imported from Japan had a defect rate one tenth that of American-made ones. In the British computer market only four of the top ten suppliers of services and software were British-owned by the early 1990s, a situation ascribed not to any lack of creativity on the part of software engineers, but rather to the restricted availability of finance for expansion, limited entrepreneurial ambition, and lack of basic management skills (Holway, 1992). Similarly, it was the superiority of Japanese production and productivity that lay behind the massive export boom in the 1980s. In vehicle manufacture, for example, Japan still enjoyed a huge productivity advantage over the West, turning out a car every seventeen hours as compared to thirty five in Europe (Wilkinson, 1990: 189).

Whatever the validity of the foreign complaints about Japanese attitudes towards competition – and they were by no means all unjustified – Japan felt obliged in an increasingly global economy to respond, the more so perhaps because her trade balance was so much healthier than in the 1950s and 1960s when international discontents were first voiced. One set of responses was contained in a five year plan for 1988–92 entitled *Economic Management within a Global Context*. The targets included improvements in individual lifestyles through the provision of more land for housing and reduced working hours, a simplified distribution system to lower prices, the dismantling of agricultural protection, the development of regional economic centres, the rectification of external imbalances, and increased contributions to development aid and Western defence. Although resolutely refusing to deploy troops overseas (most controversially when the United Nations intervened to repel the Iraqi invasion of Kuwait), Japan had already begun to shoulder more of its own defence costs. In 1981 responsibility was assumed for protecting the sea lanes for a thousand nautical miles around the home islands, and in 1986 defence spending breached (by 0.004 per cent) the self imposed 1977 ceiling of 1 per cent of the GNP. Depending on which accounting measures are used, Japan's defence spending in 1991 was between the third and sixth highest in the world in gross terms, although it is worth pointing out that only about a quarter of this went on actual weaponry.

As for trade, exports had been subject to some restriction even from the 1970s in a series of arrangements known as VERAS (voluntary export restraint agreements). After 1975 an industry to industry understanding restricted the Japanese to taking only 10 per cent (increased to 11 per cent in 1977) of Britain's domestic car market. By the mid-1980s between 30 and 40 per cent of Japan's exports were covered by such agreements. In practice, however, these had little real effect because relatively few of them applied to the newer high technology goods in which Japan was leading the way (Tatsuno, 1986). On the import side, negotiations through the 1970s and

1980s did produce a slightly more open domestic market in the sense that formal tariffs and quotas were reduced. As a result, by 1993 Japan Schick razor blades had 70 per cent of the Japanese market, Coca Cola was the top soft drink, and American firms such as McDonald's, Levi's, and Kodak were familiar household names. In 1994 the government approved a scheme to allow open bidding for public works contracts, a move expected to increase the foreign share of such work to about 20 per cent. Japan also made a number of concessions involving primary produce during the Uruguay round of GATT talks between 1987 and 1993, although the decision to allow rice imports was driven as much by internal considerations as by external ones. The practice of buying up home produced rice at official prices had become increasingly expensive as domestic consumption declined. Importing foreign rice was thus part of a broader government strategy designed to encourage agricultural diversification in Japan itself. Nevertheless, import quotas on a number of commodities were relaxed and Japan became the largest foreign consumer of American farm produce.

Few of these measures had much impact on the mounting trade surpluses, however. Japan's export superiority rested primarily upon higher levels of productivity and better quality control. As for the home market, it might be argued that Western complaints revealed a misplaced confidence in the inherent appeal of Western goods to the Japanese, for it by no means followed that any greater openness would have automatically benefited Western producers. Throughout the 1980s Southern Asia alone provided about half of all Japan's manufactured imports. Furthermore, it is a moot point as to whether non-tariff barriers to imports such as the setting and administration of industrial standards, or customs procedures, were driven primarily by considerations of trade protection or a determination to ensure that imports complied with Japan's own high qualitative requirements. After all, as early as 1899, long before Japan had any significant industrial base, the British engineer, J. S. Ransome, had noted that 'while we find it an easy matter to purchase any Japanese goods which we may require, the problem which puzzles us is that which concerns the best methods of maintaining and increasing our sales in Japan' (Ransome, 1899: 188). He then described how most of the Belgian and a third of the British pipes ordered for the Tokyo Waterworks had been rejected, following a rigorous inspection for quality and specification (Ransome, 1899: 193–6). Nor was it at all obvious that late twentieth-century Japanese practices in these respects were any worse than elsewhere. The French, for instance, devised similar strategies to restrict Japanese imports and did not immediately intervene to prevent popular action designed to keep out Italian wine or British lamb.

In the final resort, therefore, the criticism perhaps came down to suggesting that Japan's internal market was effectively closed by the complexity of the Japanese language and the traditions of group solidarity, cooperative working, and hard work that characterised Japanese society – and had always done so. The answer to the language problem was in the hands of Westerners themselves and one study has certainly suggested that the failure of foreign banks to establish themselves reflected their own ineptitude as much as any inherently defensive instincts on the part of the Japanese (Brown, 1994). Similarly, Western complaints that the Japanese worked too hard and saved too much, thereby reducing both leisure time and consumer expenditure which might have gone on imported goods, revealed a startling lack of cultural awareness. Government attempts to bring down working hours in Japan were constantly frustrated by a workforce accustomed to work long hours out of a sense of camaraderie and company loyalty. Such characteristics, it has been argued, derived from the Japanese peasant concept of time as a social, rather than an individual possession and had been translated quite smoothly into modern industrial Japan.

Ironically, one of Japan's attempts to respond positively to Western complaints produced another associated source of friction, particularly with the Americans. As part of the general international effort to drive down the overvalued dollar in the mid-1980s, the Japanese government urged its people to buy foreign goods. In addition, monetary policy was directed to appreciating the yen against the dollar. This was so successful that between 1985 and 1987 the dollar fell from Y260 to Y140. Although this helped to bring down the American trade deficit with Japan, it also made it relatively cheap for the Japanese to buy up property and plant in the United States. This heralded an expansion of Japan's overseas investment, further facilitated by savings. From the mid-1970s private saving in Japan declined but more slowly than investment levels and some portion of the resulting excess was channelled abroad.

Japan in the British economy

The rate at which Japan's overseas investments grew was astonishing. Direct investments between 1951 and 1983 totalled $61,277 million. At current prices, investment over the next decade was almost six times larger, and by 1992 Japan had more than 12 per cent of the world share of direct overseas investments, marginally behind Britain with 14.2 per cent (JISEA, 1995: 55–7). In 1986 Japan surpassed Britain as the country with the largest volume of assets of all kinds around the world. Most of these took the form of foreign government bonds, property, or overseas industrial capacity. Sony was the first Japanese company to set up an overseas manufacturing plant, at San Diego in 1972. It was also the first to open a factory in Britain, a television plant at Bridgend in 1974. Japanese car production in the United Kingdom was pioneered by Honda, followed by Toyota, Mazda, Isuzu, and Nissan. By 1991 almost 200 Japanese-owned companies directly employed about 1 per cent of Britain's manufacturing labour force. It has been estimated that although Britain's own television producers were destroyed by foreign competition, overseas sales of Japanese sets made in the United Kingdom contributed some £466 million to the balance of trade (Eltis and Fraser, 1992: 2–19). Japanese expertise revitalised the British car industry by helping to raise productivity levels. Those firms who set up in Britain felt that their working practices had been successfully transplanted, further indication perhaps that a key difference between British and Japanese manufacturing performance in the postwar years lay not so much in trade union structures and attitudes, as in management quality. The Nissan plant at Sunderland, for instance, claimed to have achieved high productivity by introducing Japanese values of consensus and company commitment. Critics were not so sure, however, suggesting that passive workers living in the shadow of the dole queue were driven hard by excessive surveillance and exploitation (Garrahan and Stewart, 1992).

Britain was second only to the United States as a recipient of Japan's outward investment, receiving $31.6 million between 1951 and March 1994, 40 per cent of all Japanese investment in the countries of the EEC (JISEA, 1995: 55). During the same period, however, British investment in Japan amounted to just $1.4 million, less than 5 per cent of the total Japan received. The reversal of roles which these figures signified over the course of the century was most tellingly epitomised in the Japanese acquisition of Turnberry golf course and Bracken House, then the headquarters of the *Financial Times*. Equally symbolic were the fortunes of Dunlop Rubber, a company whose presence in Japan predated the Second World War. In 1963, however, its Kobe-based company was turned into a jointly owned venture with Sumitomo. When Dunlop became one of Britain's many manufacturing casualties in the 1980s, Sumitomo first bought up the 40 per cent British share of the joint enterprise and then acquired Dunlop's tyre factories in Britain, France, and Germany. As the Sumitomo chairman later said: 'we have changed the master/student relationship' (Davenport-Hines and Jones, 1989: 237).

Certainly by the 1970s it was the British who were looking to Japan for ideas on industrial regeneration, another neat inversion of the situation prevailing a century earlier. In 1977 a parliamentary committee was charged with examining Japanese industry to see what could be learned about production and development and to assess the reasons for Japan's success. One long run outcome was the emergence of a number of direct industrial link-ups, as for example between the car makers, Honda and Rover. Another became clear from a 1987 survey suggesting that in some British firms management training was also developing along Japanese lines. Despite the proliferation of business schools and MBA programmes, less than a third of the large enterprises sampled placed much credence in these formal management qualifications, preferring, like the Japanese, to train their own senior staff (Constable and McCormick, 1987: 85). British firms were also experimenting with Japanese production techniques. An analysis of sixty six such firms, published in 1988, revealed that about 90 per cent were already using or planning to introduce group working and statistical process control, while 95 per cent were using or intending to use total quality control. Just in Time production was less frequently employed, although it was operational in 34 per cent of the sample firms and planned by another 30 per cent (Oliver and Wilkinson, 1988). This was perhaps not surprising, given that in Britain generally, contractual relationships between manufacturers and subcontractors were very different from those prevalent in Japan. Significantly, however, in those manufacturing activities in which subcontracting was common, notably engineering, textiles, and clothing, analysis suggested that British firms were reluctant to change their attitudes 'away from the short-termism implicit in the willingness to renege on a partner for immediate gain at the expense of the long-term benefits of cooperation' (Thorburn and Takashima, 1993: 12).

The system of reproduction

Occupational structure

By the early 1990s the pattern of employment in both Britain and Japan was typical of all advanced industrial societies, with the tertiary sector providing the majority of jobs (table 6.2). Important differences still remained, however. First, although agricultural employment continued to diminish in Japan, farming remained relatively labour intensive. Government efforts to eliminate the so-called weekend farmers and the growth of primary imports both helped to reduce the number of farm households to 2.9 million by 1991 as against some 4.5 million in 1981, but the proportion of the Japanese workforce engaged in agriculture remained more than twice as large as in Britain (Waswo, 1996: 145).

Second, Japanese industry accounted for a third of all employment, a greater share than it had absorbed in the 1950s and 1960s. Although its distribution was much changed, 55 per cent of manufacturing employment was still provided by small enterprises, employing between four and ninety nine people (Waswo, 1996: 128). In Britain whole swathes of the industrial infrastructure were laid waste by foreign competition and other economic forces. Between 1963 and 1981 employment in chemicals, for example, fell by 25 per cent, in metal, clothing, and footwear by almost a half, in shipbuilding and motor vehicles by a third, and in textiles by almost 60 per cent (Pollard, 1992: 235). With industry providing jobs for just over a quarter of the workforce by 1993, talk of de-industrialisation now seemed more justified, though as the consequence rather than the cause of slow growth. Certainly the rising volume of imports suggested that domestic manufacturing capacity was incapable of satisfying the home market.

By 1985 nine of the United Kingdom's eleven regions had unemployment rates in excess of the EEC average of 9.9 per cent, although internal disparities were considerable. The South West, Wales, and East Anglia escaped relatively lightly while the exploitation of North Sea oil created some 100,000 new jobs in the Grampian region. On the other hand, the problems of the car industry were reflected in rising unemployment in the West Midlands which had had the lowest rates of all as recently as 1965. Northern Ireland remained consistently the worst off, with double the national average of unemployment, but Yorkshire and Humberside suffered badly from the continuing decline of their traditional heavy industries. The comparative disadvantage from which such regions suffered was worsened by British entry to the European Community which accelerated the shift of trade towards Europe. Between 1973 and 1984 the volume of exports going to the EC grew 60 per cent, with imports from the Community rising 300 per cent (Armstrong, 1991: 309). Yet as the most westerly member of the community Britain's own western peripheries were doubly disadvantaged, being relatively remote from the central regions which provided the community's manufacturing core. Any countervailing long run benefits of EC regional policy were not yet clear but in the shorter term there occurred an urban–rural shift in the distribution of employment and of population. Physically closer to Europe, regions such as the South West, East Anglia, and the East Midlands had lower unemployment and actually received influxes of population in these years. As employment opportunities increasingly concentrated in smaller towns and rural areas, the major cities, which had expanded continuously until the early 1960s, lost population. Inner city Birmingham lost 17.6 per cent of its inhabitants between 1971 and 1981, Manchester 24.5 per cent, London 17.6 per cent, Liverpool 26.6 per cent (Armstrong, 1991: 308). This contributed significantly to inner city decay which emerged as a major social problem from the 1970s onwards.

Given Japan's very different topography (two thirds of the land area was still covered by forest) and historical development, similar degrees of population movement were never likely. Even so, before Tanaka unveiled his 1972 blueprint for the New Japan, the decline of the Osaka textile industry was accompanied by falling population and the rate of increase in Tokyo was slowing. Conversely, north and south Kyushu were gaining population, and the postwar demographic decline of Hokkaido was arrested. However, almost a third of the population remained crammed onto just 1 per cent of the land area in 1970, a situation which the Tanaka plan was designed in part to remedy. In the event his ambitious schemes, which had in any case not been unopposed by other politicians, went into partial abeyance during the oil crisis. By 1990, therefore, only the Honshu–Hokkaido tunnel, five of the planned bullet train lines, and three of the bridges were open. Two thirds of people still lived in towns of more than 50,000 inhabitants, but half of the population, by then in excess of 120 million, lived in districts officially classified as densely populated, most of them still packed into the eastern seaboard. Overall population density, therefore, was among the highest in the world at 334 persons per square kilometre in 1994. It is worth noting, however, that in *England* in 1995 population density was actually higher than this, each square kilometre supporting 363 people (*Spectator*, 28 October 1995).

The quality of life

The officially commissioned 1971–72 *Economic Survey of Japan* identified unacceptably high urban densities, high living costs, and a lack of social overhead capital as major contributors to the welfare gap which it perceived to exist between Japan and other advanced countries. A couple of years later the Japanese Economic Council sought to measure the social costs of rapid growth by devising a Net National Welfare (NNW) measure, recalculating the GNP by inserting welfare indicators into it. The result showed consistent growth in both NNW and GNP between 1955 and 1968, after which the NNW declined below the GNP. More crudely, a much quoted EEC report in 1979 described the Japanese as workaholics who lived in rabbit hutches. Such insensitivity caused considerable annoyance within Japan although few disputed the general point being made. The 1988 five year plan conceded that

> The economic progress that has been achieved has not always redounded to the benefit of the individual Japanese, and there is a disparity between the nation's economic strength and the individual's perceived quality of life, as seen, for example, in the spartan housing, the long hours of work, and the high cost of living. (Wilkinson, 1990: 236)

There was plenty of evidence to suggest that, from a British perspective, the quality of Japanese life left something to be desired in these particular respects. Per capita income was higher but a comparison of living costs between Tokyo and London at the end of 1993 showed that Japanese consumers were paying dearly for agricultural subsidies. which left some food prices three times the world level. Bread, milk, beef, and sugar were all far more costly in Tokyo than in London, and only eggs of the basic foodstuffs were cheaper. Inefficiencies in distribution ensured that high food costs prevailed throughout the country. Electricity, gas, and petrol were also more expensive in Tokyo and only those in search of a permanent hairwave or dry cleaning were better off there than in the British capital (JISEA, 1995: 72).

As for working hours, the monthly average in small enterprises fell from 215 in 1960 to 185 in 1980, and in large ones from 199 to 174, but workers were reluctant to slacken their efforts on behalf of their employers. In 1985 a Ministry of Labour survey calculated that the average working year in manufacturing industry was still 2,168 hours, compared with the 1,888 hours then current in Britain, where working hours remained the longest in Europe even in the mid-1990s. Long working hours in Japan were compounded by extensive commuter journeys on massively crowded trains; 20 per cent of Tokyo's workforce in 1991 commuted for more than three hours each day, although as in Britain, commuting times in provincial cities were generally much shorter. Fewer than a fifth of Japanese took a two day weekend while the average annual paid leave of nine days compared equally unfavourably with the UK average of twenty four. From the 1980s a new word, *karoshi*, meaning death from overwork, entered the Japanese vocabulary, and suicide rates in 1980 were exactly twice as high as in Britain. Not surprisingly, few Japanese had much time for leisure or recreation, even when land scarcity permitted the provision of facilities. Japan had only 7,771 public libraries, or one for every 125,230 people, in the early 1980s. In Britain nearly a third of the population in the 1970s were registered library users.

Children were not exempt from this intensive life style either. The typical school year lasted 243 days and the system's inbuilt competitive ethos was increasingly believed by the Japanese themselves to be inimical to individual development. Repeated references to the 'exam hell' were accompanied by developing dissatisfaction with the emphasis on rote learning, memory, and rigid standardisation, as well as concern at mounting evidence of bullying and absenteeism in schools. The recommendations of an ad hoc Council on Education, established in 1984, did produce some liberalisation, although neither the system's basic tenor nor its associated problems were fundamentally changed. By the 1990s, 100,000 pupils were dropping out of secondary education every year while lower down as many as 10,000 children were said to be refusing to attend primary school. The school service, admitted the Minister of Education in 1992, was 'preventing the growth of free individual personalities' (*Independent*, 10 August 1992). On the other hand, 4.4 million children were still enroled in *juku*, the private cramming establishments designed to enhance the prospects of the 50 per cent of the eligible age cohort intent on sitting university entrance exams. The *juku* intensified the pressure on time still further, since they taught children at night after regular school was over, and also over weekends.

Unattractive as such a pressurised existence may appear in British eyes, it has to be set into the appropriate Japanese cultural context, one in which suicide was regarded as honourable, loyalty and education both highly prized, hard work deemed a worthy end, and time viewed as a social rather than an individual commodity. The examination hell at least was nothing new, having first been debated in the national legislature before the First World War. Similarly, it is in the context of Japan's particular social organisation that the apparent paucity of public leisure facilities must be seen. In recreation as in welfare, the company often provided what government, whether local or national, provided in Britain. In the early 1980s 80 per cent of all sports clubs outside of schools were company run, and only 729 of the country's 8,897 swimming pools were public ones.

It was the scarcity of suitable building land above all else which condemned the densely populated Japanese to urban conditions well short of British standards. Only 12 per cent of the area of Tokyo was given up to roads, half as much as in London, although there was some compensation for choked roads in the form of litter and graffiti free, cheap, and highly efficient urban railways, a significant contrast with the British capital. Lack of appropriate planning controls had also allowed unrestrained urban development, adding to the competition for land, in the process littering the cities with tangled skeins of overhead cabling and further reducing the available amount of recreational space. In 1976 London had more than thirty square metres of parkland per inhabitant, twelve times as much as each Tokyoite. By 1982 the UK had a sewerage rating of 95 per cent as against only 44 per cent (in 1990) in Japan where even some cities of 50,000 remained largely dependent on cesspits. The Japanese coped with far more equanimity than similar conditions might have produced in Britain, where localised urban blight was steadily rendering some major city centres almost uninhabitable, particularly after dark. Furthermore, the resurgence of respiratory disease, particularly asthmas, suggested that atmospheric pollution was a developing problem in Britain, even though she had been chronologically ahead of Japan in terms of clean air legislation, as well as in cleaning up the rivers and designating national parks.

British housing provision was similarly advanced. The first town planning legislation dated from 1909 and the New Towns Act of 1946 had tried to create integrated communities in pleasant environments. Japanese housing still tended to be small, overcrowded, and very expensive. In 1971 there were 1.1 people per room of dwelling house as compared with 0.6 per room in the United Kingdom. Seventeen years later Japan had 342 residential buildings per thousand people, not all that far behind the UK's 400, but the average floor area was only 85.6 square metres, considerably smaller than the British average.

Even in the 1950s urban housing costs had been high but the soaring price of land in the 1980s threatened to make them prohibitive. A 1990 report showed that metropolitan housing was oversubscribed forty times, while the average price of a small fifty seven square metre flat in Tokyo was Y80 million, more than twelve times the average salary of a middle-aged working person (*Japan Times*, 9 December 1990). Those Japanese desirous of buying accommodation increasingly had to take on mortgages with a potential repayment span of three generations. Yet even this did not prevent the spread of owner occupation, which reached 60 per cent of all dwellings as the proportion of household income devoted to housing quadrupled to 18.8 per cent between 1980 and 1993. Even at the height of the property boom in the 1980s, British residential prices did not get so out of line with incomes and the number of owner occupiers grew steadily, encouraged further by the

Conservative policy of selling off municipal housing. By 1988 almost two thirds of houses in Britain were owner occupied, an increase of 8 per cent since 1981.

The standard of living

In most other respects, however, Japan's standard of living was pulling ahead of Britain's. An international analysis carried out in 1983 on the basis of several indicators, including demographic trends, per capita income, consumption patterns, and welfare provision, placed Japan in third place and Britain in ninth (*Economist*, 24 December 1983). There was little contesting most of the statistics. By 1994 Japan's infant mortality rate, at 7.5 deaths per thousand live births, was considerably lower than the 12.1 per thousand current in the United Kingdom. Life expectancy was also superior and among the highest in the world at 76.3 for males and 82.5 for females born in 1993. Comparable figures for Britain were about four years lower at 72.7 and 78.2 respectively. Diseases of prosperity were responsible for most deaths in Japan, with cancers, heart, and cardiovascular disorders accounting for about 60 per cent of the total in 1993 (Health and Welfare Statistics Association, 1995: 49).

As far as income was concerned, the total household earnings of Japanese workers in 1975 exceeded their expenditure by 20 per cent: by 1994 the excess was almost twice as much (Health and Welfare Statistics Association, 1995; 189). Per capita gross domestic product in Japan consistently outgrew that of Britain after 1973, and in the same period forged ahead in absolute terms as well (table 6.9). The consumption benefits of this were somewhat reduced by two influences. First, while saving levels were falling, the typical Japanese household still saved a substantial portion of its income, an average of 15.0 per cent in 1994 as against only 5.7 per cent in the United Kingdom (Takahashi, 1994: 13).

Table 6.9: *Britain and Japan: annual per capita GDP growth rates (%)*

	1950–73	1973–89
Britain	2.5	1.8
Japan	8.0	3.1

(Maddison, 1991: 49–50)

Second, Japanese food prices were kept artificially high by government subsidies to farmers and distributors. Nevertheless, in accordance with Engels' law, the consumption of basic foodstuffs such as rice continued to fall, as did the total amount spent on food. It reduced by a third between 1970 and 1993 (JISEA, 1996: 100). By 1994, food, beverages, and tobacco absorbed 20.4 per cent of household income in Japan as against 21.0 per cent in the UK (Takahashi, 1994: 12).

Other types of consumption were similarly convergent. Geography and an historical legacy of isolation both meant that the Japanese were relatively slow to join the growing queues of international holiday makers. In this respect they remained behind the more favourably located and more experienced British, seventeen million of whom took foreign vacations in 1986. Only twelve million Japanese travelled abroad in 1993 although this did represent a significant advance on the comparable figure of 600,000 for 1970. In both countries the ownership of some consumer goods approached saturation point, despite a flattening of British expenditure during the troubled 1970s. By 1985 95 per cent of British households had refrigerators, 82 per cent washing machines, and 97 per cent televisions. Comparable ownership figures in Japan in 1993 were respectively 98 per cent, 99 per cent, and 99 per cent. Possession alone, however, was not a sufficient indicator of the standard of life. In Britain rising levels of ownership depended far more heavily than in Japan upon credit arrangements and they were also offset to some extent by rapidly escalating levels of domestic theft (Maxfield, 1984).

The only significant respect in which the British still appeared to be better off than the Japanese was in terms of expenditure on medical care and health expenses. In 1994 only 1.5 per cent of British household income was devoted to this compared with more than a tenth in Japanese households (Takahashi, 1994: 13). Particular care must be exercised in the interpretation of such figures, however, since like is not always being compared with like. Discrepancies in welfare expenditure, whether at the national or personal level, must take into account the different traditions of welfare provision which had developed in the two countries. The priority given to economic growth, the low rates of benefit payable in what was only a limited system of state provision, and low dependency ratios, ensured that with the exception of health and medical care, Japan's national expenditure on welfare was well behind that of other countries in 1970. In that year 2.86 per cent of GNP went on health and medical care, 2.59 per cent on income and employment security, and 5.45 per cent on social security and retirement benefits.

However, it was clear to the Japanese that the economic miracle had bypassed some social groups. In particular, the *Economic Survey of Japan* for 1971–72 singled out the old, families with no fathers, the handicapped, and the chronically ill, adding that recent extensions of the welfare system had done little to improve the ratio of transfer income, which remained small. Thereafter, welfare provision was reformed and upgraded, assuming recognisably modern forms and dimensions. Restructuring increased the benefits payable under the compulsory health insurance scheme and introduced free medical care for the aged. In 1973 legislation raised and partly indexed old age pensions. Pensioners in the wage earning category received about two fifths of the previous year's average wage, compared with slightly more than a third payable to British pensioners. Unemployment insurance, originally introduced in 1947, was extended in 1976. By the end of the 1970s social security payments were as developed in Japan as in Britain, while by 1990 the level of medical provision was comparable if not superior in some aspects. The number of doctors per person was roughly equal, 17 per 10,000 of the population in Japan in 1991, 16.4 in the UK in 1981. On the other hand, in 1991 Japan had a hospital bed for every 74 inhabitants, whereas the number available to the British National Health Service had declined such that by 1989 283,000 beds serviced some 56 million people, not far short of one for every two hundred citizens.

Just how much the Japanese state increased its direct contribution to welfare provision in these years is apparent from the growing share of central expenditure devoted to it. In 1970 the budget for health and welfare was slightly larger than that for agriculture: by 1983 it was three times larger (Smith, 1995: 120). Nevertheless, gaps remained, particularly in terms of nursing care for the elderly and disabled, while relatively little help was available for working mothers with small children. At the beginning of 1994 the Ministry of Health and Welfare asserted that while medical and pension provision were first rate, welfare remained third class (Iwabuchi, 1994: 2). Most worrying were the long run implications of the growing proportion of the elderly in the population. This was a problem emerging in most advanced societies towards the end of the twentieth century but in Japan it was made particularly acute by the combination of high life expectancy and low birth rates. In 1994, only 15.6 per cent of the population was under fourteen years old, well under half the figure for 1950 (Health and Welfare Statistics Association, 1995: 22). Just over sixteen million people, 13 per cent of the population, were aged over sixty five in 1992 and the economically active portion of the population was paying out some 14 per cent of its income to support the burden of pensions. By 2025, it was estimated, the required percentage would be 35. One by-product of this, perhaps, was that whereas in 1963 Japan possessed only 690 institutions for the elderly, by 1984 there were 2,814 with 100 being built each year (Tobin, 1992: 17).

Along with the sick and disabled (39.9 per cent) and single parent families (9.9 per cent), the elderly (43.3 per cent) made up well over 90 per cent of the 881,000 Japanese receiving public assistance in 1993 (Health and Welfare Statistics Association, 1995: 152). This still included a disproportionate number of *burakamin*. Japan's long reluctance to admit immigrant labour and a niggardly attitude regarding refugees from Cambodia and Vietnam had prevented the development of any significant immigrant underclass, but the number of *burakamin* on welfare was six to eight times the national average, while in 1980 their unemployment levels were often as high as 20 per cent (Herzog, 1995: 549). Urban casual workers, historically very numerous in Osaka, also remained vulnerable. At the end of 1992 a number of the 25,000 day labourers working on the city's construction sites rioted. Mostly recruited by the *Yakuza*, they were being paid at about two thirds of the going rate for regular day labourers and protested when the local welfare centre stopped their emergency loans, although their real target was the state. 'As we photographed them queuing for the soup kitchen, they shouted at us "Tell the world how the Japanese Government is"' (*Independent*, 8 November 1992).

Such demonstrations were generally as infrequent as the poverty and vulnerability which caused them, although it remains a moot point as to how far the extension of state welfare reduced individual hardship and poverty. The perceived need to present a particular image to the world in the interests of national dignity perhaps caused the Japanese to underplay the extent of deprivation in their midst. On the other hand, income equality was reinforced by the system of spring wage bonuses which rested on the assumption that workers in different industries should all receive similar percentage rises and in international terms Japan's income distribution certainly remained relatively egalitarian. One estimate suggested that in the 1980s the typical chief executive in Japan was paid seventeen times as much as his average worker, whereas in America the differential was eighty five (Wilkinson, 1990: 386). Another calculated that the average company president in Japan had an income seven or eight times as large as that of his employees as against a thirty to fifty times differential in Europe and the United States (Tasker, 1989: 300).

Nevertheless, there were signs of growing unease within Japan as some evidence of widening income disparities began to surface. Between a quarter and a third of the workforce, full time regular employees in large enterprises, were well paid and received extensive company benefits. At the other end of the spectrum were the seasonal, part time workers in the big companies, receiving lower wages and fewer benefits. The majority of the workforce comprised full time employees in smaller scale enterprises. In the mid-1980s workers in small firms (up to 100 people) earned 55 per cent as much as those working in units of more than a thousand: the equivalent differential in Britain was 73 per cent (Waswo, 1996: 132). By 1993 average annual household income in Japan was Y7.575 million, the median Y5.5 million. Significantly, however, nearly 26 per cent of households received less than Y4 million a year, while 18 per cent had more than Y10 million (Health and Welfare Statistics Association, 1995: 29–30). Such differences were said to be reflected in an increasingly skewed distribution of property and in the growing ability of rich parents to buy the educational opportunities which would ensure high future incomes for their children.

At the beginning of the 1970s British welfare accounted for slightly under a half of all public expenditure and a fifth of the GDP (table 6.10). The cutbacks introduced at the end of the 1970s by a financially straitened Labour Government had little real long term effect. Neither did the actions of the succeeding Conservative Governments, despite their avowed intent of reducing what they believed to be the nationally and individually harmful culture of dependency fostered by comprehensive welfare provision. The view that welfare subverted initiative and enterprise was an old one, traceable back at least as far as the seventeenth century, and ever since its foundation the welfare state had been subjected to this type of attack (Harris, 1990: 175–96). The convictions of Mrs Thatcher's administrations thus had a long pedigree but they generally rested on very shaky empirical assumptions. They overlooked the fact that between 1960 and 1981 Japan had both the fastest growing economy *and* the most rapid rate of increase in social expenditure; conversely, both had increased at low rates in Britain where the period of fastest economic growth had also actually coincided with the highest increases in social expenditure. Although there was certainly a good case for trying to simplify a Byzantine system which by the mid-1970s had evolved more than forty different means tests, it proved far harder to achieve genuine cuts in actual expenditure. For good or ill, the British public had a general empathy for the welfare state and the health service in particular, even though the provision of medical care was socially and geographically skewed. It was also difficult to conceive of alternative machinery for tackling deprivation. The commercial insurance companies, for example, responded lukewarmly to suggestions that parts of the system might be privatised under their aegis. The existence of non-cash limited budgets along with the steady increase in the number of elderly and unemployed also served to keep expenditure high. Between 1978/79 and 1986/87 spending on social security, health, and personal social services rose respectively by 36, 24, and 28 per cent (Page, 1991: 488). By the mid-1980s the unemployed represented almost half of those on Supplementary Benefit, pensioners made up another quarter, and lone parents 17 per cent (Abercrombie and Warde, 1988: 99).

Table 6.10: *Britain: welfare expenditure*

	% of public expenditure	% of GDP
1971–72	47	20
1981–82	52	24
1987–88	56	23

(Lowe, 1994: 361)

The effectiveness of efforts to reduce expenditure by directing help to such particularly needy groups was undermined by the lack of coordination between the income tax and social security systems and by the complex patchwork of universal and means tested benefits which comprised Britain's welfare network. Resistance to change was evident both among interested professionals and the local authorities responsible for delivering many of the services. Re-elected for a third term in 1987, the Conservatives launched a determined assault on these obstacles, trying to weaken the professions, reduce the power of local authorities, and transferring financial oversight to small, non-elective bodies such as GP fundholders or hospital trusts. Supplementary Benefit was transformed into Income Support and its additional Exceptional Needs Payments became the Social Fund, with claimants expected to repay 70 per cent of any grants received. Provision was rationalised, too, one result being a reduction in the number of hospital beds from 455,000 in 1959 to 283,000 in 1989. Even so, health service expenditure grew faster than real GDP during the 1980s but still could not keep pace with a demand fuelled by the rising number of elderly people, the development of new but invariably expensive treatments, and rising popular expectations. Exactly the same problems were faced by the Japanese, although the underlying strength of their economy suggested that in the foreseeable future they would be better able to cope with them.

The original aim behind Beveridge's welfare scheme had been the elimination of poverty. Evidence that it had been unsuccessful was first compiled by sociologists in the 1960s and it continued to accrue thereafter. Although the estimated 'real' shortage of housing fell by two thirds between 1971 and 1986, 40,000 families were still officially homeless by the early 1990s. Main streets in some of the major cities once again resembled those of the late nineteenth century as they became refuges to a growing number of homeless. More than four million people were in receipt of means tested benefit by the early 1980s as against two million in 1966. Many more – one estimate put the figure in 1983 at 16.3 million – were living on or only marginally above the poverty threshold, now defined as income at 140 per cent of supplementary benefit level (Digby, 1989: 107). Such figures prompted one sociologist to conclude in 1987 that despite the growth of welfare expenditure, 'the burden of poverty has increased grotesquely over the last eight years' (Piachaud, 1987: 28). Another calculation, measuring poverty in terms of what people themselves thought essential in a modern society, concluded that about 2.6 million people, including one million children, were acutely poor, and between six and twelve million relatively so (Mack and Lansley, 1985). Not all of this, however, was attributable simply to inadequate benefit levels or delivery mechanisms. Low takeup remained a problem, while the emergence of new categories of need, especially single parent families, could be properly tackled only across a broad front involving cash payments, employment opportunities, and the provision of childminding facilities. By 1987, 14 per cent of all families with dependent children had only a single parent. About two thirds of them were living in poverty, victims, it was asserted, of changing sexual behaviour and the breakdown of traditional family ties.

Poverty had an ethnic dimension, too. Immigrant communities as a whole were disproportionately represented among the poor, the badly housed, and the unemployed although there were considerable differences of experience between the various racial groups. Generally, however, discrimination, large families, and educational under-achievement combined to condemn them to over-representation in the relatively low paid semi- and unskilled manual labouring classes (table 6.11).

Table 6.11: *Britain: ethnic origins of semi-skilled and unskilled workers, 1981 (%)*

White males	20.4
Non-white males	30.7
White females	31.5
None-white females	39.1

(Halsey, 1988: 584–5)

Rising welfare expenditures in the 1980s then did not result in any substantial reduction of poverty nor in any significant redistribution of income in Britain. Indeed, table 6.12 shows that between 1976 and 1985 the share of total household income taken by the bottom 40 per cent of households actually fell in terms of original income (income from employment, pensions, etc.), disposable income (income adjusted to allow for tax and national insurance and state benefits), and final income (disposable income remaining after payment of indirect taxes and adjustments to allow for government expenditures on health, education, etc.).

Table 6.12: *Britain: distribution of total household income, 1976–86*

	Share of income by household group (%)					
	Bottom 20%		Bottom 40%		Top 20%	
	1976	1986	1976	1986	1976	1986
Original income	0.8	0.3	10.2	6.0	44.4	50.7
Disposable income	7.0	5.9	19.6	16.9	38.1	42.2
Final income	7.4	5.9	20.1	17.3	37.9	41.7

(Page, 1991: 450)

Whatever the intention of government policy, the outcome was the creation of an economic underclass. This contrasted sharply with the personal and corporate gains made by those at the top of the social scale during the 1980s. While the growth of white collar and white blouse employment may have served to blur the occupational basis of class, a strong sense of class remained. Most public surveys in the 1980s confirmed this and at times of particular tension, such as the miners' strike, as many as three quarters of respondents admitted to a belief in class conflict (Abercrombie and Warde,

1988: 163). The uneven distribution of wealth may have confirmed this view (table 6.13). Estate duties and capital gains taxes had little effect in this respect, perhaps because, as a poll conducted by the magazine, *New Society*, showed, there was actually little popular support for wealth redistribution, even among those who might have been expected to be most sympathetic. Less than half of the most likely beneficiaries, social classes D and E, and of those likely to be most ideologically favourable, Labour Party supporters, were in favour of radical redistributive measures. With the possible exception of those few individuals involved in pressure groups supporting the homeless, single parent families, or low income groups, wealth inequalities, it seemed, did not trouble the British unduly at the end of the twentieth century.

Table 6.13: *Britain: wealth distribution (%)*

	1923	1938	1950	1960	1970	1984
Top 1%	60.9	55.0	47.2	33.9	29.7	21.0
Top 10%	89.1	85.0		71.5	68.7	52.0
Bottom 80% (+bottom 75%)	5.8	8.8		16.9	15.5	25.0+

(Page, 1991: 452)

Women and family

Politically, at least women made some further advances in these years. They accounted for almost a fifth of local councillors in 1982 and if the sixty elected as MPs in 1992 represented less than a tenth of the total number, over a hundred were returned in the election of May 1997. Women also became more active participants in higher education. Relatively few took degrees in science-based disciplines, but they accounted for 41 and 31.5 per cent of undergraduates and postgraduate students respectively in 1983–84 compared with 27.6 and 20.6 per cent in 1965–66.

More radical feminist thinking emerged out of the interplay between the Campaign for Nuclear Disarmament, the anti-Vietnam war movement, and various socialist groups. The first Women's Liberation Workshop was held in 1970 and attended by 600 delegates, giving a more strident edge to the growing advocacy of female rights which was coming from women in trade unions, professional associations, and interest groups such as the National Council of Married Women. The women's movement was particularly active in trying to secure welfare rights for low paid women, for instance. Ultimately it developed an important critique of the welfare state on the grounds that its operation reinforced women's dependence on men and thus their conventional role as unpaid carers and mothers.

In the early 1960s one sociological analysis of north London housewives suggested that relatively few women of whatever social class still saw their primary role as that of wife and mother. Little conflict was perceived between functioning concurrently as both a wife and a worker (Thane, 1991: 202). A broader study twenty years later reached the contrary conclusion that the large majority of women still saw marriage and motherhood as their main career (Martin and Roberts, 1984). Another analysis suggests that in middle-class families at least, the distribution of responsibilities and duties between husbands and wives remained fairly traditional (Edgell, 1980). Such findings do not altogether tie up with those of other surveys and are also difficult to square with the fact that between 1961 and 1981 the proportion of married women at work rose from 35 to 62 per cent (Lewis, 1992: 65)

Whatever women in the aggregate actually felt about their social role, longer life expectancies, smaller families, greater material expectations, and the changing nature of work all helped to draw them more fully into the labour market. By 1981 they formed about 50 per cent of the workforce and almost a half of those over the age of sixteen were working. Among ethnic groups the proportion was much higher, about two thirds in the case of Afro-Caribbeans, for example (Abercrombie and Warde, 1988: 216). By the 1990s all the major political parties had accepted some of women's aspirations for equal pay and work rights, child benefits, and maternity provision.

In the manufacturing industries women had long been subject to discrimination and prejudice. The Donovan Commission had observed in 1968 that

> many of the attitudes which support the present system of craft training and discrimination against women are common to both employers and trade unionists and deeply ingrained in the life of the country. Prejudice against women is manifest at all levels of management as well as one the shop floor. (Royal Commission, 1968: 93)

Such conclusions helped prompt the passage in 1970 of the Equal Pay Act. A modest measure, imperfectly because so hurriedly drafted to get through the House of Commons before the general election, it was intended to remove discriminatory pay discrepancies. Its effects were difficult to disentangle from other influences and varied according to occupations and ethnic group. The 1984 *New Earnings Survey* showed that on average women received three quarters of the average hourly rate for men, two thirds of males' weekly gross earnings. This was an improvement since 1970 but still fell far short of equality, reflecting the continued sexual segregation of the labour force. Nor did the act seek to address those barriers which effectively excluded women from high earning occupations. This was left to the Equal Opportunities Commission established by the 1975 Sex Discrimination Act. In the course of the 1980s the commission's powers were strengthened by decisions handed down from the European Commission and Court of Justice. By 1988 half the entrants to the British legal profession were women while just over a fifth of solicitors and doctors were female, although significant differences still remained in the gender composition of professions such as surgery and engineering (Thane, 1991: 207). Likewise, only 5 per cent of company directorships were held by women in the early 1990s and if 60 per cent of Lloyds Bank staff were female, only 2.5 per cent of its managers were (Giddens, 1993: 173).

A similar tale of mixed progress was unfolding for Japanese women in the last quarter of the twentieth century. Parliamentary representation remained low with women making up 8 per cent of the upper house and 1.4 per cent of the lower in the 1980s, although none of them represented the ruling LDP (Tasker, 1987: 180). Probably more an exercise in image building than in equal rights, Doi Takako was elected as the first female leader of the Japan Socialist Party in 1986. More significant perhaps were the appointments of two women to cabinet posts in 1987 and of a third to a senior post in the LDP. Changing attitudes were also suggested when Prime Minister Uno Sosuke was pushed to resign in 1989 on charges of womanising. There was a 50 per cent increase in the number of women holding management positions in business between 1970 and 1986 as pressure on the male labour supply led employers to start more women on fast management tracks. By 1994 nearly 51,000 Japanese companies, about 5 per cent of the total, had female chief executives (Kuriki, 1994: 13).

By this time just over a half of all Japanese women worked, representing 38.3 per cent of the workforce, proportions comparable with the situation in Britain. Between 1970 and 1984 the number of part time female workers increased four fold, particularly in small scale enterprises. In part at least this was the result of the Working Women's Welfare Law of 1972, an attempt to counter the national labour shortage by getting employers to be more sensitive to the welfare needs of working mothers. In 1992 the number of families in which both spouses worked overtook single income households for the first time. Despite the passage in 1986 of an Equal Opportunity Law, women's relative status in the workforce did not change much, however. They still dominated traditional occupations such as teaching but were overwhelmingly concentrated in the lower grades. As a result, they were generally precluded from the lifetime employment system. Many women started off on roughly equal terms with men, but by the age of thirty or so their wages were between 20 and 30 per cent lower, although even that was a substantial advance on the ratios prevailing in the early 1970s. Overall, women's average monthly earnings were slightly more than 50 per cent of the male average. Employers justified such discrepancies on the grounds that women tended to leave work to have families, making it difficult to give them equal treatment (Lo, 1990: 71). Interestingly, a survey of young women in the early 1990s revealed that half of them agreed with such sexual inequalities in the workforce, a marked contrast with Britain where only about a tenth did so (Mifune, 1995: 18–19).

This suggests that the subordinate status of women in the Japanese workplace did not rest solely on male prejudice or the ease with which employers could evade the 1986 legislation because it was not backed by any significant legal sanction. Except perhaps among that very small minority of intellectuals who embraced feminist liberation ideology in the 1970s, the situation was accepted by most women because marriage and family life were still widely regarded as the ultimate feminine ideals. Although about a third of all women entered higher education in 1984, not far behind the proportion of men at 38 per cent, the majority still took two year courses in subjects such as home economics, more geared to marriage than careers. In 1982 one survey of women in their twenties revealed that almost four fifths considered marriage as the ultimate source of female happiness compared with less than a half of British women (Mifune, 1995: 18–19). By the late 1980s it appeared that only 15 per cent of Japanese women wished to work on a long term basis. It was significant, too, that 93 per cent of all Japanese women over 25 in 1985 were or had been married (Hunter, 1989: 152). The evidence also suggests that women regarded their earnings as supplementary to those of their menfolk, their primary function in a marriage perceived as that of homemaker. A half of the women asked in 1994 to rank the ideal qualities of a potential wife, put in first place the ability to understand the demands made on a husband by his job. In second place (49 per cent) was the diligent carrying out of housework and child rearing (Tanifuji, 1995b: 25). Traditional gender roles within the family remained far stronger than in Britain where only a fifth of respondents agreed with the proposition that husbands should be the breadwinner and wives stay at home. Studies of the financial arrangements within families revealed that almost a half of Japanese wives were charged with full financial responsibility for the family budget, an arrangement operative in only 14 per cent of British families where shared responsibility was much more common (Mifune, 1995: 18–19). This may reflect the rather compartmentalised nature of Japanese family life in which the demands placed upon male breadwinners by the intensity of working life inevitably left wives carrying the main responsibility for domestic arrangements and child rearing. Effective family life was restricted to Sundays and public holidays.

That an increasing number of Japanese women went to work cannot by itself, therefore, be taken as evidence of fundamentally changing social aspirations, which remained strongly traditional, particularly in the countryside. It is true, however, that marriage continued to develop as primarily a romantic rather than a primarily contractual relationship, the proportion of arranged marriages falling between the 1960s and the 1980s from about a half to a fifth. Within marriage, too, gender roles were affected by demographic trends, just as they were in the labour market (Atoh, 1994: 19–22). Longer life expectancy and smaller families (the average Japanese couple had only 1.5 children in 1992) left women with more free time. After marriage they tended to work until the birth of their first child, returning to employment in their mid-thirties when their families were usually mature. Their personal freedom to work was further enhanced by the reduction in the number charged with responsibility for looking after elderly parents-in-law. About 60 per cent of households were nuclear by 1991, a rise from 1955 when the proportion was 45 per cent. This still left a significant number of retired people living with their children. Nevertheless, in 1973 less than one in five of Japanese mothers regarded their own current dependants as potential sources of support during their own old age (*Japan Report*, 16 October 1973).

The strength of the nuclear family in Japan reflected the progress of urbanisation and the declining significance of rural households. It did not experience anything like the growth of illegitimacy and divorce which in Britain left under a half of all families consisting of married couples with dependent children and about a fifth of them with a single parent. Only 1.4 per cent of households in Japan had a lone parent, a good number of them created by the death of the other parent (Health and Welfare Statistics Association, 1995: 25). Only 1 per cent of Japanese babies in 1994 were born out of wedlock, compared with 16.5 per cent of infants in England and Wales some ten years earlier. Against this, however, the number of induced abortions among those under twenty in Japan more than doubled between 1965 and 1993, a period when the national total fell by more than half as the Family Planning Federation of Japan (1954) offered advice on alternative forms of birth control (Health and Welfare Statistics Association, 1995: 80). As for divorce, by 1981 the number reached 159,000 in Britain, up by 132,000 on the 1961 figure. While this was in part the natural outcome of the greater number of marriages, the divorce rate also rose, by a factor of six between 1961 and 1991. By the mid-1990s 40 per cent of all marriages were destined to end in legal separations. This reflected the declining stigma attached to divorce, legal changes which made it easier, and the weakening of the wider social support mechanisms which in the past might have held faltering relationships together.

In Japan, there was a similarly rising trend with divorce numbers doubling from 1950 to reach just over 188,000 by 1993 but this represented a much lower rate of termination than in Britain (Health and Welfare Statistics Association, 1995: 62). Internal disciplines and ties within Japanese families were probably stronger anyway and as social units they were buttressed by the external groups with which individual members identified – the company, agricultural cooperatives, or professional associations for husbands; school and college for children; parent teacher associations and consumer groups for wives, dominated by the ubiquitous Women's Association to which more than half of Japanese women in these years belonged.

7

Power and ritual, 1945–*c*.1995

Introduction

At the end of the Second World War Britain's political and social infra-structures remained essentially intact. Those of Japan were radically revised as part of an American policy consciously intended to immunise the country against any resurgence of extreme nationalism and militarism. Although occasionally disturbed by outbreaks of nationalist sentiment, democratic government was successfully established. Thereafter, some aspects of post-war Japanese political development mirrored to a greater or lesser degree those of Britain, in particular the growth of centralisation, the emergence of corporate decision-making and the general parliamentary predominance of one party. In both countries, too, there were signs from the 1970s of growing disenchantment with formal political processes. Associated with this was a more general rejection by the first postwar generation of the values on which their parents had rebuilt their respective societies after 1945. While it would be unwise to discount entirely explanations for such phenomena couched in national terms, similar developments were apparent in many advanced industrial countries. This suggests that broader international influences were also at work as communication technology and economic imperatives pro-gressively reduced the significance of geography and helped to undermine or refashion some of the legacies of the past.

The system of power

Formal structures: Britain

The return of peace in 1945 saw the election of the first majority Labour Government in Britain's history, prompting the unwise and much quoted claim of one radical that 'we are the masters now' (Howard, 1964: 15).

However, little major alteration occurred in the country's formal structures of power. The medieval Courts of Assize were replaced by a system of high court and circuit judges, the quarter sessions by recorders. Later changes included the introduction of life peerages in 1958 to enhance the social and intellectual standing of a comparatively weak House of Lords. Both main political parties introduced more open and democratic ways of selecting their leaders. In 1948 residential qualifications for the franchise were ended while the abolition of university and business votes eliminated the last vestiges of plural voting. A far more significant measure was the reduction of the voting age to eighteen in 1969.

The prestige of the monarchy, apparently under a cloud as recently as 1936, was much strengthened both by the refusal of the royal family to leave the country during the war and by its direct public involvement in morale-boosting activities. Coinciding as it did with the ending of postwar austerity, the accession of Elizabeth II in 1952 produced much romantic talk of a new Elizabethan Age. If this never materialised, the young queen set about her state duties with a vigour and charm that prompted admiration even from critics (Martin, 1962). Some diminution in the global authority of the crown was inevitable as the process of dismantling the empire gathered momentum from the late 1940s onwards. In the longer run, entry to the European Community was much more fundamental to the constitutional position of the monarchy and indeed to every other institution of power and authority in Britain. Although the full implications of entry emerged only gradually as the community itself evolved, it was becoming apparent by the 1990s that the supremacy of the Houses of Parliament and the British courts was increasingly passing to European institutions.

Formal structures: Japan

For Japan, defeat in 1945 resulted in radical changes to the system of power and authority as the occupying authorities determined to establish a democratic society secure against militarism and extremism. Hardly an aspect of Japanese life was left untouched in pursuit of this objective. The ownership of land and industry was reorganised on democratic lines. The *ie* was abolished and the subordination of women outlawed, while the state's ability to control popular opinion was reduced by scrapping the dangerous thoughts legislation and decentralising education and policing. The armed forces were dismantled, the new constitution formally renounced war as an instrument of policy, and Shinto was deprived of its privileged status as the state religion. The chief innovation in the legal system was the vesting of all judicial power in a new Supreme Court. In practice, the court proved reluctant to exercise its right of determining the constitutionality of laws, but it was important in safeguarding the individual rights which, it was purposed, should replace the prewar concept of personal responsibility as the basic tenet of citizenship.

Popular sovereignty was basic to SCAP's vision of Japanese democracy and entailed a major change in the constitutional position of the emperor. Some wished to abolish the whole imperial system on the grounds that the emperor's theoretically absolute powers had allowed the prewar military to usurp his authority in the name of patriotism. Others demanded that Emperor Hirohito be tried as a war criminal, although this was successfully resisted by General MacArthur. A poll in December 1945 indicated that 95 per cent of Japanese wished the Showa emperor to remain on the throne, support perhaps for MacArthur's claim that a royal execution would provoke guerilla warfare on such a massive scale that a million extra troops would be required to contain it. But there were other good reasons for allowing Hirohito to retain his position. He represented a way of legitimating SCAP's reforms, providing an important psychological bridge with the past and bringing an element of stability and continuity to the political system.

In the event, therefore, both Hirohito and the imperial system survived, though mainly as symbols of the state and shorn of effective power. The royal family was restricted to the emperor and his three brothers, imperial property was transferred to the state, and the royal finances subjected to Dietary control. The Privy Council was disbanded and the Imperial Household Ministry brought under the direction of the Prime Minister's Office. The new constitution vested sovereignty in the people. The electorate was to include women for the first time and the voting age was lowered from twenty five to twenty. The peerage was abolished and the upper house of the Diet reconstituted as a House of Councillors elected to serve for six years. Three fifths of the members were to be returned from the forty seven prefectures each with at least two seats, the rest being elected by the nation at large. The lower House of Representatives was left with 466 members as in 1925, but the first peace-time election led to an influx of fresh political blood, only a fifth of those elected having served before. One important element of the prewar system which did survive was the use of multi-member electoral districts, most of which returned between three and five representatives to the lower house. Some later adjustments to allow for population shifts raised the total membership of the House of Representatives to 512 by 1986 but even then there were still 130 constituencies each electing between three and five members.

Under the previous constitution Japan's prime ministers had been legally answerable to the emperor. The new system made them responsible to the lower house, from whose majority party cabinets were to be drawn. Political parties, effectively suppressed under the old regime, began to re-form. Seiyukai was reorganised as the Liberal Party while Minseito became first the Progressive and then the Democratic Party, although it shared the Liberals' broadly conservative outlook. On the left, old prewar groups re-emerged in a Socialist Party whose appeal was at once evident in the 1946 election when it took almost a fifth of the vote, almost twice the share secured in the final prewar electoral contest of 1937. In the first election held under the new constitution, the socialists did well enough to form a government. Rather to SCAP's relief, however, they were not strong enough in the Diet to carry through their radical policies and in 1948 the government split and resigned. At the ensuing election socialist representation in the Diet fell by more than half and the Liberals came to power.

From October 1948 Yoshida Shigeru guided Japan through the remainder of the Occupation, using his influence to ensure that some of the more radical SCAP reform schemes, most notably those concerning the *zaibatsu*, were watered down. By the time Yoshida resigned in 1954, the revitalised Japan Socialist Party (JSP) appeared once more as a serious political threat. Faced with this possibility of a renewed socialist challenge, the two conservative parties merged into a single party, the Liberal Democrats. This broad alliance against socialism and communism held unbroken power in Japan until the early 1990s. Even when it was finally ousted by an eight party coalition, it was still the largest single party in the Diet with 36.6 per cent of the vote and 223 seats. The second party, the JSP, secured 15.4 per cent of the vote and only seventy seats.

Single party dominance

The LDP's long dominance in the postwar period has often been attributed to the vagaries of the electoral system. One vote, multi-member electoral districts naturally encouraged parties to put up several candidates. This raised the risk that one might receive so much popular support that the chances of party colleagues were seriously weakened, but in a constituency with say five seats a shift of more than 20 per cent in the number of votes cast was required in order to gain an extra representative. This explains why it was very difficult to oust the party in power, but not why that party was for so long the LDP. For that, we must look first to the party's record of economic achievement. Almost two thirds of the Liberal Party's successful Dietary candidates in 1946 were from a business background and this close connection with the commercial community ensured that the party's consistent success in promoting growth on the basis of private enterprise brought handsome electoral returns. Such policies appealed not only to the business elements, the major source of political funding in Japan, but also to the mass of the electorate whose rising living standards were the natural outcome of high growth rates. Few were going to reject a government which presided over such significant and rapid improvements as Japan experienced from the 1950s onwards.

Equally important, however, was the strength of the LDP's rural support. The designation of the electoral districts drawn up in the 1940s naturally reflected the existing distribution of population. Although more seats were subsequently created in recognition of developing urbanisation, the country areas generally remained over-represented. By the mid-1980s industrial constituencies had only 190 or 37 per cent of the seats in the lower house. The political significance of this lay in the fact that the countryside usually returned over 60 per cent of the LDP's Diet members and all nine premiers who served between 1960 and 1987 held rural seats. Furthermore, the uneven size of electoral districts also worked to the LDP's advantage. A rural seat, for example, might represent 115,000 voters whereas in some urban areas it could be as many as 500,000. Thus the party usually won more seats than its share of the popular vote would indicate simply because a large number of them were elected from comparatively small rural districts.

Not surprisingly, therefore, the LDP took good care of Japan's agriculturalists. Inflation rapidly reduced the real debt burden acquired by those farmers who bought land after the war. High protection and the provision of central subsidies ensured that most of them shared in the economic miracle. By the 1980s soaring land values had combined with the lack of any compulsory purchase system and low land taxes to give farmers annual incomes a third higher than the national average. Their Co-operative Union had a bigger turnover than Toyota and their bank was the ninth largest in the world. The LDP was equally careful to direct investment to the countryside. By 1982 public investment in the Niigata district, for example, was six times higher than the district's tax yield. Conversely, in the same year Tokyo residents paid twice as much in taxes as they received in spending on public works.

A third reason for the LDP's long monopoly of power lay in the nature of the parliamentary opposition. In the main, the predecessors of the LDP had represented small town and rural Japan while the progressive parties on the left had drawn most of their support from the cities and Marxist intellectuals, who had been suppressed in the 1930s. In the straitened economic circumstances of the Occupation years, ideological differences between left and right were sharp, manifest in endemic industrial unrest and the threat of a general strike. It may well be that the potential for violence was checked only by the presence of the Occupation army and MacArthur's dictatorial powers. Growing prosperity, however, narrowed the gap. Gradually both left and right drifted towards the political centre and it was significant in this respect that by the late 1950s the majority of bills went through the Diet unopposed. Only occasionally did issues such as the renewal of the American Security Treaty in 1960 or the Vietnam War expose underlying divisions with a capacity for degenerating into violence. Economic recovery effectively emasculated the general political appeal of left wing parties.

Equally importantly, however, the left was no more able in the postwar years than it had been in the 1920s to overcome its own internal wrangling in order to mount a united challenge to LDP hegemony. The significance of this was underlined by the fact that in every election between 1971 and 1983 the LDP vote was always lower than that given to the four main opposition parties combined. On the far left was the Communist Party whose espousal of Marxist-Leninism had a perennial fascination for a hard core of intellectuals. The movement's political influence was much weakened in June 1950 when, following allegations of communist-inspired disruptions to the national railway system, SCAP purged communists from public office. Thereafter, communism apparently had little appeal to the masses, more and more of whom were able to satisfy their aspirations to a middle-class life style as their living standards rose. The communists enjoyed something of a revival from the 1960s under the leadership of Miyamoto Kenji, but after his death in 1982 this support diminished and in the 1993 election only 7.7 per cent of the vote and a handful of seats were secured.

The main party of the left, the JSP, did patch up its internal differences in 1955 but they were opened up again by disagreements about the renewal of the American security treaty in 1960. Right wing members defected to form the Democratic Socialist Party, and its appeal to the more moderate of the major labour federations, *Domei*, split the trade union movement. The more radical *Sohyo* continued to back the JSP which lurched to the left, losing much of its electoral support in the process. In 1958 it had 32.9 per cent of the popular vote but only 21.9 per cent in 1972, by which time it was actually doing better in rural and small town constituencies than in its traditional heartlands of the Kanto and Kansai industrial belts.

In the same election 8 per cent of the total national vote went to another opposition group, the left of centre *Komeito* or Clean Government Party. It was formally established in 1964, although its sponsor, a Buddhist lay organisation called *Soka Gakkai*, had been participating in elections since 1955. In 1993, by which time *Soka Gakkai* had about 7.5 million members, *Komeito* captured fifty one seats in the Diet and played its part in bringing to an end, at least briefly, the long rule of the LDP (Morita, 1993: 22–4).

While the postwar dominance of the LDP in Japanese political life was remarkable, it was matched, albeit to a lesser degree, by the achievements of the British Conservative Party which won eight of the fourteen general elections held between 1945 and 1992, each time with a sufficient majority to implement its programme. The Conservatives held parliamentary power for two thirds of the time between 1945 and 1995. By contrast, Labour had parliamentary majorities of more than ten for only four years, winning only two elections with comfortable working majorities. This was all the more remarkable, given that the British first-past-the-post electoral system required only a small shift in voting patterns to produce significant changes in party representation. Since this general preference for the Conservatives had prevailed in the interwar period as well, it might be taken as evidence for the existence of some innate conservatism in the British psyche. Against this it can be noted that, like the LDP in Japan, the Conservatives seldom gained a majority of the total votes cast in general elections. This was also true of Labour's crushing victory in 1997, even though the party had moved decisively to occupy the political middle ground usually dominated by the Tories.

Others have attributed the Conservatives' dominance to the influence of the press because with the exception of the group owned by Cecil King and the *Daily Herald* which collapsed early in the 1960s, it was overwhelmingly Tory in sympathy. However, the implication of such an argument – that voters were incapable of independent political thought or electoral judgement – is to say the least, unflattering. More significant perhaps was the weakness of the opposition and in particular the Labour Party's inability to resolve its own internal ideological differences. After 1950 the party did well at the polls only when it ignored its own left wing. Here was another obvious parallel with Japan, where the fragmented state of the opposition parties worked to the electoral advantage of the LDP. More mundanely, perhaps, the British Conservative Party resembled the LDP in that it benefited from the consistent aggregate improvement in voters' average living standards, although this suggestion does not always square very easily with electoral defeats in 1964 and 1974.

Democracy

The lack of any effective opposition to the LDP has sometimes been taken to imply that Japan's postwar democracy was something of a sham, failing to guarantee popular sovereignty through the disposition of political parties in the Diet. It is certainly possible to marshall evidence for such a point of view. First, the Supreme Court never really challenged the executive. Although the Court adjudged that several general elections were unfair and unconstitutional because the electoral districts were so unequal, it was unwilling to take the logical step of declaring the results void. The relatively recent tradition of an independent judiciary, fear of appearing to revert to the prewar position of interference with Dietary sovereignty, and the generally conservative tendencies of the judges may all help to explain this reluctance (Eccleston, 1989: 123–9).

Second, Japan's ethnic minorities remained in a subordinate position in the political structure. They could be ignored relatively easily because, unlike equivalent groups in Britain, they were not, with the exception perhaps of the Ainu, physically very distinctive. Nor were they very numerous. Some 24,000 Ainu hunters in Hokkaido could thus be safely ignored, as could the *burakamin*, officially numbered at slightly more than a million in 1987, and 700,000 ethnic Koreans. The latter in particular were subject to discrimination in terms of housing, education, and employment. Effectively, they were simply denied citizenship, regardless of the fact that many were Japanese-born. But if this was a defect in Japanese democracy, the contrast with Britain was less sharp than might appear. British racial minorities were certainly not subjected to formal official discrimination, and indeed appeared to be protected by legislation. It was often argued, however, that the various immigration controls introduced from the 1950s were themselves discriminatory, while laws governing racial equality could not overcome popular xenophobia. Nonwhites remained under-represented in major professions (98.7 per cent of Britain's 48,500 solicitors were white in 1987) and over-represented among the socially deprived. Even by the 1990s ethnic groups had scarcely penetrated the system of power and authority, only a few MPs of immigrant stock having emerged.

Critics of Japan's democratic credentials point also to the strong political factionalism which, among other things, produced a very high turnover among prime ministers – no fewer than twenty between 1946 and 1994 as against ten in Britain. Yet factionalism was not inherently incompatible with democracy. It worked well, first as a way of selecting prime ministers and second as a means of restraining any autocratic tendencies which premiers might subsequently reveal. Party consensus could be more easily achieved on the basis of the views of a group of faction leaders rather than of the whole party. At the same time, membership of a particular faction allowed relatively junior members to secure a better hearing than they could hope for in the party at large. Furthermore, faction was the product of a specific cultural context. In Japan's earlier social structure support for an individual's immediate *samurai* leader was in practice more important than the higher loyalty nominally due to the emperor. In this sense, perhaps, factionalism was the political equivalent of the company system, faithful service being rewarded in both cases by patronage and other benefits. So integral were factions to Japanese politics that they were actually officially registered organisations with offices and activities independent of the central party. Since political contributions tended to be made to faction leaders rather than to parties, the influence of prominent individuals was further strengthened, in some cases outlasting their own tenure of high political office. Even after his own premiership ended in 1974 Tanaka Kakuei continued to dominate the LDP, deciding who its – and thus the nation's – leader should be. In this way he was able to operate behind the scenes rather in the manner of the old *genro*.

The existence of multi-member constituencies also encouraged factionalism. Before reforms in 1994 raised the number of single seat districts in the lower house to 300, a party wishing to win a Diet majority had to field sufficient candidates to secure the majority of seats in each electoral district. As electors had only one vote, however, candidates from a particular party had to fight each other as well as their opponents. For this reason it was essential to build up local support groups or *koenkai*, although the country's strict electoral laws often compelled them to masquerade as cultural organisations. Close connections between politicians and local industries or interests were thus an integral part of parliamentary politics. Dietmen rarely changed constituencies and the carpet bagging so typical of British parliamentary candidatures was relatively uncommon in Japan.

With the estimated cost of winning a seat as high as Y7 billion and with parliamentary salaries and expenses (plus free housing and secretarial assistance) five and a half times the national average wage in the mid-1980s, Dietmen needed and could well afford to keep their local support machines well oiled. The system thus carried with it an obvious potential for corruption. In 1986 10,500 individuals were questioned on suspicion of vote buying, a figure reckoned to represent merely the tip of a substantial iceberg. Nine out of Japan's first sixteen postwar premiers were investigated for graft but the problem became more newsworthy from the 1970s as the result of some particularly spectacular revelations. In December 1974 Prime Minister Tanaka resigned after a magazine exposed his somewhat cavalier acceptance of political contributions and the use of his own money to influence decisions. Further allegations that he had taken bribes from the American Lockheed Corporation led to his indictment and conviction. In the following decade Takeshita Noboru was similarly caught up in corruption involving illicit business dealings. The ensuing defections from the LDP led ultimately to the formation of various new parties.

Although these aspects of political life were sometimes interpreted as being incompatible with democratic government, they were nothing new. As early as 1918 one Japanese thinker had observed that in the East political parties quickly became factions 'pursuing private and personal interests' (Tsunoda, de Bary and Keene, 1958: 690). Just as factional politics have to be understood in the context of Japan's own history, the same is true of what appears at first sight to be bribery and corruption. The giving of gifts and favours traditionally incurred mutual obligations. It is significant that even after he was indicted, Tanaka was re-elected by supporters obviously untroubled by ethical considerations of a Western type. His political methods, said one commentator, were at the heart of the system, 'the embodiment of today's Japan' (Tasker, 1987: 230).

It might also be argued that compared with the situation in Britain the alleged flaws in Japanese democracy represented differences of degree rather than of kind. After all, neither faction nor graft were entirely absent from British politics, though their forms may have been more subtle. Undeclared institutional and individual donations to party funds could well be seen as possessing at least a potential for corruption, as might the honours system with which such contributions were sometimes linked. Nor were all MPs or ministers above allowing personal considerations to influence political actions. It was also revealing that until 1996 members of parliament resisted proposals to compel full disclosure of their extra-parliamentary incomes and activities, which included for the average Conservative MP in 1988 two company chairmanships and four directorships (Abercrombie and Warde, 1988: 494).

Equally, both main British parties were riddled with factions which, though usually crystalising around individuals, generally had more to do with issues than personalities. As in Japan, the nature of the electoral process was influential in this respect. The first-past-the-post system effectively marginalised all ideological extremists, thus compelling the Conservative and Labour Parties to accommodate the full spectrum of thought within their own ranks. Thus Labour was always divided between those wanting to offer an electable, reforming alternative to Conservatism, and those who preferred to hold out for more fundamental change (Norton, 1980). Only in 1945–50 did the party programme satisfy both wings. In the 1950s this underlying ideological division manifested itself in disputes about the need for further nationalisation and rearmament. From the mid-1960s onwards the left gained an increasing prominence through the Tribune Group and the capture of a number of major unions, while Trotskyists infiltrated the party via the Militant Tendency. From 1974 the left was almost a separate entity from the parliamentary party, gaining even more influence following the Conservative victory in the 1979 general election. When the Campaign for Labour Party Democracy handed the election of the leader over to an electoral college, leading right wingers broke away to form the Social Democratic Party (SDP) in 1981. A sustained campaign through the 1980s by an erstwhile left wing leader, Neil Kinnock, regained control for the centre. Paradoxically, his unexpected election defeat in 1992 strengthened the moderates' hand still further, so much so that his successor, Tony Blair, was able to rewrite what had hitherto been regarded as a cardinal tenet of the socialist faith, the commitment to nationalisation of the means of production, distribution, and exchange, contained in clause four of the party's constitution. Moving decisively into the political centre, Blair led his party to a landslide victory in May 1997.

Conservative factions were also ideological rather than personal. At different periods overlapping tendencies, whether progressive, moderate, new right, neo-imperialist, or old right, dominated the party. At least four major changes of emphasis in the postwar period prompted one expert to suggest cynically but not inaccurately that Conservatism's only ideology – and certainly its most enduring one – was the retention of power (Seldon, 1991: 249). On the other hand, the last phase, which sought to embrace the free market philosophy, was so closely identified with the party leader that it became widely known as an 'ism' in its own right. Thatcherism was never such a coherent ideology as this suggests and it was in any case fundamentally misconceived. Another important ideological rift within Conservatism, and one apparent also within Labour ranks, if more muted and tightly controlled, involved objections to the perceived loss of British sovereignty entailed in moves towards greater European integration.

Corporatism

It has been argued that the influence most corrosive of popular sovereignty in postwar Japan was corporatism, the decision-making process in which power rested not exclusively with the Diet but rather with a triumvirate consisting of the politicians, business interests, and the bureaucracy. Inputs to policy came from all three, were turned into concrete proposals by the civil service, and put into effect by the ruling political party. The LDP was always closely identified with business, while businessmen themselves were subjected to considerable influence and pressure from a bureaucracy which, despite SCAP's initial purges, retained much of its prewar power. Retribution was certainly one of the occupying Americans' initial objectives and a number of national leaders and war criminals were in fact executed. Some 200,000 individuals designated for removal from high office included a number of civil servants selected on the grounds that they had been among the chief agents of prewar policy. In the event, however, only about 2 per cent of those investigated were actually purged and while these included a number of senior civil servants, the influence of the national administration itself largely survived. Both the language problem and the fact that the bureaucracy had become well attuned from the 1930s to functioning as a subordinate of the military, made it inevitable that the Americans should have to rely on it during the Occupation. Once the Americans withdrew, Japanese bureaucrats continued to play an important role in the formulation and implementation of policy.

The symbiotic relationship between business, politics, and administration was expressed in the interflow of personnel between them. The tendency of retired bureaucrats to gravitate towards business or politics was so common that the Japanese even gave it a name, *amakudari* (the descent from heaven), but the flow was two way. As early as 1949 17 per cent of Liberal Dietmen were former bureaucrats, and most prime ministers before 1972 began their careers as civil servants. Thereafter, the tendency was for prime ministers to come up directly, like Tanaka, through the party ranks although successors such as Fukuda Takeo (1976–78) and Ohira Masayoshi (1978–80) began their careers in the civil service. It was also true that from the late 1970s bureaucratic influence on big business weakened somewhat, but the decision-making process still remained essentially a three-sided one, the political dimension to the notion of Japan Incorporated.

Similar tendencies have been identified in Britain as early as the 1920s, when a 'corporate bias' is said to have emerged, mainly out of government efforts to resolve differences between labour and capital informally rather than through institutionalised systems. Long before 1945, it is suggested, parliament ceased to be the supreme governing body, becoming instead the electoral source of the political majority and merely the provider of the party element in government (Middlemas, 1979). The gradual shift towards corporatism was accelerated during the Second World War which conferred enormous power on organised labour, epitomised perhaps in Bevin's role and the creation of a tripartite Production Council. After 1945 the trend became still more pronounced with the proliferation of the administrative agencies needed to support the formal planning associated with Keynesian economics. By the 1960s one eminent political scientist could refer to the 'vast, untidy system of functional representation that has grown up alongside the older system of parliamentary representation' (Beer, 1965: 337). In the process, the House of Commons was diminished, becoming little more than

> a theatre for the presentation of policy and legislation, and for belated and usually ineffectual criticism by the Opposition only after discussion behind the scenes between ministers and civil servants and the functional interests concerned. The real decisions were agreed on behind closed doors by 'unassuming experts'. (Perkin, 1989: 328)

As parliamentary debates declined in significance, the voices of MPs were increasingly submerged beneath a flood of opinions emanating from the media. But as individuals they no longer counted for very much anyway as they were effectively reduced to lobby fodder, professional career politicians increasingly detached from meaningful links with their constituencies. At the same time, the power of the cabinet expanded and it appeared to become ever less accountable to the House of Commons. Under Labour in the 1960s and 1970s it was frequently complained that British Government was becoming almost presidential, while the high attrition rate among Conservative ministers from 1979 also suggested that the first female prime minister in British history had a highly developed instinct for self preservation. It became increasingly common for ministers to ignore the tradition which demanded their resignation in the event of major blunders by the departments for which they were responsible.

Superficially, the corporatist hypothesis does combine quite neatly two different analyses of the distribution of power in modern Britain, the pluralist and the elitist. The first argues that effective power was fragmented with many different groups competing to influence policy. The second suggests that most of the key power groups were dominated by elites of white males, sharing a common educational background (usually private school and Oxbridge), moving in the same restricted social milieu, and between them determining the agenda of national political life. Nevertheless, as an interpretation of postwar British politics corporatism is open to question. First, although the unions were undoubtedly consulted widely on policy issues, especially in the 1940s, and again in the 1960s and 1970s, leaders were frequently unable to control their rank and file members, or to deliver their promises and commitments. Perhaps the most that can be said is that for part of the postwar period British unions were more involved in the decision-making process than in Japan where independent organised labour, after its initial postwar flourish, was largely transmogrified into company unionism. The continued growth of the service sector and small company employment helped to reduce Japanese union membership from 45 to 28 per cent of the workforce between 1970 and 1985. Even the unions' role in negotiating annual wage bonuses gradually diminished over the years. From the 1980s onwards British trade unionism also lost much of its influence under the combined impact of mass unemployment, industrial decline, and restrictive legislation.

Second, the business element in what has been termed Britain's 'wartime triangle' was weak compared with its Japanese equivalent. Smaller scale business organisation, the relative frailty of employers' federations, and the tendency for firms to act individually meant that the role of business in national politics was probably less significant than that of the TUC. In any case, the inclination of the Treasury-dominated civil service to subjugate the interests of industry to those of finance almost certainly meant that even after the establishment of the Confederation of British Industry in the 1960s, the collective political influence of manufacturing was weaker than that of the well organised business lobbies in Japan.

It may also be suggested, though with less certainty, that the civil service element in the British system was less influential than its Japanese counterpart, notwithstanding its greater size. In the late 1980s, for example, Japan had forty four civil servants per thousand people as against just over a hundred per thousand in Britain. However, decision-makers in Britain frequently consulted professional experts outside as well as inside the civil service. Observing both this and the increasingly professional composition of the House of Commons, Professor Perkin has argued in *The Rise of Professional Society* that British corporatism might be more accurately interpreted as the triumph of professional society. Certainly by 1979 almost two thirds of MPs were drawn from the professions.

Finally, while by the early 1990s corporatism was widely believed in Japan to be breaking down, with one diplomat referring to the 'collapse of the triangle of politics, business and the bureaucracy', its earlier operation was generally smoothed by an underlying social ethic of harmony and consensus (Thomas, 1996: 303). This was in contrast to the more confrontational, individualistic nature of British decision-making. The Conservative politician, Anthony Barber, exaggerated in claiming that the miners' strike of 1973–74 presented the nation with a choice between parliamentary government on the one hand and 'chaos, anarchy and a totalitarian or Communist regime' (Porter, 1994: 339). But it was true that British corporatism always had to contend with a social ethic in which, as a leading French scholar pointed out, the 'them and us division is still fundamental' (Bedarida, 1979: 290). This helps explain why the priorities of economic policy in postwar Britain were never so unanimous as those of Japan. Its persistence probably reflected the fact that historically the average Briton valued liberty far more than egalitarianism. Interestingly, opinion polls in Japan in the 1990s showed exactly the reverse – that of all advanced peoples, the Japanese had the strongest preference for equality over freedom (Tanifuji, 1995a: 25).

Finally, even if it is allowed that some version of corporate government operated in Britain for part of the postwar period, it was much weakened, if not actually destroyed, by the advent of the Thatcher administrations after 1979. The contrast between the Britain of the early 1960s and that of the early 1990s was well described by Anthony Sampson who noted how since 1979 'the national cast of public characters has narrowed. The earlier drama', he went on, referring to his 1965 book, *The Anatomy of Britain Today*,

> included a range of major speaking parts, including trade unionists, local coun-
> cillors, vice-chancellors, scientists, regional leaders and maverick politicians.
> Now the story line and supporting characters have been pared down to the cen-
> tral plot, revolving round money, the Treasury and – above all – Downing Street.
> (*Independent on Sunday*, 29 March 1992)

Dealignment

Whatever the validity of arguments concerning corporatism and the erosion of popular sovereignty, there were indications in both Britain and Japan from the 1960s of a growing disaffection with formal politics, revealing itself initially in falling levels of party activism and support. A declining propor-
tion of Japanese was willing to acknowledge allegiance to a particular party. Only 19 per cent of those polled in 1953 declared that they had no specific political affiliation but by 1993 the proportion had risen to 41 per cent (table 7.1). A survey carried out by the Federation of Iron and Steel Unions showed that only 10 per cent of members professed to support the JSP, the party to which the Federation was formally pledged. The LDP had the support of 16 per cent of the members, the Democratic Socialists 11 per cent. Most telling of all was the 55 per cent who supported no party at all (Tasker, 1987: 177).

Table 7.1 *Party political support in Japan (%)*

	1953	1963	1973	1983	1993
LDP	41	43	33	39	27
SDP	23	22	17	13	9
None	19	22	33	32	41

(Tanifuji, 1995c: 25)

Similar tendencies were also discernible in Britain. It 1963 it was possible for two political scientists to argue that the country had a highly differenti-
ated political culture and that the regime enjoyed wide support from a population content to work within existing political channels (Almond and Verba, 1963). Subsequently, however, the intensity of voter loyalty to the main parties diminished. In the 1960s about 45 per cent expressed very

strong attachment to a party as against only 21 per cent by 1979 (Sarlvik and Crewe, 1983). Party support also declined in the 1970s with Labour membership going down from 1.3 million to 600,000. This was said to be linked to the putative process of working-class embourgeoisement and the declining number of white male manual workers, but such developments cannot explain the similar fall in Conservative membership, which dropped by about half from two to one million in the same period. A more likely explanation for diminishing party enrolments, therefore, is that activists in both camps were becoming progressively more disillusioned by the growing tendency of MPs to vote according to party whips rather than their con-stituency wishes. The consequent shrinkage of local support was one reason why followers of ideologues such as the Tory Keith Joseph and the socialist Tony Benn were able to capture control of constituency organisations.

These indications of disenchantment with established political institutions and processes were accompanied in both countries by the tendency of a minority to resort to extra-parliamentary methods in pursuit of political ends. Probably the worst instance in Japan occurred in the summer of 1960 when the Security Treaty with the United States came up for renewal. There was strong resistance to the new agreement, which proposed no restriction on the uses to which American bases in Japan might be put. Opposition sur-faced in the Diet, there was fighting in the streets, and a right wing zealot assassinated the leader of the socialist party for suggesting that China and Japan had a common enemy in America. Even so, while the Japanese Government had to face the embarrassment of postponing a proposed visit from President Eisenhower, the overall situation was not nearly as serious as, for example, the 1918 Rice Riots. Most people remained unaffected and were soon distracted by Ikeda's announcement of the income doubling plan and then the staging of the 1964 Olympic Games in Tokyo. Student unrest, on the other hand, was a more persistent problem. Growing out of broad opposition to the Vietnam War it eventually came to focus most sharply on the construc-tion of Narita Airport on the outskirts of Tokyo. From 1966 the students worked so effectively with farmers and environmentalists that completion of the airport was delayed until 1978. The ultimate expression of direct action in Japan appeared in the form of the terrorist Red Army. Although it attracted a good deal of media coverage and appeared to have links with similar terror groups abroad, it never represented a serious threat to national stability.

Britain had its own share of student unrest in the course of the 1960s and 1970s, much of it also driven by opposition to American foreign policy and leading to street demonstrations and the wholesale disruption of some uni-versities. Other forms of violence, which flared up intermittently in the form of internecine brawls between mods and rockers or competing gangs of foot-ball supporters, were shortlived and usually very localised disturbances, generally manifestations of over-indulgence in alcohol, representing high spirits and hooliganism rather than philosophical rejection of parliamentary government. A more serious threat was presented, however, by the developing violence of industrial unrest. The adoption of the so-called flying picket tactic gave strikers victory at the Saltley Coke Depot in 1972. Its use during the miners' strikes in 1973–74 and again in 1984–85, both of which had strong political overtones, prompted some wildly exaggerated discussion of whether Britain was in the process of becoming ungovernable. High levels of unemployment from the 1980s soon helped to take the edge off industrial militancy, however. The unemployed proved generally as acquiescent as they had in the 1930s and largely for the same reasons – regional concentration, the destructive psychology of unemployment, and a perpetual hope that a benign providence would bless a gamble on the pools, the horses or – from 1995 – the National Lottery, on which the socially deprived spent proportionately more heavily than the better off. Even so, unemployment played some part, as did racial tensions, in sparking off inner city riots. These were costly in terms of damage to property and were sometimes ascribed to frustration with parliamentary means of securing economic and social change, although vandalism and boredom were also contributory factors.

The most potent rejection of parliamentary authority, though of a most singular kind, occurred in Northern Ireland where a determined campaign by the Catholic minority to secure civil rights ultimately led to the abolition of the province's own parliament in 1972. Equal rights were then guaranteed by the Westminster parliament. In the accompanying civil disorder the struggle was hi-jacked, becoming a bloody three sided struggle between the crown forces, a resurgent Irish Republican Army, and pro-Union terror groups. While resort to terrorism might be seen as a rebuttal of parliamentary democracy, from a nationalist perspective it was generally portrayed as a colonial freedom fight and a rejection only of the *British* parliament.

What general reasons can be identified for the apparent disillusionment with prevailing constitutional practices and institutions in Britain and Japan from the 1960s? In Japan loss of confidence in the political process has been variously attributed to the continuing revelations about corruption within the faction-riddled LDP, the more volatile state of the economy, and also to general uncertainties about the nation's role in the post Cold War world, seen best perhaps in the government's inept response to the Gulf War crisis. Such considerations may help to explain the indications of discontent apparent in the 1990s, but most postdate a process which, measured by party affiliations, first began to develop much earlier. More plausibly, an explanation usually advanced in the British context might be applicable in some measure to Japan. Britain's experience fits well with the post-materialist hypothesis that by the early 1970s a postwar generation was rejecting the material concerns of the preceding generation in favour of higher needs, such as personal fulfilment and growth, abandoning hierarchy and formalism in favour of participatory decision-making. It is in this light, it has been argued, that unconventional protest movements should be viewed. Certainly, support for extra-parliamentary forms of political activity was strongest among the young, the affluent middle classes, and the educated. By and large these were the groups most involved in Britain and, though to a lesser extent, also in Japan. Disenchantment with party politics in that country, therefore, might also be seen as part of a wider, international, post-materialist movement (Inglehart, 1977).

Centralisation

On the other hand, in so far as this post-materialist hypothesis implies also a popular rejection of the centralising tendencies of modern democratic governments, Japanese experience does not fit quite so neatly. There was certainly a general belief that the actions of the bureaucracy frequently ignored local or special interests, but against this Japan had a long tradition of central control. In prewar times the Home Ministry had supervised local government closely, controlling the police and the appointments of prefectural governors. The content of education was also centrally determined. SCAP sought to change this, abolishing the Home Ministry, increasing the powers of elected local bodies, and transferring responsibility for the police and education to local control. But the localities were not provided with adequate financial resources and the tide of centralisation began to flow strongly again once the Occupation ended. Only the multi-seat electoral districts acted as a sort of breakwater by ensuring that local interests were kept well to the fore in the politicians' minds. Education and the police were effectively brought back under central control. A series of referenda resulted in many of the smaller forces being merged into the National Rural Police. From the mid-1950s the police were organised at prefectural level while the distribution of ranks and stations, and the appointments of police chiefs were decided centrally.

In Britain, while the advent of the welfare state and national economic planning necessarily entailed a considerable extension of government activity from the 1940s, centralisation did appear to gather pace in the 1960s and 1970s, thus supporting the post-materialist thesis. In 1972 the historic structure of local government was abolished and replaced by six metropolitan and forty seven non-metropolitan counties. Six years before, a more centralised policing system had resulted from the compulsory amalgamation of local forces in England and Wales, reducing their number from 117 to 49 (down to 43 by 1986). As central government acquired more power and disillusionment with the existing political structures set in, so minority parties attracted support. Between 1950 and 1970 92 per cent of the votes cast in general elections went to the main two parties. In four elections between 1970 and 1983, however, only 75 per cent did so. The corollary of this was rising support for the Liberal and nationalist parties. Plaid Cymru began to win seats in Wales from 1966 and in the 1970s the Scottish Nationalist Party added to its first seat won in 1967. Although the pressure for devolved regional government in the Celtic fringes was sufficient to secure the passage of enabling legislation, neither the Welsh nor the Scots people gave it the required degree of popular support and in 1979 the legislation was repealed.

The Conservative Government voted into power in 1979 was committed to reducing the influence of central government, mainly by reducing public expenditure. Yet the attempt failed, largely because the policy rested on a paradox. Cutting state expenditure by reducing the level of public provision was politically sensitive and potentially damaging in electoral terms. The alternative was to deliver services more cheaply and thus more efficiently. But this could be achieved only by extending central control over local expenditure. Contrary to government intentions, therefore, Thatcherism led to greater interference from Whitehall. Every tier of education, for example, was subjected to more pervasive intervention than ever before (Gamble, 1994). Local government was increasingly emasculated by the imposition of limits on expenditure and the transfer of traditional responsibilities to the centre, following which the outlays actually rose faster (Jenkins, 1995). With the exception of a couple of years, state expenditure during the Thatcher and Major years continued to account for about 43 per cent of the nation's wealth, the same proportion as it had taken in 1979. Whether a symptom or cause of declining support for traditional democratic processes it is difficult to know, but in the 1980s there was a general stripping out of elected representatives in favour of personal patronage, with many appointments being vetted for political soundness. Privatisation and the introduction of incentives, accountability, and league tables, all led to the proliferation of non-elected and non-accountable bodies such as the Child Support Agency, the Student Loan Company, the Crown Prosecution Service, and training and enterprise councils.

The system of ritual

Militarism

Unconditional surrender in 1945 created a crisis of morale for the Japanese people. Initially, there was an understandable loss of confidence in the traditional values and institutions which had led to Hiroshima and until the 1960s at least, main stream Japanese thinking continued to focus on the notion that the nation must fully embrace both Westernism and modernism (Pyle, 1982: 223–64). Yet defeat also bequeathed a long and divisive ideological legacy, apparent in varied and ambivalent attitudes to both the war and the Occupation. The left blamed a military clique for leading an unwilling country into a war of imperial aggression, while the right interpreted the conflict as an attempt to drive European colonisers out of Asia. These differences were even enshrined in the designations given to the war, with rightists favouring the 'Great East Asian War' as opposed to the more common

'Pacific War'. As for the peace, the left argued that too little changed in postwar Japan, as witness the revival of prewar economic structures, the constraints eventually placed upon independent labour organisation, and the survival of the bureaucracy. Right wingers asserted that the compulsory renunciation of war, the effective abolition of the army, and the disestablishment of state Shinto deprived Japan of its national soul and dignity.

They were equally angered by the initial reduction of government control over the educational curriculum, in particular the exclusion of anything deemed to glorify militarism. The teaching of history in schools was briefly banned until the textbooks could be cleansed of jingoism, yet the version of the war presented to subsequent generations of Japanese school children continued to be controversial. Many intellectuals regarded the overthrow of militarism as the major benefit of the Pacific War, viewing with suspicion anything that smacked of imperialism, war, or rearmament. Their attempts to be more open and self critical about Japan's wartime role were a constant source of provocation to the pro-imperialist right. When Emperor Hirohito died in 1989 the Mayor of Nagasaki was among those who opined that he might have done more to prevent or terminate the war. He was thereupon shot by a right wing gunman for his temerity. Others defended the emperor's reputation with more subtlety, urging that as a good constitutional monarch he had not opposed the rise of the army in the 1930s because it was so obviously a manifestation of the popular will.

The persistence of the old militaristic-imperialist ethos in Japan was also evident at official level in a long standing reluctance to acknowledge any responsibility for the war or the perpetration of war crimes such as the rape of Nanking. Even when a formal apology was finally made in 1995, it almost managed to avoid mentioning the war at all and included critical references to British colonialism. In part at least the cause of this official reticence lay in the fact that right wing organisations such as the Bereaved Families Association, still 1.5 million strong in the 1980s, were powerful lobbies, rallying annually at the memorial services held at the Yasukuni shrine. It was there that in 1979 the spirits of General Tojo and other war criminals were collectively enshrined. A prominent right wing Dietman, Okuno Seisuke, justified this on the grounds that the war crimes trials had been merely 'the victors' revenge upon the defeated', adding for good measure that no national apology for the war was necessary since it had been 'a war of self-defence' (Byrne, 1995: 13–14). Even among less committed Japanese, there was often an unwillingness to discuss the war in terms of guilt and responsibility, prompting one unsympathetic journalist to write that she did not 'want to hear any more of the "shikata ga nakatta" ("it couldn't be helped") justification for not thinking from the wartime generation' (Halloran, 1993: 14–15).

By the time he expressed them, opinions such as Okuno's were certainly those of a minority but they nonetheless constituted an influential current in the stream of postwar political sentiment and were capable of exposing divisions among the Japanese. Emperor Hirohito's death in 1989 was followed by his burial in accordance with the Shinto funeral rights customary for the imperial family. This, it was objected, violated the constitutional separation of state and religion. Similar protests were voiced when crowning of the new emperor, Akahito, included participation in the *daijosai*, the most sacred of Shinto's royal rituals. The official line was that this was a merely a traditional and ceremonial formality. The objectors said it that since it was supposed to symbolise the emperor dining with the gods and entailed his being reborn as a manifest god himself, it represented a return to the notion of royal divinity, a major feature of the old military-imperialist ethos.

Monarchy

In a way, however, these objections were superfluous, for they, too, represented only a minority opinion. SCAP's reforms had effectively succeeded in their purpose of reducing to mortal dimensions an emperor, many of whose subjects had actually knelt down to hear his understated declaration of surrender, this being the first time they had heard his voice, still less seen him. The new postwar constitution and the demotion of state Shinto stripped Hirohito of his quasi-religious status, denying imperial divinity and establishing the sovereignty of the people. The abolition of the army and of compulsory moral education in schools removed two more important supports of the prewar imperial cult. As part of the demythologising process, Hirohito was also required to appear more frequently in public, and the imperial house was restricted in size to his own immediate family and brothers. Hirohito's oldest son carried the process a stage further by marrying a commoner who broke another imperial convention by insisting on raising her children herself. By the 1980s the Japanese were fairly neutral towards their royal family. A 1984 poll found only 34 per cent declaring themselves well disposed to the emperor. Significantly, 70 per cent of those who expressed indifference were in their twenties (Fennema, 1993: 14–15).

This should not be taken to imply any significant diminution of respect, however, for the imperial household by no means forfeited all its mystique. In 1990 a court photographer lost his job for publishing a picture of the emperor's second son having his hair rearranged by his bride, a photograph deemed 'unrespectful'. A year or two later in response to requests from the Imperial household, the Japanese press voluntarily restricted coverage of the Crown Prince's search for a wife, 'out of consideration for the human rights and privacy of the candidates' (Suzuki, 1993: 17). The marriage of Crown Prince Naruhito to Owada Masako, another commoner, prompted one American magazine to observe that 'the imperial family enjoys the nation's respect, unlike the beleaguered Windsors, who may be only a few tapes away from oblivion' (*Time*, 7 June 1993).

This was an overstatement, for the British monarch still retained an important place in the ritual process. Divorced from politics, the throne continued to provide a symbol of national unity, a token of stability, and an emotional and psychological link with the past reinforcing a sense of history. The VE day celebrations in London in 1945 culminated with the public appearance of King George VI and his family, many still in military uniform, before the cheering masses packed into all the approaches to Buckingham Palace. The accession of his daughter in 1952 prompted notions of a second Elizabethan age and twenty five years later *The Times* confidently claimed that Elizabeth II was 'our best professional monarch for . . . many generations' (Havighurst, 1985: 626). Nevertheless, the constitutional position of the monarchy was somewhat diminished by the contraction and virtual disappearance of the empire, and then by entry into the European Community. More significantly, perhaps, the reputation of the royal family itself became somewhat tarnished from the 1980s. This was mainly the product of personal problems among the Queen's children, particularly the failure of the heir apparent's marriage, and their ruthless exposure by the popular press. 'The British media', it was noted by a Japanese commentator, 'especially the tabloid papers, treat the royal family like celebrities such as movie stars, rock singers and sports heroes. They sell the private lives of the royal family. The British media coverage is excessive' (Togo, 1993: 17).

Press

The near obsession of Britain's popular press with the activities of royalty was in marked contrast with its restraint at the time of the 1936 abdication crisis and indicated just how far this particular shaper of values had altered in the intervening years. Only in the sense that individual newspapers tended to target particular social classes and that they remained overwhelmingly Conservative in sympathy was there much continuity between pre- and postwar newspapers. Unlike their predecessors of the 1930s, modern press magnates possessed interests and ambitions that were global rather than purely national in scope. New technology, new owners, rationalisation, and changing public taste resulted in the demise of nine major national papers between 1955 and 1975. The physical presentation of the news also changed with the introduction of colour photography, glossy supplements, and the decision of *The Times* in 1966 to print news on its front page. Above all, there was a gradual change of emphasis in the postwar years. Although joined by a newcomer in the form of the *Independent*, the quality papers, described by Francis Williams in 1957 as being 'secure in their position', never achieved circulations to match those whose primary concern was to pander more openly than ever before to their readers' (often prurient) tastes (Williams, 1957: 247). In 1981 the average daily sales of *The Times* and the *Guardian* amounted to 297,000 and 400,000 respectively, while the *Telegraph* did rather better with 1.3 million. All fell well short of the 3.4 million sold each day by the *Mirror* and the 4.1 million copies of the *Sun*. The British remained among the most avid consumers of newspapers in the world, but much of what the press was offering by the last decade of the century was gossip and trivial. Even those papers which tried to maintain the loftier aspirations of an earlier generation had now to compete as opinion formers against the ubiquitous voices of proliferating television stations, some of them controlled by the same individuals who owned the papers.

The same was true in Japan where newspaper readership also remained very high, with three quarters of all households taking a daily paper. In the 1960s the morning editions of the three great national papers, *Asahi Shimbun*, *Mainichi Shimbun*, and *Yomiuri Shimbun* each sold between four and seven million copies with about half that for the evening editions. By the 1980s the circulation of *Yomiuri* was three times that of the British *Mirror* and *Star* combined. Before the war Japanese papers had generally been subservient to the establishment – or suppressed. In the freer climate after 1945, the mainstream press usually adopted a left of centre, mildly critical stance towards government, but in practice it became an integral part of the country's intellectual establishment. Investigative journalism was rare and it was a magazine, not a newspaper, which first drew attention to high level political corruption in the 1970s. Press writers saw their primary role as purveyors of factual information, most of which they acquired through that most distinctive of Japanese institutions, the press club. These associations of reporters were attached to every government agency at national, prefectural, and even local level, as well as to political parties, business firms, unions, and educational and social organisations, providing each with a channel through which information could be passed to the readers. Journalists nudged popular opinion along, feeding government ideas to the people, moulders rather than mirrors of public opinion. The main exception to this was at the bottom end of the market catering far more openly than was possible even in the British press to the Japanese taste for violence and pornography. *Nikkan Gendai*, for example, sold a million copies a day in the 1980s. Interestingly, most of them were purchased by the same people who bought the quality publications, indicative of the way in which the Japanese press lacked any specific class appeal. More generally the emphasis on fact, the deference to authority, and the lack of overt political partisanship gave them a uniformity of appearance and content. In these ways the press contributed to the perpetuation of the mass culture which was so important in fostering and preserving a strong sense of national identity in postwar Japan.

Education

The education system performed a similar function. It had been successfully used as a potent means of social control ever since Meiji times, and SCAP reforms were intended both to weaken its potential in this respect by decentralising control, and also to alter its emphasis by imbuing the curriculum with different values. Responsibility for universities was transferred to the prefectures, for secondary schools to elected education boards. A three tier schooling system was introduced, based on the American model of a compulsory six years at elementary school, three at middle school, and three voluntary years of high school. More than half of Japanese children were attending high school by 1955 compared with only 7 per cent in 1940 under the highly elitist prewar system. By 1975 over 90 per cent of children were being educated beyond middle school level. During the Occupation the content of education was reformed to foster Western values often at odds with Japanese tradition, such as sexual equality, and freedom of religious and political belief. History teaching was briefly prohibited, classes in English and other languages, banned under the military regime, were reintroduced, and textbook content was freed from central scrutiny. A strong left wing teachers' union protected these changes against a conservative Ministry of Education. However, many of the reforms were diluted when Japan regained independence. The powers of the Ministry of Education were in some measure restored, elected education boards replaced by appointed ones, textbook screening was strengthened and secondary school teachers were required to follow detailed daily teaching guidelines for each subject.

Whatever its problems, postwar Japanese education serviced the economy satisfactorily and acquired an international reputation for academic quality. More pertinently in the context of the ritual and value system, while central control was certainly weaker and less direct than before the war, education provided a uniform curriculum through a uniform structure, thereby offering equality of opportunity and acting as an important shaper of national identity. As a result high culture was, by British standards, popular rather than elitist, unifying rather than divisive.

Little of this was true of British education where by the 1990s growing problems of classroom discipline sometimes tended to overshadow issues of quality. By the age of nine British children were already falling behind their Japanese equivalents in terms of mathematical ability. In addition to its alleged failure to provide an adequate supply of appropriately trained workers, the system of education in Britain remained socially divided and divisive for a long time. It was in fact not one but three systems, with Northern Ireland and Scotland each operating independently. The socially exclusive (because expensive) fee paying public and private schools, along with the tripartite division of grammar, technical, and secondary schools established in the 1940s, mirrored class divisions and sustained unequal opportunity. Far from contributing to any sense of national cohesion, secondary level schooling in Britain served for a long time to perpetuate the 'them and us' syndrome, defensible only in so far as it provided a limited degree of upward social mobility (Halsey, 1978: 111–38). Not until the 1960s did a common school model begin to emerge as the first steps were taken towards constructing a system of comprehensive education. By the end of the 1980s 88 per cent of all secondary pupils were in such schools. The content of education also became more uniform in that a national curriculum was introduced in 1988 while the dual system of leaving examinations was recast as a single General Certificate of Secondary Education (GCSE). Uniformity was further encouraged by the advent of mass higher education in the 1990s. Yet whatever the educational virtues of these changes – and they were by no means uncontested – their social impact was diluted by the survival of fee paying schools, the maintenance in some local authority areas of grammar schools, and by streaming and banding within the comprehensive system which tended to reflect and perpetuate the divide between middle- and working-class children. The survival of a narrowly based, academic examination for eighteen year olds sustained the division between academic and vocational qualifications, while the progressive winding down of student grants threatened to place serious financial barriers in the way of working-class and minority groups desirous of pursuing tertiary level education. Although Conservative Governments after 1979 succeeded in significantly raising the numbers in higher education, the experience of it was hardly a very unifying one, since the availability of resources, facilities, and expertise varied hugely between institutions.

Religion

If education and the press thus contributed more significantly to national identity and cohesion in Japan than in Britain by providing more uniform social contexts and ideologies, the reverse might appear to be true of religion. The coexistence of several major faiths and the failure of Christianity to make significant inroads over the course of the twentieth century probably served to confirm the views of early observers that the Japanese did not take religion very seriously. J. S. Ransome referred, for instance, to their 'want of conviction . . . about religion in any form' (Ransome, 1899: 35). This appeared as a marked contrast with the impeccable Christian credentials of the British. Furthermore, the established position of the Church of England continued to provide a central national focus for religious life, whereas such a focus disappeared in Japan when state Shinto was abolished by the SCAP reforms.

Yet the realities of religious life after 1945 were far more complex than such a summary suggests. Generalisations about a lack of religious impulse in the Japanese psyche were misplaced. Monthly public surveys revealed that in 1978 40.4 per cent of people claimed to believe that spiritual health was more important than material affluence. Slightly fewer ranked the two the other way round. By 1994 spiritual health was given first place by 57.2 per cent, material progress by only 30.0 per cent (Tanifuji, 1995d: 25). This suggests that even almost fifty years of uninterrupted economic growth had not proved wholly satisfying. One reflection of this was the progress made in postwar Japan by new religious groups, including the homicidal Aum cult. Generally small in membership, these movements mainly appealed, as in Britain, to those alienated from mainstream society whether by the growth of urbanisation, a sense of individual isolation, or rejection of the materialist and competitive ethos inherent in modern society.

Such groups, however, were still overshadowed by the old. In the 1980s 80 per cent of Japanese described themselves as followers of Shinto. Many business enterprises remained sufficiently circumspect to operate under the patronage of a specific *kami* or spirit. At the same time, however, 80 per cent of people also described themselves as Buddhists. At first sight these apparently incompatible statistics might be taken as further proof of religious indifference on the part of the Japanese. From a different perspective, however, they reveal how through the centuries contending foreign religious influences had been absorbed and then moulded in accord with Japan's own ideals and needs. Shinto and Buddhism (and for that matter Confucianism) were complementary, each satisfying different aspects of the religious impulse and all amenable to the high value placed upon social harmony. It was precisely because Christianity with its claim to exclusivity could not be fitted into this framework that it had so little impact. MacArthur actively encouraged Christianity to fill what he saw as the spiritual vacuum left by the disestablishment of state Shinto, but most of the bibles imported with his encouragement probably ended up as black market cigarettes papers. By the time he left in 1951, the Christian population was still under 1 per cent of the population. Forty years later, they remained a minority.

Matters were similarly complex in the case of Britain. Enduring communal conflict in Northern Ireland from 1969 might suggest that Christianity was not inherently a socially unifying influence. Statistics might imply that postwar Britain provided a prime example of secularisation theory in operation, with urbanisation, scientific advance, new forms of leisure, and the sanitising of death all helping to dilute religious belief and reduce its formal observance. Whereas in 1900 almost two thirds of live babies had been baptised in the Church of England, the proportion was less than a quarter by 1995 (*Spectator*, 28 October 1995). Except in Scotland and Northern Ireland, membership of the established churches certainly fell away (table 7.2). The decline was particularly marked from the 1960s, and by 1985 only 15 per cent of the adult population were members of a Christian church compared with slightly more than 20 per cent ten years earlier (Abercrombie and Warde, 1988: 433). As far as beliefs were concerned, 73 per cent of those asked in 1982 professed a belief in God but only 43 per cent believed in Jesus Christ as his son, a major reduction since 1947. The growth of some 450 new religious movements and the emergence of non-Christian faiths, usually associated with immigrant minorities and numbering almost two million adherents by 1988, appeared as further evidence of the diminishing hold of Christianity on postwar Britain.

Table 7.2 *Britain: church membership (millions)*

	Anglican	Methodist
1950	2.96	0.74
1960	2.86	0.73
1970	2.56	0.62
1980	1.82	0.49

(Wolffe, 1994: 428)

Yet secularisation theory is both complex and internally contradictory (Davie, 1994: 165–78). New vigour was introduced into the Christian establishment by immigrants and also by an evangelical and charismatic revival, the latter manifesting itself strongly in the form of the house church movement, which claimed over 100,000 adherents by the late 1980s. General public interest in Christian affairs was still readily aroused, as by the Pope's visit in 1982, the allegedly heretical utterances of the Bishop designate of Durham, and the agonising within the Church of England about the ordination of women and homosexuals. Finally, while the established church had not been manipulated in the twentieth century for social and political purposes in the same way as Shinto in prewar Japan, it remained prominent in terms of national ritual and ceremony. Christian festivals such as Christmas, Easter, and Remembrance Day were still important in giving national life a pattern, while the association between the nation and the church was perpetuated in the continuing role of the monarch as head of the Church of England. If only in these ways, the values and rituals associated with Christianity did continue to act as a form of underlying social cement in Britain, albeit weaker than in the previous generations.

Crime

The decline in formal Christian observance was accompanied, particularly from the 1950s, by some weakening of its associated behavioural norms and restraints, although direct cause and effect cannot simply be assumed. Crime statistics, for example, soared upwards. From the mid-1950s offences against the person, which had risen about 6 per cent a year since the mid-1930s accelerated annually at about 11 per cent (Marwick, 1982: 148). Contemporary research attributed this to broad social change as well as to the greater temptations to crime presented by an affluent society. Whatever the cause, the statistics underestimated the true extent of the problem. A comparison between the official figures and those compiled by the Crime Survey in 1983 showed that only 8 per cent of the occurrences of vandalism, 11 per cent of sexual offences, 38 per cent of thefts from property and about half of all burglaries were officially reported and recorded (Abercrombie and Warde, 1988: 455). This makes even more striking the contrast with Japan, where crime rates were among the lowest in the civilised world (table 7.3).

Table 7.3: *England and Japan: crime and arrest rates, 1989 (per 100,000 of population)*

	England and Wales	Japan	Arrest rates per 1000 offences in Japan
Murder	9.1	1.2	95.9
Rape	12.1	1.3	83.6
Robbery	65.8	1.3	75.9
Theft	5077.9	1203.7	41.7

(Hendry, 1995: 214)

Although this might be attributable to a general reluctance on the part of the Japanese to report offences or to become involved with the law, it owed something as well to the survival of a strong sense of local community and identity, manifest in a general willingness to accept collective responsibility for law and order offences which breached conventions of harmony and consensus. Whether this was the product of history or, as some have argued, indoctrination, remains a moot point. Even more remarkably, perhaps, low rates of crime coexisted with a police service which, proportionate to the population, was far smaller than its British counterpart. Indeed, Japan had a higher ratio of people to police than almost every other industrial nation. Furthermore, the forces of law enforcement enjoyed a high reputation. While this might perhaps be a reflection of the deference generally accorded to figures of authority, it probably owed more to a highly effective community policing system. The force's high standing was apparent in the fact that in the 1980s a quarter of the annual intake were university graduates and the National Police Agency was the third most popular bureaucratic career after MITI and the Ministry of Finance.

The quality of personnel might also explain the high arrest and clear up rates achieved by the Japanese police. Alternatively, success might have resulted from the fact that suspects could be held for twenty three days without formal indictment. Nor should the influence of a culture which stressed the resolution of disputes by discussion between the concerned parties be overlooked. This was a survival from Tokugawa days when the negotiated settlement of disagreements was seen as essential in order to avoid bringing shame on the individuals or groups concerned. Issues of absolute right and wrong, on which much Western litigation rested, were comparatively unimportant in Japan. Judges, lawyers, and even police officers acted as conciliators within the system. As a result, relatively few cases ever reached court. When they did, the conviction rate by the judges (there was no jury system) was almost 100 per cent, a further incentive to earlier settlement via arbitration. Even then, less that 3 per cent of convicted individuals received prison sentences. One other indirect outcome was that in the late 1980s Japan had ten lawyers for every hundred thousand people: Britain had ninety four (Haley, 1992: 265–81).

Of those who actually went to prison in Japan, roughly a third were connected with organised crime, notably the *Yakuza* gangs. These probably never had more than 100,000 members but they were highly structured and responsible for a level of organised criminal activity far higher than anything in Britain: in crime, as in business and government, it seemed, the Japanese were the more efficient. It was indicative of the somewhat ambivalent role played in Japanese society by the *Yakuza*, that they also had a respectable, public persona, for as organisations they were not in themselves illegal. They occupied proper offices, engaged publicly in ceremonials such as funerals, and frequently hired themselves out to businesses, politicians, and even the police, to help with security, as well as supplying contract labour to the building trade. Their criminal activities were most certainly illegal but they generally tended to eschew those which conflicted with the interests of society at large, sticking mainly to extortion, pornography, and loan sharking. Furthermore, their absorption of social misfits gave such individuals that all important sense of group identity denied to them in the law abiding world outside. From one point of view, therefore, the *Yakuza* could be said to play an important role in controlling the underside of Japan, even moulding it in accord with accepted social norms. This, however, may be another example of the distinction made by the Japanese themselves between *tatamae* and *honne*, the outward and the inward thinking about a situation. To all intents and purposes the *Yakuza* were accepted at one level as performing a useful social function. At a different level of social thinking, however, especially among the police, they were probably regarded as parasites worthy only of prosecution.

British decline

In Britain the ending of the Second World War was accompanied by nothing reminiscent of the sense of betrayal and threat to the status quo which followed the return of peace in 1918. On the contrary, the war appeared to have vindicated British values and ways of life, strengthening ritual institutions such as the monarchy and the empire. This was seen, for example, in British films which, for a decade or so after 1945, purveyed notions of an essentially decent, law abiding, and tolerant society in which communal cooperation transcended acknowledged differences of wealth and status (Richards and Aldgate, 1983). In the longer run, the war probably worked in the same way as the earlier conflict, releasing or strengthening forces ultimately corrosive of what were believed to be traditional beliefs, institutions, and behavioural patterns. By the 1970s, symptoms of this were thought to include the apparent decline of the church, the diminishing reputation of the monarchy, disillusionment with the parliamentary process, the progressive vulgarisation of the media, the dissolution of the empire, the resort to violence in industrial relations, along with rising rates of divorce, illegitimacy, and crime. Combined with mounting evidence of economic malaise, such trends helped to spark talk of national decline and assertions that the institutions and values which had traditionally held British society together were decaying. These ideas were given an aura of respectability by a stream of learned studies whose general tone was well caught in the title of Isaac Kramnick's edition of *Is Britain Dying?* (1979). An interesting later twist on the debate came in 1995 from Will Hutton, who suggested that modern economic problems arose from the inappropriate nature of the country's political institutions (Hutton, 1995).

The notion of a national crisis was certainly sharpened by the economic difficulties of the 1970s but for the majority of people talk of national decline was meaningless in material terms. Equally, the idea of moral decay could be sustained only from an absolutist perspective, since change was not necessarily the same thing as deterioration. Nor were references to decline anything new, having surfaced in various guises and at different times from the late nineteenth century onwards (Tomlinson, 1996: 731–57). At root the whole debate might be interpreted as part of the contemporary attempt to adjust simultaneously to long term changes in social values and to Britain's changing international status. Similar concerns at the turn of century, when a leftish critique of contemporary society coincided with economic difficulty and military reversal, contributed eventually to similar symptoms of disillusionment with prevailing political processes. Now in the second half of the twentieth century the dominant set of cultural values, broadly Christian in ethos and pretty well intact since its emergence in the Victorian era, was apparently under threat. The Suez debacle in 1955 exposed the frailty of the military strength on which Britain's great power aspirations rested. It was followed by the rapid shedding of colonial territories. At all levels of society the decline of church attendance and a more open repudiation of the evangelical nonconformist moral code began to undermine the shared values of the past. This was apparent in the writings of the so-called angry young men and the acquittal in 1959 of Penguin Books on an obscenity charge for publishing *Lady Chatterley's Lover*, previously unavailable in Britain. The moral revolution was later advanced apace by legislative changes which removed or weakened official proscriptions on many forms of gambling, as well as on homosexuality and abortion. As a perceptive foreign scholar put it in the mid-1970s, 'old England's mask of formality was undergoing radical change' (Bedarida, 1979: 249). Countercultures and alternative values began to jostle for a place in the social fabric. Some were ethnic, associated with particular immigrant groups. Others were regional, manifest in a growing Celtic assertiveness from the 1960s which challenged the old assumption that England was Britain. Others, most notably the new religious movements, represented cultures of withdrawal. Whatever particular form they took, the new cultures were espoused most enthusiastically by the young who appeared, therefore, as the most significant challengers of existing orthodoxies.

The challenge of youth

Although a distinctive youth culture in Britain predated the Second World War, what came after it was a much more comprehensive phenomenon. Full employment opened up new opportunities which neither manufacturers nor advertisers were slow to exploit. With more disposable income than ever before, the young were in the vanguard of consumerism, in the process appearing to reject almost wholesale the values and life styles of earlier generations. Among the collective expressions of this apparent revolt which sparked some of the most agonised soul searching on the part of the establishment, were the outbreaks of vandalism accompanying showings of Bill Haley's film *Rock Around the Clock*. The American film star, James Dean, personified this rebellion, distilling, as one writer put it, 'the essence of youthful non-belonging' (Lewis, 1978: 123). Ultimately in the 1970s consumerism provoked its own anti-materialist reaction on the part of later radical youngsters, such as hippies, skinheads, feminists, environmentalists, and adherents of new religions. These were more ideological than the earlier protesters but all offered a similar challenge to the value systems of the older generation.

Inevitably the publicity generated by the discovery of the 'youth problem' in the 1950s served to obscure important realities and continuities. Society had been perceiving youth problems ever since the late nineteenth century but the majority of young people remained strongly conformist (Springhall, 1986). Despite popular impressions of the 'swinging' sixties and the liberated, drug-driven seventies, a survey of 1971 showed that while sexual behaviour was changing, permissiveness was by no means as widespread as was commonly assumed (Gorer, 1971). Similarly, the most outlandish expressions of adolescent assertiveness, teddy boys, mods and rockers, hippies, skinheads, punks and their later successors never involved more than a small proportion of the nation's youth. Neither their violence nor their rejection of the old order were ever serious political threats. Nevertheless, all represented wider currents of social change and along with ethnic minorities they played an important part in helping to fragment and diversify what had previously been a more uniform set of social values.

In Japan, too, the burden of a similar challenge to aspects of prevailing value systems was carried almost entirely by the young. It became apparent in the 1960s with the maturing of the first postwar generation of children. Even by the late 1950s attitudes to such matters as the choice of marriage partner or the role of the family as a cross-generational support base had not changed very much (Chiye, 1962). The traditional etiquette of neighbourly obligations also survived, well into the 1970s in the rural areas where, as one anthropologist observed, 'just as individual interests give way to those of the household, so household interests give way to those of the community and village as a whole' (Moeran, 1985: 152). Yet surveys showed that almost three quarters of Japanese believed that in the cities the custom was in retreat (Stoetzel, 1955: 272). Traditional attitudes were increasingly challenged as a new generation of Japanese children were educated in a system and reared in a society strongly influenced by the new constitution's emphasis on personal rights and individualism. These were unfamiliar concepts to those taught by an earlier and more traditional regime to distinguish between individual feelings and social and civic obligations.

As the consumer opportunities provided by the economic miracle were increasingly embraced, so it appeared to many older Japanese that the life styles of the young were being overly influenced by Western style hedonism and increasingly supported by all the same props, whether musical, dietary, or sartorial. Young urbanites seemed to have lost the willingness to sacrifice themselves for the future, becoming less idealistic and more self centred, and giving far too high a priority to self fulfilment and personal comfort. The slowly accumulating evidence of the young's reluctance to take on responsibility for the elderly was viewed as another similar straw in the wind: so, too, was the growing preference for love marriages. Equally disturbing, though for very different reasons, was the way that some of those who rejected consumerism and its associated values, particularly students and environmentalists in the 1970s, seemed so willing to reject traditional conciliation in favour of violence.

As in Britain, much of this was a rerun of the past, similar youthful misdemeanours having attracted adverse comment even before the First World War (Yoshikate, 1982: 206–15). In the longer run, too, the challenge to the prevailing social norms was far more muted in Japan than in Britain. As the national economic achievement increasingly left the West behind, so there was a fresh acknowledgement of the important contribution made by 'traditional' Japanese norms, in particular the emphasis placed on harmony and social consensus rather than individualism. By and large, therefore, Japan in the 1990s remained an ethically and culturally homogeneous society. The economic – and by implication the social – significance of this was drawn out by a prime ministerial study group in 1980.

This basic characteristic permeates, and acts as a living foundation of, the workings and the system of the Japanese economy . . . the Japanese economy relies on 'collegial groups' that are based on various relationships created within and between companies. This tends to give rise to a phenomenon of dependence that is induced by mutual reliance among persons. (Pyle, 1982: 231–2)

Similar explanations for Japan's success have been advanced by some Western scholars as well (Lazonik, 1991). Postwar Japan may have embraced Western consumerism while some of its social institutions and practices also increasingly resembled those of the West. Always, however, fundamental Japanese values remained strong, imposing their own shape and demands (Tobin, 1992; Waswo, 1996: 99–103). Therein, perhaps, lay the secret of Japan's progress. Of course social practices and structures, values, ideas, and beliefs cannot explain everything. They constantly interact with specific and changing circumstances, most notably perhaps in the case of twentieth-century Britain and Japan the outcomes of two world wars. Equally, however, their enduring strength and influence cannot be discounted. By 1995 little had changed in this respect since Clive Holland observed eighty years earlier that

Although modern Japan is so changed from what it was even twenty five or thirty years ago, and although 'modernity' and all that the word may be held to imply, has so great and apparently irresistible an attraction . . . workaday life . . . has little to do with . . . Western civilisation. (Holland, 1913: 144)

References

Abe, E. and Fitzgerald, R. (1995), 'Japanese economic success: timing, culture and organizational capability', in Abe, E. and Fitzgerald, R. (eds), *The Origins of Japanese Industrial Power*, Cass.

Abercrombie, N. and Warde, A. (1988), *Contemporary British Society: A New Introduction to Sociology*, Polity Press.

Abramovitz, M. (1986), 'Catching up, forging ahead and falling behind', *Journal of Economic History*, 46.

Abrams, P. (1963), 'The failure of social reform, 1918–1920', *Past and Present*, 24.

Ackrill, M. (1987), *Manufacturing Industry Since 1870*, Philip Allan.

Addison, P. (1975), *The Road to 1945: British Politics and the Second World War*, Cape.

Aldcroft, D. H. (1970), *The Inter-War Economy: Britain 1919–1939*, Batsford.

Alford, B. W. (1981), 'New industries for old? British industries between the wars', in Floud, R. and McCloskey, D. (eds), *The Economic History of Britain Since 1700. 2. 1860 to the 1970s*, Cambridge University Press.

Alford, B. W. (1988), *British Economic Performance, 1945–1975*, Macmillan.

Alford, B. W. (1996), *Britain in the World Economy since 1880*, Longman.

Allen, G. C. (1961), *British Industries and their Organisation*, Longman.

Allen, G. C. (1981a), *A Short Economic History of Modern Japan*, Macmillan.

Allen, G. C. (1981b), *The Japanese Economy*, Weidenfeld and Nicolson.

Almond, G. A. and Verba, S. (1963), *The Civic Culture*, Princeton University Press.

Andreski, S. (1954) *Military Organization and Society*, Routledge.

Aoki, M. (1987), 'The Japanese firm in transition', in Yamamura, K. and Yasuba, Y. (eds), *The Political Economy of Japan*, Stanford University Press.

Armstrong, H. W. (1991), 'Regional problems and policies', in Crafts, N. F. R. and Woodward, N. (eds), *The British Economy since 1945*, Oxford University Press.

Ashworth, W. (1960), *An Economic History of England, 1870–1939*, Methuen.

Atoh, M. (1994), 'An era of later marriages, fewer kids', *Economic Eye*, 15,

Bacon, R. and Eltis, W. A. (1976), *Britain's Economic Problem: Too Few Producers?*, Macmillan.

Bairoch, P. (1982), 'International industrialization levels from 1750 to 1980', *Journal of European Economic History*, XI.

Barnett, C. (1986), *The Audit of War*, Macmillan.

Bedarida, F. (1979), *A Social History of England, 1851–1975*, Methuen.

Beer, S. (1965), *Modern British Politics: A Study of Parties and Pressure Groups*, Faber.

Benson, J. (1995), *The Rise of Consumer Society in Britain, 1880–1980*, Longman.

Berghoff, H. (1990), 'Public schools and the decline of the British economy, 1870–1914', *Past and Present*, 129.

Berghoff, H. and Muller, R. (1994), 'Tired pioneers and dynamic newcomers? A comparative essay on English and German entrepreneurial history, 1870–1914', *Economic History Review*, XLVII.

Bethel, D. (1992), 'Alienation and reconnection in a home for the elderly', in Tobin, J. J. (ed.), *Re-Made in Japan. Everyday Life and Consumer Taste in a Changing Society*, Yale University Press.

Bisson, T. A. (1945a), *Japan's Wartime Economy*, Institute of Pacific Relations.

Bisson, T. A. (1945b), 'The increase of zaibatsu predominance in wartime Japan', *Pacific Affairs*, XVIII.

Black, C. E. (1966), *The Dynamics of Modernization: A Study in Comparative History*, Harper and Row.

Blackaby, F. T. (1979), *De-Industrialization*, Heinemann.

Blumenthal, T. (1987), 'Depressions in Japan: the 1930s and the 1970s', in Dore, R. and Sinha, R. (eds), *Japan and World Depression Then and Now. Essays in Memory of E. T. Penrose*, Macmillan.

Bowden, S. (1994), 'The new consumerism', in Johnson, P. (ed.), *Twentieth Century Britain: Economic, Social and Cultural Change*, Methuen.

Bowley, A. L. and Hogg, M. H. (1925), *Has Poverty Diminished?*, P. S. King.

Bowley, A. L. and Stamp, J. C. (1938), *The National Income 1924*, London School of Political and Economic Science Reprints.

Boyle, J. H. (1993), *Modern Japan: The American Nexus*, Harcourt, Brace and Jovanovich.

Braybon, G. (1981), *Women Workers in the First World War*, Croom Helm.

Braybon, G. (1995), 'Women and the war', in Constantine, S., Kirby, M., and Rose, M. (eds,) *The First World War in British History*, Arnold.

Briggs, A. (1981), 'Social history, 1900–45', in Floud, R. and McCloskey, D. (eds), *The Economic History of Britain Since 1700. 2. 1860 to the 1970s*, Cambridge University Press.

Brittain, V. (1933), *Testament of Youth*, Gollancz.

Brown, J. R. (1994), *Opening Japan's Financial Markets*, Routledge.

Brown, K. D. (1971), *Labour and Unemployment, 1900–1914*, David and Charles.

Brown, K. D. (1974), *Essays in Anti-Labour History*, Macmillan.

Brown, K. D. (1982), *The English Labour Movement, 1700–1951*, Gill and Macmillan.

Brown, K. D. (1985), *The First Labour Party, 1906–1914*, Croom Helm.

Brown, K. D. (1990), 'Modelling for war? Toy soldiers in late Victorian and Edwardian Britain', *Journal of Social History*, 24.

Brown, K. D. (1993), 'The collapse of the British toy industry, 1979–1984', *Economic History Review*, XLVI.

Brown, K. D. (1995), 'The strange death of Liberal England 1910–1914: a re-interpretation', *Shakai-Keizai Shigaku*, 61.

Brown, K. D. (1996), *The British Toy Business: a History Since 1700*, Hambledon Press.

Burnett, J. (1969), *A History of the Cost of Living*, Pelican.

Buxton, N. K. (1980), 'Economic growth in Scotland between the wars; the role of production structure and rationalization', *Economic History Review*, XXXIII.

Byrne, D., 'This is your torturer', *Spectator*, 29 July 1995.

Cairncross, A. (1971), *Britain's Economic Prospects Reconsidered*, Allen and Unwin.

Calder, K. E. (1973), *Strategic Capitalism: Private Business and Public Purpose in Japan*, Princeton University Press.

Capie, F. (1978), 'The British tariff and industrial protection in the 1930s', *Economic History Review*, XXXI.

Capie, F. (1983), *Depression and Protectionism in Britain Between the Wars*, Allen and Unwin.

Capie, F. and Collins, M. (1992), *Have the British Banks Failed British Industry? An Historical Survey of Bank/Industry Relations in Britain, 1870–1990*, Institute of Economic Affairs.

Cassar, G. H. (1994), *Asquith as War Leader*, Hambledon Press.

Chandler, A. D. (1990), *Scale and Scope: The Dynamics of Industrial Capitalism*, Belknap Press.

Channon, D. F. (1973), *The Strategy and Structure of British Enterprise*, Macmillan.

Charles, R. (1973), *The Development of Industrial Relations in Britain, 1911–1939*, Hutchinson.

Chiye, S. (1962), 'Changing values of the Japanese family', in Silberman, B. (ed.), *Japanese Character and Culture*,

Chubachi, M. and Taira, K. (1976), 'Poverty in modern Japan; perception and realities', in Patrick, H. (ed.), *Japanese Industrialization and its Social Consequences*, California University Press.

Coates, D. (1994), *The Question of UK Decline: The Economy, State and Society*, Wheatsheaf.

Coates, D. and Hillard, J. (1986), *The Economic Decline of Modern Britain: The Debate Between Left and Right*, Wheatsheaf.

Coleman, D. C. and Macleod, C. (1986), 'Attitudes to new techniques: British businessmen, 1800–1950', *Economic History Review*, XXXIX.

Constable, T. and McCormick, R. (1987), *The Making of British Managers*, British Institute of Management.

Cooper, S. (1964), 'Snoek piquante', in Sissons, M. and French, P. (eds), *Age of Austerity, 1945–51*, Pelican.

Corley, T. A. B. (1994), 'British overseas investments in 1914 revisited', *Business History*, 36.

Crafts, N. F. R. (1991), 'Economic growth', in Crafts, N. F. R. and Woodward, N. (eds), *The British Economy since 1945*, Oxford University Press.

Crouzet, F. (1982), *The Victorian Economy*, Methuen.

Cullen, L. (1993), 'Tokugawa economy and society in historical perspective', in Matsuo, T. (ed.) *Comparative Aspects of Irish and Japanese Economic and Social History*, Institute of Comparative Economic Studies, Hosei University.

Currie, R., Gilbert, B., and Horsley, L. (1977), *Churches and Churchgoers: Patterns of Church Growth in the British Isles Since 1700*, Clarendon.

Curwen, P. (1990), *Understanding the UK Economy*, Oxford University Press.

Daly, A., Hitchens, D., and Wagner, K. (1985), 'Productivity, machinery and skills in a sample of British and German manufacturing plants: results of a pilot inquiry', *National Institute Economic Review*, 111.

Dangerfield, G. (1961), *The Strange Death of Liberal England, 1910–1914*, Capricorn.

Daniel, W. W. and Millward, N. (1983), *Workplace Industrial Relations in Britain: The DE/PDSI/SSRC Survey*, Heinemann.

Davenport-Hines, R. P. T. and Jones, G. (eds) (1989), *British Business in Asia since 1860*, Cambridge University Press.

Davie, G. (1994), 'Religion in post-war Britain: a sociological view', in Obelkevich, J. and Catterall, P. (eds), *Understanding Post-War British Society*, Routledge.

Deane, P. and Cole, W. A. (1962), *British Economic Growth, 1688–1959*, Cambridge University Press.

Digby, A. (1989), *British Welfare Policy: Workhouse to Workfare*, Faber.

Donajgrodzki, A. J. (1977), *Social Control in Nineteenth-Century Britain*, Croom Helm.

Dore, R. (1959), *Land Reform in Japan*, Oxford University Press.

Durcan, J. W., McCarthy, W. E. J., and Redman, G. R. (1983), *Strikes in Post-War Britain. A Study of Stoppages of Work Due to Industrial Disputes, 1946–73*, Allen and Unwin.

Eccleston, B. (1995), 'The Japanese polity', in Megarry, T. (ed.), *The Making of Modern Japan: A Reader*, Greenwich University Press.

Edgell, S. (1980), *Middle Class Couples: A Study of Segregation, Domination and Inequality in Marriage*, Allen and Unwin.

Elliott, J. H. (1991), *National and Comparative History: an Inaugural Lecture Delivered before the University of Oxford*, Oxford University Press.

Eltis, W. and Fraser, D., (November 1992), 'The contribution of Japanese industrial success to Britain and Europe', *National Westminster Bank Quarterly Review*.

Eltis, W., Fraser, D., and Ricketts, M. (February 1992), 'The lessons for Britain from the superior economic performance of Germany and Japan', *National Westminster Bank Quarterly Review*.

Feinstein, C. H. (1989), 'Economic growth since 1870: Britain's performance in international perspective', *Oxford Review of Economic Policy*, 4.

Feinstein, C. H. (1994), 'Success and failure: British economic growth since 1948', in Floud, R. and McCloskey, D. (eds), *The Economic History of Britain Since 1700. 3. 1939–1992*, Cambridge University Press.

Fennema, E. (1993), 'Right hand ban', *Japan Update*, 22.

Floud, R. and McCloskey, D. (eds), (1981), *The Economic History of Britain since 1700. 2. 1860 to the 1970s*, Cambridge University Press.

Fowler, D. (1995), *The First Teenagers: The Lifestyle of Young Wage-Earners in Interwar Britain*, Woburn Press.

Francks, P. (1984), *Technology and Agricultural Development in Pre-War Japan*, Yale University Press.

Francks, P. (1992), *Japanese Economic Development. Theory and Practice*, Routledge.

Fruin, W. M. (1992), *The Japanese Enterprise System: Competitive Strategies and Co-operative Structures*, Clarendon.

Fukutake, T. (1995), 'Agriculture and the villages before World War II', in Megarry, T. (ed.) *The Making of Modern Japan: A Reader*, Greenwich University Press.

Gamble, A. (1994), *The Free Economy and the Strong State: The Politics of Thatcherism*, Macmillan.

Garrahan, P. and Stewart, P. (1992), *The Nissan Enigma: Flexibility at Work in a Local Economy*, Mansell.

Giddens, A. (1993), *Sociology*, Polity Press.

Glynn, A. and Sutcliffe, B. (1972), *British Capitalism, Workers and the Profits Squeeze*, Penguin.

Glynn, S. and Booth, A. (1996), *Modern Britain: an Economic and Social History*, Routledge.

Gordon, A. (1985), *The Evolution of Labor Relations in Japan: Heavy Industry, 1853–1955*, Harvard University Press.

Gorer, G. (1971), *Sex and Marriage in England Today*, Nelson.

Gospel, H. and Littler, C. (1983), *Managerial Strategies and Industrial Relations*, Heinemann.

Gourvish, T. R. (1980), *Railways and the British Economy, 1830–1914*, Macmillan.

Guagini, A. (1991), 'The fashioning of higher technical education in Britain: the case of Manchester, 1851–1914', in Gospel, H. (ed.), *Industrial Training and Technological Innovation*, Routledge.

Haley, J. (1992), 'Unsheathing the sword: law without sanctions', *Journal of Japanese Studies*, 8.

Halliday, J. (1975), *A Political History of Japanese Capitalism*, Monthly Review Press.

Halloran, F. M. (1993), 'War's memory: battle of souls', *Japan Update*, 19.

Halsey, A. H. (1972), *Trends in British Society since 1900*, Macmillan.

Halsey, A. H. (1978), *Change in British Society*, Oxford University Press.

Halsey, A. H. (1988), *British Social Trends Since 1900*, Macmillan.

Hanley, S. B. and Yamamura, Y. (1977), *Demographic Change in Pre-Industrial Japan, 1600–1868*, Princeton University Press.

Hannah, L. (1994), 'Crisis and turnaround, 1973–1993', in Johnson, P. (ed.), *Twentieth Century Britain: Economic, Social and Cultural Change*, Methuen.

Harada, S. (1928), *Labor Conditions in Japan*, Columbia University Press.

Harris, J. (1990), 'Enterprise and welfare states', *Transactions of the Royal Historical Society*, 40.

Hasegawa, H. (1996), *The Steel Industry in Japan: A Comparison with Britain*, Routledge.

Havighurst, A. (1985), *Britain in Transition: The Twentieth Century*, Chicago, University Press.

Health and Welfare Statistics Association (1995), *Health and Welfare Statistics in Japan*.

Hendry, J. (1995), *Understanding Japanese Society*, Routledge.

Herzog, P. (1995), 'Minorities', in Megarry, T. (ed.), *The Making of Modern Japan: A Reader*, Greenwich University Press.

Hiratu, T. (1936), 'Municipal unemployment in Japan', *Journal of Osaka University of Commerce*, IV.

Hobsbawm, E. J. (1969), *Industry and Empire*, Penguin.

Hoggart, R. (1965), *The Uses of Literacy*, Pelican.

Holland, C. (1913), *Things Seen in Japan*, Seeley and Co.

Holway, R. (1992), *A Review of the Financial Performance of the UK Computing Services Companies*, Richard Holway Ltd.

Hopkins, H. (1963), *The New Look: A Social History of the Forties and Fifties in Britain*, Secker and Warburg.

Horsley, W. and Buckley, R. (1990), *Nippon: New Superpower. Japan Since 1945*, BBC.

Howard, A. (1964), 'We are the masters now', in Sissons, M. and French, P. (eds), *Age of Austerity, 1945–51*, Penguin.

Howson, S. (1981), 'Slump and unemployment', in Floud, R. and McCloskey, D. (eds), *The Economic History of Britain since 1700. 2. 1860 to the 1970s*, Cambridge University Press.

Hunter, J. (1989), *The Emergence of Modern Japan. An Introductory History since 1853*, Longman.

Hunter, J. (1991), 'British training for Japanese engineers: the case of Kikuchi Kyozo (1859–1942)', in Cortazzi, H. and Daniels, G. (eds), *Britain and Japan, 1859–1991: Themes and Personalities*, Routledge.

Hunter, J. (1992), 'Textile factories, tuberculosis and the quality of life in industrialising Japan', *LSE Working Papers in Economic History*, 4/92.

Hutton, W. (1995), *The State We're In*, Cape.

Inglehart, R. (1977), *The Silent Revolution*, Princeton University Press.

Iwabuchi, K. (1994), 'Social security today and tomorrow', *Economic Eye*, 15.

James, H. (1990), 'The German experience and the myth of British cultural exceptionalism', in Collins, B. and Robbins, K. (eds), *British Culture and British Economic Decline*, Weidenfeld and Nicolson.

Jenkins, S. (1995), *Accountable to None: The Tory Nationalization of Britain*, Hamish Hamilton.

JISEA (Japan Institute for Social and Economic Affairs) (1993), *Japan, 1993: An International Comparison*.

JISEA (1994), *Japan 1994: An International Comparison*.

JISEA (1995), *Japan 1995: An International Comparison*.

JISEA (1996), *Japan 1996: An International Comparison*.

Johnson, C. (1982), *MITI and the Japanese Economic Miracle: The Growth of Industrial Policy, 1925–1975*, Stanford University Press.

Johnson, C. (1991), *The Economy under Mrs Thatcher, 1979–1990*, Penguin.

Johnson, P. B. (1968), *Land Fit For Heroes: The Planning of British Reconstruction, 1916–1919*, Chicago University Press.

Kaldor, N. (1966), *Causes of the Slow Rate of Economic Growth in the United Kingdom*, Cambridge University Press.

Kemp, T. (1989), *Industrialization in the Non-Western World*, Longman.

Kennedy, W. P. (1987), *Industrial Structure, Capital Markets and the Origins of British Economic Decline*, Cambridge University Press.

Kirby, M. (1994), 'Britain in the world economy', in Johnson, P. (ed.), *Twentieth Century Britain. Economic, Social and Cultural Change*, Methuen.

Kitson, M., Solomu, S., and Weale, M. (1991), 'Effective protection and economic recovery in the United Kingdom during the 1930s', *Economic History Review*, XLIV.

Koike, K. (1987), 'Human resource development and labour-management relations', in Yamamura, K. and Yasuba, Y. (eds), *The Political Economy of Japan*, Stanford University Press.

Kropotkin, P. (1900), 'The small industries of Britain', *Nineteenth Century*, 48.

Kuriki, C. (1994), 'Distaff bosses: women take charge', *Japan Update*, 33.

Kuznets, S. (1971), *Economic Growth of Nations: Total Output and Production Structure*, Harvard University Press.

Laybourn, K. (1995), 'The rise of labour and the decline of liberalism: the state of the debate', *History*, 80.

Lazonik, W. (1991), *Business Organization and the Myth of the Market Economy*, Cambridge University Press.

Lewis, J. (1992), *Women in Britain since 1945*, Oxford University Press.

Lewis, P. (1978), *The Fifties*, Heinemann,

Littlewood, I. (1996), *The Idea of Japan: Western Images, Western Myths*, Secker and Warburg.

Livingston, J., Moore, J., and Oldfather, F. (eds), (1976), *The Japan Reader*, two volumes, Pelican.

Lo, J. (1990), *Office Ladies, Factory Women: Life and Work at a Japanese Company*, M. E. Sharpe.

Lockwood, W. W. (1955), *The Economic Development of Japan: Growth and Structural Change, 1868–1938*, Oxford University Press.

Lowe, R. (1994), 'Postwar welfare', in Johnson, P. (ed.), *Twentieth Century Britain. Economic, Social and Cultural Change*, Methuen.

Lukes, S. (1969), 'Durkheim's "individualism and the intellectuals"', *Political Studies*, XVII.

McClintock, F. H. and Avison, N. H. (1968), *Crime In England and Wales*, Heinemann.

McCloskey, D. (1970), 'Did Victorian Britain fail?', *Economic History Review*, XXIII.

McCune, S. (1942), 'Recent growth in Japanese cities', *Geographical Review*, 32.

Macintyre, S. (1980), *Little Moscows: Communism and Working Class Militancy in Inter-War Britain*, Croom Helm.

Mack, J. and Lansley, S. (1985), *Poor Britain*, Allen and Unwin.

Mackenzie, J. M. (1986), *Imperialism and Popular Culture*, Manchester University Press.

Mackenzie, N. (1978), *The Letters of Sidney and Beatrice Webb: II: Pilgrimage, 1912–1947*, Cambridge University Press.

McKibbin, R. (1974), *The Evolution of the Labour Party, 1910–1924*, Oxford University Press.

Macpherson, W. J. (1987), *The Economic Development of Japan, c.1868–1941*, Macmillan.

Maddison, A. (1991), *Dynamic Forces in Capitalist Development: A Long-Run Perspective*, Oxford University Press.

Maizels, A. (1963), *Industrial Growth and World Trade*, Cambridge University Press.

Maraini, F. (1960), *Meeting with Japan*, Viking.

Marsh, R. M. and Mannari, H. (1976), *Modernization and the Japanese Factory*, Princeton University Press.

Marshall, B. K. (1982), 'Growth and conflict in Japanese higher education', in Najita,

T. and Koschmann, J. (eds), *Conflict in Modern Japanese History*, Princeton University Press.

Martin, J. and Roberts, C. (1984), *Women and Employment: A Lifetime Perspective*, HMSO.

Martin, K. (1962), *The Crown and the Establishment*, Penguin.

Maruyama, M. (1963), *Thought and Behaviour in Modern Japanese Politics*, Oxford University Press.

Marwick, A. (1967), *The Deluge: British Society and the First World War*, Pelican.

Marwick, A. (1982), *British Society since 1945*, Pelican.

Mason, M. (1994), *The Making of Victorian Sexuality*, Oxford University Press.

Matsuo, T. (1989), 'Solidarity in rural community and totalitarian regime in the 1930s', *Hosei University Economic Review*, LVII.

Matthews, R. C. O., Feinstein, C. H., and Odling-Smee, J. C. (1982), *British Economic Growth, 1856–1973*, Oxford University Press.

Maurette, F. (1934), *Social Aspects of Industrial Development in Japan*, International Labour Organization.

Maxfield, M. G. (1984), 'Fear of crime in England and Wales', *Home Office Research Study*, Home Office.

Middlemas, K. (1979), *Politics in Industrial Society: The Experience of the British System since 1911*, Andre Deutsch.

Mifune, M. (1995), 'Household harmony', *Japan Update*, 41.

Miles, C. (1968), *Lancashire Textiles: A Case Study of Industrial Change*, Cambridge University Press.

Millward, R. and Singleton, J. (1995), *The Political Economy of Nationalisation in Britain, 1920–50*, Cambridge University Press.

Minami, R. (1986), *The Economic Development of Japan: A Quantitative Study*, Macmillan.

Mitchell, B. R. and Deane, P. A. (1971), *Abstract of British Historical Statistics*, Cambridge University Press.

Moeran, B. (1985), *Okubo Diary: Portrait of a Japanese Valley*, Stanford University Press.

Morgan, K. O. (1979), *Consensus and Disunity: The Lloyd George Coalition Government, 1918–1922*, Oxford University Press.

Morikawa, H. (1992), *Zaibatsu: The Rise and Fall of Family Enterprise Groups in Japan*, Tokyo University Press.

Morishima, M. (1982), *Why Has Japan 'Succeeded'?*, Cambridge University Press.

Morita, M. (1993), 'Dietmen of the cloth', *Japan Update*, 27.

Mosk, C. (1983), *Patriarchy and Fertility: Japan and Sweden, 1880–1960*, Academic Press.

Moulder, F. (1977), *Japan, China and the Modern World Economy*, Cambridge University Press.

Mowatt, C. L. (1955), *Britain between the Wars*, Methuen.

Muto, S. (1919), *Employers and Workers: An Appeal*, International Labour Organization.

Nakamura, T. (1983), *Economic Growth in Prewar Japan*, Yale University Press.

Nakamura, T. (1994), *Lectures on Modern Japanese Economic History*, LTCB International Library Foundation.

Nakane, C. (1970), *Japanese Society*, California University Press.

Nakase, R. (1981), 'Some characteristics of Japanese-type multi-national enterprises today', *Capital and Class*, 13.

Napier, R. (1982), 'The transformation of the Japanese labour market, 1894–1937', in Najita, T. and Koschmann, J. (eds), *Conflict in Modern Japanese History*, Princeton University Press.

Nicholas, S. (1984), 'The overseas marketing performance of British industry, 1870–1914', *Economic History Review*, XXXVII.

Nish, I. (1987), 'Britain's view of the Japanese economy in the early Showa period', in Dore, R. and Sinha, R. (eds), *Japan and World Depression Then and Now. Essays in Memory of E. T. Penrose*, Macmillan.

Norton, P. (1980), *Dissension in the House of Commons, 1974–1979*, Clarendon.

OECD, (1990), *Historical Statistics*.

Ohbuchi, H. (1976), 'Demographic transition in the process of Japanese industrialization', in Patrick, H. (ed.), *Japanese Industrialization and its Social Consequences*, California University Press.

Ohkawa, K. and Shinohara, M. (1979), *Patterns of Japanese Economic Development: A Quantitative Appraisal*, Yale University Press.

Ojala, E. M. (1952), *Agriculture and Economic Progress*, Oxford University Press.

Okayama, R. (1983), 'Japanese employer and labour policy: the heavy engineering industry in 1900–1930', in Gospel, H. and Littler, C. (eds), *Managerial Strategies and Industrial Relations*, Heinemann.

Okimoto, D. (1989), *Between MITI and the Market: Japanese Industrial Policy for High Technology*, Stanford University Press.

Okimoto, D. and Saxonhouse, G. (1987), 'Technology and the future of the economy', in Yamamura, K. and Yasuba, Y. (eds), *The Political Economy of Japan*, Stanford University Press.

Oliver, N. and Wilkinson, B. (1988), *The Japanisation of British Industry*, Blackwell.

Olson, M. (1982), *The Rise and Decline of Nations: Economic Growth, Stagflation and Social Rigidities*, Yale University Press.

Ono, A. and Watanabe, T. (1976), 'Changes in income inequality in the Japanese economy' in Patrick, H. (ed.), *Japanese Industrialization and its Social Consequences*, California University Press.

Orwell, G., (1962) *The Road to Wigan Pier*, Penguin.

Osaka City University Research Institute of Economics (1989), *Osaka Economic Data Over Sixty Years*.

Osaka Municipal Office (1920), *Municipal Social Welfare Work in the City of Osaka*.

Page, R. M. (1991), 'Social welfare since the war', in Crafts, N. F. R. and Woodward, N. (eds), *The British Economy since 1945*, Oxford University Press.

Patrick, H. (1971), 'The economic muddle of the 1920s', in Morley, J. W. (ed.), *Dilemmas of Growth in Prewar Japan*, Princeton University Press.

Patrick, H. and Rosovsky, H. (1976), *Asia's New Giant. How the Japanese Economy Works*, Brookings Institute.

Pearse, A. (1929), *The Cotton Industry of Japan and China, Being the Report of the Journey to Japan and China*, International Federation of Master Cotton Spinners' and Manufacturers' Associations.

Peden, G. (1986), *British Economic and Social Policy: Lloyd George to Margaret Thatcher*, Philip Allan.

Perkin, H. (1969), *The Origin of Modern English Society, 1780–1880*, Routledge.

Perkin, H. (1989), *The Rise of Professional Society: England Since 1880*, Routledge.

Phelps Brown, E. H. (1975), 'A non-monetarist view of the pay explosion', *Three Banks Review*, 105.

Piachaud, D. (1987), 'The growth of poverty', in Walker, A. and Walker, C. (eds), *The Growing Divide. A Social Audit, 1979–1987*, Child Poverty Action Group.,

Pollard, S. (1970), *The Gold Standard and Employment Policies Between the Wars*, Methuen.

Pollard, S. (1981), *The Wasting of the British Economy: British Economic Policy 1945 to the Present*, Croom Helm.

Pollard, S. (1983), *The Development of the British Economy, 1914–1980*, Arnold.

Pollard, S. (1989), *Britain's Prime and Britain's Decline: The British Economy, 1870–1914*, Arnold.

Pollard, S. (1990), 'Reflections on entrepreneurship and culture in European societies', *Transactions of the Royal Historical Society*, 40.

Pollard, S. (1992), *The Development of the British Economy, 1914–1990*, Arnold.

Porter, B. (1994), *Britannia's Burden: The Political Evolution of Modern Britain 1851–1990*, Arnold.

Pratten, C. F. and Atkinson, A. G. (1976), 'The use of manpower in British manufacturing industry', *Department of Employment Gazette*, 84.

Priestley, J. B. (1934), *English Journey*, Heinemann.

Pugh, M. (1982), *The Making of Modern British Politics, 1867–1939*, Oxford University Press.

Pyle, K. (1982), 'The future of Japanese nationality: an essay in contemporary history', *Journal of Japanese Studies*, 8.

Ransome, S. (1899), *Japan in Transition: A Comparative Study of the Progress, Policy and Methods of the Japanese Since Their War With China*, Harrap.

Redmond, J. (1984), 'The sterling overvaluation in 1925: a multilateral approach', *Economic History Review*, XXXVII.

Reid, A. (1986), 'The impact of the First World War on British workers', in Wall, R. and Winter, J. (eds), *The Upheaval of War: Family, Work and Welfare in Europe*, Cambridge University Press.

Richards, J. and Aldgate, A. (1983), *Best of British: Cinema and Society, 1930–1970*, Blackwell.

Richardson, R. (1991), 'Trade unions and industrial relations', in Crafts, N. F. R. and Woodward, N. (eds), *The British Economy since 1945*, Oxford University Press.

Robbins, K. (1988), *Nineteenth-Century Britain. Integration and Diversity*, Oxford University Press.

Roberts, E. (1984), *A Woman's Place*, Oxford University Press.

Roberts, J. G. (1973), *Mitsui, Three Centuries of Japanese Business*, Weatherhill.

Robertson, A. (1990), 'Lancashire and the rise of Japan, 1910–1937', *Business History*, 32.

Rosovsky, H. (1966), *Industrialization in Two Systems*, Wiley.

Rostow, W. W. (1971), *The Stages of Economic Growth*, Cambridge University Press.

Royal Commission on Trade Unions and Employers' Associations, 1965–1968 (1968), Cmnd. 3623, HMSO.

Rubinstein, W. D. (1993), *Capitalism, Culture and Decline in Britain, 1750–1990*, Routledge.

Runciman, W. G. (1966), *Relative Deprivation and Social Justice*, Routledge and Kegan Paul.

Saito, O. (1996), 'Gender workload and agricultural progress', in Leboutte, R. (ed.), *Proto-Industrialization: Recent Research and New Perspectives*, Librairie Droz S.A.

Sanderson, M. (1994), 'Education and social mobility', in Johnson, P. (ed.), *Twentieth Century Britain. Economic, Social and Political Change*, Methuen.

Sarlvik, B, and Crewe, I. (1983), *Decade of Dealignment: The Conservative Victory of 1979 and Electoral Trends in the 1970s*, Cambridge University Press.

Sato, K. (1987), 'Saving and investment', in Yamamura, K. and Yasuba, Y. (eds), *The Political Economy of Japan*, Stanford University Press.

Searle, G. R. (1977), *The Quest for National Efficiency*, Oxford University Press.

Seki, K. (1956), *The Cotton Industry of Japan*, Japan Society for the Promotion of Science.

Seldon, A. (1991), 'The Conservative Party since 1945', in Gourvish, T. and O'Day, A. (eds), *Britain Since 1945*, Macmillan.

Sheridan, K. (1993), *Governing the Japanese Economy*, Polity Press.

Silberman, B. (1974), 'The bureaucratic role in Japan, 1900–1945: the bureaucrat as politician', in Silberman, B. and Harootunian, H. (eds), *Japan in Crisis: Essays on Taisho Democracy*, Princeton University Press.

Singleton, J. (1991), *Lancashire on the Scrapheap: The Cotton Industry, 1945–1970*, Oxford University Press.

Skocpol, T. and Somers, M. (1994), *Social Revolutions in the Modern World*, Cambridge University Press.

Smethurst, R. J. (1986), *Agricultural Development and Tenancy Disputes in Japan, 1870–1940*, Princeton University Press.

Smith, D. B. (1995), *Japan Since 1945: The Rise of an Economic Superpower*, Macmillan.

Smith, M. (1995), 'The war and British culture', in Constantine, S., Kirby, M., and Rose, M. (eds), *The First World War in British History*, Arnold.

Smith, S. R. (1992), 'Drinking etiquette in a changing beverage market', in Tobin, J. J. (ed.), *Re-Made in Japan. Everyday Life and Consumer Taste in a Changing Society*, Yale University Press.

Smith, T. C. (1988), *Native Sources of Japanese Industrialization, 1750–1920*, California University Press.

Smithies, E. (1984), *The Black Economy in England since 1914*, Gill and Macmillan.

Springhall, J. (1986), *Coming of Age: Adolescence in Britain, 1860–1960*, Gill and Macmillan.

Stead, A. (1906) *Great Japan: A Study of National Efficiency*, John Lane.

Stevenson, J. (1984), *British Society, 1914–45*, Pelican.

Stoetzel, J. (1955), *Without the Chrysanthemum and Sword: A Study of the Attitudes of Youth in Postwar Japan*, UNESCO.

Stone, N. (1983), *Europe Transformed 1878–1919*, Fontana.

Storry, R. (1990), *A History of Modern Japan*, Penguin.

Sugihara, K. (1989), 'Japan's industrial recovery, 1931–6', in Brown, I. (ed.), *The Economies of Africa and Asia in the Interwar Depression*, Routledge.

Sugiyama, S. (1995), 'Work rules, wages and single status: the shaping of the

"Japanese employment system"', in Abe, E. and Fitzgerald, R. (eds), *The Origins of Japanese Industrial Power: Strategy, Institutions and the Development of Organizational Capability*, Cass.

Supple, B. (1963), *The Experience of Economic Growth: Case Studies in Economic History*, Random House.

Supple, B. (1988), 'The political economy of demoralization: the state and the coalmining industry in America and Britain between the wars', *Economic History Review*, XLI.

Supple, B. (1994), 'British economic decline since 1945', in Floud, R. and McCloskey, D. (eds), *The Economic History of Britain since 1700. 3. 1939–1992*, Cambridge University Press.

Suzuki, K. (1993), 'Unhappy media', *Japan Update*, 16.

Tachi, R. (1991), *The Contemporary Japanese Economy*, Tokyo University Press.

Takahashi, E. (1994), 'Daily life. How do different countries stack up', *Japan Update*, 31.

Tanifuji, E. (1995a), 'Democratic values', *Japan Update*, 43.

Tanifuji, E. (1995b), 'Feminism', *Japan Update*, 42.

Tanifuji, E. (1995c), 'Lowering opinions', *Japan Update*, 45.

Tanifuji, E. (1995d), 'Spiritual affluence', *Japan Update*, 40.

Tasker, P. (1989), *Inside Japan. Wealth, Work and Power in the New Japanese Empire*, Penguin.

Tatsuno, S. (1986), *The Technopolis Strategy: Japan, High Technology and the Control of the 21st Century*, Prentice Hall.

Taylor, A. J. P. (1965), *English History 1914–1945*, Oxford University Press.

Thane, P. (1991), 'Towards equal opportunities: women in Britain since 1945', in Gourvish, T. and O'Day, A. (eds), *Britain Since 1945*, Macmillan.

Thomas, J. E. (1996), *Modern Japan: A Social History Since 1868*, Longman.

Thomas, M. (1983), 'Rearmament and economic recovery in the late 1930s', *Economic History Review*, XXXVI.

Thompson, F. M. L. (1981), 'Social control in Victorian Britain', *Economic History Review*, XXXIV.

Thompson, F. M. L. (1988), *The Rise of Respectable Society: A Social History of Victorian Britain, 1830–1900*, Fontana.

Thompson, F. M. L. (1990), 'English landed society in the twentieth century: I: progress, collapse and survival', *Transactions of the Royal Historical Society*, 40.

Thorburn, J. and Takashima, M. (February 1993), 'Improving British industrial performance: lessons from Japanese subcontracting', *National Westminster Bank Quarterly Review*.

Tobin, J. J. (ed.) (1992), *Re-made in Japan: Everyday Life and Consumer Taste in a Changing Society*, Yale University Press.

Togo, S. (1993), 'The princess and the press', *Japan Update*, 18.

Tolliday, S. (1987), *Business, Banking and Politics: The Case of Steel, 1918–1936*, Harvard University Press.

Tomlinson, J. (1990), *Public Policy and the Economy Since 1900*, Oxford University Press.

Tomlinson, J. (1996), 'Inventing "decline": the falling behind of the British economy in the postwar years', *Economic History Review*, XLIX.

Totten, G. O. (1967), 'Collective bargaining and works councils as innovations in industrial relations in Japan during the 1920s', in Dore, R. (ed.), *Aspects of Social Change in Modern Japan*, Princeton University Press.

Trewartha, G. T. (1945), *Japan: A Physical, Cultural and Regional Geography*, Wisconsin University Press.

Tsunoda, R., de Bary, W. T., and Keene, D. (1958), *Sources of the Japanese Tradition*, Columbia University Press.

Uchida, H. (1991), 'Japanese technical manpower in industry, 1880–1930: a quantitative survey', in Gospel, H. (ed.), *Industrial Training and Technological Innovation*, Routledge.

UNESCO (1971), *Technological Development in Japan*.

Utley, F. (1931), *Lancashire and the Far East*, Allen and Unwin.

Utley, F. (1936), *Japan's Feet of Clay*, Faber and Faber.

Waller, P. J. (1983), *Town, City and Nation: England 1850–1914*, Oxford University Press.

Warshofsky, F. (1989), *The Chip War: The Battle for the World of Tomorrow*, Scribner.

Waswo, A. (1977), *Japanese Landlords*, California University Press.

Waswo, A. (1989), 'Japan's rural economy in crisis', in Brown, I. (ed.), *The Economies of Africa and Asia in the Interwar Depression*, Routledge.

Waswo, A. (1996), *Modern Japanese Society, 1868–1994*, Oxford University Press.

Wells, S. J. (1964), *British Export Performance: A Comparative Study*, Cambridge University Press.

Westergaard, J. and Resler, H. (1975), *Class in a Capitalist Society: A Study of Contemporary Britain*, Heinemann.

White, M. (1985), 'Japanese management', in Lawrence, P. and Elliott, K. (eds), *Introducing Management*, Penguin.

Wickham, E. R. (1957), *Church and People in an Industrial City*, Lutterworth Press.

Wiener, M. J. (1981), *English Culture and the Decline of the Industrial Spirit, 1850–1980*, Pelican.

Wigen, K. (1995), *The Making of a Japanese Periphery, 1750–1920*, California University Press.

Wilkinson, E. (1991), *Japan Versus the West: Image and Reality*, Penguin.

Williams, F. (1957), *Dangerous Estate: The Anatomy of Newspapers*, Arrow.

Williams, L. J. (1971), *Britain and the World Economy, 1919–1970*, Fontana.

Wilson, J. (1995), *British Business History, 1720–1994*, Manchester University Press.

Winter, J. (1986), *The Great War and the British People*, Macmillan.

Wolf, M. (1984), *The Japanese Conspiracy: Their Plot to Dominate Industry Worldwide and How to Deal with It*, Empire.

Wolffe, J. (1994), 'Religion and "secularization"', in Johnson, P. (ed.), *Twentieth Century Britain. Economic, Social and Cultural Change*, Methuen.

Woronoff, J. (1996a), *Japan As – Anything But – Number One*, Macmillan.

Woronoff, J. (1996b), *The Japanese Economic Crisis*, Macmillan.

Wrigley, C. J. (1976), *David Lloyd George and the British Labour Movement: Peace and War*, Harvester Press.

Wrigley, C. J. (1982), 'The Ministry of Munitions: an innovatory department', in Burk, K. (ed.), *War and the State: The Transformation of British Government, 1914–1919*, Allen and Unwin.,

Wrigley, C. J. (1987), *A History of British Industrial Relations, 1914–1939*, Harvester Press.

Wrigley, C. J. (1996), 'Trade unions, strikes and the government', in Coopey, R. and Woodward, N. (eds), *Britain in the 1970s: The Troubled Economy*, UCL Press.

Yamamura, K. (1967), 'The role of the samurai in the development of modern banking in Japan', *Journal of Economic History*, XXVII.

Yamamura, K. (1968), 'A re-examination of entrepreneurship in Meiji Japan, (1868–1912)', *Economic History Review*, XXI.

Yasuba, Y. (1976), 'The evolution of dualistic wage structure', in Patrick, H. (ed.), *Japanese Industrialization and its Social Consequences*, California University Press.

Yonekura, S. (1994), *The Japanese Iron and Steel Industry, 1850–1990*, Macmillan.

Yoshikate, O. (1982), 'Generational conflict after the Russo-Japanese war', in Najita, T. and Koschmann, J. (eds), *Conflict in Modern Japanese History*, Princeton University Press.

Young, M. and Wilmott, P. (1973), *The Symmetrical Family: A Study of Work and Leisure in the London Region*, Routledge and Kegan Paul.

Zimmeck, M. (1988), 'Get out and get under', in Anderson, G. (ed.), *The White Blouse Revolution*, Manchester University Press.

Index